John Stuart Mill and

the Writing of Character

John

and the Writing of Character

JANICE CARLISLE

The University of Georgia   Athens & London

FOR KATE AND JOEY

© 1991 by the University of Georgia Press
Athens, Georgia 30602
All rights reserved
Designed by Richard Hendel
Set in Baskerville by Tseng Information Systems
Printed and bound by Thomson-Shore
The paper in this book meets the guidelines for permanence and
durability of the Committee on Production Guidelines for Book
Longevity of the Council on Library Resources.

Printed in the United States of America
95 94 93 92 91   C   5   4   3   2   1

Library of Congress Cataloging in Publication Data
Carlisle, Janice.
    John Stuart Mill and the writing of character / Janice Carlisle.
        p. cm.
    Includes bibliographical references and index.
    ISBN 0-8203-1295-9 (alk. paper)
    1. Mill, John Stuart, 1806–1873. 2. Philosophers–England–
Biography. 3. Mill, John Stuart, 1806–1873–Contributions in
concept of character. 4. Character. I. Title.
B1606.C37 1991
192–dc20
[B]   90-40734
                        CIP

British Library Cataloging in Publication Data available

Contents

Preface

This study began as an essay on Mill's *Autobiography,* but the more I worked on the project and developed the context in which I wanted to read his account of his life, the more convinced I became that, as a single text, it provides a highly misleading key to all Mill's mythologies. Part of the reason for this situation lies, I think, in the nature of autobiographical writing itself, a question with which I deal in the last part of this study. Yet the deceptive qualities of the *Autobiography* also result from the way in which it was written. Because Mill first drafted and then revised the work in such genuinely difficult circumstances—first under the threat of his own supposedly impending death, later after the death of his wife, Harriet Taylor Mill, and in her honor—it can hardly begin to do justice to the diversity of his experience or to the complexities of his relation to his cultural context. The length of the composition history of the *Autobiography* creates similar problems. Wordsworth comments eloquently on the fact that the time involved in writing one's life is itself a shifting medium when he portrays the autobiographical writer as a man looking at the bottom of a lake from a slow-moving boat. Because the various parts of Mill's *Autobiography* were written at different points in his life, the boat in his case moved in fits and starts, with his perspective altering as he changed place in time. The first part, drafted and revised in 1853–54, recopied and extended in 1861, was not finished until the completion of Chapter VII in 1869–70. The "instinct for closeness" that Mill confessed in his *Early Draft* (1853–54)—and whose effects he demonstrated by deleting the confession—combines with the temporal complexities of the composition history of the *Autobiography* to create a greater challenge for its readers than its apparent simplicity would suggest. Because it was intended originally to stand at the head of a collection of miscellaneous essays on ethics, religion, society, and philosophy, the *Autobiography* was meant to be the foreword to, not the last word on, Mill's experience.

Unfortunately for Mill's reputation and his current status in literary studies, the *Autobiography*—along with the second of his two canonical and most difficult works, *On Liberty*—is the one most often granted the fullest authority. It is not surprising, therefore, that the study of Mill, so often limited among literary critics to the analysis of the *Autobiography,* has left unsolved and even unexplored many of the more mysterious and intriguing of the relations between his life and his work. Evaluations of Mill's famous crisis, for instance, are frequently misled by their tendency to take his word, the only word available, for gospel. To address these issues, I have had to go beyond Mill's version of his life. The *Autobiography,* however, necessarily receives in the following pages a good deal of attention because it, along with his letters, is the central primary source on his experience. I hope, however, that the attention I give Mill's account of his life serves the function of putting it in its proper place.

At the end of his long and tortuous analysis of the writings of a contemporary, *An Examination of Sir William Hamilton's Philosophy* (1865), Mill comments that one can earn the right to evaluate a writer's thought only if one has read all of his or her works and has tried, with as much empathy as possible, to see each one of the ideas presented in the context that is created for it by the corpus as a whole. This comment recapitulates a point that he made in 1833 when he claimed that an author's works can be read only by "the light they reflect on each other." Mill made such statements about the work of other writers, I think, because they are so eminently true of his own. Because of the range of the subjects on which Mill wrote, my own work, which began as an exercise in literary criticism, has turned inevitably into an interdisciplinary project. In the following chapters, forays into philosophy and science, discussions of political and intellectual history, and psychological and rhetorical analysis alternate so that I can examine his writings from a number of perspectives. As my work on this project progressed, it became clear to me that the "light" that Mill's diverse works cast is focused on the subject of character—the characters of individuals and their diversities, the characters of various groups and the circumstances that have made them what they are.

Although Mill never devoted an essay or a treatise solely to the study of character, it constituted the principal subject of his long career as a writer. Whether he was writing on economics or education, politics or philosophy, whether he was reviewing a work of fiction or formulating a system of logic, his inquiries almost invariably declared their psychological and social orientation and his preoccupation with character, not as a literary concept or phenomenon, but as the central fact of human experience. According to Mill, diverse disciplines join in a common pursuit of this subject. The philosopher, more a psychologist than a theorist of abstract principles, attempts to understand the complexity of human behavior and establish those laws of character that might lead to its reformation. Similarly, as Mill explains in an early review, the function of the literary critic is to analyze how the writer "figures himself" in his writings and how "the age, and his individual circumstances, have influenced the formation of his character as a man and as a writer." Mill even projected the establishment of a science that would examine these issues with something approaching the rigor and clarity of the physical sciences: Ethology, the field in which he wished to make his mark, was to be the science of the formation of character by its circumstances. In Mill's view, there was nothing abstract or bloodless about these issues. They were intimately connected with the most significant political questions of his day, indeed of any day, and they deserved to constitute their own field of inquiry because they could identify the conditions that yield either human misery or human happiness.

Treating Mill as an analyst of character necessarily involves analysis of the analyst. As he said of Sir William Hamilton, a writer's opinions have their "foundation in the author's individuality." One of the most profound of Mill's insights into the subject of character, to which I revert in several contexts, provides a telling perspective on his own character. In an article written in 1846, he claims, "What shapes the character is not what is purposely taught, so much as the unintentional teaching of institutions and social relations." Although he always avoided a recognition of the formative influence of the particular contingent conditions of his own personal experience, Mill's theories about character were, I argue, very much a reflection of his own character. In this study, I examine Mill as a writer whose work consistently bore the impress of "the unintentional teaching of institutions and social relations." The personal questions posed by Mill's career are related, in ways he ignored, to the larger presuppositions of the culture in which he was raised, and I focus accordingly on the attitudes of that culture toward the relative value of theory and practice, the status of the writer, the relation of gender to profession, and contemporary debates over freedom and necessity. In the introduction, I examine Mill's first principles, his propensity to equate his own character with the individuality evidenced in his published writings and the source of that self-definition in his training in associationist psychology. The two chapters that follow deal with the issues that Mill usually rejected as irrelevant to the understanding of an author's work: family, parentage, station, choice of profession, and, as one even more personal determinant and proof of character, choice of mate.

Because these factors were central to Mill's lifelong but frustrated attempts to found a science of character, my discussion of them precedes my examination of his ethology, a science that turns out to be, in the works in which he most fully realized its potential, a political science that can deal more effectively with marginal groups than with the individuals whose birth or station or profession gives them a place in the dominant classes. To understand the force of circumstance on such privileged individual characters, one has to turn, I think, to the issues that were central to Mill's conception of his own status as a writer, the questions of intellectual influence and authority. In responding to the pressures exerted by such questions, he reveals some of his conclusions about character in general, and I treat a specific text, *On Liberty*, both as an example of Mill's analysis of these issues and as a demonstration of their power over him.

Finally, the last two chapters of this study treat Mill as an artist of character. He continually distinguishes between theory and practice, science and art; and his practice of character, his attempts to sketch the characters of other individuals, most fully reveal the traits of his own character and his most profound yet painful conclusions about character. Mill spent his long career as a writer and the length of his autobiographical description of that career in an attempt to prove his freedom from the social, intellectual, and institutional forces that controlled his actions. His work on character ultimately points toward a recognition on his part that such control over even as powerful a mind as his own was a condition that neither he nor anyone else could escape.

Before turning to Mill's first principles, however, I should declare my own. In discussing the issues I have outlined, I have chosen not to use the term *identity* or, to be more *au courant*, the terms *subject* or *Subject*. Instead, I have adopted the old-fashioned term *character*, first, of course, because Mill used it, but also, paradoxically, because *character* avoids even the hint of essentialist thinking that terms like *subject* still too often imply. To talk of "the subject" is to evoke a definite theory of the process that constitutes the phantom called "identity" or "individuality": a subject is the fiction of identity created from without by the forces to which the individual is subjected. Such a formulation is particularly pertinent to the study of a writer both formed by his culture and engaged in creating the forces that would form others. Yet, as I demonstrate in my introduction, the term *character*, for Victorian writers, implies a shared understanding of what constitutes individuals without specifying how they are so constituted. I also, of course, adhere throughout to Mill's definition of *ethology*, though he might have been dismayed to realize that the science for which he had such hopes is now devoted to the study of expressive behavior, both human and nonhuman.

Secondly, this study focuses both on what Mill knew about character and on what he revealed about that subject without knowing that he had done so. It treats his self-conscious analysis of character as well as his often stunningly unselfconscious revelations of character. There is, of course, a crucial difference between such acts of analysis and of revelation. In one case, Mill does the work of inquiry; in the other, he leaves it to be done by his reader. As Bentham once put it so well, a writer's work may "afford a rich fund of materials; but a quarry is not a house." Mill's attitude toward the East India Company, for instance, reveals the extraordinary power of such institutions to mold the thinking of those who are supported by them, and it does so precisely because he was so thoroughly unaware of this power in his own case, despite his frequent statements of disdain for the "depraving influence" that social and professional positions exert on others. Although I make no attempt in this study to treat the writing that Mill did at the India House, I do argue that his position there was crucial in determining the work he undertook for more general publication. Had he been any less aware of how such influences work on others, his blindness to the limitations on his own thinking, resulting from the same causes, would have been far less revealing. I am not in any sense, however, suggesting that Mill's twentieth-century readers adopt a kind of bemused pity for the confusions and contradictions in his thought. They constitute, indeed, the most convincing evidence of the validity of his analysis.

Despite the fact that I have followed Mill's injunction to consider his whole work rather than its parts, the character that emerges from this study is not always one that he himself would have found flattering. My emphasis on his acceptance of some of the more short-sighted and prejudiced attitudes in Victorian culture suggests that he was not quite the thinker able to withstand the pressures of his age that he thought himself to be. Particularly in his responses to the marginality of his role as a writer, Mill was often more the victim of his culture than its master. Paradoxically, however, he turned that marginality into the basis of his authority, using not only the lessons it taught but the rhetorical methods that it enjoined to produce in *On Liberty* the book that was recognized by his contemporaries as the "gospel" of the nineteenth century. A very strange gospel it is, the work of an odd prophet who thought himself the voice of wisdom crying unheeded in the streets. Yet unless Mill's complex negotiations with Victorian culture are examined, it is impossible to understand either his modest conception of his role or the elevated status that he did achieve.

Too often Mill is summed up and dismissed as the Saint of Rationalism. After nearly one hundred and fifty years of commentary on his life and work, he has become too much the sad and wizened man who looks out from the late, touching portrait by George Frederick Watts. Mill repeatedly claims in the *Autobiography* that his story has no interest in itself, that he is an unremarkable individual, and many readers have taken him at his word. The subjects that Mill understood best—subjection and power, authority and influence—he understood because he had lived their consequences. His thought and the example of his experience as a thinker in Victorian England should be of more use than they are to contemporary scholars and critics. The autobiographer who took analytic psychology as one of his main fields of endeavor offers a great deal, I think, to those interested in Victorian autobiography. The writer who planned as his magnum opus a work on the formation of character provides a telling perspective on the work of those novelists who also took that subject as their main field of inquiry. And the man who took as his principal concern—in psychology, sociology, and politics—the relation between the individual and his or her historical context deserves the attention of those who see a new value in historical perspectives on Victorian culture. Far from the detached thinker Mill thought he had embodied in his writings, he emerges as a man whose personal limitations were confirmed and complicated by the culture in which he lived, yet a man whose failures of vision on certain issues are as revealing and compelling as his insights into others.

Acknowledgments

Of all the personal and institutional debts that I have incurred in writing this book, I am pleased to acknowledge first Professor John M. Robson, his fellow editors, and the editorial staff of *The Collected Works of John Stuart Mill.* During the many months that I have spent with the volumes of this edition, I have often thought that if any editorial labors deserved to be called heroic, the efforts of Professor Robson and his colleagues would surely be among the most prominent contenders for that title. In generously responding to an inquiry I made, Professor Robson also provided timely words of encouragement for my project. Jonathan Arac, Jay Clayton, Naomi Lebowitz, Linda H. Peterson, Mary Poovey, and Daniel Schwarz gave their support at various stages of this work. Two of my colleagues at Tulane, Molly Rothenberg and Teresa Toulouse, were particularly instrumental in helping me sort out several complex issues. Jonathan Arac and Jonathan Loesberg both offered thoughtful and extremely useful readings of the manuscript from which it has greatly benefited, although they are not responsible for any deficiencies that remain.

A revised version of an essay originally published in *Victorian Studies* is reprinted by permission of the Trustees of Indiana University. *Studies in the Literary Imagination* kindly granted permission to reprint part of an essay that first appeared in its pages. The National Endowment for the Humanities deserves acknowledgment for the fellowship that allowed me to complete this study, as does Tulane University, which added its support during the year of leave when I held the fellowship. Much of my research could not have been completed without the courtesy of the interlibrary loan office at the Northwestern University Library. The Newberry Library granted permission to reprint two cartoons from *Judy*.

Finally, Joseph Roach surely knows without my saying so that his support, in both practical and intellectual terms, has made it possible for me to write this book; for his efforts, this expression of appreciation is a poor return. To my children, Catherine Roach and Joseph Roach III, I offer this book in affectionate thanks not only for their forbearance when the writing of it interfered with their just claims on my time, but also for the daily pleasures of their companionship as it was being written.

Note on Citations

Unless otherwise noted, all references to Mill's works in the text are to *Collected Works of John Stuart Mill* (Toronto and London: University of Toronto Press and Routledge and Kegan Paul, 1963–). The following list is arranged numerically by volume number.

1. *Autobiography and Literary Essays*. Edited, with an introduction, by John M. Robson and Jack Stillinger. 1981.

2, 3. *Principles of Political Economy: With Some of Their Applications to Social Philosophy*. Edited, with a textual introduction, by J. M. Robson. Introduction by V. W. Bladen. 1965.

4, 5. *Essays on Economics and Society*. Edited, with a textual introduction, by J. M. Robson. Introduction by Lord Robbins. 1967.

6. *Essays on England, Ireland, and the Empire*. Edited, with a textual introduction, by John M. Robson. Introduction by Joseph Hamburger. 1982.

7, 8. *A System of Logic Ratiocinative and Inductive*. Edited, with a textual introduction, by J. M. Robson. Introduction by R. F. McRae. 1973.

9. *An Examination of Sir William Hamilton's Philosophy and of the Principal Philosophical Questions Discussed in his Writings*. Edited, with a textual introduction, by J. M. Robson. Introduction by Alan Ryan. 1979.

10. *Essays on Ethics, Religion and Society*. Edited, with a textual introduction, by J. M. Robson. Introductions by F. E. L. Priestley and D. P. Dryer. 1969.

11. *Essays on Philosophy and the Classics*. Edited, with a textual introduction, by J. M. Robson. Introduction by F. E. Sparshott. 1978.

12, 13. *The Earlier Letters of John Stuart Mill, 1812–1848*. Edited by Francis E. Mineka. Introduction by F. A. Hayek. 1962.

14, 15, 16, 17. *The Later Letters of John Stuart Mill, 1848–1873*. Edited, with an introduction, by Francis E. Mineka and Dwight N. Lindley. 1972.

18, 19. *Essays on Politics and Society*. Edited, with a textual introduction, by J. M. Robson. Introduction by Alexander Brady. 1977.

20. *Essays on French History and Historians*. Edited, with a textual introduction, by John M. Robson. Introduction by John C. Cairns. 1985.

21. *Essays on Equality, Law, and Education*. Edited, with a textual introduction, by J. M. Robson. Introduction by Stefan Collini. 1984.

22, 23, 24, 25. *Newspaper Writings*. Edited by Ann P. Robson and John M. Robson. Introduction by Ann P. Robson. Textual introduction by John M. Robson. 1986.

26, 27. *Journals and Debating Speeches*. Edited, with an introduction, by John M. Robson. 1988.

28, 29. *Public and Parliamentary Speeches*. Edited by John M. Robson and Bruce L. Kinzer. Introduction by Bruce L. Kinzer. Textual introduction by John M. Robson. 1988.

30. *Writings on India*. Edited by John M. Robson, Martin Moir, and Zawahir Moir. Introduction by Martin Moir. Textual introduction by John M. Robson. 1990.

31. *Miscellaneous Writings*. Edited, with an introduction, by John M. Robson. 1989.

Introduction

In his essay "Nature" (1853–54), Mill asks, "What is meant by the 'nature' of a particular object? as of fire, of water, or of some individual plant or animal?" His answer involves no hint of essence or spirit: the nature of an object or being is, rather, the "*ensemble* or aggregate of its powers or properties: the modes in which it acts on other things (counting among those things the senses of the observer) and the modes in which other things act upon it." If the object in question is a "sentient being," Mill adds, its nature also includes "its own capacities of feeling, or being conscious." The word *nature* may be historically "one of the most copious sources of false taste, false philosophy, false morality, and even bad law," but for Mill it holds no mysteries. He sums up his explanation in an authoritative phrase: "The Nature of the thing means . . . its entire capacity of exhibiting phenomena" (10:373–74). Although Mill never offered a comparably complete and systematic definition of *character,* the formulation he arrives at in "Nature" illuminates his understanding of the term he associated with it. *Character* for Mill is, most often, a specifically human version of his definition of *nature,* and it signifies a thoroughly conditioned phenomenon known by its "powers or properties," not by an unchanging essence imperceptible to others. Character involves how one human being acts or is acted upon by other human beings and by their shared circumstances. Character inevitably comprises one's thoughts, desires, and impulses, but it is known most accurately through one's choices and actions.

For Mill, character suggests the qualities that distinguish one individual from another or one group of people from another group. Yet it is more than a mere synonym for *individuality*. Mill's classic statement on that trait, canonized as the lengthiest citation offered in the entry on *character* by the *Oxford English Dictionary*, is too often taken as a sufficient summation of his conception of the proper use of the term: the author of *On Liberty* declares, "A person whose desires and impulses are his own—are the expression of his own nature, as it has been developed and modified by his own culture—is said to have a character. One whose desires and impulses are not his own, has no character, no more than a steam-engine has a character" (18:264). Although Mill's phrasing is almost crafty in its equivocations—what exactly is the relation envisioned here between "nature" and "culture"?—this assertion does treat character as the *sine qua non* of human experience. To be human, to avoid the nonentity of mechanical existence, one must express one's nature, one must have a forceful and distinctive character. Yet more often in Mill's work, the word *character* represents precisely what his definition of *nature* suggests: no matter if they are unusual or commonplace, the qualities that distinguish the individual's or the group's "entire capacity of exhibiting phenomena" constitute its character. In "Nature," Mill eloquently rejects any idealist or essentialist mystifications: there is no innate "nature," no essence that is not already a demonstrable capacity.

Mill's understanding of his own nature depended almost exclusively on his identification of himself as a writer. If he had been asked to characterize his "entire capacities of exhibiting phenomena," he would have responded by pointing unhesitatingly to the body of his written work. His "writings," he told one curious correspondent, provide the only "materials" available for an account of his life (17:1641). In the great mass of his periodical essays, newspaper writings, and multivolume studies on politics, society, and philosophy, he embodied the only "powers or properties," the only "capacities of feeling, or being conscious" that mattered. It was quite possible, he believed, to "put on paper [one's] entire mind" (1:253n), as if writing could effect a kind of transubstantiation. According to Mill, in his own case and particularly after the death of his wife, there was no life beyond the writing—no life in the flesh, no life in the feelings—that would be worthy of comment or consideration.[1] The written word takes precedence not only over speech but also over sensation; once freed from the physical and emotional and social context from which it emerges, writing validates and establishes individuality as no other activity can.

Mill's identification of writing with character was in his own case, he thought, a statement of fact, a fact that provided the basis of his grandest hopes for his works. The process of writing a character, of making one's nature a "power" or giving it "properties" through writing, was central to Mill's conception of his career and to all his major works. This equation was also, for Mill, a corollary of his first principles, principles of such obvious validity and utility that he adopted and adhered to them without question. To conceive of all the works he published in these terms was simply, he assumed, a deduction from the more general laws of character that he found to be universally applicable to all human beings. Writing, in Mill's thought, came to stand not only as a figure for character, but also as an explanation of the relation between the individual and his or her circumstances.

To understand what may seem, at first glance, an oddly reductive form of self-definition, it is necessary to place it in the context of the culture and the personal experience that encouraged its development. For all Mill's either pained or prideful sense of his divergence from the conventional norms of Victorian thought, he shared with his contemporaries a notion of character whose publicity encouraged the equation between an individual's writing and his or her nature. Although Mill's statements about his work provide ample evidence of the extent to which he accepted this identification—and I offer in this introduction the analysis required to gauge its significance for him—its sources in his early experience, in the methods and systems of thought that James Mill inculcated in his son during his famous education, also demand attention: in his training, Mill found confirmed and explained the more general cultural notion that one's writings constitute one's character because, he came to believe, character itself is written onto one by one's experiences.

WRITING AS CHARACTER

Though Mill differed from most of his contemporaries by taking an empirical or, as he called it, experientialist stand, he and his fellow Victorians agreed on the public dimensions of their shared conception of character. Unlike the twentieth-century definitions of *identity* or *the self, character* in Victorian usage was irreducibly public in its manifestations, equivalent to an individual's reputation or to a written reference, the "character" that a servant takes from one situation to the next. Whether their perspective on the subject was moral, economic, religious, or scientific, Victorians used the word in surprisingly similar fashions. Even a writer like Samuel Smiles, who declares that character is the "moral order embodied in the individual," also insists that the test of character is one's behavior toward others. In "Character.—The True Gentleman," the last chapter of *Self-Help* (1859), Smiles combines the language of moral uplift and a recognition of his readers' worldly interests when he explains that character may reveal one's moral nature, one's "righteartedness and kindly feelings," but unless such qualities are demonstrated in behavior, they cannot gain the high repute that is their goal. As he says more bluntly in the later volume called *Character* (1871), "Character is property," property that should win for its owner "reward in esteem and reputation."[2]

The only "System of Character" current in the mid-Victorian period was phrenology; according to this self-declared science, personal qualities are so obviously demonstrable that they can be felt in the size and contours of the skull. When Mill's associate Alexander Bain wrote his critique of phrenology, *On the Study of Character* (1861), he demonstrated a scientific interest that could not be more removed from Smiles's concern for the moral ingredients of worldly success, but Bain's test of character is much the same: "How does a man spend his days?"[3] If one answers that question, one can describe and analyze the constituents of character. For Bain, as for Mill, the primary ingredients of character are the capacities that can be recognized because they have been demonstrated in action or behavior. Bain, therefore, concludes his own attempt to classify the features of character by focusing on the special capabilities exhibited by those with talent and genius, and the examples that he brings forth seem like nothing if not a more intellectualized version of the exemplary men and women whom Smiles describes so that he can teach his readers how to display the qualities that will prove that they themselves have attained similar exemplary status.

The practice of Victorian novelists also witnesses to the public dimensions of character. A figure like Wemmick in *Great Expectations* has one character at the office, another at home. His devotion to his father and his affection for Miss Skiffins are as much public demonstrations of his capabilities as are the coldness and rigidity of his demeanor in Jaggers's presence. Together, the two public forms of behavior reveal Wemmick's "entire capacity of exhibiting phenomena." He is not suffering from the pathological condition of multiple personalities; one supposedly authentic self does not battle against another supposedly inauthentic identity. Rather, Dickens charts the easy transition made from one character to another as Wemmick walks from London to Walworth and back again. Even a novelist like Charlotte Brontë, whose central characters cannot initially be known through their public behavior, endeavors through her plots to offer figures like Jane Eyre and Lucy Snowe the justice of situations in which they can display their capacities.

In two early reviews of the pseudonymous writer Junius Redivivus (1833), Mill reveals the extent to which such an emphasis on the public dimensions of character provides the grounds on which writers are able to establish their individuality through their work. For Mill, as for many of his contemporaries, writing involves the publication of character. His analysis of the work of a pseudonymous author allows him to prove this point. Focusing on the "distinctness with which the individuality of the writer [Junius Redivivus] preserves and paints itself in all that issues from his pen," Mill discusses the array of opinions that reveals the "general character of his mind" (1:381,383). His democratic convictions, his unconventional views on property, his emphasis on the self-improvement open to the working classes, and his respect for learning—all these attitudes are "phenomena" that "exhibit" his character. Mill is impressed that the writer combines "something of the spirit of ancient heroes" with the "superior humanity" and "superior refinement of modern times" (1:372). The analysis of the causes behind this admirable combination of characteristics is fairly specific. The originality of the work suggests a writer self-taught, but wide experience has protected him from the "self-conceit" typical of the autodidact (1:383). Junius Redivivus's bitterness arises from his sympathy with the oppressed. The quickness of his intellect and the expansiveness of his views have been fostered by his appreciation of beauty both as an end in itself and as an agent of human improvement.

In confidently drawing this detailed portrait of the writer, Mill testifies to his acceptance of the commonplace that the Victorians inherited from Romantic critical theories: writing and character are one and the same. He also raises one of the central questions associated with character in Victorian debates on the subject: How is character formed? In these two reviews, Mill answers that question without hesitation: character is formed by its circumstances. Junius Redivivus, both in his lack of training and his longing for improvement, is the product of social institutions badly in need of reform. In short, he reveals one of Mill's firmest convictions: the subjection of the individual to the conditions of his or her historical period. With some condescension, Mill claims that Junius Redivivus's role as a popularizer of the "thought and experience of the few" is the only role open to him. He can do no other, more "eminent" work because he has done the "fittest" and only possible work open to him in "the present epoch" (1:372–73). In fact, the characteristic that clearly betrays the historical positioning of Junius Redivivus is one that he shares with his reviewer: both writers recognize the "depraving influence upon human character" exerted by unjust social and political institutions (1:384).

Although these early essays clearly bear the impress of the thinking of Thomas Carlyle, Mill sets himself off from his would-be mentor by insisting that the character of Junius Redivivus demonstrates the "depraving influence" of his circumstances. For Carlyle, character is self-generated: it reflects each person's unique and essential nature; more important, it can reveal the divinity that is inherent in each individual if the individual has the will to make his or her spirituality manifest. When Carlyle addresses the relation between character and its circumstances, he asks, "What shape . . . must [divine truth] assume with such a man, in such an era?" The "era" does not produce the "man"; the "man" must triumph over the limitations that his historical situation imposes on him. "Great men" are, according to Carlyle, great because they are "Texts of [the] divine BOOK OF REVELATIONS," because their spiritual essence can be read in their actions.[4] Mill, however, wants to understand the historical forces that create individuals so that such an understanding can establish more positive circumstances and, therefore, encourage the formation of improved characters. In his essays on Junius Redivivus, Mill's antiessentialist thinking is uncompromising: in the same way that Junius Redivivus has no character worth analyzing that is not evident in his writings, he has no character that his circumstances have not created.

Mill believed that he, like Junius Redivivus, published his character in his writings. The full extent and the implications of this equation emerge, however, most clearly in Mill's private writings, the diaries, letters, journals, and notebooks that he did not intend for publication, as well as in the passages of the *Early Draft* that were deleted from the *Autobiography*. In such works Mill was essentially preparing the character in which he would appear before the public, studying his part, and sorting out the assumptions that came to underlie his career as a writer. Before turning to that career and to the pressures in it that further encouraged the identification of character with its writings, I want to examine, first, how that identification comments on Mill's character and, then, how his early experience encouraged such thinking.

Mill most explicitly equates the value of his life with the writing he could do in the private or provisional statements he made in the mid-1850s when he was convinced that both he and Harriet Taylor Mill were dying. In particular, the diary that he kept in 1854 reveals how consistently Mill reversed the conventional conception of the relation between experience and writing and gave unquestioned priority to the latter. He began the diary to see if he could come up with "one thought per day which is worth writing down." These thoughts could not be the mere detritus of daily life; rather, they must address issues of "life . . . feeling . . . high metaphysical speculation" (27:641). The apparent absurdity of such a mechanical exercise is offset by the clarity, intensity, and honesty of the feelings that it allowed Mill to record. In this diary, he appears in a character considerably more outspoken and direct than that in which he appeared in public: the man who planned to make public his debt to Wordsworth in the autobiography he was writing explained in his diary that poets ought to be banished from his republic because the "regeneration of the world in its present stage is a matter of business" (27:647). The man who so adamantly demanded the toleration of all opinions admitted that he would, if he could, "blot out entirely" German philosophy, Christian theology, and English law (27:652). But the subject that interested him most, at a time when he found art long and life short, was the reputation earned by a writer's work. The fact that his father was no longer known and respected seemed only the most "striking example" of the fickleness of "posthumous reputation" (27:642). Such considerations could lead him to reveal a writer's petulant jealousy of his more successful contemporaries, and the example of Macaulay evoked signally unattractive expressions of envy. In this private context, which encouraged Mill to express his most intimate fears and hopes, his comments on his own writing are particularly telling.

In January 1854, Mill added to his diary one of his more forceful formulations of the relation between experience and writing. Now that time was running out, Mill noted, "I feel bitterly how I have procrastinated in the sacred duty of fixing in writing, so that it may not die with me, everything that I have in my mind which is capable of assisting the destruction of error and prejudice and the growth of just feelings and true opinions" (27:644). In one of his letters in the same year, he used the same formulation, hoping that more time would be granted him so that his ideas could be "fixed in writing" (14:168). The genuine oddity of this formulation deserves attention. Writing is not a vehicle for communicating ideas; such terminology emphasizes the relation between writer and audience. Nor is writing a form of self-expression: the individual does not speak in and through texts; such a metaphor places the emphasis on the writer and on the writer's need to make external or public what resides in the mind or, as his contemporaries would have added, in the heart. Rather, Mill's term *fix* suggests the physical rigidity and supposed permanence that writing attains when it is printed in an article, pamphlet, or book. Mill seems to have imagined that the contents of his mind, "everything that I have in my mind," could be physically emptied out and "fixed" onto paper much as a botanical or entomological specimen is attached to paper with glue and labels. The writer who ignores so many of the irreducibly physical constituents of experience—bodies, faces, gestures, houses, clothes simply do not exist in his works—seems to have reserved that physicality so that he could locate it in the one fact of his experience to which it might seem to be least relevant: his writing. In this context, the conventional assertion that the writer's work becomes his or her "memorial" takes on new force. The deathly implications that the term *fix* might suggest are here fully appropriate. The books written during the writer's life are "fixed" into rigid immobility by the writer's death, and as Mill said of his father's work, they become "the best monuments" to the life that has yielded them (12:321).

This trope is, characteristically, the writer's gesture in defiance of mortality—one need go to no more arcane source than Shakespeare's sonnets to find a generous array of similar figures—but for Mill it depended on an equation of character and writing that was not simply a conventional figure of speech. Although such a formulation might seem, at first, merely the inevitable outcome of a life devoted, in one form or another, to writing, it is much more than that. The equation between writing and character that appears repeatedly in Mill's work exhibits the complexity of his own distinctive character as no other quality can. Other writers resisted such reductive identifications of themselves with their work. In the *Biographia Literaria,* Coleridge laments the difficulties of having become "*merely* a man of letters," an individual who appears "in conversation, and in print" in forms that he cannot control or contest. Similarly, although John Henry Newman valued an individual's writing as the "lucid mirror of his mind and life," he refused to be bound within the confines of his own words. Even the documents that Newman adduces in the *Apologia pro Vita Sua,* even the earlier writings that testify to the changes in his beliefs, can too easily become a form of "paper logic" that simply misrepresents the "concrete being . . . the whole man."[5]

Rather than resent being reduced to print and paper, Mill actually extended and elaborated the process in revealing ways. Because he granted a certain independence and integrity to the successive stages of an individual's intellectual development, he could also conceive of separate works written at separate times as the monuments to those stages. In his diary, he confessed that he thought of his earlier works as marks of a different character, "the writings of some stranger whom I have seen and known long ago" (27:655). His early essays, collected first in the 1859 edition of his *Dissertations and Discussions,* were, therefore, "memorials of the states of mind in which they were written" (10: 493). Even within a specific intellectual stage, it might be necessary to "fix" an idea in writing like a bug in amber: in his *Autobiography,* Mill explains that as soon as he developed his theory of the syllogism, he "immediately fixed [it] by writing it out" (1:191), and the first provisional description of this act in the *Early Draft* clarifies his motives:

Mill thought of the theory as having been made "safe" by its having been written down (1:190). Earlier ideas in the *Logic,* he has already explained, had been "put on paper" and were therefore "secured . . . from being lost" (1:167). Since Mill makes this statement about a period in the 1830s when death did not seem imminent, it is hard to determine from what these ideas have been "secured" if not from the mutability of thought to which he was particularly susceptible during that decade.

Mill repeatedly emphasized two apparently contradictory attitudes: because ideas arise out of the welter of one's contingent experience, all thought is necessarily provisional—as time and place alter, so does one's thinking—but writing involves the rigidification of thought. He tried to reconcile these contradictions by continually and substantially revising each of his major and many of his minor works as they went into new editions. Each call for a new edition gave Mill the opportunity to ask himself if his ideas had changed since the last. He devoted extraordinary care and effort to revising his works, often delaying completion of other, new works so that such revision could be undertaken. His *System of Logic* (1843) and his *Principles of Political Economy* (1848), to name only his two major treatises, went through eight and seven editions respectively during his lifetime, many of them including extensive and substantial revisions. As long as life lasted, work could be revised. To facilitate that process, for instance, Mill left as an open question in the seventh edition of the *Principles of Political Economy* the issue of a wages fund (4:xxxix), an issue he ultimately found no opportunity to clarify. Mill even entertained the bizarre idea of developing a system of "marks" for the "alterations and additions" that such revision entails, a kind of typographical equivalent to Faulkner's fanciful notion about using different colors of ink to mark the temporal shifts in *The Sound and the Fury.* With regret, however, Mill gave up such a scheme: "one could scarcely give distinctive marks to all the successive strata of new matter" (16:1108). One's past thought is like a cross section of still malleable geologic matter: it offers evidence of the changes that have already occurred, but remains open to further evolution.[6]

Mill invariably thought of his writing in terms of the physical form that would establish its identity as a book. Even in the first entry of the 1854 diary, he described the collection of thoughts that had not yet been written as a "little book" (27:641). More telling still are the lists that Mill drew up of his writings. In four of the five bound volumes of his copies of the *Examiner* (1830–34), Mill listed the articles he had contributed on the flyleaf of the volume. The list for 1833, a tortuously neat and methodical account entitled "Index to my own Articles," seems to function as a table of contents. In three of the volumes, Mill marked his writings with brackets as if he were making a book to conform to that table of contents. The much longer and more comprehensive list that Mill kept in a separate notebook, first published in 1945 as a *Bibliography of the Published Writings of John Stuart Mill Edited from his Manuscript,* covers his entire career.[7] In it, Mill recorded all the published dispatches that he wrote as an employee of the East India Company from 1825 on as well as his books, articles, and reviews. Mill's exercise in authorial bookkeeping was in part, perhaps, the result of impulses developed by his training in the civil service. It resembles nothing more closely than the list of his novels that Anthony Trollope appended to his *Autobiography,* complete with notations on the income that each novel had produced. The differences between these two records, however, are revealing: Trollope attempts to prove his worth by totaling up the pounds he has earned; Mill seems to be content simply to survey the quantity of the writing he has done.

The most famous—or infamous—of Mill's attempts to figure the physicality of his writing is the reference that he made in a letter to Harriet Mill when he called his works "a sort of mental pemican" (14:141). The idea of Mill's thought serving as emergency rations for intellectual Arctic explorers or North American Indians, admittedly egotistical and faintly absurd, does point to an important quality in his attitude toward his work. Just as fruit and meat can be dried in the present for use in the future, the monument constituted by one's writing transcends its original function as a witness to the life that has been lived and becomes a source of instruction to those in future generations who will behold it. Some months before drawing this analogy between writing and sustenance, Mill had explained its implications in more general terms in another letter to Harriet Mill: "We must finish the best we have got to say, & not only that, but publish it while we are alive—I do not see what living depositary there is likely to be of our thoughts, or who in this weak generation that is growing up will even be capable of thoroughly mastering & assimilating your ideas, much less of reoriginating them—so we must write them & print them, &

then they can wait till there are again thinkers" (14:112). The emphasis here on the need, not only to write down ideas, but to publish them as well, suggests how radically isolated the Mills felt themselves to be in their "weak generation." There was available to them neither an individual who could serve as a human safe-deposit box for their ideas nor anyone who could be trusted even to prepare them for publication.

In his *System of Logic*, Mill describes as a "perpetual oscillation in spiritual truths" the way in which the "meaning [of ideas] is almost always in a process either of being lost or of being discovered." Mill clearly thought that his ideas would be lost after his death, but the passage in the *Logic* goes on to point out in general terms the optimistic turn that Mill, at times, could give to this wheel of fortune: "words and propositions lie ready to suggest to any mind duly prepared" the full "meaning" of such "spiritual truths." "Such individual minds are almost always to be found: and the lost meaning, revived by them, again by degrees works its way into the general mind" (8:682). The terms that Mill uses here—propositions "lie ready" to be "revived"—are not vague abstractions. As his uses of "fix" and "monument" and "pemican" suggest, the ideas lie buried, rigid, inert until they are made to live again by the mind able to understand their significance. Ideas, then, even "spiritual truths," are phenomenal, not spiritual: their "nature" is like that of any other existent "thing"—it consists in their ability to act and to be acted upon. Written ideas, if they are unread or misread, are what Mill in the essay on "Nature" calls "unused capabilities," entities whose "powers and properties" are potential rather than actual (10:374).

This concept led to some of the more extreme statements that Mill made about his work—statements, as I have noted, that he presumed would be protected by the privacy of the context in which he made them. Three days after he recorded in his diary his response to the "piece of excellent good fortune" that he enjoyed in having "the whole summer . . . to die in" (27:665), he remarked: "It is not surprising that in ages of ignorance the principal instrument of a magician's arts was supposed to be his books. Books are a real magic, or rather necromancy—a person speaking from the dead, and speaking his most earnest feelings and gravest and most recondite thoughts" (27: 666). This highly uncharacteristic analogy—the rationalist is invoking realms of medieval magic to figure forth the power of books—explains his more characteristic references to their physicality. When he did use a metaphor that suggests communication, it does not involve writers speaking to their contemporaries; rather, the dead are raised so that the voice of the past can speak to those who will live in the future. Death and the passage of time allow writers to voice their "most recondite thoughts": Mill's faith in the gradual but inevitable improvement in human understanding over generations authorized this faith that future readers would be able to comprehend ideas that in his own time seemed impossibly difficult. This process is the reverse of Darwinian evolution: fossils are preserved, not as the record of forms that have outlived their viability, but as forms that will find their use only in the future.

Mill's contempt for his contemporaries and the extent of the cynicism to which it could lead are evident in another passage in the 1854 diary: "Those who are in advance of their time need to gain the ear of the public by productions of inferior merit—works grounded on the premises commonly received—in order that what they may be able to write of first-rate value to mankind may have a chance of surviving until there are people capable of reading it" (27:660). According to Mill, authors should actually set out to write second-rate books in the hope that the celebrity gained by such popular works will preserve their first-rate books for the posterity capable of understanding them. Such condescension, the reverse of claims by a novelist like Dickens that the Victorian audience was equal to the best that could be offered it, reveals both self-satisfaction and self-pity. Although Mill does not say whether he had any of his own books in mind here, the general import of this entry is clear: Mill valued only his future audience, and his consistent emphasis on the physicality of his writing as fixed and monumental allowed him to hope that his work would survive long enough to reach that audience.

That Mill identified his ideal audience with readers yet to be born was the painful result of his public career and the limited opportunities offered by that career during the late 1820s and throughout the 1830s. Tracing in Mill's early training the source of his definition of his works in physical terms as well as his identification of his individuality with his writings provides, however, an appropriate introduction to any discussion of his professional dilemmas. Such definitions constituted, for Mill, deductions from his first principles, arguments from a premise upon which all others are founded, a premise that could be neither proved nor disproved. James Mill was, of course, the source of such first principles. Accounts of the celebrated experiment that he performed on his son and that he required his son to perform on his younger siblings are numerous enough. Chilling images of the father's severity survived even Mill's attempt to soften the portrait of James Mill originally drawn in the *Early Draft* of the *Autobiography*. His was certainly an educational experiment that entailed the emotional and social deprivation of its subject. Yet I would like to focus on what that education included, both in its methods and its content, rather than on what it lacked. Mill was trained according to psychological methods and in a system of psychological beliefs that encouraged him to think of his writing as a physical entity, an entity that conferred the only value available on the experience from which it arose.

Throughout his account of his extraordinary education, Mill stresses the physical quality of James Mill's methods, and the son seems to have developed the propensities that such methods encouraged in ways that might have surprised the father who initially put them into practice. James Mill began by writing out Greek words or "Vocables" and their English equivalents for his son—there being, at the time, no such thing as a Greek/English dictionary—and his son soon imitated this early version of the flash card by turning what he learned into a physical form that he could show to his father. First, the son began recording "on slips of paper" what he was reading so that he could recount the information to his father. This process, Mill claims, began as a "voluntary rather than a prescribed exercise" (1:9,11). In an earlier version of the *Early Draft,* however, Mill admits that it was behavior copied from James Mill: "Passing my time in the room in which he wrote, I had fallen into an imitation of many of his ways and as in reading for his history he made notes on slips of paper of the main facts which he found in his authorities, I made, as I fancied, similar notes on all the books I read" (1:10n). As a child Mill had been able only to imagine that his notes were like his father's.

Faced with a teacher as demanding as James Mill, John Mill logically turned to such a device to aid him in the "*compte rendu*" (1:31), the daily examination of his progress that their walks constituted, but this device was part of a larger pattern of imitative writing. In another passage of the *Early Draft* that did not survive to be published in the

Autobiography, Mill explained that because his father wrote his *History of British India* in his presence and had his son read the manuscript, "Almost as soon as I could hold a pen I must needs write a history of India too." This project gave way to the writing of "what I called a Roman history," and after that, an abridged *Ancient Universal History,* and, before his eleventh or twelfth year, a history of Holland (1:16). Mill shaped his idea of himself as a writer by modeling it after his conception of the powerful figure by whose side he sat from at least the age of three until he was fifteen, when he left for a year's visit with Sir Samuel Bentham's family in France. Soon the young Mill was writing down the substance of his father's peripatetic lectures on the subject of political economy. These notes became the basis for James Mill's *Elements of Political Economy,* the organization of which John Mill helped its author to test by writing out marginal notes on the contents of each paragraph, a practice of making visible the structure of an argument, one that James Mill had in turn learned from Bentham (1:31,65).

When Alexander Bain describes in his *Autobiography* the outmoded pedagogical methods current when he served in the 1840s as a teaching assistant at a Scottish university, he indirectly provides evidence about the source of James Mill's insistence that learning be textually recapitulated. The morning hours of the course in Moral Philosophy were taken up with "diting," as the assistant read an abstract of the course and the students wrote it down verbatim. In the afternoon, the professor "read lectures, repeated from year to year in identical form." One professor in particular took "whole chapters" verbatim from his sources and read them to his students; once they learned where the lectures had come from, they would entertain themselves by reading the text itself as the professor read from his copy as if the words were his own. Bain specifically notes that the "verbal copying" indulged in by this elderly professor and "the diting of notes" were holdovers from the late eighteenth century; presumably this is the kind of teaching to which James Mill himself was subjected.[8] His demand that his son put the ideas he learned into his own words seems, in this context, a radical liberation from old methods. When as an adolescent John Mill was writing a dialogue on his father's essay on government, he was at least putting old wine into new wineskins (26:11).

James Mill's educational practices—with their emphasis on synoptic tables and marginal notes and slips of paper—all equated learning and writing, and his son soon understood that one can prove what one knows on a particular subject by writing about it. In the journal that Mill kept of his visit to France in 1820–21, he noted that the "best exercise" in subjects like political economy and logic consists of writing treatises on them (26:46). Such an attitude also explains the long composition history of his *System of Logic,* a work that he began to write to find out what he needed to know so that he could complete his writing of it. Yet his training often issued in results that went beyond such rational practices. At times Mill suggested that, for him, writing was not merely identified with learning: it usurped the place of perception. In one of his lengthy accounts of a journey through Italy, he told Harriet Mill that he was able to savor the beauty of the scenery more fully "when I am *not* looking at it": "now in this bedroom by candlelight I am in a complete nervous state," a state into which he had worked himself by writing about, rather than seeing, the scenery in question (14:322).

The journals that Mill kept during his walking tours in the late 1820s and the 1830s continually witness to this reversal of priorities. Frequently, Mill notes that he has not mentioned a particular sight or geologic feature in its "proper place" in the journal. Such careful emendation of what is usually assumed to be an *ad hoc* form of composition reveals again Mill's concern with the physical nature of his record: a specific hill or bay or waterfall has a location, not only in the landscape, but in the journal that records that landscape, and it was more important to Mill to find the "proper" location in his writing than in his walking. Such scrupulosity would have struck James Mill, an admittedly more casual, even sometimes mechanical writer, as wasted and perhaps pedantic effort. At one point in his journal of a walking tour in 1832, John Mill describes his writing in terms of his walking: "Thus far have I ventured though without much confidence of success, to attempt to convey an idea of what I saw; but here I hardly dare proceed. . . . Yet having once begun I am ashamed to turn back" (27:619). The descriptive skill required by the writing of the journal threatens a more perilous passage than the landscape itself, and again a commonplace, almost tritely appropriate metaphor that equates making one's way through a text with completing a journey seems to reverse in Mill's case the usual priority given to the tenor over the vehicle: the writing is a journey more physically palpable to its conductor than the actual distance covered, in this case, between London and Falmouth.

CHARACTER AS WRITTEN

If James Mill's educational methods led to such unforeseen outcomes—with his son apparently finding writing more substantial than the materiality it purports to represent—the content of the education that he drew out for his son's benefit had, even more forcefully, the same effect. Along with Greek, mathematics, logic, political economy, and history, James Mill instructed his son in the principles of associationist psychology, the "analytic psychology" (1:71) for whose adaptation and propagation in the early nineteenth century James Mill undoubtedly deserves major credit. Moreover, of all the subjects that John Mill learned at his father's side, associationist psychology was the one about which the student was least free to raise questions.

Repeatedly in his mature years Mill attacked the practice of "principling," a term that James Mill had adopted from Locke to express a teacher's imposition of his or her ideas on the docile mind of the pupil. This practice was, John Mill said in 1836, an "abuse of the human faculties" (18:141). But James Mill clearly "principled" his son when it came to the study of psychology. John Mill could read on his own as much history and poetry and even fiction as he chose; later, he could even perform the intellectual experiment of tasting the thought of the German intuitionist school of "metaphysics," as Mill often called psychology, in the works of Coleridge and Carlyle. But by the time Mill read these authors, his conviction of the undisputed and indisputable validity of his father's brand of empiricism was so strong that the effect of such self-motivated reading in alien doctrines was more apparent than actual, more temporary than long-lasting. Throughout his life, Mill was willing to reconsider and to disavow some of his father's most deeply cherished beliefs—Francis Place thought John Mill's apostasy on the question of the ballot enough to make his father spin in his grave—but associationism was not subjected to such a process of reconsideration and revision.

Mill's *Autobiography,* even in all its various stages and with all its emendations, supports this point. He defines his father's "fundamental doctrine" in psychology as a belief in "the formation of all human character by circumstances, through the universal Principle of Association, and the consequent unlimited possibility of improving the moral and intellectual condition of mankind by education. Of all his doctrines none *was* more important than this, or *needs* more to be insisted on" (1:111, emphasis added). The use of both the present and the past tenses in the final sentence here is telling: this doctrine has been preeminently important in James Mill's lifetime and still is as his son writes the narrative of his own life. Throughout the *Autobiography,* father and son are linked as champions of psychological enlightenment in an age darkened by the superstitions and sophistries of intuitionism. Once in the section of the *Autobiography* completed in 1854 and again in the section added in 1869–70, Mill explains that he has undertaken a particular work to prove the fallaciousness of any psychology not based on a doctrine that "derives all knowledge from experience, and all moral and intellectual qualities principally from the direction given to the associations" (1:233; cf. 1:270); the repetition of this definition offers one of the few evidences in the *Autobiography* of the various stages of its composition. Mill's earlier comments on his enthusiasm for Hartley's *Observations on Man* betray him into an equally atypical gracelessness of style: James Mill "made me study" the book he "deemed the really master production in the philosophy of mind" (1:71).

Significantly, Mill began sustained study of associationism, "under my father's direction," after his return from France in 1821 and according to the methods that had already equated writing and learning in his earlier training. The sixteen-year-old read Locke's *Essay on Human Understanding* and "wrote out an account of it, consisting of a complete abstract of every chapter, with such remarks as occurred to me: which was read by, or (I think) to, my father, and discussed throughout." The student voluntarily "performed the same process" on Helvetius's *De l'esprit* and, at his father's instance, on Hartley's *Observations on Man.* "It was at this very time," Mill notes somewhat disingenuously, "that my father commenced writing his *Analysis of the Mind*" (1:71). The younger Mill was clearly serving as his father's unacknowledged research assistant; the process of recapitulation that he performed on these works was as much for James Mill's benefit as for his own. As the elder Mill worked on his *Analysis of the Phenomena of the Human Mind* (1829) over the next seven years, his son read the manuscript. Being present at the creation of the *Analysis* must have contributed to the force with which his father was able to "principle" his son in the significance of his "fundamental doctrine."

In the version outlined by Hartley and elaborated upon by James Mill, associationism explains thought in terms of its relation to the parallel realm of matter. Physical vibrations in the nervous system account for all sensations and ideas; the individual is the sum of the impressions that have been made on him or her. *Character*—the word that derives from the Greek root meaning an instrument for making an impress, a stamp—epitomizes the assumptions of this theory. Educational systems that attempt to form character take on, therefore, preeminent importance in associationist thought. As James Mill explained in his *Encyclopædia Britannica* article on "Education," "the character of the human mind consists in its sequences," and education, defined as "everything, which acts upon the being as it comes from the hand of nature," can form certain sequences and prevent the formation of others. He continues, in a sentence that evokes the similar cadences of his son's mature prose, "if education does not perform everything, there is hardly anything it does not perform." According to James Mill, "skillful employment of the early years" may render "certain trains" of association "so habitual as to be uncontrollable by any habits which the subsequent period of life could induce." For the absolutism of his faith in the practical potential of associationist training, James Mill may indeed deserve the priority in the field that John Mill granted him.[9]

Indeed, after his father's death and after he had established himself as a thinker in his own right, Mill defined as crucial his father's role in keeping the "truth" of associationism alive. In the last decade of his life, Mill undertook, as an act of filial piety, to establish James Mill as the "reviver and second founder of the Association psychology" by preparing a new edition of the *Analysis*. Mill enlisted the aid of his younger colleague Alexander Bain and his old friend George Grote so that they could bring James Mill's theories into line with more recent developments in physiology, "illustrat[ing] and enforc[ing]" but also correcting the original text (31:99,102). In the *Analysis*, he claimed elsewhere, his father had "done far more for Hartley's theory, than

Hartley himself" (10:24), and James Mill's sense of the value of his work in this field is clear from his boast that he could "make the human mind as plain as the road from Charing Cross to St. Paul's."[10] James Mill's treatise was, to John Mill's mind, the work that raised his father above the level of Bentham's other disciples and proved his originality.

In 1869, then, John Mill was doing for his father's thought what he had hoped to do for his own in the 1850s: he was "fixing" it in writing and republishing it in the form in which James Mill would have written it in the 1860s if he had lived two lifetimes instead of one. Such a republication was required because, as Mill recognized, Hartley's "suggestive" outline of associationism had undergone its own process of being lost and recovered: "his book made scarcely any impression upon the thought of his age" because Hartley lacked the expository skills necessary to fix his ideas in monumental form and because his work was published inauspiciously at "the commencement of the reaction against the Experience psychology." In a claim rendered suspect by John Mill's decision to revise the *Analysis,* he asserted that James Mill's treatment of the system "gave it an importance that it can never again lose" (31:102,98). In fact, John Mill's anxiety to preserve associationism in a form that would be useful to future readers outweighed, as it did in his *Autobiography,* his jealous desire to promote and preserve his father's reputation. At times as he worked on his annotations, Mill feared that he might appear in his notes "too much in the character of an assailant," but he persevered in updating his father's work despite the "uncomfortable feeling" that he was betraying his father in the interests of preserving his system of psychology (16:1526).

Mill's footnotes, along with Grote's and Bain's, ultimately do more, I think, to support James Mill's text than to undercut it, and they do so because John Mill had long before granted associationism a central place in his own thought. Associationism was for Mill what he said Comte's version of history was for the French thinker, "the key to [his] other generalizations . . . the backbone . . . of his philosophy" (10: 269). It was one of those "ultimate truths" upon which other truths depend (31:95). It was itself both supported by the highest authorities and tested on each individual's pulses. As Mill points out in his preface to the *Analysis,* associationism had its beginnings in authorities no less formidable than Aristotle, Hobbes, and Locke; it had reached the status of a "mental science" when Hartley attributed the power of experience to impress itself on the mind to the "great fundamental law of Association of Ideas." James Mill had further clarified and classified the workings of this law. In his son's time, Herbert Spencer and Alexander Bain had done much to achieve its "completion" as a science (31:97,102).

Associationism, however, ultimately did not need this distinguished pedigree, according to Mill, because anyone of even moderate sophistication can examine the patterns of his or her own thoughts and recognize the validity of its precepts. The method of inquiry on which associationism rested was simple observation—of "our own minds [and] a few others," as Mill put it in 1827 (26:393). Unlike the fallacious introspection practiced by the intuitionists, which was intended to reveal which states of mind or assumptions "felt" inborn, the associationist asked each individual to examine complex patterns of thought in order to determine that they are "acquired impressions, mistakenly deemed intuitive" (9:141). As James Mill points out in the first page of the first chapter of the *Analysis*, "It is necessary . . . that the learner should by practice acquire the habit of reflecting upon his Sensations, as a distinct class of feelings; and should be hence prepared to mark well the distinction between them and other states of mind, when he advances to the analysis of the more mysterious phenomena." [11] With a little practice, then, associationism becomes an open truth; anyone not already hopelessly blinded by metaphysical obfuscations should be able to apprehend it. Such a conviction of the simple and absolute cogency of these principles explains the intensity of Mill's bewildered impatience with the vast majority of his contemporaries who could not be impressed by it. The disrepute into which associationism had fallen and remained throughout the nineteenth century was, after all, one of the principal reasons Mill despaired of his own "weak generation."

Associationism, simple and convincing as it might be, was not without its problems, and in much of the writing that Mill did, he attempted to solve those problems without forsaking the system that had created them. His equation of character and writing and his conception of the rigid physicality of the written word both resulted from this impulse. Starting with Hume, to whose "hardy scepticism" Mill attributes the disregard into which "Experience psychology" had fallen (31:98), associationist thinking had called into question the integrity of individual identity. The individual is merely a "bundle" constituted by the impressions to which it has been subject. Impressions are like beads on a string, except that, as the associationist would argue, the presence or absence of the string that holds them together can never be ascertained. In Mill's early and indirect statements on this issue, particularly in his letters to his friend John Sterling, he tried to side-step this problem by focusing on individuality in a way that would emphasize its stability in spite of its constant openness to change. Thus, in 1832, he asked Sterling to supply "a knowledge of *you,* namely of what has passed and is passing in your own mind, and how far your views of the world and feelings towards it, and all that constitutes your individuality as a human being, are or are not the same, are or are not changed" (12:99). Both Hume's skepticism and Mill's desire to escape its implications are evident here. Thoughts, feelings, attitudes—"all that constitutes . . . individuality"—may change, but that individuality, *"you,"* remains mysteriously constant and able to communicate such changes.

In later, more carefully formulated treatments, the evasion of this problem remains the same. In his *System of Logic,* Mill admits that on the subject of mind or consciousness or "the thinking principle," as he labels this elusive concept, "we are . . . entirely in the dark." Only a substantial quotation of this passage reveals the extent of the difficulties that this issue raises:

All which we are aware of, even in our own minds, is (in the words of James Mill) a certain "thread of consciousness;" a series of feelings, that is, of sensations, thoughts, emotions, and volitions, more or less numerous and complicated. There is a something I call Myself, or, by another form of expression, my mind, which I consider as distinct from these sensations, thoughts, &c.; a something which I conceive to be not the thoughts, but the being that has the thoughts, and which I can conceive as existing for ever in a state of quiescence, without any thoughts at all. But what this being is, though it is myself, I have no knowledge, other than the series of its states of consciousness. As bodies manifest themselves to me only through the sensations of which I regard them as the causes, so the thinking principle, or mind, in my own nature, makes itself known to me only by the feelings of which it is conscious. I know nothing about myself, save my capacities of feeling or being conscious (including, of course, thinking and willing): and were I to learn anything new concerning my own nature, I cannot with my present faculties conceive this new information to be anything else, than that I have some additional capacities, as yet unknown to me, of feeling, thinking, or willing. (7:64)

This passage attains something of the sense of profound mystery, if not the eloquence, of St. Augustine's meditations on the nature of memory in his *Confessions*. Although Mill's conception of the "thinking principle" or mind is predictably similar to his definition of the nature of a being as its "entire capacities," such a formulation does not adequately answer the questions it raises. He constantly qualifies the subject he is trying to discuss here—at one point, consciousness is "a something"—as he tries to understand how a capacity that he refuses to conceive of as dependent upon the sensations it registers can exist except through those sensations.

This analysis, which accords with Hume's treatment of the issue, is repeated more than twenty years later in the *Examination of Sir William Hamilton's Philosophy*. Here Mill acknowledges that consciousness is the opposite of a first principle: it is a "final inexplicability." If "we speak of Mind as a series of feelings . . . a series of feelings which is aware of itself as past and future . . . we are reduced to the alternative of believing that the Mind, or Ego, is something different from a series of feelings . . . or of accepting the paradox, that something which *ex hypothesi* is but a series of feelings, can be aware of itself as a series." All Mill can do at this point is to "accept the inexplicable fact" without any theory that will explain it (9:194). Jonathan Loesberg is, therefore, quite justified in his conclusion that Mill based much of his thinking on a "fiction of consciousness." As Alan Ryan, another of the most cogent of recent commentators, notes, Mill's mechanical, phenomenalist psychology "destroys our concept of personal identity; the agent disappears, to be replaced by a spectator of events occurring at a location which we somehow continue to call 'him.'" A contemporary satire in *Blackwood's* put the point in more personal terms, "If there's neither Mind nor Matter, / Mill's existence, too, we shatter."[12] According to the writer of this ditty, Mill's analysis simply reduces Mill himself to a nullity.

At times, Mill dealt with this problem simply by ignoring it and focusing on questions of character, the individual's "capacity for exhibiting phenomena," but the difficulties raised by associationism could not be dismissed quite so easily, particularly by the man who had been trained in associationist principles by the leading associationist of his generation. Significantly, James Mill's harshest criticisms of his son's failures as a student were couched in the associationist terms most likely to arouse anxiety on precisely this point. In the rejected leaves of the *Early Draft,* Mill confessed, "I was, as my father continually told me, like a person who had not the organs of sense: my eyes and ears seemed of no use to me, so little did I see or hear what was before me, and so little, even of what I did see and hear, did I observe and remember" (1:609). Even the most cursory acquaintance with associationist thought suggests how devastating such a criticism is. James Mill conceives of mental functions as a hierarchy, beginning in sensation, proceeding to ideas, then to trains of ideas, through complex variations on consciousness such as affections, motives, and dispositions, to end in the will and intention, the projection of will into the future. Unlike idealist models of consciousness that conceive of a battle between flesh and spirit, associationism does not aim at the annihilation of the lower functions by the higher. The higher, more complex function is "compounded" of the more "elementary" (*Analysis* 2:321), and its goal is to use the information and energy created by sensation and idea in the service of the higher powers such as reflection and moral sense. Without sensation—the capacity to register impressions—there is no "series of feelings" out of which even a "fiction of consciousness" can be developed. James Mill's most withering criticisms denied his son the organs of sense that would have allowed him, according to associationism, to be formed by impressions. Blind and deaf, the young Mill is reduced to imbecility. Without organs of sense, he is, in associationist terms, no one and no thing.

Writing, fixing one's ideas in print, clearly offers a solution to this ultimately annihilating dilemma. John Mill could effectively prove to James Mill that he was mistaken about his son's insensibility by showing his father or by reading to him the record of the impressions that his reading had made on him. Writing makes permanent one's transient impressions—*impression* is a word that recurs repeatedly in the *Autobiography*—and writing can therefore serve as a monument more tangible and satisfying than the "thread of consciousness" that James

Mill defined as the individual mind. The chapter in John Mill's *System of Logic* in which he considers the problem of that "something" called "Myself" is entitled "Of the Things Denoted by Names." By putting the same name on one's various works, by recording each of them in ledger-like fashion, or by meticulously revising new editions of the same works, one can establish both a stable and a changing identity.

Such a conception of writing explains, at least in part, Mill's ambivalence about the anonymity characteristic of periodical publication during this period. In 1834, he complained that newspaper writers were encouraged to be irresponsible because they wrote anonymously, but the intensity of his statement of this problem recalls his father's earlier complaints about his son's insensibility: "A newspaper-writer nobody knows; nobody thinks about him, or inquires who he is; nobody remembers to-day what he wrote yesterday, nor will remember to-morrow what he may choose to write to-day" (6:183). The anonymous writer simply does not exist; he might as well be the figment of some editorial imagination. For this reason, Mill was one of the first to support the idea of signing one's contributions to the periodical press.[13] For this reason, he praised Junius Redivivus for at least using a consistent pseudonym; if every "periodical writer" followed such a practice, he "would then have a character to lose or to gain" (1:370). Appearing publicly in a consistent authorial identity gives a writer a "character" in more than the simple sense of a reputation; it may actually grant one the identity that associationism questions or denies. Any comfort offered to the individual by being able to point to the character embodied in writing would be, of course, emphasized by the physicality of print. Even when Mill laments in 1846 that a poet can no longer, like a Greek bard, write "his poem, as it were, on the memory of the younger bards," his reference to the modern "habit . . . of recording all things in permanent characters" suggests that he is not quite as nostalgic for preliterate times as he claims (11:291). Writing insures the permanence of character.

To understand the full implications of the substantiality that Mill attributed to writing, it is necessary to see that this concept evolved from his associationist definition not only of mind, but also of matter. In both the *Logic* and the *Examination*, Mill claims that "we" are equally "in the dark" about the "inmost nature" of both the interior realm of consciousness and the exterior realm of physical existence (7:64). The status of either as a reality is inexplicable. But in the *Examination,* Mill defines matter in a way that allows him to escape the solipsism inherent in such a formulation, and this definition further reveals why it is so important to Mill to conceive of writing as a record of consciousness that achieves the status of matter. Matter is, according to Mill, the "Permanent Possibility of Sensation" (9:183), by which he means the permanent possibility of being sensed by consciousness. It is no different than the cause of any other sensation except in its potentiality— only the act of naming it *matter* makes it seem a "different thing" than feeling, and for that reason Mill does not give it its "special name" until three pages after he has defined its qualities. Because it can be sensed not once, but again and again, matter gains a significance beyond that of any individual capable of experiencing sensation. Present sensations are "fugitive" and therefore "of little importance." Matter is "permanent" and therefore "important" (9:180).[14]

Moreover, matter transcends the solipsism that associationism might impose on each sensitive agent by being capable of being experienced, not by one person only, but by many: "Other people do not have our sensations exactly when and as we have them: but they have our possibilities of sensation. . . . The permanent possibilities are common to us and to our fellow-creatures: the actual sensations are not." This, Mill claims, is the quality that grants matter the status of "the fundamental reality in Nature" (9:182). Because the act of writing transforms thought into its physical form, it grants thought the status of a "fundamental reality" that may at any time be experienced. And, as Mill continues to demonstrate in his chapter on "The Psychological Theory of the Belief in an External World," because the power of conventional associations persuades people to think of sensation as an effect, matter—the permanent possibilities of sensation—comes to be viewed as "Cause," and "these Possibilities" therefore seem to be "independent and substantive entities" (9:186). Thus, while grounding an understanding of the status of matter and therefore of writing in consciousness, Mill explains why matter, through association, comes to assume a priority over sensation and why he should have wished that his thought might attain such a status when it became writing.

Mill emphasizes the relation of his definition of matter to the physicality of writing through the only example he offers of that definition: "I see a piece of white paper on a table. I go into another room, and though I have ceased to see it, I am persuaded that the paper is still there." In the third edition of the *Examination,* he adds: "If the phænomenon always followed me, or if, when it did not follow me, I believed it to disappear *è rerum naturâ,* I should not believe it to be an external object. I should consider it as a phantom—a mere affection of my senses: I should not believe that there had been any Body there" (9:179). This amplification of the original example suggests what the white paper might represent. Mill's careful notation of the color of the paper—it is white, unmarked—implies that the paper on the table is paper waiting to be written on, but unless the paper can be apprehended by anyone who enters the room, it is a "phantom." Such an example seems to come almost inevitably to the writer of philosophy. William James uses the same illustration in his *Principles of Psychology* when he wants to demonstrate the variety of the "true ways" in which individuals conceive of a "concrete fact": "Now that I am writing, it is essential that I conceive my paper as a surface for inscription."[15] Because Mill, like James, was writing this passage, it is logical, if not essential, to define the paper in question as "a surface for inscription." In that case, the white paper, once written upon, confers physicality on the writer and therefore insures the writer's potentiality. It grants the "permanent possibility" of being sensed, a possibility that is, as Mill argues, "independent of our will, our presence, and everything which belongs to us" (9:182). Without the potentiality that writing insures, one could even argue, the writer might not exist at all.

The second major problem posed by associationist psychology is its inherent determinism, a problem that Mill took more seriously than the first. After all, the mysteries of identity can be ignored as an imponderable that has no practical effect on what one thinks or does. But if thoughts and actions are simply the result of impressions formed in accordance with the universal laws of association, laws to which all human beings are subject equally, there is no room in which to exercise the faculty of will; and "willing and thinking" are the only capacities of consciousness that Mill, in the long passage from the *System of Logic* that I have quoted, feels compelled to identify specifically. He labored early and late to solve this problem, expending ultimately vast resources of time and mental energy so that he could carve out from associationist doctrine a space in which an individual's impulses and desires could gain the freedom they needed if they were to have an effect on character. In his *System of Logic*, Mill dogmatically concludes, "We are exactly as capable of making our own character, *if we will*, as others are of making it for us." Because, he argues, an individual's desires contribute to the "circumstances" that "mould" character, one can change one's character simply by desiring different circumstances: "The work is not so irrevocably done as to be incapable of being altered" (8:840–41). But this answer satisfied Mill no more than it has satisfied generations of his readers. His confidence in the solution he had reached in the *Logic* was clearly premature: the *Examination* includes a later and even longer treatment of this issue, but the results are no more conclusive. How can one desire what circumstances have not already taught one to desire? [16]

The ability of the sequences of association to form character and the inescapability of the effect of sequences already formed were precisely the deductions from the laws of association that Mill found so tormenting in the years of his famous crisis: "There seemed no power in nature sufficient to begin the formation of my character anew" (1:143). This problem became, as Mill explains in the *Autobiography*, one of the burdens that during his crisis made death seem preferable to life—the choice of suicide might seem at least an indisputable act of will. Significantly, however, his misery never prompted him, according to his later account, to question the validity of the psychological system whose precepts he found so paralyzing. Rather, his record of the crisis in Chapter V of the *Autobiography* is cast solely in associationist terms to prove that he found wanting, not the system, but its advocates.[17] In one of the more difficult passages in his account of his life, Mill differentiates between associations that are "artificial and casual"—associations issuing from the "old familiar instruments, praise and blame, reward and punishment"—and "natural" associations based on scientific principles of cause and effect, means and ends. Mill explains that his father depended too much on the former and not enough on the latter; because artificial associations can be undone by the analytic methods in which he was indoctrinated, analysis became a "perpetual worm at the root both of the passions and of the virtues" (1:141,143). If James Mill had been a better teacher, if he had known to associate in his son's mind the pursuit of virtue with its natural consequences, his son would have become a contented, energetic, determined individual. It was no fault of the system that the Frankenstein in charge of this act of creation was unequal to its challenges.

The central problem of the determinism inherent in associationism permeated every area of Mill's thought; its impress is as evident in his work in economics, for example, as in his treatments of psychology. His insistence on the distinction between the laws of production and the laws of distribution in his *Principles of Political Economy* merely recapitulates as it proposes to solve the apparently insoluble contradiction between necessity and freedom. The laws of production are universal and unchanging, imposed on human communities as irrevocably as the law of gravity; the laws of distribution, however, reflect human decisions that may be based on motives like greed or on standards like justice. Yet even Mill's economic theory suggests how evasive such accommodations ultimately prove. The testimony he gave in 1850 before a special committee of the House of Commons offers a telling instance of just how slippery such a distinction might be. When asked to evaluate the possible effects of allowing workers to form a corporation that they themselves would own and control, Mill answered that even if a small number of associations succeeded, they would have the "same salutary effect on [the workers'] minds as if they embraced" all the workers: "Those who might continue to be receivers of wages in the service of individual capitalists, would then feel that they were not doing so from compulsion but from choice, and that taking all the circumstances into consideration their condition appeared to them preferable as receivers of wages" (5:412). In fact, of course, the alternative offered such workers would be merely an appearance, not an actuality, of choice: the number of corporations run by workers would be too small to accommodate all of them if all workers chose to join, and the corporations owned by the capitalists would still have insuperable advantages over those run by workers. But Mill recognized only the importance of allowing workers to "feel" that they have choices when, even in improved circumstances, they would have so few alternatives as to render them meaningless. What Mill reveals here in his consideration of an economic issue emerges with equal clarity when he treats matters that are subject to psychological or philosophical investigation.

Mill's analysis of the relative claims of the doctrines of freedom and necessity in Chapter V of the *Autobiography* is a case in point. He rejects the word *necessity,* almost as if out of a superstitious fear that its use would grant illimitable power to the concept it represents; but he directs his reader to the "chapter on Liberty and Necessity" in the *Logic* to substantiate his claims "that we have real power over the formation of our own character; that our will, by influencing some of our circumstances, can modify our future habits or capabilities of willing" (1:177). One has to look no further than the passage earlier in the chapter in which Mill explains the consolation he found in Wordsworth's poetry to be able to refute this confident claim. Mill specifically states that he found in Wordsworth the power to surmount his depression, not by creating new associations, but by strengthening the old ones. Precisely because the subject of Wordsworth's poetry draws on the "love of rural objects and natural scenery" and, particularly, of mountain vistas, it could appeal to a young man whose most pleasurable associations involved Jeremy Bentham's summer residence, Ford Abbey, and an adolescent tour of the Pyrenees with Sir Samuel Bentham's family. Wordsworth's poems offered the "medicine" that Mill required because they built on a foundation of early associations involving "states of feeling, and of thought coloured by feeling, under the excitement of beauty" (1:151). They offered, in short, not new capacities, but continued proof of preestablished capacities. As Mill says of another art, music, Wordsworth's poetry can "wind . . . up to a high pitch those feelings of an elevated kind *which are already in the character*" (1:147, emphasis added). Mill concludes that the "delight which these poems gave me, proved that with culture of this sort, there was nothing to dread from the most confirmed habit of analysis." But the Wordsworthian "culture of the feelings" that Mill envisions here is itself an associationist formulation (1:153,151).[18] The strong associationist bent in Wordsworth's theory of poetry, as his Preface to the *Lyrical Ballads* proves and as Mill confirmed in his 1829 debate on Wordsworth, makes this conclusion all the more inevitable. Wordsworth's poetry, for all its talk of a "power . . . far more deeply interfused," therefore joins the associationist school as a vehicle for the formation of character, proving once more of the inevitability of its being formed by circumstances beyond its control.

Mill repeatedly pointed out that Christians avoid the most debilitating implications of their beliefs simply by ignoring them, and his handling of the determinist implications of associationist thought in the *Autobiography* suggests that he was not above evasions of the same kind—but stronger medicine was, after all, required. One of the earliest formulations of what Mill called "Experience psychology" suggests how writing might allow at least a partially satisfying solution to this problem. In one of his treatments of the human mind as a *tabula rasa*, Locke suggests: "Let us suppose the Mind to be, as we say, white Paper, void of all Characters, without any *Ideas;* How comes it to be furnished? . . . To this I answer, in one word, From *Experience:* In that, all our Knowledge is founded; and from that it ultimately derives it self."[19] Experience inscribes its characters on the white paper of the mind, and, as Mill continued to follow this line of argument, the result is "character." By using this example in his *Examination* over forty years after he had abstracted and annotated each chapter of Locke's *Essay,* Mill testified to its force. By the mid-nineteenth century, this figure had gained the status of a cliché: experientialists and intuitionists alike described character, as Mill did, by likening it to a book "legible enough" to be "read" (10:96). Throughout Victorian literature, puns on the double meaning of *character* abound. According to Mill, poets, for instance, look within themselves and find there "specimen[s] of human nature, on which the laws of emotion are written in large characters, such as can be read off without much study" (1:346). In exceptional circumstances, Mill might be tempted to reverse the direction of the associationist process inherent in the metaphor—a particularly forceful individual like Lord Durham, for instance, could use Canada as a "tabula rasa" and "inscribe" his own character upon it (6:429–30), but for more ordinary mortals, cause and effect are not reversible: experience impresses itself upon the individual, and the result is character, the identity that issues in the behavior and ideas that can be read by others.

This formulation gained force in the case of the young John Stuart Mill because experience had come to him most often in the form of writing. In the *Autobiography* he takes quite seriously the obligation to "mention . . . all the books which had any considerable effect on my early mental developement" (1:73), the result of which is the inclusion of several numbingly list-like paragraphs in the first chapter. Mill seems to think that such lists will tell the whole story—much to the annoyance and frustration of readers who rightly want to know about other kinds of experience, about the effects of being raised, for instance, in a small house with too many siblings and a mother who served as the maid-of-all-work. Yet the "impressions" received from books are, to Mill, the ones that matter, and his story, as he tells it, offers one of the most forceful examples of the power of such impressions, an example that is comparable even to that of St. Augustine reading the life of St. Anthony or of Newman reading the writings of Thomas Scott. When Mill first read the *Traité de législation*, Dumont's redaction of Bentham's thought, he was not only transfigured and translated, "taken up to an eminence from which I could survey a vast mental domain"—he was transformed. "When I laid down the last volume of the *Traité* I had become a different being" (1:69). Books do not simply constitute part of the circumstances that form character; remarkable books can alter character, create a new being to take the place of the old by demonstrating that the old character is either naive or irrelevant. One might have thought that a person who had read as many books as John Stuart Mill had by the winter of 1821/1822 would have become inured to their effects. Quite the contrary, his training seems to have made him only more impressible.

This striking example of the power of books to inscribe themselves on the reader's character offers, of course, no proof that the individual has a role in determining the circumstances to which he or she will be subject. After all, it was James Mill who decided when and if his son would read the *Traité*. Among the very few references to physical acts in the *Autobiography*, Mill mentions on six separate occasions that his father "put [a particular book] into my hands" as if to emphasize, by noting the physicality of that action, the power of both the reading he did and of the father who determined its course.[20] Once more, however, if one examines Mill's private writing, the work he did not intend for publication, a more satisfying solution emerges, and once again, it is based on a process that equates character and writing.

Mill's journals reveal throughout the strength of the impress that his reading had made on his character. Particularly in the journal that he kept during his 1831 walking tour of Yorkshire and the Lakes, Mill imitates Wordsworth's turns of phrase as obsessively as he has imitated his father's writing of history. A pile of stone on the summit of a mountain makes of Mill the garrulous sea captain of "The Thorn": "No one could have resisted the temptation of imagining it to be the abode of some unfortunate being" (27:514). Although Mill spent four days in Wordsworth's company, he describes that time in only the most general of terms; there is no sketch of the poet's manner, talk, person, or home. But the effect of Wordsworth's poems, which Mill had read before their meeting, is registered throughout the journal and particularly in Mill's account of his "melancholy" farewell to Windermere: "The image of the lake and mountains remained impressed upon the internal eye, long after the physical organs could see them no more" (27:556). This awkward paraphrase of "The Daffodils," a poem that Mill had specifically defended in his speech on Wordsworth before the Debating Society in 1829, suggests that the scene is "impressed" on Mill only because his reading has made him capable of registering it in the terms that Wordsworth's poem has offered.

Yet Mill's journal seems also to propose writing as a way of reversing this process and gaining at least a temporary surcease from the tyranny of impressions. In his introduction to Mill's accounts of his walking tours, John M. Robson argues, quite rightly, that they contain evidence that implies that they might have been written with at least a private audience in mind (26:li). Yet no intended audience could account for the relentlessly obsessive quality of these journals, a characteristic, indeed, that makes reading them, unlike most of Mill's writing, a chore. At night, after long days of walking or after additional evening rambles, or during a rainy day, Mill recorded what he had seen. He piles long, numbingly minute descriptions of the turn of a mountain or the massing of a geologic formation, one on top of another, until it seems that the only purpose of writing these passages must inhere in the act of writing itself. Such, I think, is the case. The daily entries into the journals serve as a kind of aesthetic exercise. Mill is constantly trying to explain why he considers a particular building or view beautiful.[21] Especially in the entries written just before Mill meets Wordsworth, he is testing his ability to find the figurative language that will not do an "injustice" to one sight or another (27:550). Struck by a view of some "curious rocks," he tries one metaphor after another: the rocks resemble "a monkey feeding her cub" or "a bear devouring some small animal." Mill is genuinely pleased to discover an account of this sight in Jonathan Otley's *Concise Description of the English Lakes;* Otley's account proves that Mill's metaphors, which together imply an interesting collocation of nurture and cruelty, "were but a type of the diversity of the images the objects suggested to different observers" (27:526). The Utilitarian on foot in the Lake District is, therefore, like other tourists in his power to invent creative figures. As his meeting with Wordsworth approaches, Mill's journal entries strive even more devotedly to make him worthy of the meeting by proving that he has developed an acute aesthetic sensibility. Writing not only records how experience impresses itself on character: it is an activity, Mill seems to hope, that allows the character to inscribe on itself the features that it hopes to find there.

A year later, Mill remarked, "I learn every day by fresh instances, that only when I have a pen in my hand can I make language and manner the true image of my thoughts" (12:97). Although this comment might be dismissed as a merely conventional invocation of a Romantic theory of self-expression, its implications go beyond such a formula. Here Mill invalidates spoken language and wordless gesture as forms of communication. Wielding a pen seems to allow him to create the only image of his thought that he chooses to recognize as his own. The graceless, stilted shadow of Wordsworthian language that haunts the pages of the journal of Mill's tour in the Lakes proves how faint the hope of rewriting one's character through writing could, at times, be. Wordsworth's poetry is less instrumental in "saving" Mill than in suggesting the kind of character he could never quite become.

Yet, as following chapters demonstrate, the power of writing, exerted over others and not directly over oneself, did indeed offer Mill more than a faint hope of freedom. Sketching portraits of one's contemporaries is a way of rewriting oneself. Although such sketches are, for Mill, more self-involved and more self-serving than he would have wanted to admit, they are a genuine, if qualified, assertion of imaginative freedom. Moreover, writing offers a kind of associationist's revenge. One's printed work can, if one is skilled enough, exert the influence that books have had in one's own life. Power that cannot be escaped can, at least, be used on others. Such, precisely, was the effect of a work like *On Liberty*. Charles Kingsley, in words that recall although they cannot echo the account of the effect of Bentham's *Traité* on Mill, described Mill's book as a force he could not resist. Picking up a copy of *On Liberty* at a bookseller's shop, Kingsley felt compelled to sit down, then and there, and read it from beginning to end. *On Liberty* made of Kingsley "a clearer-headed, braver-minded man on the spot," nothing less than a new man.[22]

At twenty-one years of age, Mill commented on the "power of early impressions [to] decide the whole character, the whole life of the man" (26:411). That judgment, rendered at so young an age, might seem to have been somewhat premature if it were not for its applicability to the entire course of Mill's career. Such a statement is, of course, an article of associationist faith. Mill's equation of character and writing along with his emphasis on the physicality of the printed word are the constants of his thought that attest to the strength of the early impressions that his study of associationism made on him. Once he took his place in the wider public world beyond the room in which James Mill wrote, John Mill would have to find ways to accommodate his belief in the validity of associationism to a culture that was appalled by its implicit atheism and disgusted by its unabashed materialism. As William James put it, the Mills, preceded by Hume and followed by Bain, had "constructed a *psychology without a soul*" (*Principles* 1:15).

Nearly twenty years later, at the midpoint of his fifty-year career as a writer, Mill gave a twist to his earlier statement about the power of "early impressions." In the middle of a paragraph of a newspaper article that was not reprinted until its appearance in the Toronto *Collected Works*, Mill explains, "What shapes the character is not what is purposely taught, so much as the unintentional teaching of institutions and social relations" (24:955). This claim is, of course, in line with associationist doctrine, though it puts in question utilitarian convictions about the extent to which the training of the individual can be planned and controlled. The emphasis on "unintentional teaching" certainly runs counter to the dominant "spirit of the age": Mill's contemporaries believed firmly in the intentional improvement that could be gained by amassing parliamentary blue books and self-help manuals, by instituting poor laws and charitable organizations, and by establishing schools and projects for colonization—all in the name of the purposeful pursuit of improved individual lives and a world made safe for free trade. Mill himself was one of the voices—or pens— most devoted to such causes. After all, he pointed out the power of "unintentional teaching" in 1846 only so that he could encourage his contemporaries to recognize its untoward effects and substitute for it the kind of intentional teaching he advocated.

Yet, as I demonstrate in the following chapters, Mill's mature experience taught him the power exerted by institutions and social relations over the feeble wishes and impulses of the individual. If Mill's identification of his character with his writing was the result of his father's intentional teaching, it was a lesson hammered home by the institutions and social attitudes of Victorian culture, a lesson that he had been forced to learn, a lesson whose implications he continued to try to ignore. Because associationism is now a dead letter, an idea granted the physicality of text but so petrified as to be beyond hope of revivification, it would be easy to ignore what it shared with other currents of Victorian thought that, even then, seemed more vital. Yet both Mill's early training in associationism and his later experience in the public sphere had the same effect: they tended to convince the man who wanted to study character that his own character was most fully, even adequately, embodied in his writings.

Part 1

A Career in Theory
and Practice

Responding to an inquiry for biographical information from an American journalist, just as he was to write the final segment of his *Autobiography*, Mill claimed that his personal history was of no interest to the general public. Yet the summary of his career that he offered the journalist, which I quote in full, is in many ways more revealing than the much longer and more self-protective official life that was to be published posthumously in an attempt to forestall any "pretended biographies" that others might write (31:329):

My life contains no incidents which in any way concern the public; and with the exception of my writings, which are open to every one, there are no materials for such a biographical sketch as you contemplate. The only matter which I can furnish is a few dates. Born in London, May 20, 1806. Educated wholly by my father, James Mill, author of History of British India, Analysis of the Phenomena of the Human Mind, and other works. In 1823 received an appointment in the East India House, and rose progressively to be the head of the principal office of correspondence between the home authorities and the local government of India, a post which had been held by my father. Quitted the service in 1858, when the functions of the East India Company were transferred to the Crown. Married in 1851 to Harriet, daughter of Thomas Hardy Esq. of Birksgate, near Huddersfield and widow of John Taylor Esq merchant of London; who died in 1858. Elected to Parliament for Westminster in 1865; was an unsuccessful candidate for that city in 1868.

On that note and with the usual "I am Dear Sir yours ever faithfully" (17:1641), the letter ends.

Mill here offers but a "few dates." Any selection of facts is, no doubt, an interpretation, and this selection of the primary facts of birth, career, and marriage in a particular life is no exception. "Incidents" are nonexistent; the writings, "open to all," constitute the life. That these sentences lack a subject—"Quitted . . . Married . . . Elected . . ."— epitomizes the self-effacement typical of Mill's directly autobiographical remarks. Moreover, the emphases of the "few dates" that Mill does provide here are telling. Unlike several chapters in the *Autobiography*, in which James Mill has no place and no power, this summary links the father's career and his writings to the career of the son. In the

Autobiography, John Stuart Mill is born "the eldest son of James Mill, the author of *The History of British India*" (1:5); here James Mill is equally the author of the classic nineteenth-century text in association psychology. The son's position in the East India Company is given a prominence here that the *Autobiography* studiously denies. The peculiarities of Mill's statement about his marriage reveal lingering doubts about the propriety, even the legitimacy, of that bond: his wife is simply "Harriet," not Harriet Taylor, more the daughter of Thomas Hardy than the wife of John Taylor, even though by the time she married Mill, she had not lived in her father's house since she was eighteen, and her father had died in the same year as her husband. The grammar of the sentence, though strictly correct despite its incompletion, is equally slippery in its implications. If one does not pay careful attention to the semi-colon before the final clause, Mill seems to be saying that John Taylor died in 1858, seven years after Mill married his wife. Mill and those later commentators jealous of his intellectual stature have tried either to see only the advantages of Mill's relation to Harriet Taylor or to ignore it completely. But even this factual statement reveals how little such optimistic accounts or such discreet silences tell of the strains and uncertainties that Mill imposed on himself by making his relationship to Harriet Taylor "the most valuable friendship of my life" (1:193). His sketch encompasses not birth and death—the latter, of course, being outside his ken—but birth and political defeat. The brief, but final note—"unsuccessful candidate for that city in 1868"— had profound meaning for Mill, a meaning that he chose to explore only indirectly in the segment of the *Autobiography* that he was to write in 1869–70.

The "biographical sketch" that follows confirms the implications of the skeletal account that Mill offered in this letter. It claims that the "materials" for a biographical account of his life are to be found in his writings, that they are more "open to every one" than the *Autobiography* is. It focuses less on the education that Mill received from his father than on his father's role in determining his son's later career, less on Harriet Taylor Mill as the "joint" author of Mill's works than as the cause and the symbol of the dilemmas he faced as a writer. It attempts, accordingly, to pay attention to what Mill himself called "those facts in human life which tend to influence the depths of the character . . . such, for instance, as the sexual relations, of those of family in general, or any other social and sympathetic connexions of an intimate kind" (10:98). Yet any attempt to chart the "depths" of character through analysis of such "intimate" connections cannot take for granted the conventional categorization of some factors in an individual's experience as private and of others as public. Indeed, as the following chapters argue, Mill's work as a public figure was as much a response to his relation to Harriet Taylor Mill as that relation was the result of the same cultural and material forces that determined his vocational alternatives. No understanding of Mill's "intimate" experience is possible, therefore, unless it is seen in relation to Victorian debates on the competing claims of theory and practice, the alignments of work and gender, and the value of disinterested thought and heroic action. Although Mill continually counseled the need to move beyond "the narrow bounds of individual and family selfishness" as if there were a wider public sphere in which such motivation would simply evaporate (19:322), his story witnesses to the inextricable connections between personal history and public concerns as they both affect and reflect the "depths" of his character.

One

Vocation

In 1843 when Mill published his first book, *A System of Logic Ratiocinative and Inductive: Being a Connected View of the Principles of Evidence and the Methods of Scientific Investigation,* he could hardly have been expected to foretell the success it would become. Mill's *Logic,* no doubt, owed its contemporary acclaim, particularly at Oxford and Cambridge, to its clear and cogent exposition of a method of inquiry that would bear fruit throughout the century. Part of the charm that the work still retains—and *charm* is, I think, the appropriate term here—results from the assured tone of its author, his conviction that he knows what he wants to accomplish and how to go about the task. Yet another quality, equally unexpected in a work that deals with "abstract truth, & the more abstract the better" (12:78), is its participation not simply in the current debates of Victorian intellectual life, but in the debates surrounding its popular and conventional attitudes. Some of the cultural assumptions that make their way into the *Logic* are, however, the reverse of charming. In illustrating how a syllogism can prove a negative, Mill offers an example that concludes, "Mr. A's negro is not necessarily vicious" (7:169). This example stood unrevised through eight editions of the *Logic,* even after the abolition of slavery in America, a new age at whose dawning Mill rejoiced particularly when it was heralded by Lincoln's reception of the first African-Americans to visit the White House. In this syllogism, Mill is offering evidence of the power of popular assumptions: the only way to counter racism is to claim that at least one black is not a savage. If the *Logic* records the impress on Mill of the psychological system he had learned during his years of private tuition with his father, it also reveals the pressures exerted on Mill by the larger culture in which he was attempting to find his place.

The most striking revelation of popular assumptions in the *Logic*, for my present purposes at least, testifies to the status of the speculative thinker in Victorian England. In speaking of common fallacies, Mill turns to the mistaken belief that "whatsoever has never been, will never be." To illustrate the inadequacy of this presupposition, Mill offers the following examples: Women can never have the intellects of men, Negroes can never be as civilized as whites, and philosophers can never be "fit for business." "Bookish men, taken from speculative pursuits and set to work on something they know nothing about, have generally been found or thought to do it ill," just as women have proven that they cannot learn and blacks that they cannot be tamed (8:788–89). Mill is, of course, objecting to such failures of reasoning. Indeed, the way in which he describes the test used to prove the practical inadequacy of bookish men reveals the narrowness of the prejudice against them: even those well accustomed to "business" would fail when "set to work on something they know nothing about." Yet the conjunction of these examples—women, blacks, and philosophers—demonstrates the common disabilities suffered by members of all three groups. Like blacks and women, theorists in Victorian Britain were too often dismissed as powerless and marginal figures whose views were easily rejected but more often simply ignored.

In undertaking to write *A System of Logic*—a massive work on the "science of science itself, the science of investigation" or "method" (12:79)—Mill had, of course, defined himself as a theorist and had settled into what he later calls in the *Early Draft* of the *Autobiography* his "literary existence" as a writer on speculative questions (1:616). To a certain extent, Mill inherited from his father the conviction that theory could be successfully defended against the opposing claims of practice. It was, in fact, a subject on which James Mill entertained no doubts. Alexander Bain recorded that the elder Mill's commonplace book brought together a "mass of authorities to check the overween-ing presumption of the 'practical' man."[1] Once when the young Mill had casually used the "common expression that something was true in theory but required correction in practice," James Mill responded with "indignation." After humiliating his son by making him attempt to define the word *theory,* the father defined the term properly as he exposed the fallacy behind the "vulgar form of speech" through which his son had betrayed his "unparalleled ignorance" (1:35).

In 1836 James Mill published in the *London and Westminster Review* a dialogue called "Theory and Practice," and its form suggests that it might have recapitulated and idealized this uncomfortable conversa-tion with his son. Y plays the Socratic role in the dialogue, developing definitions and narrowing the discussion, all for the benefit of poor, benighted X, who believes that to follow theory is simply to follow one's fancy. By proving that all theories are based on past experience, Y is able to demonstrate that "those people who condemn others by saying you follow theory, and extol themselves by saying we follow practice, only show the wretched state of their own minds. . . . All men . . . in every rational action of their lives are followers of theory." X capitulates completely: "What a revolution you have produced in my mind," he tells Y.[2] The adolescent Mill responded to his father's anger with less gratitude than X lavishes on Y's rational demonstra-tion, but both forms of indoctrination support the same lesson: that the "vulgar" privileging of practice over theory is simply a proof of ignorance and folly.

Throughout his career, John Stuart Mill registered his awareness of the "ancient feud" between theory and practice as well as his dismay at the vehemence of its expression during his own times (4:324), but his elaborate and frequent comments on this issue reveal how close to the bone it cut. His attitude toward the question in general tended, naturally, to alter as he altered his specific conception of his own role as a theorist. In his early essays, John Mill was content to adopt both the absolutism and self-assurance of his father's attitudes. Writing in 1824, he denounced so-called "practical men" as the most "unsafe" and "bigotted," the "most obstinate and presumptuous of all theo-rists" because they erect their principles on the "small number of facts which come within the narrow circle of their immediate observation" (4:19). In an essay written in 1837, Mill uses the same terminology that would later appear in the passage in the *Logic* in which he equates philosophers to the other marginal groups composed by blacks and women. He claims that the thinker "whose business it has never been to act" may have "originate with him" thoughts "for which the world may bless him to the latest generation," but only if they are "recast in the mould of other and more business-like intellects" (20:173). In 1837, before he had settled into his "tranquil and retired existence as a writer of books," as he describes his life in the *Autobiography* (1:272), he could afford to be scathing about the unlimited "chimeras" produced by the thinker untested by the exigencies of practical life. Revising this passage extensively for the 1859 edition of his *Dissertations and Discussions,* he is much more sympathetic to the individual who, according to both versions, "thinks without any experience in action, or without having action perpetually in view" (20:173). Although the motivation for this revision may seem a "little mysterious" (20:cxii), it becomes less so when it is located in the context of Mill's emerging definition of himself as a man of thought rather than a man of action.

If his attitude toward the challenges created by such prejudices was more ambivalent than James Mill's, John Mill's defense of theory was also more subtle and sophisticated. Knowing as he did that *theory* was to many Victorians a dirty word—Mill himself once uses it in such a way in *The Subjection of Women* (21:264)—he often tried to avoid its use and the unattractive implications that it conjured up by speaking of a debate, not between theory and practice, but between science and art.[3] Thus Book VI, Chapter XII of the *Logic* treats the "Logic of Practice, or Art." At times in his more polemical works, the debate becomes one between science and quackery, or between "general principles" and "tricks" (4:111,115). Some of Mill's commentary on this issue suggests the extremes to which he felt he had to go before he could establish the claims of theory. In his *Principles of Political Economy,* he rejects the traditional categories that distinguish agricultural, manufacturing, and commercial endeavors; instead, he develops a hierarchical categorization that has at its acme the "labour of investigation and discovery." To defend this new classificatory scheme, he first breaks down the distinction between mental and physical labor—even Newton had to push a pen across the page—so that he can break down the distinction between speculative and practical thought. Even "purely speculative and apparently merely curious enquiry" results in practical applications:

"No limit can be set to the importance, even in a purely productive and material point of view, of mere thought" (2:42–43). Both the organization and terminology of this passage suggest how important and how difficult it is for Mill to defend "mere thought." Instead of resting its claims on standards opposed to those that justify practice, Mill has to resort to such practical standards to make his case.

At several points in his career, it became important to Mill to believe that a reconciliation between theory and practice was possible. In his important essay "On the Definition of Political Economy," published in 1836 but written in 1831, Mill muses on the benefits that could be offered society by a "speculative politician" or a "practical philosopher" (4:335–36), reversing the conventional arrangement of nouns and adjectives to suggest the new hybrid he has in mind. Such an accommodation to the status accorded practice in Victorian culture had its basis, certainly, in Mill's reformist goals, but a better-known essay, his most careful evaluation of Bentham, reveals Mill's stake in this issue.

Mill's handling of the relation between theory and practice in the essay "Bentham" (1838) offers the most remarkable instance of the power of popular prejudice. He brings up the issue in the first sentence: Bentham and Coleridge are the two men who have achieved a revolution in "thought and investigation," whose ideas dominate the "thinking men in their time." Almost immediately—in the next sentence, in fact—the popular prejudice appears: both men are "closet-students—secluded in a peculiar degree, by circumstances and character, from the business and intercourse of the world: and both were . . . regarded . . . with feelings akin to contempt." This widespread contempt is a monster that rears its ugly head, not so that Mill can cut it off, but so that he can allow it to hover triumphantly over the rest of the essay. In his first paragraph Mill makes a faint effort to allay this prejudice, saying that Bentham and Coleridge have proven what must be proven anew in every generation—that thought is "the thing on earth" that "most influences" the "business of life" (10:77). Yet the rest of the essay undercuts that stand.

In fact, the first authority that Mill cites to prove Bentham's value is an unnamed "man of great knowledge of the world and of the highest reputation for practical talent and sagacity" (10:78). No closet-student has sufficient authority to pass judgment on another closet-student.

"Our idea of Bentham," as the essayist says, involves a man remarkable, not for his abstract thought, but for his "essential" practicality (10:93). Although Mill spends a great deal of time analyzing the limitations of Bentham's understanding of human nature, limitations that inevitably compromised his thinking, Mill claims that there is no reason to distrust Bentham: his thought is capable of "organizing and regulating" the "*business* part of . . . the social arrangements" (10:99). Mill continues to appeal to his readers by stressing Bentham's "intensely practical turn of mind" (10:103); his writings will "long form an indispensable part of the education of the highest order of practical thinkers" (10:115). Near the end of the essay, Mill concedes that "it may surprise the reader" that he has said nothing about the "first principle" of Bentham's philosophy, a principle "with which his name is more identified than with anything else." This first principle may have been necessary to Bentham, but it is not "in reality necessary for the just estimation of Bentham" (10:110). The speculative thinker who devoted a lifetime to exploring the implications of the principle of utility can best be understood by ignoring the principle itself. The essay on Bentham was, as Mill said, written at the height of his reaction against his Utilitarian training; even so, its betrayal of his father's faith in the priority of theory over practice is striking. The prejudice against the closet-student is so compelling that Mill himself assents to it.

When Mill came to write the *Early Draft* of his autobiography in the mid-1850s, his allegiance to the life of the theorist was at its strongest and least ambivalent. He offers little direct evidence, either in the draft or in the final version of the *Autobiography,* that he has ever wavered in his loyalty to the life of thought. His unquestioning acceptance of his role as a speculative thinker dominates his mature perspective on his past experience. Mill makes the story of his progress from reader to writer, from student to author, seem natural, even inevitable. On its surface, indeed, the *Autobiography* unashamedly records the life of a self-styled "bookish man." Mill presents his education as the sum of the books he read, his mature achievement as the sum of the books he wrote. The *Autobiography* is, as he notes, the "tale of [his] writings" (1:207), and the boy trained more "to *know* than to *do*" becomes in its pages the author of "books destined to form future thinkers" (1:39,85). Beneath this explicit, official account of Mill's life, however, lies another story. Through telling indirections and hints, significant silences, and transpositions of chronology and subject matter, the *Auto-biography* conveys the extent to which Mill not only felt threatened by the prejudice that valued practice over theory, but also often shared that prejudice.

Although his writings hardly display the impractical aridity of the stereotypical "bookish man"—no Mr. Casaubon, he—Mill himself often measured his efforts against the standard of practical action and found them wanting. Even though his voluminous output of books and essays was consistently motivated by his desire to change the social and political conditions he deplored, he could not avoid recognizing the distinction between a writer who encourages reform and a politician who makes it happen. In fact, Mill's uneasy recognition of the marginality of the theoretical thinker in Victorian society illuminates a number of the more troubling and mysterious cruxes of his experience, including such well-known conundrums as his famous crisis and his relation to Harriet Taylor. Understanding these problems, however, depends on being able to gauge the distance between Mill's mature role as a writer and his youthful ambitions for quite another sort of life.

VOCATIONAL CHOICE

In one of the passages cancelled from the *Early Draft* of the *Autobiography,* Mill confesses that his "instinct for closeness" and "reserve" had become "habitual" from an early age (1:612–13). His reticence in the *Autobiography* is, at once, both overly scrupulous and ultimately ineffectual. Closeness—the instinct of the clam to shut itself tightly up in its shell at the approach of any prying force—is indeed what most readers recognize as the principal strategy of self-presentation in the *Autobiography.* In some cases Mill's reticence can be particularly confusing because it masquerades as openness: his effusive account of his intellectual debt to Harriet Taylor is, like his detailed rendition of his years of crisis, more disguise than revelation. In some instances, Mill's silence is so absolute as to cry out for comment: his deletion of his mother from the *Early Draft* is only the most obvious example of such an omission. Yet there are other instances in which Mill seems to say just enough to convince his readers that no more need be said. Nowhere in the *Autobiography* has the partial reserve that he practices there more effectively closed off discussion than in his treatment of his youthful ambitions about the work that he hoped he would later undertake when he became an adult.

As the mature narrator of his own story, Mill invariably presents such ambitions in an oblique and condescending fashion. When he alludes vaguely to his earlier "aspirations," he labels them "juvenile" in both the literal and the pejorative senses of that word (1:65). One "boyish ambition" that he locates in his late adolescence led him to unspecified "great excesses" that would require "a useless waste of space and time" to relate (1:111). But like every other autobiographical narrator, Mill must live not only with what has happened, but with ever-present imaginative constructions of what might have happened, and the regrets attendant on such thoughts ultimately do make themselves felt in ways that reveal his dissatisfaction with his "bookish" life. Even the complexity of the composition history of the *Autobiography* and the different pressures exerted on it at the different points in its drafting did not alter the centrality of these questions. Mill's sensitivity on the subject of his failed ambitions never altered, although the different forms in which it evidenced itself varied considerably.

To follow the fate of Mill's youthful aspirations in the *Autobiography*, the reader must continually shift perspective backward and forward: forward to the specific later circumstances that shaped the interpretation of a given event and backward to the yet earlier circumstances that created the context in which the younger Mill experienced the event. Only then can one do justice to his "juvenile aspirations." In his brief, glancing account of his earliest ambitions, Mill is, of course, revealing that the question of vocation—of what he will do in the world—was important to him, but he refuses to think of it as a question, as a choice that at one time had not already been made for him. The significance of Mill's early ambitions, both in terms of the shape of the *Autobiography* and the trajectory of his later career, cannot be overstated.

One of the alternatives that Mill does not mention at all suggests the power of his impulse toward reticence, particularly on the issue of vocation. According to "family tradition," James Mill's patron, Sir John Stuart, gave his namesake a gift of £500 to allow him to attend Cambridge University, but either father or son declined, if not the gift, at least the purpose for which it was intended. Mill's silence about this gift perhaps reflects the protective instincts that dominate so much of the *Autobiography*. In this case, he might be trying to protect the memory of his father, who raged often enough against the privileges of money and class to have been convicted of self-contradiction for even entertaining the idea of profiting from them. More likely, however, is the possibility that Mill is protecting himself from a recognition of one of the alternatives that would have changed the direction of his later experience. In 1823 a Cambridge professor revived the idea behind Sir John Stuart's gift when he "urgently" pleaded with James Mill to allow his son to attend the university and mix there with his "Patrician contemporaries."[4] That Mill did not have an opportunity to prepare himself for a public career through the conventional route of university attendance is a fact pertinent to the questions of vocation that he found too important and too painful to be treated directly. To understand the import of this omission, one needs to read the hints suppressed but contained in his account of his unconventional training for the career that did await him.

Mill seems to have been as precocious in developing ambitions for himself as he was in learning Greek, but he carefully conceals that fact from the reader by referring to his ambitions in only the vaguest of terms and only at points in the narrative when those terms are likely to be misunderstood. Mill confesses his early desire to be a "reformer of the world" in Chapter V in a reference to the founding of the *Westminster Review* and directly after his account of his "youthful propagandism" (1:137). In this context the confession clearly refers to the work he had been doing as his father's lieutenant in the field of political journalism. Yet is the pen the instrument by which the young Mill had proposed to reform the world? Was writing the role into which he planned to pour what he confesses were his considerable stores of both energy and ambition? Earlier passages in the *Autobiography* suggest an answer other than the one implied by the placement of this confession.

In Chapter III, Mill explains that he did not have access to a history of the French Revolution until after his return in the spring of 1821 from his fourteen-month stay in France. In the winter of 1821 or 1822, he read for the first time about the "great commotion" of which he had had only a "very vague idea": "From this time, as was natural, the subject took an immense hold of my feelings. It allied itself with all my juvenile aspirations to the character of a democratic champion. What had happened so lately, seemed as if it might easily happen again; and the most transcendant [*sic*] glory I was capable of conceiving, was that of figuring, successful or unsuccessful, as a Girondist in an English Convention" (1:65,67). This passage, placed prominently at the beginning of the third chapter of the *Autobiography*, is interesting both for what it says and for what it reveals about previous silences. In 1821 France had fallen from the democratic grace in which it had stood, but Mill could "easily" imagine the revolution that had happened there happening even in England, and then he would be swept up in the "most transcendant glory" of serving as a delegate to a popularly elected constitutional convention. There he would do for England what the Girondins had tried and failed to do for France. In Mill's construction of their role, which may reflect less his attitudes in the early 1820s than the reading he did about them in the 1840s,[5] the Girondins were relatively moderate supporters of the republic, champions of liberty of both thought and trade, who had hoped to disseminate democratic principles across Europe. In the event, however, they had paid with their lives in the Reign of Terror for their refusal to accommodate the party of extreme republicanism. Why such martyrs to the cause of democracy should have so impressed Mill as a youth seems clear. He has already confessed the "delight" he took in "animated narrative" (1:18), and their story, with all its emphasis on heroic integrity and self-sacrifice, could not but appeal to his adolescent longings for "transcendant glory."

In this passage, however, Mill also admits that he has not been candid about the ambitions he had previously and silently nurtured before his journey to France and his reading about the French Revolution. The image he created of the Girondins "allied itself with all my juvenile aspirations to the character of a democratic champion." Presumably, Mill here refers to ambitions he developed in his first decade, but he has not, until this moment, mentioned them at all. If one uses this later comment to illuminate the earlier commentary on his reading, what Mill hints at here seems obvious enough. Roman history had "delight[ed]" him, and by the age of ten or eleven he had written a "history of the Roman Government, compiled . . . from Livy and Dionysius: of which I wrote as much as would have made an octavo volume. . . . It was, in fact, an account of the struggles between the patricians and plebians, which now engrossed all the interest in my mind which I had previously felt in the mere wars and conquests of the Romans." Mill expands on the pleasure afforded him by "this useful amusement" (1:17), but he is quite discreet about the imaginative pull exerted on him by his own retelling of the conflicts between patricians and plebians. He does not admit, as Rousseau does in his account in the *Confessions* of his reading of Plutarch, that he has seen himself among the figures whose heroic deeds he recounts. Rousseau might say, "I . . . pictured myself as a Greek or Roman. I became indeed that character whose life I was reading," but Mill has been trained by his father's severity to avoid "the chilling sensation of being under a critical eye" (1:17), and he keeps the extent of his enthusiasm from his reader and, perhaps more importantly, from the older self who recalls his former enthusiasms. That he read himself into the chronicles of Roman history that he was writing Mill admits only after this image of heroic struggle has been transformed into the French model proposed by his reading about the National Convention.

By analyzing these two passages at such length, I am emphasizing the importance of points that Mill himself plays down in the account that he offers of his early years. In fact, Mill in his *Autobiography* seems to be trying to deny what is obvious to a reader of his other mature works: his early reading developed in him a decided taste for military valor and heroic display, a taste that evidences itself in his writings almost as often as does his anxiety over the debate between theory and practice—such reading, indeed, probably fueled that anxiety. There are, however, a few hints in the *Autobiography* about how such a taste was developed. One of the histories that first caught his attention did so because it was filled with "wars and battles." In reading another, "an intense and lasting interest" was "excited" in him by "the heroic defence of the Knights of Malta against the Turks, and of the re-volted provinces of the Netherlands against Spain." James Mill's desire to inculcate the attractiveness of virtue encouraged—inadvertently, I think—this taste for the heroic when he had his son read accounts of the voyages of various explorers as examples of "men of energy and resource in unusual circumstances, struggling against difficulties and overcoming them" (1:11). From Mill's eighth through his twelfth year, he adopted history as his "private reading" (1:15), in contrast to the reading he did with his father; and he notes with a certain naiveté how surprised he was later to discover that Pope's Homer did not appeal universally to what he considered "a taste apparently so natural to boyhood" (1:13). By the time the young Mill was in France, the art that took his fancy was the statue of the Fighting Gladiator and David's painting of Leonidas and the Spartans at Thermopylae (26:7,10). Later in the *Autobiography*, Mill explains that he benefited from a "poetic culture" of sorts by reading accounts of the "heroes of philosophy" (1:115)—reading to which I turn in the last chapter of this study—but many comments throughout his career suggest that he was drawn first to the heroes of the battlefield or the agora; only later did he substitute in the place they held in his imagination those other figures of philosophic courage and integrity. When he wanted to praise Bentham in the essay of 1838, Mill compared him to Hercules and St. George. His highest praise for a contemporary involved calling him a hero worthy of inclusion in Plutarch's *Lives*, a laurel that he typically awarded to Lafayette (23:716).

This lasting penchant for heroic display explains, perhaps, Mill's odd taste in drama. During his adolescence, he confesses in the *Autobiography*, he wrote tragedies "under the inspiration not so much of Shakespeare as of Joanna Baillie, whose *Constantine Paleologus* in particular appeared to me one of the most glorious of human compositions. I still think it one of the best dramas of the last two centuries" (1:19n). *Constantine Paleologus* may not be "glorious," but its subject certainly is heroic glory. Of the many dramas that Baillie wrote during her long life, it was one of the few that actually reached the stage, quite successfully in 1820 in Baillie's native Scotland, but less so as a melodrama at the Surrey in London. Baillie herself realized that her plays were more noteworthy for their instructive than their dramatic powers, but *Constantine Paleologus* exerted a profound effect on the young Mill because of its grandiose displays of noble self-sacrifice. Baillie adapts her plot from Gibbons's treatment of the Turkish siege of Constantinople. Constantine, a gentle and urbane man of peace, is forced by circumstances to become warlike, and he rises to the challenge

> To sustain in heaven's all-seeing eye,
> Before my fellow men, in mine own fight,
> With graceful virtue and becoming pride,

> The dignity and honour of a man,
> Thus station'd as I am, I will do all
> That man may be. . . .[6]

"All / That man may be" involves, predictably, the ultimate sacrifice of Constantine's life. His enemy and destroyer, Mahamet, is so impressed by Constantine's dignity that he responds in kind—thus do Englishmen civilize by example the infidels they meet. Mahamet grants Constantine the "military pomp" of a hero's burial and frees those of his "brave band" still living (421). The play closes on an echo of Demosthenes: heaven favors the virtuous even in defeat, and Constantine becomes a "glorious lesson" in the "high ennobling power" that is best revealed by a "dying man" (438).

Such heroics would easily appeal to a youth who had in more than good measure a "taste apparently so natural to boyhood," but Baillie's treatment of one character in particular—Othus, the "soft letter'd sage" who, in challenging circumstances, becomes a "valiant soldier grown" (405)—is, I think, what won her the footnote in Mill's *Autobiography* that grants her play its status as a dramatic work as great as any written since the 1650s. Othus proves that, when put to the test, the "bookish man" is a more than capable soldier. He, too, dies with Constantine, but not, of course, before delivering the last words of the play on the exemplary power of the dying man. Earlier, when Constantine plans to face a group of rebellious citizens—the play emphasizes Constantine's greatness by contrasting him to the cowardly townspeople he is trying to defend and to masses of sniveling and deceptive Turks—one of the nobles argues that the people should be beaten with sticks. Othus has a better plan:

> Words will, perhaps, our better weapons prove.
> When us'd as brave man's arms should ever be,
> With skill and boldness. Swords smite single foes,
> But thousands by a word are struck at once. (304)

The young Mill, who had been beaten often enough with the words that were his father's weapons, the boy whose life was already defined by the words he read and by the words he wrote, would have found such a passage comforting. It elaborates on the old saw that the pen is mightier than the sword, and in doing so, it ends the contest between theory and practice, thought and action, by attributing to words all the military grandeur of heroic deeds. It is a resolution to which Mill pays tribute, at the same time concealing his admiration by relegating his comments on the play to a footnote. Below the text, suppressed by his allegiance to theory, his relish for heroic display is allowed to persist. Once more Mill avoids "the chilling sensation of being under a critical eye," either his own or the reader's.

Mill never specifies how his identification with either the heroes of ancient history or the Girondins relates to his later desire to be "a reformer of the world," but an answer to that question emerges if the reader puts together pieces of information that the narrator is careful to offer only separately. The title of Chapter III, which begins by covering this period, advertises it as a time of transition: Mill moves from the "Last Stage of Education," overseen by his father, to the "First of Self-Education," for the form and content of which he himself is presumably responsible. James Mill, however, still determined the course of events. At approximately the same time that the young Mill was reading about the French Revolution, his father decided on his son's career: "During the winter of 1821/2, Mr. John Austin, with whom at the time of my visit to France my father had but lately become acquainted, kindly allowed me to read Roman law with him. My father, notwithstanding his abhorrence of the chaos of barbarism called English Law, had turned his thoughts towards the bar as on the whole less ineligible for me than any other profession" (1:67). The phrasing here is revealing: James Mill did not arrange that his son read law with John Austin; Austin "kindly" allowed it. The bar was not the best profession for John Mill, just the least "ineligible." The narrator seems anxious not to attribute the power of decision to his father and not to display any enthusiasm for the profession marked out for him by his father. As a "needful accompaniment" to that study, James Mill set his son to read Dumont's *rédaction* of Bentham's work, the *Traité de législation*. This, the first significant "epoch in my life," gave, as Mill notes, "a definite shape to my aspirations" (1:67,71). But, again, this comment is tantalizing in its vagueness. If Bentham's *Traité* gave "definite shape" to Mill's aspirations, what did he aspire to be?

The older narrator's account of this reading hints at an answer to this question even as it refuses to be specific. As I have noted, Mill felt himself transformed into a "different being" by his introduction to the extent and detail of Bentham's thought. He was also transported. Here, for Mill, were the Pisgah sights—"I felt taken up to an eminence from which I could survey a vast mental domain," the "most inspiring prospects of practical improvement in human affairs." Clearly meant as a further indoctrination in the ideas that James Mill valued, this reading, however, was to lessen rather than to increase the father's authority. The young Mill had known the general outlines of Bentham's thought—"My previous education had been . . . a course of Benthamism"—but the *Traité* allowed him to grasp for the first time the specific and practical implications of ideas that appeared to him "extremely general and abstract" in his father's works. His father treated the "logic" of the law, Bentham its "ethics." His father treated jurisprudence; "Bentham's subject was Legislation, of which Jurisprudence is only the formal part." If Mill imagined himself transformed by the impression that this reading made on him, it was not simply Bentham's thought that had such power to reform the young Mill's sense of his character; it was the difference between James Mill and Jeremy Bentham that made of John Stuart Mill a "different being." "I now had . . . a religion; the inculcation and diffusion of which could be made the principal outward purpose of a life" (1:67,69).

Mill carefully omits to say exactly how that "outward purpose" would define his vocation, but the context in which he read Bentham, as part of his study of the law, and its subject, legislation, both suggest that as early as 1822 Mill might have been looking to Parliament as the place where he could put Bentham's practical goals into practicable form.[7] James Mill's decision to have his son study law would have given him ample justification for such hopes. After the lean years before the publication of *The History of British India*, James Mill was clearly rising in the world. Even before John Mill returned from France in 1821, his father had been promoted at the India House and was earning £1000 a year. His son may well have hoped eventually to do what other sons of moderately well-to-do men had done: follow his ambition for unremunerated public service in the House of Commons. This very likely was the "definite shape" that Bentham's *Traité* gave to Mill's "aspirations."

Mill indirectly confirms this interpretation by contrasting the modes of change offered by the model of French revolutionary action, about which he read "this winter or the next," and the model of more gradual

English reform. Although the word *reform* is not used until Chapter V, Mill does admit here that he was taken by the way in which Bentham "at every page . . . seemed to open a clearer and broader conception of what human opinions and institutions ought to be, how they might be made what they ought to be." Bentham set, for the young Mill, a pattern of "studiously moderate" reform to be pursued and achieved (1:65,69). The shortcoming of Mill's earlier revolutionary goals—to be a Girondin in an English convention—is that they depended on a revolution. Without such a wholesale destruction of existing institutions, no individual could serve in the assembly that would build them anew. But the model of reform that Bentham offered did not require any such uncontrollable turnings of the historical tide. In a time of "rapidly rising Liberalism," as Mill later calls the period beginning in 1819 (1:101), a young man whose vocation involved the recasting of institutions could actually envision himself as an effective and prominent leader in that movement—if he had a seat in Parliament. This is the "most transcendant glory" he could now imagine. In the early 1820s he was far too young to think that such a role would be immediately available to him, but by studying law with John Austin, Mill was set on a course that could make that vision a reality.

The material that Mill treats in the rest of Chapter III suggests not only the strength of this ambition but the autobiographical narrator's desire not to acknowledge it. He goes on, not to define the "definite shape" of his ambitions, but to outline the reading that he did during subsequent years. Bentham became his "private reading"; in public, "under my father's direction," he read widely, as I have emphasized, in analytic psychology (1:71). Mill's "private" enthusiasm for Bentham had to be nurtured and protected from the "chilling" effect of his father's "critical eye" just as his earlier enthusiasm for Roman history had been protected. These were the years in which the relation between James Mill and Bentham had already shown signs of considerable strain, and John Mill probably knew that his interest in Bentham should be confined to the work on which his father had placed his imprimatur.

More telling, however, than even this note of secrecy—a Utilitarian version of the romances that Rousseau devoured in private—is the way in which Mill describes the young men with whom he now came in contact. He first describes George Grote and John Austin—slightly older contemporaries, bridges between his father's generation and his own—and then the Cambridge men he met through John Austin's younger brother Charles: Macaulay, Hyde and Charles Villiers, Edward Strutt, and Samuel Romilly. With Charles Austin and his friends, Mill tells us, he first felt himself "a man among men" (1:79), and by founding the Utilitarian Society in 1822/23, he became a "sort of leader" of men. To his earlier list, he adds the names of those members who had become his "intimate companions," William Eyton Tooke, William Ellis, and George Graham; and Mill concludes the roster, in an unmistakable tone of condescension, with the name of "a man who has made considerably more noise in the world than any of these, John Anthony Roebuck" (1:83).

This list of peers, less meaningful to readers now than to those of Mill's contemporaries who first read it in 1873, is remarkable for the hidden vocational agenda it suggests and for Mill's complete refusal to acknowledge its implications. Each of these men is included in the narrative because each was prominent in the ferment of thought taking place in the 1820s and early 1830s. These young men gathered principally to talk and to test their principles in talk; such debate served as their preparation for public life. Charles Austin is singled out as a "brilliant orator and converser." His effect on "the élite of the Cambridge youth" is "an historical event" worthy of being recorded in Mill's story. Austin was, despite Macaulay's later celebrity, "the really influential mind among these intellectual gladiators" (1:79). Like the Utilitarian Society, which provided Mill with "practice in oral discussion" (1:83), the London Debating Society offered its members the opportunity to come together so that they could contend like warriors in verbal combat, but Mill never reveals the purpose of all this discussion and debate. The answer, again, is obvious: Macaulay, Roebuck, Tooke, and Graham were all in training for Parliament. As one of the participants more candidly explained, "Our proceedings were conducted with the forms that prevailed in the House of Commons. . . . We had even opposition and ministerial sides."[8] Mill never explicitly makes that connection.

The men whom Mill chooses to mention in Chapter III at this crucial transition in his experience almost all conform to the same profile: they were all liberals—Mill does say that much—but, more importantly, they were the liberals on whom the fate of reform would depend; most of them were gentlemen, sons of men of property or, in a majority of the cases, descendants of noble lines; many were university-educated, "the élite of the Cambridge youth"; most of them were studying law, and most of them were future M.P.s. Indeed, Charles Austin, John Austin, Romilly, Charles Villiers, Thomas Hyde Villiers, and Macaulay all had either been called to the bar or had entered Parliament by 1827. Roebuck was practicing law by 1831 and in Parliament by 1832. Strutt was studying law by 1825, an M.P. by 1830. The remarkable similarity of their activities and of the timing of their entrances into public life suggests the importance to Mill of the alternatives that these men represented. They were all what John Stuart Mill by the late 1820s was not. The leisure for study, epitomized by Grote, and the freedom of choice conferred by money and position, epitomized by Hyde and Charles Villiers, were not to be Mill's, however much he might have thought so in the winter of 1821/22 when he first began reading law with John Austin.

In one of the most poignant juxtapositions in the *Autobiography*, Mill moves from his description of Roebuck, the man who made "noise in the world," to an account of his own fate:

> In May 1823, my professional occupation and status for the next thirty-five years of my life, were decided by my father's obtaining for me an appointment from the East India Company, in the office of the Examiner of India Correspondence, immediately under himself. I was appointed in the usual manner, at the bottom of the list of clerks, to rise, at least in the first instance, by seniority; but with the understanding, that I should be employed from the beginning in preparing drafts of despatches, and be thus trained up as a successor to those who then filled the higher departments of the office. My drafts of course required, for some time, much revision from my immediate superiors, but I soon became well acquainted with the business, and by my father's instructions and the general growth of my own powers, I was in a few years qualified to be, and practically was, the chief conductor of the correspondence with India in one of the leading departments, that of the Native States. This continued to be my official

duty until I was appointed Examiner, only two years before the time when the abolition of the East India Company as a political body determined my retirement. (1:83,85)

In four bloodless sentences, Mill offers the entire course of his professional career, looking ahead here as he rarely does elsewhere in the early chapters of the *Autobiography*. Knowing the intellectual eminence to which Mill would rise, the reader may overlook the depths to which his father's decision had condemned him: at seventeen, he was a junior clerk whose only distinction was that he did less scurrying to and fro than the other clerks. He was to receive no salary for the first three years, only a gratuity of £30, as if to show that in his apprenticeship, his work was not worth pay. The position itself was a favor to his father, whose severity, terrible in its unrelenting proximity, Mill perhaps had hoped to escape by studying and practicing law. The passive voice and the strings of prepositional phrases, still so much the marks of bureaucratic prose, bespeak his awareness of his subjection to his father's will. The parent who displayed such "decision and energy of character" in "every action of life" (1:39) was now determining the arena of practical action in which his son would compete, the arena, moreover, in which he had already proven his own dominance. Here, Mill determines nothing for himself; even the end of his term at the India House is decided for him when the East India Company is abolished.

Years later, in writing the narrative of his life, Mill is almost silent about his initial response to the decision that installed him at the India House. He stresses the advantages that, as he later discovered, accrued to the public servant who wished to follow "private intellectual pursuits" and to work as a "theoretical reformer." The "chances of riches and honours" he gave up, he says, without regret. Mill devotes only part of one sentence and an apologetic double negative to the effect he most lamented: "But I was not indifferent to exclusion from Parliament, and public life" (1:87,85). By closing the prospect of the bar as his profession, his father had not, of course, denied his son his religion. The son still believed in the cause. What he had lost was the opportunity to participate directly in its achievement. The disciple who might have hoped to become the leader of a new generation of believers was now relegated to an ancillary role at best. That recognition must have been particularly painful to Mill since James Mill, "very anxious" later on to secure a seat in Parliament for Charles Austin, had pulled strings to do so, and Austin was indeed offered a seat, a position for which, ironically, he had no desire.[9]

The narrative in the *Autobiography* continues to register the effects of the momentous decision to place Mill in the India House even as its narrator seeks to downplay them. If Chapter III deals almost exclusively with talking, Chapter IV deals almost exclusively with writing, and many of the figures who populate Chapter III reappear here not as political neophytes, but precisely as versions of what John Stuart Mill has now defined himself to be: a writer and a theorist. Mill names among the contributors to the *Westminster Review* Charles and John Austin, Grote, and Roebuck, and he then concludes in modest triumph, "I was myself the most frequent writer of all" (1:99). By recasting the identities of these men, he can declare his prominence among them. He also records yet another French version of his earlier ambitions. He still speaks of the "abundance" of his "ambition and desire of distinction" (1:113), but as an active career eludes Mill's grasp, the Girondins are replaced by the philosophers whose theoretical work of destruction preceded the Revolution: "The French *philosophes* of the eighteenth century were the example we sought to imitate, and we hoped to accomplish no less results" (1:111). Mill then recounts the founding of the *Parliamentary History and Review,* and he does so, not by describing the material covered in the review, the debates in Parliament, but by listing the contributors—Peregrine Bingham, Charles Austin, Strutt, Romilly, and "several other liberal lawyers"—so that he can again predominate: "It fell to my lot to lead off the first number." In describing his articles, he claims that they reveal a "maturity" of thought, that their "execution" is "not at all juvenile" (1:121,123). The terms he uses suggest the distance he has come, not only from the derivative and juvenile writings of his youth, but from his juvenile desire to figure in, not to write for, a parliamentary review.

This desire does eventually surface in the *Autobiography,* but it does so three chapters after Mill gives his account of the "official duty" at the India House that presumably kept him out of the House of Commons. In Chapter VI, Mill describes the failure of the Philosophic Radicals to take advantage of the "fair opportunity" afforded them by their election to the reformed Parliament of 1832. The charity of hindsight allows Mill to concede that these men were less to blame than their "unfavourable circumstances": "It would have required a great political leader . . . to have effected really great things." At this point, Mill engages in a revealing speculation: "Such a leader there would have been, if my father had been in Parliament." In 1832 James Mill was no more likely to have entered Parliament than his son, but this political ambition is one that in retrospect the son allows himself to have in the name of the father. To Mill himself, the question is not relevant: "I laboured from this time till 1839, both by personal influence with some of [the Philosophic Radicals], and by writings, to put ideas into their heads and purpose into their hearts."[10] And then he finally opens to his reader and to himself a vision of alternatives: "On the whole . . . my attempt was vain. To have had a chance of succeeding in it, required a different position from mine. It was a task only for one who, being himself in Parliament, could have mixed with the radical members in daily consultation, could himself have taken the initiative, and instead of urging others to lead, could have summoned them to follow" (1:203,205). Here, long delayed and protected by the generality of the terms in which Mill presents it, is a confession of the ambitions that may or may not have been genuinely beyond his reach.

VOCATIONAL CRISIS

Mill so carefully disguises his "juvenile aspirations" in the *Autobiography* that their relevance to its one great event, his mental crisis of 1826–28, is almost completely hidden from view. That effect is, I would argue, precisely what Mill hoped to achieve, though it is open to debate whether he himself, his wife, or his future readers constitute the audience he might have wanted to mislead. The mysterious nature of this crisis and the importance that Mill himself attributed to it have encouraged a great deal of ultimately unsatisfying explanation. The three most prominent approaches look to physical, psychological, or emotional causes. Alexander Bain speaks of overwork, the result particularly of Mill's editing of Bentham's *Rationale of Judicial Evidence*.[11] Readers with the least acquaintance with Freud have pointed to the passage in which Mill records his response to Marmontel's account of the death of his father, and they conclude that

Mill's crisis was the result of guilt over his death wish for his father—
an idea that my own emphasis on his vocational dilemmas would support.[12] Clearly, Mill's memories of the 1826 crisis bear the weight of
the ambivalence and guilt he experienced ten years later during the
greater, but unmentioned, crisis that occurred at the death of his
father. But the explanation of the event as an affective crisis is the one
that still has the greatest currency precisely because it is the one that
Mill himself offers, and he is, after all, the only authority on this event.

The emotional poverty of Mill's education had created "a mere reasoning machine" (1:111), a machine with yet enough sentience to recognize that something was missing, a machine that broke down under
the weight of that recognition. According to this scenario—the one
offered in the *Autobiography*—the cure came gradually with the realization that the machine could retool itself, that it could enhance its
life with an "internal culture" of feeling to offset the deadening effect
of analysis (1:147). Poetry, in the form of Wordsworth, offered a kind
of exercise of the feelings, and the machine, now more nearly a man,
ran smoothly again, though perhaps without its earlier unconscious
assurance that it would always run well.

I rephrase this account in a reductive fashion—using, however, the
terms that Mill himself uses—to suggest both its simplicity and its
inherent contradictions. Mill's continued loyalty to associationist psychology is the source of some of these contradictions. A being so completely formed by external forces cannot easily decide to form himself
anew without calling into question his own explanation of his initial
formation. But Mill's emphasis on poetry and emotions serves to obscure the relation of his specifically vocational problems to his crisis. In
1853–54 when he first drafted his account of this event, he was undergoing yet another period of transition that would have highlighted
once again his dissatisfactions with the earlier vocational decisions that
had been made for him: after his youthful propagandism, the death
of his father, and his strenuous work as the unacknowledged editor of
the *London and Westminster Review,* he had published his *System of Logic*
and gained, quite unexpectedly, a respectful following of readers. His
equally impressive *Principles of Political Economy* had followed in 1848.
In 1851 he had married Harriet Taylor and put an end to the questions and eyebrows raised by their long intimacy during the life of
her husband. One would have thought that the happy resolution of

the painful ambiguities of their relation would have freed Mill for his magnum opus, the study of ethology that he had outlined at the end of the *Logic*. But no such work was forthcoming. Instead, ill health and distractions and perhaps the unrealizable vagueness of the great work intervened, and Mill did little more than plan and draft a number of essays on topics about whose importance to future readers both he and Harriet Mill agreed.

If the record of the crisis of 1826 bears some of the weight of the events of 1836, it also bears, I think, the impress of the uncertainty and relative lack of achievement that Mill was experiencing as he wrote about that crisis. In his 1854 diary, he recorded his harsh and despairing recognition that he had "frittered away the working years of [his] life in mere preparatory trifles" (27:665), as if the *Logic* and the *Principles of Political Economy* were no more than easily dismissed gestures toward the work not yet done. This dissatisfaction was closely connected to the frustration of his earlier ambitions, a frustration that he does not mention in his account of the years of his crisis. Despite the clarity and intensity of the pain that Mill describes, there is something forced, vague, and indefinite about his account of this period.[13] An examination of Mill's crisis, not from the later perspective from which he views it, but in relation to the earlier events that actually preceded it, suggests that the famous upheaval was less a crisis of emotion than a crisis of vocation.

The chronology that Mill offers in the earlier chapters supports such an interpretation. The crisis, Mill tells us, began in the fall of 1826. In May of 1826, Mill completed his apprenticeship at the India House and, in place of the £30 gratuity he had been receiving, was awarded a salary of £100 a year.[14] As Mill says in his earlier account of his "professional occupation," he was at this time "qualified to be, and practically was, the chief conductor of the correspondence" in the Department of Native States (1:83,85). As long as Mill was working as an apprentice in his position, he may have been able to think of it as a temporary or an incomplete definition of his professional self. As soon as he was promoted and formally recognized for his efforts, no doubt that illusion became more difficult to sustain. In 1825 and 1826, he had been hard at work editing Bentham's *Rationale of Judicial Evidence*. Like Bain, I would stress the importance of this labor, but not simply as a source of physical strain; rather, it offered Mill unavoidable evidence that he was not doing with his life what he had thought he could do. Bentham instructed his young editor to fill any gaps in the argument that the older man had left, "and at his instance I read, for this purpose, the most authoritative treatises on the English Law of Evidence" (1:117). In short, he was studying law again, this time under the tutelage of Jeremy Bentham rather than John Austin. If the young Mill still harbored any desire to set out on a career that could be distinguished from his father's dual role as India House official and writer, the arduous duty of editing the work of his father's mentor must surely have made him recognize the difficulty of such an escape. Although Chapter V, which deals with his crisis, does not contain a word about the East India Company, its impress is, I think, evident in the terms in which Mill casts his account of his suffering.

There is, first, the famous moment of self-examination that precipitated Mill into profound and lasting depression:

> In this frame of mind [a dull state of nerves] it occurred to me to put the question directly to myself, "Suppose that all your objects in life were realized; that all the changes in institutions and opinions which you are looking forward to, could be completely effected at this very instant: would this be a great joy and happiness to you?" And an irrepressible self-consciousness distinctly answered, "No!" At this my heart sank within me: the whole foundation on which my life was constructed fell down. All my happiness was to have been found in the continual pursuit of this end. The end had ceased to charm, and how could there ever again be any interest in the means? I seemed to have nothing left to live for. (1:139)

What is remarkable but previously unremarked about this question is the assumption on which it is based. Mill imagines a kind of magical and instantaneous transformation during which all his goals as a "reformer of the world" would be accomplished. What is missing from this vision of a dream achieved is his active role in its achievement. Like his position in the India House, this vision of fulfillment puts him on the sidelines. Reform occurs without his having offered his life in its service, and the dream becomes a nightmare. He can find no personal happiness in a world not needing improvement because he sees no role for himself there, just as he no longer can imagine for himself the "transcendant glory" of being a champion of democracy. "The end had ceased to charm" because the "means" had already been put beyond his reach.

Both Mill's appointment at the India House and his imaginative conception of a fully improved world result in the same condition: inactivity. When he adds, "The fountains of vanity and ambition seemed to have dried up within me" (1:143), he specifically recalls his muted complaints about the disadvantages of his work for the East India Company in Chapter II: his official duties deny him any role that would satisfy ambition. The manuscript of Mill's 1828 speech on perfectibility offers a revealing commentary on his state of mind at the time: he suggests that "those who speak of perfectibility as a dream do so . . . because they are conscious that they themselves are doing nothing to forward it and are anxious to believe that great work impossible, in which if it were possible they know it would be their duty to assist" (26:429). Here, in one of those flashes of psychological insight that can so clearly reveal the power and honesty of Mill's analytic abilities, he censures attitudes that mirror as they distort the state of mind that he attributes to himself in the *Autobiography*. Those who label progress a dream do so because their despair relieves them of the responsibility to work for its achievement. Mill despaired of the effects of progress because he could not contribute directly to its achievement. That, precisely, is the subterranean story of Chapter V. This point emerges with particular clarity when Mill's experience is compared to the two similar accounts of crisis that he mentioned in a letter to Carlyle in which he hinted at the mysteries of his "spiritual history" (12:224): John Sterling's *Arthur Coningsby* (1833) and F. D. Maurice's *Eustace Conway* (1834). In both novels, the heroes repent their specifically Benthamite reformist goals. Mill's suffering, by contrast, resulted from his inability to further such goals through his own directly political efforts.

Mill's interpretation of this period as a time of emotional crisis depends on exactly that contrast between activity and passivity, doing and knowing, that provides the hidden agenda of Chapters III and IV. He must find a way to stimulate passive enjoyment because he is precluded from the active achievement of his goals. A John Stuart Mill who could have looked forward to his eventual election to Parliament would hardly have had either time or occasion to worry about the condition of his contemplative powers; he would have been too much engaged in preparing himself for the exercise of his active abilities as a leader in the cause of reform. As it was, however, Mill turned to Wordsworth, the "poet of unpoetical natures," to find the solace of "tranquil contemplation." Significantly, Byron "did not suit my condition." The poet who had recently died in active pursuit of political freedom in Greece is certainly not the kind of imaginative mentor that Mill needed. Wordsworth, on the contrary, was soothing less because he offers "the very culture of the feelings" that Mill says he represents than because he mourns the defeat of youthful desires. "He too," Mill explains, "had had similar experience to mine" (1:151,153). In the "Intimations of Immortality" ode, which Mill quotes, Wordsworth writes a hymn to the continuing power of such youthful visions to intoxicate those who remember them; at the same time, he struggles to honor the lesser, passive pleasures of the "philosophic mind." The transition he charts parallels Mill's movement from his dreams of being a Girondin to his acceptance of the more settled, less dramatic role of a writer on political questions.

Contrary to the impression that the *Autobiography* makes, Mill, in his notes for his debate with Roebuck in 1829 on the relative virtues of Wordsworth and Byron, spoke of the poet he championed in terms that identify Wordsworth as proof of his despair, not its solace. Wordsworth teaches that it is possible to take pleasure without moving forward; but since such a state of "being stationary" is not yet possible, "I fear in the present state of society something stronger is required." This comment is echoed in the confession Mill makes to his 1854 diary, but the debating notes more clearly reveal the frustration experienced by the man of thought who longs for the opportunities for heroic action: "At present great struggles are necessary and . . . men who were nourished only with [Wordsworth's] poetry would be unnerved for such struggles" (26:441–42).

The contrast between activity and passivity informs as well the most significant part of Chapter V that Mill later excised from the *Early Draft:* the lengthy analysis of the character and career of John Roebuck. Roebuck still figures prominently in Chapter V of the published *Autobiography,* but primarily as a participant in the Debating Society. In opposition to Mill's advocacy of Wordsworth, Roebuck is the champion of Byron because his own "instincts were those of action and struggle" (1:153). But in the *Early Draft,* that difference in tastes and instincts reveals a difference both in character and in vocation. Roebuck is an original: he has a "decided character of his own." The youth he spent in Canada has "formed" him "to self help, to self assertion, and to be ever ready for conflict." His story is proof of his determination and energy: "He came to England to qualify for the bar, and finding that he could maintain himself by writing, remained there" (1:154). Mill goes on to describe Roebuck's pugnacity, his one-sidedness, and his indifference to the "culture of the feelings." As Mill sketches the career of his former friend, he is forced to acknowledge that this "mental type" had become "more and more alien to my tastes and feelings":

> To conclude here my notice of Roebuck; when three years afterwards he under almost every disadvantage of fortune and position took his seat in the House of Commons, he fulfilled my expectation and prediction at the time, viz. that he would fail, apparently irretrievably, half a dozen times and succeed at last. . . . Notwithstanding his many defects of judgment, he succeeded by perseverance and by really having something to say, in acquiring the ear of the house. He conquered all external obstacles, and if he ceased rising it was because he had got to the end of his tether . . . he did not labour to master the special questions of legislation . . . and his voice, at last, was heard almost solely on personal questions, or on such as he was able to make personal. He made no progress in general principles; like the Parliamentary Radicals generally, made no addition to his original stock of ideas. . . . Even on English matters, when he had succeeded in being somebody, and above all when he had married and become involved in the petty vanities and entanglements of what is called society, he gradually ceased to be the champion of any important progress; he became a panegyrist of England and things English, a conformist to the Church, and in short merged in the common herd of Conservative Liberals. (1:156,158)

In this passage, Mill sets out all his differences from Roebuck, but he does so in a way that reveals not only his disapproval but his unspoken envy. Roebuck is the man of action who, despite all obstacles, achieves what he wants, a seat in the House of Commons, and who, once there, makes himself heard. He is fatally limited by his lack of a speculative capacity, so he squanders his heroic potential on merely "personal questions." In a final act of self-condemnation, Roebuck becomes a shorn Samson when he meets his Victorian Delilah and is reduced to the "petty vanities and entanglements of what is called society."

Mill's account of Roebuck surely bears the animus occasioned by Roebuck's outspoken opposition to his friend's "ill-judged passion" for Harriet Taylor,[15] but there are other, more important psychological forces at work here. Roebuck is genuinely the opposite of his opponent in the Debating Society. Like Bentham and Coleridge in being each other's "counter-pole" (13:405), Mill and Roebuck would define all that is best in Philosophic Radicalism if they comprised one man, not two: Roebuck's energy and will to succeed, Mill's speculative understanding of the issues; Roebuck's career, Mill's wife. The passage was obviously a prime candidate for deletion, not because of what it said about Roebuck, but because of what Mill had said in it about his own failed ambitions. The crisis that led Mill to read Wordsworth and defend him against Roebuck resulted from the desire to have the opportunities that Roebuck had created for himself, opportunities, Mill notes as if commenting on sour grapes, of which Roebuck had made as little as those who had never had the chance to make anything.

This reading of the famous crisis sheds light as well, I think, on the philosophical question that Mill defined as central to the "later returns" of his suicidal despair, "returns" that, significantly, coincided with his 1828 promotion to Assistant in the East India Company at a salary of £600. During this time, Mill explains, he was oppressed by the "incubus" of associationism: "I felt as if I was scientifically proved to be the helpless slave of antecedent circumstances; as if my character and that of all others had been formed for us by agencies beyond our control, and was wholly out of our own power." The embodiment of the "antecedent circumstances" at work here is, of course, James Mill, the father who had required of his son continued study of the psychological system that holds that "character is formed by circumstances." The young Mill longed for the "inspiriting" effect of the "doctrine of freewill," and, as I have suggested, Mill's attempts to find such inspiration within the confines of the associationism in which James Mill had "principled" his son demonstrates how much he needed to escape the "depressing and paralysing influence" of his training (1:175,177), but the dilemma Mill describes here in abstract terms found its more immediate and palpable embodiment in the question of vocation.

What Mill longed for was proof that his will was strong enough, his desires distinctive enough, to make a difference in his circumstances. He wanted the opportunity to make a choice that was genuinely free of external interference, to feel that there are internal forces capable of exerting themselves against circumstance. He wanted, in short, to be John Roebuck. The choice of vocation raises these issues as no other choice can. Choice of marriage partner is contingent—one marries X because one has met X and because Y has not crossed one's path. Choice of habitation depends on factors such as work, income, marriage. Choice of family is, of course, no choice at all. But choice of vocation comes at the liminal point between childhood and adulthood: it is both the result of choices made for one in the past and the promise of autonomy in the future. As Mill claims in *On Liberty*, the person who lets another "choose his plan of life for him, has no need of any other faculty than the ape-like one of imitation" (18:262). Vocation signals the relation between character and volition, between what one is and what one desires to be. George Eliot, for instance, made the subject central in *Middlemarch* because it encapsulates these issues so neatly and so complexly. For many individuals, vocation bears a significance that can hardly be overstated. And it is, at least as Mill tells his story in the *Autobiography,* the one choice he can never admit that he might have had the opportunity to make.

Mill's concern with the annihilating effects of a belief in Philosophical Necessity simply transposes this vocational problem into generalized terms, and the philosophical solution that he discovered to it— that one can will a change in one's circumstances and therefore will a change in oneself—was ultimately no more satisfying to him than his continued role as a "helpless slave" at the India House could be. The late 1820s for the young Mill were not merely years in which his father was continuously supervising his activities—his hours at the office, his teaching of the younger children in his father's house where he continued to live, his readings in associationism, the large output of articles and essays in which he voiced his father's ideas—they were years in which his father's past choices for him determined the course of his future efforts. That the terms *free* and *slave* should dominate his thinking at this time and concerning this time seems, to use his own words, almost a philosophical necessity. Although James Mill claimed in 1823 that his son was free to study law after his entry into the service of the East India Company[16]—in effect, that his son had had the choices that the narrator of the *Autobiography* silently but conclusively denies him—Mill prefers to see himself docilely and inevitably imprisoned by his career as a civil servant.

The question of vocation does not appear in the *Autobiography* as a question open either to discussion or to regret, but if one turns from the account of Mill's career as it appears there to the more nearly contemporary account in his letters, a clearer picture emerges of the process by which this question turned from a live issue into a predetermined outcome engraved in stone. If little recorded comment remains from the crucial period of the late 1820s, subsequent comments shed light on that dark age. In the fullest statement he was to make on this subject, in a letter of August 1837 to John Robertson, Mill admitted not only the specific shape of his earlier ambitions but their longevity: "For the present politics are wonderfully dull; and for the first time these ten years I have no wish to be in Parliament" (12:345). Ten years before 1837 locates this desire in the midst of the famous crisis and shortly after the time when Mill had completed his apprenticeship at the East India Company. The desire, he confessed, had continued through the agitation over the passing of the First Reform Bill and through the tenure of the first Reform Parliament. Interestingly enough, in this letter Mill also admitted that he did not know if his employment at the India House actually did preclude his accepting a seat in the House of Commons. He referred to a possible offer of a seat and noted, "I shall not accept it unless I find by inquiry here that I can hold it with my situation in this house." He was ready, he claimed, to let his family "go down" in the world, but he would not sacrifice the "speculative pursuits which I like, and in which I can do great things, for the position of a Radical member of this coming Parliament" (12:346). For even a man of Mill's capacity for work, such a prospect might have been daunting, but he seems to have imagined that it was possible for him to pursue his speculative work, hold a seat in the House of Commons, and keep his desk at the India House.

Earlier that year, he had seen his alternatives as more clearly opposed to each other. He told John Pringle Nichol that he "often wish[ed]" he were "among" the Radicals in Parliament, and he imagined that he was the only one who held "the scattered threads" of the party "in his hands" at a time "for knitting together a powerful party": "But that cannot be while I am in the India House. I should not mind leaving it if I had £300 a year free from anxiety and literary labour, but I have at most £100. *Sed tempus veniet*" (12:324). But that time never did come. The conflict between his service in the East India Company and his desire to serve in Parliament remained unresolved. By the mid-1850s, when he was drafting the *Autobiography*, his question about this alternative was no longer unanswered, either because he had discovered that the Board of Control of the East India Company would not countenance any political activity on his part or because he no longer wanted to think that such opportunities had continued to be open to him.

The two lengthy letters that Mill wrote to John Sterling in October 1831 and May 1832 offer the fullest evidence of his ambivalence and uncertainty at the very moment when events themselves seemed to offer the greatest opportunities for bold initiatives. Sterling, who was superintending a sugar plantation on St. Vincent in the West Indies, was the logical recipient for Mill's confessions simply because his distance from the scene of events decreased the possibility of interference and therefore increased Mill's candor. Sterling, indeed, was so far from England that Mill might as well have been talking to himself. In these letters, Mill expressed both the agitation into which the country had been thrown by the idea of reform and the agitation it had caused him as an individual who had no definite role to play in its achievement. In the earlier letter, Mill speculated that if the bill did not pass, "I am firmly convinced that in six months a national convention chosen by universal suffrage, will be sitting in London." Here, at last, was his opportunity to serve as a Girondin in an English convention. But Mill hesitated: "Should this happen, I have not made up my mind what would be best to do." He preferred to let fools finish off the destruction of old institutions "if one could but get a shilling a day to live upon meanwhile." He envisioned a "coalition . . . between the wisest radicals & the wisest anti-radicals," and then, before he could speculate on the new world they would create between them, he dropped the subject and defensively told Sterling that his "long prosing rambling talk about politics" could not convey "how little I really care about them." Principles, he claimed, were his only real concern: "the investigation of abstract truth, & the more abstract the better" (12:78). He even fantastically envisioned a time when "the East India Company is abolished and funded property confiscated, [and] I shall perhaps scrape together the means of paying my passage to St Vincent's & see whether you will employ me to teach your niggers political economy" (12:80). The prospect of becoming a teacher of the disenfranchised once his work at the East India Company was over suggests, perhaps, the impotence of Mill's current position; this self-mocking ambition certainly was one that would have relegated him to irrelevance in the world of English politics. Such a comment reveals at once Mill's self-contempt and his contempt for the marginalized groups with which he aligns the philosopher in his *System of Logic*.

Writing to Sterling again in May of 1832 after the Reform Bill had progressed "through a sea of troubles . . . in safety to within sight of land," Mill claimed that there was now "a clear field to work in and a consequent duty on all whose vocation is not different, to address themselves to the work." Yet he seemed almost disappointed that the change had come "through other means than anarchy & civil war." Instead of rejoicing at the prospect of this "clear field," Mill added a melancholy assessment of "our common acquaintances" as "sadder and wiser men," although the picture he painted has less relevance to "The Rime of the Ancient Mariner" than to the conclusion of the "Immortality" ode:

> By sadder, I do not mean gloomier, or more desponding: nor even less susceptible of enjoyment, or even gaiety; but I mean that they look upon all things with far deeper and more serious feelings, and are far more alive to those points in human affairs, which excite an interest bordering on melancholy. Their earnestness, if not greater, is of a more solemn kind, and certainly far more unmixed with dreams of personal distinction or other reward. This is also, in a measure, the case with myself; except that, so far as respects the last point, the change had taken place long before. (12:100)

In suggesting that his associates had given up "dreams of personal distinction," Mill referred to a time in the past, "long before," when he had renounced the pursuit of similar visions of personal achievement, but the pain of such a sacrifice was still one that Mill could feel vicariously for others and, more importantly, could remember in relation to himself. It is almost as if Mill had been hoping throughout the agitation over reform that existing institutions would crumble around him and that the times themselves would force him to create new opportunities for himself, though the nine years he had already spent in the India House made it difficult for him to imagine a more central role for himself than the teaching of political economy to the West Indian counterparts of the East Indian inhabitants of the Native States.

Throughout the 1830s into the 1840s as he worked on the *System of Logic,* it became more important for Mill to define both the times he lived in and the work he did as incompatible with his earlier goals. As the possibilities for action decreased, he became more and more willing to accept his role in the East India Company as a convenient explanation for his lack of engagement in public affairs. In a letter to Thomas Carlyle in 1833, he bemoaned the "infinitesimal smallness" of the good that one individual can accomplish: "Yet it seems to me that if one had a proper stage and proper tools, more is to be accomplished just now by the doer of the deed than by the sayer of the word. . . . But then, what career is open to the *doer,* if either in your position or in mine?" (12:155–56). He then, in a painful gesture of his own confusion, asked Carlyle to share his own thoughts on this question, as if to disprove what the tone of the question implies—that there is no answer. At times Mill held out hope for a change in his circumstances. Whether it involved a seat in Parliament or the editorship of a paper, the India House interposed itself and paralyzed its employee: it "hampers my freedom of action in a thousand ways but . . . shall not hamper it always" (12:200).

As the decade closed, Mill put such ambitions behind him. He told Sterling, "I quite think with you that it is no part of my vocation to be a party leader." Whether he had "any better vocation for being a philosopher," only time would tell (13:406). By 1841 not only was Mill ready to redefine his vocation, he was ready to redefine the world in which he lived: "We are entering upon times in which the progress of liberal opinions will again, as formerly, depend on what is *said* & *written,* & no longer upon what is *done,* by their avowed friends" (13:483). Mill had come full circle from the claim he made to Carlyle in 1833 that the "doer of the deed" rather than the "sayer of the word" was the man of the moment. Earning a living at the India House limited his freedom so that he could function politically only as a writer, and he was quite willing to accept and to perpetuate that outcome. At one point, he mockingly described himself as one of those "whose whole life is passing in writing either to 'Our Governor General of India in Council' or to everybody's governor general the English public" (13: 447). To be the company's servant as well as the public's servant now suited not only his character but the times as well.

No wonder, then, that Mill retained the particular brand of hero-worship that had its source in his first responses to his earliest reading of ancient and modern history.[17] Mill's version of such admiration was not, like Carlyle's, the adulation of the strong man whose might makes right, but it issued from the same source as Carlyle's—the frustration experienced by the man of letters over his own weakness and his anomalous position in his culture. Specifically in opposition to Carlyle's views, Mill held that such worship "must be the worship not of a hero but of heroes" (27:666), not of one hero who might mislead his followers, but of the human potential for heroism that the aggregate of such figures displays. In contrast, James Mill's disdain for the so-called heroic efforts of the individual was absolute: in 1817 he wrote David Ricardo to assure him that "all great changes, are easily affected, when the time is come. Was it not an individual, without fortune, without name, and in fact without talents, who produced the reformation?" Others might point to Luther's disabilities as a way to emphasize the magnitude of what he had achieved, but James Mill did so only to erase the man he refuses to name as a force in history. The elder Mill's lack of interest in the individual and the individual's feats of military valor was so overpowering that his *History of British India*, as William Thomas so justly says, consists of "large tracts of dull narrative studded with shorter and more striking passages of theory."[18]

For James Mill's oldest son, however, the man who had acquired as a child a taste for the kind of "animated narrative" that his father could not appreciate and would not write, the example of the hero was crucial. It proved that some individuals, at least, were not the slaves of their circumstances. It allowed him to rewrite his life, as I argue in the last part of this study, in ways that transform the actions of a "bookish man" into an imaginatively and emotionally satisfying portrait of the man of action. Heroism, as Mill conceived it, was ultimately central to his values and thought because it allowed him to resolve—imaginatively, conceptually, if not actually—the conflict between theory and practice. The hero is the individual who tests ideas by applying them to the "business of life." The closet-student is always limited by the closet; the man of action—and it is a *man*, not a human being, who is at issue here in the context of nineteenth-century thought—the man of action takes the idea onto the field of battle, whether it be the site of military engagement or the floor of a senate, and there he proves his mettle as it can be proved nowhere else.

Such considerations explain one of the strangest chapters in Mill's career as a writer. In the fifth edition of the *System of Logic* (1862), Mill added an entire chapter entitled "Additional Elucidations of the Science of History," and in it he explores the question of whether "the subjection of historical facts to uniform laws" diminishes the ability of certain individuals to affect the course of history. This was, in the early 1860s, a topical issue that elicited intense responses. Buckle's *History of Civilization,* published in 1857 and 1861, had excited what Mill calls the "present controversy on this subject" (9:941n), and James Fitzjames Stephen had responded to Buckle in a two-part essay called "The Study of History" that appeared in the *Cornhill* for June and July, 1861. In the early 1860s Mill was particularly attracted to what he called intellectual "combat" waged with weapons of controversy, but he chose to respond to this particular issue because it involved, for him, matters of great emotional centrality. This issue touches, certainly, on the "doctrine of Free Will" (8:931): the possibility of great men, as examples of the potential power of will over circumstances, provided for Mill a crucial demonstration of freedom in a world ruled by necessity and natural law. Yet the methods of controversy that Mill uses suggest further points of relevance. Mill does not take on Buckle as his adversary here; rather, he uses a footnote and the testimony of one of Buckle's friends to exonerate him from the charge of having denigrated great men (9:936n). Mill chooses as his opponent his father's old adversary and his own *bête noire*, Macaulay. In an early essay on Dryden, Macaulay had adopted James Mill's position on this issue and argued for the "absolute inoperativeness of great men" (9:937). Years later, despite Mill's admission that even Macaulay had not himself reprinted the essay and might, therefore, have at least qualified his assertion, Mill still uses it to exemplify the point he must attack.

Mill cites Macaulay's striking figure of the sun shining on the hills when it is below the horizon and on the valleys when it rises: the "highest minds" merely, according to Macaulay, see first the sunlight that will, in the course of nature, inevitably shine on all. This idea is more than Mill can bear: "Eminent men do not merely see the coming light from the hill-top, they mount the hill-top and evoke it; and if no one had ever ascended thither, the light, in many cases, might never be seen upon the plain at all" (8:938). Mill has to rewrite the workings of the universe in his strained attempt to disprove Macaulay's principle by reversing the import of the figurative language in which it is conveyed. Elsewhere in the chapter, Mill concedes that great men, working necessarily in accordance with the laws of history, may only speed up or slow down the advance of progress. But here he is approaching Carlyle's dogmatism: the great man commands the sun to rise; without his decision to climb up the hill, there would be no sun at all. It is as if Mill were using the experience of Moses on Mt. Pisgah—one of his favorite figures—to prove that the prophet did not merely see the Promised Land; his presence on the mountain actually called it into being. In the rest of Mill's lengthy discussion of this issue, he cites examples of heroic figures drawn equally from the realms of theory and practice. Charles the Third, Themistocles, and Caesar illustrate the principle that Mill wants to defend, and they do so along with Plato, Socrates, Aristotle, and Christ. Mill concludes by citing, as Stephen had done in his article, George Grote's *History of Greece* as proof that the "events on which the whole destiny of subsequent civilization turned, were dependent on the personal character for good or evil of some one individual" (8:942).

If Mill himself could not escape being subjected to his circumstances, if he could not leave his employ at the India House and elude the dominance of his life by the pattern set in his father's life, he could escape—conceptually, at least—into the realm of history, a realm that proved that such acts of self-assertion had been possible for others and might even be possible for him. Action, deeds of combat, would have answered Mill's needs, although he was not likely to have followed the example that Roebuck, his most envied earlier ally, had set when he fought a duel in 1835 with John Black. Mill's willingness, however, to stand for a seat in Parliament in 1865 proved that his earlier attempts to satisfy such impulses, such as the chapter added to the 1862 *Logic*, could not ultimately resolve the conflict between theory and practice. Despite all Mill's protests that an active political career would distract him from the speculative endeavors that he had defined as his chosen work, the fact that he agreed to stand for a seat was his tacit admission that a life devoted to thought, a character identified with its writing, had not been his choice. In the event, even his place in Parliament could satisfy his earliest needs for action in the realm of practice only when transmuted beyond recognition by the powers of imagination, not by the force of will. But that story I reserve for my last chapter. In the meantime, an examination of the other major determinant of Mill's career, his marriage to Harriet Taylor, will explain how that supposedly private experience made even more painful and more absolute Mill's definition of his character in terms of his writing.

Wife and Work

When John Stuart Mill adopted his father's dual career as writer and India House employee, there was no simple way to describe what he had become. In one of the Platonic dialogues that Mill published in the 1830s, Socrates sets a questioner to confront Gorgias, the rhetorician: "Ask him what he is." —"How?" —"So that, if he made shoes, he would answer that he is a shoemaker" (11:98). Similarly pressed, Mill would be hard put to find a one-word answer. He had undertaken one activity for remuneration, the other for the selfless and financially unrewarding furtherance of his ideals. Even if he had been allowed two terms, the second of these careers had no widely accepted and respectable title. Before the publication of his *System of Logic,* he was a writer for the newspaper and periodical press, but the social position of the newspaper man, in particular, was "altogether anomalous" (6:163), as Thackeray was learning to his pain at about this time.[1] Journalists, as Mill acknowledged in 1829, were reputed to be worse than brothel-keepers; theirs was the "vilest & most degrading of trades" (12:39). Despite such considerations, Mill in 1835 took on the more respectable, but equally precarious, role of unacknowledged editor of the *London Review,* which became the *London* and *Westminster Review* in 1836. Mill held onto that post until 1840, although the endeavor was financially damaging, in the hope, I think, that it would eventually offer him a living and thus the independence that his position in the East India Company denied him. By 1845 he was lamenting, "Nothing but books seems to do good now. The time for writing books seems to have come again, though unhappily not for living by doing it" (13:665). There was, of course, in Mill's case one simple answer to Socrates' probing question: when it came to his writing, as he revealed in his comment on the writer's inability to live off the proceeds of that work, Mill was an amateur.

By mid-century, the status of the amateur, so highly respected and respectable in the eighteenth century, had become ambiguous. As N. N. Feltes demonstrates, the relative value ascribed to the terms *amateur* and *professional* shifted throughout this period,[2] and no doubt such variations caused discomfort to those caught between the changing definitions and distinctions that the terms evoked. Writers were becoming more anxious to establish the authority of their books by referring to the professional standing that justified their claims to expertise. James Fitzjames Stephen, for instance, was ready to publish a volume without revealing his name but not without revealing that his were *Essays by a Barrister*. A look at the four-page catalogue of books offered by Mill's publisher, John William Parker, at the back of Mill's collected *Essays on Some Unsettled Questions of Political Economy* (1844) reveals how widespread this trend was as Mill began his career as a writer of books. Of the twenty-four authors whose works are advertised, only two appear without information about the degrees or the professional positions they hold. William Whewell, whose study of the history of science had been so important to Mill's work on the *Logic,* is identified as "Master of Trinity College, and Professor of Moral Philosophy in the University of Cambridge." The simplest citation is "A. Taylor, M.D." The most involved follows the name of W. H. Smyth: "R.N., K.S.F., D.C.L., F.R.S., F. Astron. Soc. &c., &c.; one of the Board of Visitors of the Royal Observatory." Of course, for the purpose of instilling confidence in one's readers, such apparently defensive elaborations might have been worse than no elaboration at all. But when Mill came before the public, he came with his name alone. The lack of any elaboration following his name on the title page of the *Essays on Some Unsettled Questions* sets him apart from the authors catalogued in its endpapers.[3] The title page of Mill's most celebrated work reads simply:

On Liberty

by

John Stuart Mill

By contrast, the authors of two books that Mill reviewed in 1859 for his article "Recent Writers on Reform" appear at the head of the article as "John Austin, Esq., formerly Professor of Jurisprudence at the London University, and Reader on the same subject at the Inner Temple" and "James Lorimer, Esq., Advocate" (19:342). By 1859, Mill would have needed no such professional identification. Before then, his amateur status insured that he could invoke none.

Originally, Mill had envisioned a career that would have avoided such problems. When he says in the *Autobiography* that his "object in life" was "to be a reformer of the world," he is speaking of a vocation, a calling as profound as any traditional summons issued to any believer by God himself. In studying law, Mill was on his way to a "profession": the law, along with divinity and medicine, was one of the three time-honored learned occupations. In joining the ranks at the India House, Mill gained a livelihood or, as he calls it in the *Autobiography*, a "professional occupation" (1:83). Mill was well aware of the connotations of these terms, and although he uses them in the *Autobiography* in ways that conform to the contemporary prejudices attached to them, he elsewhere refused to accept either the traditional definition of *profession* as one of the learned three or, according to its emerging definition, as a line of work that had monopoly status over a specific body of knowledge by virtue of the training, examinations, and membership in a professional organization that it required. To Mill, as to another civil servant like Anthony Trollope or to other writers insecure about their status, one's profession simply meant one's means of subsistence, the way in which one earned one's bread.[4] Only, for instance, as Mill contended in the 1830s, when work is compensated does it become a "profession: the occupation and study of a laborious life" (18:35). The writing that Mill did after he had discharged his official duties at the India House—or, indeed, often during the hours when he stood ready to do those duties—such writing was the marginal remnant of his original vocation. In fact, writing, because it did not earn his liveli-hood, was, according to his own definition, not a profession, but an avocation, the "*dilettante* work" he dismisses elsewhere when describing "unpaid" efforts (18:35).

Mill certainly would have accepted no such disparagement of his role as a writer. Later commentators on his life who choose to dis-miss or ignore his employ at the India House are simply following the lead Mill offered in the *Autobiography*. There his relative silence on the subject allows him to focus all his attention on his work as a writer as he ignores the contradictions inherent in it. One proof of his "altogether anomalous" position was the contrast between the serious-ness with which he undertook the job for which he was not paid or paid very little and his relative lack of commitment to the job for which he was paid. Mill's embarrassment on this subject appears every time he comments on those highly educated individuals devoted to thought and speculation. What does one call such individuals? As T. W. Heyck argues, the catchall term *intellectuals* did not come into wide usage until late in the century. Recent writers on Mill's work share this em-barrassment every time they invent such labels for him as "cultural critic" or "public moralist."[5] Mill seems to have been genuinely am-bivalent about the current term *man of letters:* it carried a suggestion of amateurish dabbling that was not at all appealing. Macaulay, for instance, was, according to Mill's sneering and unfair description, a "coxcombical dilettante litterateur who never did a thing for a practi-cal object in his life" (17:1970). *Literary man* was no better: it suggested trade, and as Mill proved in 1831 by quoting a passage from the *Brigh-ton Guardian*, the financial interests of the literary man put him "on the same footing as a mountebank or a puppet-showman" (22:321), a comment that again recalls Thackeray's professional dilemmas. In 1854 Mill privately mocked those who, like Carlyle, attempted to ele-vate "the literary character" into a "new priesthood"—"they aim at a sort of under-finery instead of aiming at things above finery" (27:653)—but Mill himself favored more elevated and respectful titles for writers and thinkers. Accordingly, the only authority cited in *On Lib-erty*, Wilhelm von Humboldt, is described as a man "eminent both as a *savant* and as a politician" (18:261). In his *Principles of Political Economy*, Mill also uses the term *savant*, as if an imported term would be less grating on practical sensibilities than *sage*, though even that more grandiose title was one he on occasion used, particularly if he was writing about another author, such as Coleridge, who had himself used it.

Mill found it easier to talk about such individuals as members of a group, a "learned class," but such a designation leaves unsolved another problem, a problem that again bears on the difficulties involved in writing for love, not money. If one recognizes the existence of a "lettered class," as Mill sometimes called it, how is that class to be supported? It was, of course, the question that his own experience had raised, and Mill suffered no hesitation in answering: because "the cultivation of speculative knowledge . . . is a service rendered to a community collectively, . . . it is, *primâ facie*, reasonable that the community collectively should pay" (3:968). Endowments, salaries, and fellowships should liberate those for whom "the occupation of some hours every day in a routine employment" (3:699) would constitute a prohibitive distraction from their real work of thought and discovery. Coleridge's concept of a nationally supported clerisy—as Mill defined it, "the *lettered* class; the *clerici* or clerks; who were appointed generally to prosecute all those studies, and diffuse all those impressions, which constituted mental culture" (4:220)—had great appeal for Mill.[6]

The personal implications of this idea are evident whenever Mill treats the subject. Twice in 1834, when he was still hoping for a source of livelihood other than his position in the East India Company, Mill, speaking in general, called for "a small provision" that would free the speculative thinker from "mechanical drudgery" (6:243). In one newspaper article, he vented a great deal of anger against a French writer who had misunderstood "the position of a man of letters" in England. It is not, Mill claims, that hacks cannot make a living in England—they are "almost the only prosperous persons among our public writers"— it is that "men of scientific eminence" cannot gain a living by publishing the results of their speculations. In this context, *scientific* replaces the reference to *learned* or *lettered* that Mill uses elsewhere. He objects to the thinker's involvement in getting and spending, in providing for the necessities of life: "All the men of high philosophical intellect in Great Britain depend for food and clothing upon the vulgar pursuits of some mechanical business, which could be quite adequately performed by persons with none, or with a far smaller share of their exalted qualities" (24:723–24). In this passage it is hard not to identify Mill's own restiveness with the "vulgar pursuits" and "mechanical business" of the India House.

Such a reading seems particularly apt when one realizes that in 1834 Mill was trying to proceed with his work on his *System of Logic*. When that work was going well in 1837, he wrote to Carlyle that it required "my best (or some of my best) faculties": "In truth, I have not, for years before, had a mind free from occupation with pettinesses. That is the only true meaning of leisure—*choice* of work" (12:347). Those "occupations and pettinesses" to which he referred certainly included the domestic problems created by his father's long illness and death, but they may also allude to the extra hours and days that Mill devoted to India House business during that final illness. Throughout the same decade, Mill consistently called for the payment of legislators. The legislator ought to be one of the learned class—or, in another version of the argument, the learned class ought to govern—and the business of government should be done, not by talking, but by thinking: "The *post* of a good and wise legislator is his own study" (6:159). Clearly, the man who should be translated from his study to the House of Commons and paid for the journey is the writer of this article, John Stuart Mill. Payment for members of Parliament, an idea that Mill opposed later in his career, would have solved the financial aspects of his vocational conflicts in the 1830s and would have given him a *locus standi* as a writer of books on public questions.

The amateur status of Mill's writing is, I think, directly related to the one choice of which he is so extravagantly proud in the *Autobiography*, the choice that he refused to reverse despite the vigorous disapproval of his father and of friends like Roebuck: his choice of Harriet Taylor, first as his intimate friend and later as his wife. A passage in the rejected leaves of the *Early Draft* links Mill's work as a writer to the qualities of his future wife in terms as positive as his comments on Roebuck's marriage are negative. In the words that originally conclude Part I of the *Early Draft*, he speaks of his work for the *London and Westminster Review* from 1834 to 1840 as a "new phasis" in his "literary existence [that] belongs to a different period in my personal history . . . that in which I enjoyed the friendship and was under the ennobling influence of one to whom I owe all that is best, either in me or in what I have written, and compared with whom I am in myself scarcely worthy of a passing thought" (1:616). Mill is now living a "literary existence" in which Harriet Taylor plays the dominant role. As Mill puts it at the opening of Chapter VI, in which he appears exclusively as a writer and a theorist, Harriet Taylor is "the source of a great part of all that I have attempted to do, or hope to effect hereafter, for human improvement" (1:193). Like another Harriet, Harriet Grote, who claimed to have initiated not only her husband's monumental *History of Greece*, but also Sir William Molesworth's edition of Hobbes,[7] Harriet Taylor was the motive force behind Mill's writings, but Mill, not his wife, was the one who assigned her that role. She proposed, he disposed. Yet it is clear that the relation of cause to effect might be construed differently. Precisely by defining himself as a writer and theorist, he set for himself a life's work in which Harriet Taylor could participate, one that, indeed, by mid-century her gender had come to define. In embracing the role of the writer, Mill was embracing the marginality of Harriet Taylor's condition.

In the passages in *The Subjection of Women* that deal with vocation, when Mill defines as a genuine profession only the work that earns a livelihood and establishes the individual's place in society, he concludes that "women artists," except those on the stage, are "all amateurs." "The vast superiority of professional persons over amateurs," he further explains, is a "familiar fact" (21:317). The identification Mill recognizes between women and amateurs pertained not just to the fine arts but to writing as well. More and more through the mid-Victorian period, even as certain kinds of writing, of novels particularly, became the source of substantial incomes, the career was identified with and put into question by its association with women.[8] Mill's thinking conformed to such stereotypes when he identified his writing as an activity not only in which he and his wife collaborated but in which she predominated. By stressing the exalted nature of his writing as an activity motivated by the idealistic purity and passion he attributed to his wife—no hint of filthy lucre here—Mill tried to move beyond the shortcomings of its amateur status even as he tacitly acknowledged them. Needless to say, no such elaborate defenses would have been necessary had he achieved his earlier ambitions for active political service. As it happened, Harriet Taylor became, for Mill, not, as he claimed, the symbol of the intellectual power he longed to possess, but the image of his own powerlessness.

Related to the doubt cast on writing by its amateur status and underlying the disabilities it suffered by being associated with women was the fact that much writing was done, as Mill's was done, in conjunction with other, often distracting occupations. Writing could be, as both Frances Trollope and her civil-servant son abundantly proved, undertaken without training and on a part-time basis. Robert Southey might counsel Charlotte Brontë that writing ought not be the business of a woman's life, but Brontë could object, as many women did, that writing could be combined with household duties. Whenever Mill commented on the circumstances of women's lives in Victorian England, he stressed the way in which those lives were defined by the multiplicity of the duties they involved. A woman in charge of a household had to attend to many different subjects for short periods of time. In both his *Principles of Political Economy* and his *Subjection of Women,* Mill tries to make a virtue of this necessity. Women, he says in the earlier work, have "far greater versatility than men" because their occupations are various and "general" while those of men are single and "special," and variety invigorates the "animal spirits" (2:127–28). In *The Subjection of Women,* he maintains that long concentration on one subject may not be a "normal and healthful condition for the human faculties, even for speculative uses." If Mill is seen for what he was—an intellectual generalist if there ever was one—and a man who pursued his intellectual interests during his hours at the India House when at any moment the arrival of a mail from India, like the servant's question or the child's cry, might interrupt his writing, the equation between the housewife's work and Mill's daily commitments becomes clear. Women who have such frequent calls on their attention "must steal time at odd moments for thinking" if they are engaged on "anything [that] requires longer thought" (21:310). *A System of Logic* had required ten years of thought, a period that was certainly rendered "longer" by the conditions under which Mill attempted to complete that work. His efforts to be optimistic about the invigorating effect that women's multiple duties had on them was, arguably, an attempt to place his own circumstances under the best light.

More importantly, writing aligned the work of women and that of the "learned class" by drawing on the cultural stereotype that identified the active as the masculine and the passive as the feminine. A reviewer in *Bentley's Quarterly,* for instance, noted in 1859 that the pseudonymous author of *Adam Bede* must be a woman because "the position of the writer towards every point in discussion is a woman's position, that is, from a stand of observation rather than more active participation."[9] Women observe, men participate. Although Mill frequently assigned women to the realm of practice—in *The Subjection of Women* he says they would be well suited to manage a Poor House because they know how to run a house—he often adverts to the wisdom and beauty of their passivity. In the statement "On Marriage" that he wrote for Harriet Taylor in 1832 or 1833, he argued that although women should be trained to work for a living, their "natural task" would be "to adorn and beautify" life, a task to "be accomplished rather by *being* than by *doing*" (21:43). Women are, like the men trained to speculative thought, defined by their exclusion from the realm of *doing*. The thinker is, as Mill famously said of himself, "more fitted . . . to *know* than to *do*" (1:39).

Both thinkers and women are at one remove from the active business of life. If they are allowed to participate at all, that participation must acknowledge their marginality. Harriet Martineau, who explained that she decided to "do something with the pen, since no other means of action in politics are in a woman's power," also claimed that her one direct act of participation in politics occurred when she was confined to bed by a serious illness. The image of Harriet Martineau, lying in bed, yet writing the letters that patch up a quarrel between two feuding statesmen, is particularly apt, a single woman's version of the curtain lecture through which women have traditionally exerted the indirect power open to them.[10] Mill's career yields similar, if less dramatic, images of marginality. The writer can show the legislator what laws ought to be passed; he cannot legislate directly. Mill may have been speaking of his own position when, in his 1854 diary, he proclaimed that "an intellect" like his wife's proves her to be "one who seems intended for an inhabitant of some remote heaven, and who wants nothing but a position of power to make a heaven even of this stupid and wretched earth" (27:654). Mill continually identified himself as a man who knew what to do to solve the problems around him—that was preeminently the public stance he took during the Irish potato famine of the late 1840s—but also as a man who had no power, other than the persuasive power of his pen, to implement the measures in which he had such faith. In the crisis of the famine, as he watched the British government undertake what he considered to be exactly the worst response possible, his sense of his own powerlessness became extreme. When he wrote *The Subjection of Women,* before he was elected to serve as a member of Parliament, he defined "women's writings" as "the only mode of publicity which society permits to them" (21:270). He might have said the same of himself. Such considerations point to the personal experience behind the analogy in the *Logic* that links philosophers presumed to have no practical experience with women presumed to have no intellectual capacities.

As Mill's 1854 comment on the "heavenly" but powerless intellect of Harriet Mill might suggest, Victorian culture was quite willing to grant to both thinkers and women the status of "higher" natures precisely because they were marginal and impotent. Like the token black whose acceptance is used to prove the colorblindness of a racist society, the elevation of women and thinkers was one way of making more palatable the aggressive and acquisitive energies and values of a commercial culture. The long account that Mill offers in *August Comte and Positivism* of the French thinker's plans for a new heaven and a new earth suggests just how debilitating such an elevation might be. Comte turned to the past and found there the traditional models after which to pattern his renovation of society. His treatment of the learned and of women is, therefore, simply a matter of conventional attitudes writ large. Comte defined women and thinkers, along with all their traditional disabilities, as a "Spiritual Power." The capacities of this "counterpoise" to the "absolute dominion of the civil rulers" would be exercised in the domestic sphere by women and in the public sphere by writers and thinkers. Women, in this new world, are not allowed to support themselves, they have "no powers of government, even domestic," and they are not allowed to own property. Mill emphasizes the congruity between Comte's vision of women's place and his conception of the clerisy: "Like women, they are to be excluded from all riches, and from all participation in power. . . . They are neither to inherit, nor to receive emolument from any of their functions, or from their writings or teachings of any description, but are to live on their small salaries," to be supported by the State as women are supported by their husbands—or, indeed, as women without husbands or fathers are to be supported by the State. If there could be any doubt that Comte is merely glorifying the *status quo*—and the traditionalism of the French thinker is the quality that Mill most deplores—the Spiritual Power incorporates yet one more "element" after women and the learned: the working classes or "proletaires." Because workers own no property and live on small wages, because they "are not allowed the smallest political rights," they appropriately constitute the "third element of the Spiritual Power" (10:344–47). This unholy alliance of women, thinkers, and workers recapitulates the triangle of the powerless that Mill creates in his reference in *A System of Logic* to philosophers, blacks, and women.

Since the term that Comte uses, *Pouvoir Spirituel*, was one that Mill applied to his own work and to his conceptions of the clerisy (12:40), his distress at the construction of Comte's paradise is as easily understood as his desire to change both his own situation and the status of the cleric. Harriet Taylor Mill recognized the disadvantages of such a role in her essay the "Enfranchisement of Women" (1851): "What is wanted for women is equal rights, equal admission to all social privileges; not a position apart, a sort of sentimental priesthood" (21:415). Mill's cherished ideals of a clerisy involved such a "priesthood," but it would not be merely "sentimental" because monetary compensation would provide the recognition of the work it did as valuable to the community. In writing to support women's suffrage, Mill underlines the similar disabilities of those women and men placed in a "position apart." One of the major objections to the idea of granting political equality to women involved the fear that their votes would increase the power of the clergy because women would follow their clergymen's instructions about how to vote. Mill's solution to this problem is not to change the influence of clergy over women, but to renovate the position of the clergy themselves. Here he could be speaking of the position of the speculative thinker as well: "What is it that makes clergymen in general . . . such unsafe advisers in politics and the affairs of life? It is because they are too much in the position of women; they are treated too much as women are: under a show of deference, they are shut out from the free and equal discussion of great political questions, and are taught to think themselves concerned with only one aspect of any subject—the moral and religious aspect" (29:390). A "show of deference" to the clergy does not disguise the fact that they are "shut out from" practical affairs. They are "too much in the position of women." In the case of both women and the clergy, Mill has no doubt that the effect of such exclusion is debilitating, to those who do the excluding as well as to those who are excluded.

Conventional attitudes, then, have a great deal to do with the construction that Mill put on the ideal qualities of his relation to Harriet Taylor, a relation that ultimately conformed to cultural stereotypes even as it attempted to transcend them. Mill's groveling and self-advertised intellectual subservience to his wife is well known, and its validity is generally dismissed: if he thought that she was the Bentham, he the Dumont (14:112), few readers of the *Autobiography* from Alexander Bain on have accepted the interpretation that their "joint productions" owe much to Harriet Mill's participation in them. Although I have no wish to join in the continuing debate over the amount of his writing that she actually did, a debate that Jack Stillinger has apparently placed within its proper limits by examining her pervasive but limited role as the first editor of the *Early Draft*,[11] not enough, I think, has been made of the indirect power over Mill that Harriet Mill wielded simply by being his chosen companion—power that affected not only the shape of Mill's career, but what he wrote about that career.

First, it is important, I think, to understand the strains created by Mill's intimacy with Harriet Taylor, and a single example of its effect on his personal relations will suffice to make that point only too emphatically. Among the acrimonious exchanges between Mill and members of his family over his marriage, the most painful took place between Mill and his younger brother George Grote Mill. In writing letters of bewildered congratulation to his new sister-in-law and her son, George had wondered why he had had to learn of the marriage secondhand. Using his father's authority to justify his criticism, he presumed to suggest that his older brother had been "mysterious." George had worked as a clerk under his brother at the East India Company; in touching imitation of his brother's talents, he was trying to make a living by writing. He had been sent for his health to the Continent where, in the last stages of consumption, he would die by his own hand two years later. George was understandably hurt by Mill's silence about his plans to marry Harriet Taylor, especially since George had received a letter from Mill written four days after he left his mother's house in preparation for the event and just twelve days before the event itself.

But Mill could not understand his brother's pained confusion, and he responded with an extraordinarily cruel attack on George's failures of character, his lack of manners, his immaturity, and his insensitivity— Mill had not been "prepared" for "such want of good feeling, together with such arrogant assumption," even in George. He then responded to George's musings on the strength of Harriet's principles—her ideas on the slavery inherent in marriage being enough, George had reasonably thought, to keep a widow from engaging in another round of bondage—but Mill reserved his final words and his greatest display of anger for George's claim that his eldest brother had been "mysterious" (14:73–74).

Mill's anger issued in alternate pleading. George should have known that it had "never been [his brother's] habit to talk" about his concerns. Alternatively, "every one has a right to be mysterious if they like." And, in still another form of defense, John Mill claimed that he had not done what "every one" has a right to do: "I had never anything to be mysterious about." Among these defenses come the most childish and petulant. "As for the 'mystery' which on my father's authority you charge me with, if we are to bandy my father's sayings I could cite plenty of them about all his family except the younger ones, compared with which this is very innocent." To this threat, Mill added another interpretation of his father's reading of his own character: "It could [have been] said at all but as a half joke" (14:74–75). Against the charge of mysterious silence and deceptive behavior, Mill defended himself in every way possible and, unlike the intended effect of alternate pleading in an English court of law, the sum of the defenses in this case was no defense at all.

This coldly furious letter reveals equally Mill's sensitivity about his new wife's principles and his sensitivity about his own lack of openness and candor. Twenty years of intimacy with a married woman had reduced his equanimity on both these issues to particularly low flash points. While John Taylor was alive, the anomalies of Mill's relation to Harriet Taylor were obvious: weekly or twice-weekly dinners together, sojourns on the Continent, a trial separation of husband and wife in 1833, lengthy communications between the two "friends" by post. All this activity was never mentioned or acknowledged to or by Mill's family or by any friends not within the Unitarian circle where Mill had first met Harriet Taylor. It was a relationship that both Mill and

Taylor were ready to defend as normal, innocent, and irreproachable. William J. Fox, the Unitarian minister who had introduced Mill and Taylor in 1830, used exactly the same justification for his openly adulterous relation with Eliza Flower.[12] But as John Mill's letter to George Mill reveals, such a relation, consummated or not, called for defenses and denials that could not but affect every aspect of Mill's experience.

The alienation that Mill's defensiveness caused between himself and his family extended to his professional associates as well, particularly the friends, such as Roebuck and the Grotes, with whom he had been so closely associated as one of the Philosophic Radicals. Bain's distress over this situation was evident: catching Mill for fifteen or twenty minutes of conversation at the India House was "the only way that he could be seen." Not until receiving the copy of *The Principles of Political Economy* with the effusive dedication to Harriet Taylor added to its presentation copies did Bain dare even to mention her to Mill, and in so doing, he was considered by their other friends to have done a "very rash thing."[13] The greater distance from active politics that his relation to Harriet Taylor demanded cost Mill much more than he could admit in the *Autobiography*. In 1833, he confessed to William J. Fox that "what ought to be so much easier to me than to her, is in reality more difficult—costs a harder struggle—to part company with the opinion of the world, and with my former modes of doing good in it" (12:178). His "modes of doing good" in the arena of public affairs consisted of leading the Philosophic Radicals either in Parliament or out, and the snickers about his Platonica, as Thomas Carlyle cruelly called Harriet Taylor, could only undermine his position.

There is evidence that this point was actually a topic of pained discussion between Mill and Harriet Taylor. In a letter written in 1834, she responded furiously to Mill's suggestion that she was the cause of his being "*obscure & insignificant.*" She attacked him for succumbing to the fear that he was not able "to brave the world," and she found "a touch of Common Place vanity" in such fear.[14] Mill uses much the same terminology to describe his rejection of English society in the *Autobiography*—he explains that he could retreat from the insipidity of "general society" once he gave up the editorship of the *London and Westminster Review* and thereby "indulge the inclination, natural to thinking persons when the age of boyish vanity is past, for limiting my own society to a very few persons" (1:235). Since the "very few persons" he has in mind are his unnamed "incomparable friend" and "her first husband, Mr. Taylor" (1:237), one has to conclude that what Mill hoped to escape was less the triviality of polite society than the wagging of impertinent tongues. Significantly, Mill identifies this retreat as possible only when "the age of boyish vanity" is past. Here he indirectly links the end of his earlier heroic ambitions with his role as a "thinking person" and with his devotion to Harriet Taylor. The "desire of distinction" (1:113) in the world, in the form of his earlier parliamentary ambitions, is one of those toys of childhood that he must put aside if his relation with her is to continue. Perhaps out of his extraordinary generosity to her, Mill continued in the role of the theorist so that she could remain part of his life as a writer. Any more active political involvement would have proven too obviously the disabilities she suffered because she was a woman, not to mention a married woman who had been for twenty years intimate with a man other than her husband.

Contemporary observers unfriendly to Harriet Taylor confirm this supposition. Thomas Carlyle, to whom Mill had described in moving terms his emotional isolation in 1833 as an impulse to "beat against the bars of my iron cage" (12:144), used the same image in 1836 to describe Mill's relation to his "charmer": "that he does not speak, that he never could speak, but was to sit imprisoned as in the thick ribbed ice, voiceless, uncommunicating, is it not the most tragical circumstance of all?" Harriet Grote, looking back in 1867 to the 1830s, offers a similar, though nastier, version of Carlyle's assessment. For all the failed hopes of the Philosophical Radicals in 1832, Mill's election to the House of Commons in 1865 offers some consolation: "J. S. Mill [is] only now entering upon such a political career as he longed for before he was half his present age (which I believe to have been that woman's doing, with much other mischief)." [15] "That woman" was certainly not the only reason that Mill did not gain the seat in Parliament that he "longed for" at thirty, but Mill's rejection of public life, necessitated by his relation to her, remained an important reason.

By the time Mill was writing his *Autobiography*, the distance between himself and his former political allies and between his current work as a writer and his former political ambitions could not have seemed greater. But the pain created by that distance could hardly be acknowledged in the *Autobiography* he wrote with its cause, Harriet Mill, at his side, her pencil ready to scratch out whatever she, for one reason or another, might dislike. Carlyle's image of Mill rendered silent by Harriet Taylor—sitting imprisoned without a voice—is appropriate to his writing of the *Autobiography* as well. He wanted to tell all that was necessary to justify his relation to her, but because she was superintending the writing of the *Autobiography*, he could not have been candid, even if he had wanted to, about his earlier ambitions and her effect on his chosen vocation. Given free choice between politics and life with his "precious guide philosopher & friend" (14:163), who, like the child of the "Immortality" ode, is the "best philosopher," Mill would have chosen the latter, but the censorship her presence exerted in the *Autobiography* needs to be recognized. Mill is candid about the "restraints and retinences [*sic*]" (1:215) that his father's presence had entailed on his writing for the *London Review*, but he cannot acknowledge the similar reticences required by Harriet Taylor's presence. After her death in 1858, as he revised and added to the story of his life, silence on the subject was all the more imperative: death itself had canonized Mill's "most valuable" friend.

Such a perspective explains at least some of the mysteries that surround his account of his crisis in the *Autobiography*. Unlike the later crisis of 1836, which occurred at the death of James Mill, the earlier crisis had no perceptible effect on either Mill or his routine: he kept to his daily round of work and debates and writing, though the latter did decrease in volume at this time. No one but John Stuart Mill seems to have realized that something was wrong in 1826. The very scanty record left in his letters certainly casts doubt on the gravity he ascribes to this crisis in the *Autobiography*. Mill and his constant companions, John Roebuck and George John Graham, were known as the Trijackia during these years (12:20n), a nickname that evokes visions of easy camaraderie rather than solitary pain. In the *Autobiography*, Mill focuses on the clearly less substantial crisis of 1826–1828 and ignores the crisis of 1836, even though that was the psychic event that required a lengthy leave of absence from his duties at the India House and marked him permanently with a facial tic. In 1853–54, when Mill was writing the *Early Draft*, he could not mention that later crisis because, of course, Harriet Taylor had been part of its cause, as James Mill at the time had clearly recognized when he attributed his son's "pining condition" to an unmentionable, but obvious "cause." [16] In 1836 Mill's duty to his dying father competed with his desire to be with his "intimate friend," and his own illness was both the result of that conflict and the excuse Mill needed to escape to Brighton during his father's last months and to the Continent shortly after his death. It is possible, then, that Mill cast his account of the earlier crisis in emotional terms so that he could explore without acknowledgment some of the emotional cost of his competing loyalties to James Mill and Harriet Taylor, a competition that the later crisis made all too evident.

Moreover, in 1853–54 it was crucial for Mill to define solely in emotional terms the crisis that presumably occurred before he met Harriet Taylor as a way to justify her later role as his companion. Mill attributes all his unhappiness to the shortcomings of his education, an education at the hands of the father who took him to task for being in love with another man's wife, so that he could justify the extreme measures involved in a relation with the only paragon of humanity who could cure his ills. The father taught analysis; the friend cultivated Mill's emotional garden. Mill's redefinition of Utilitarianism in 1836, after he became involved with Harriet Taylor, presents a similar accommodation: neoradicalism should include in all its earlier principles a new understanding of the importance of "Feeling" (12:312). Harriet Taylor, as she appears in the *Autobiography*, is a woman of passion, sensibility, and self-created energy. The opposite of James Mill, though his equal in critical severity, she serves as proof of John Stuart Mill's embrace of poetry and feeling. The function that Mill attributes to Wordsworth in Chapter V is simply a way of talking about the role that Harriet Mill played in Mill's life from the early 1830s on. Significantly, Mill never directly compares her to Wordsworth—she is, rather, a greater poet than either Carlyle or Shelley—because Wordsworth simply stands in for Harriet Taylor when discretion forbids that she appear in her own person. How severely limited Mill took that role to be is made clear both by his admiration for the man of action and by his repeated assertions that the times required action, not poetry. In being the reason for the explanation of the crisis that Mill offers in his autobiography, Harriet Mill was a party to its production, not as its "joint" author, but as the fact of Mill's life that, even in the mid-1850s, required more justification than any other. In this sense, she authorized the substance of the *Autobiography* more than Mill himself might have cared to recognize.

Defending the oddities of the Mills' relation was, of course, one of the primary motivations for the writing of the *Autobiography*,[17] and Mill chooses over and over again to satisfy that need by blaming his father for problems that were often at least as much the result of his relation with Harriet Taylor. The image of Mill so commonly derived from the *Autobiography* as a man crippled by the overpowering domination of his unpleasant father results, in part, from this maneuver. To some extent, that image is accurate, but it replaces the image, derived from other sources, of Mill as a man crippled by the influence of his equally unpleasant wife. Mill's reserve is a case in point. In the *Early Draft* Mill attributes his incapacity for intimacy and candor to his education—his inability to engage in easy sociability resulted both from his father's early refusal to let him mix with other boys and from his father's severity.[18] Yet my analysis points to rather different conclusions. Although the cost of his devotion to Harriet Taylor was undeniably evident even at times to Mill, he found it easier to blame his dead father for the personal qualities that contributed to that cost than his wife for being the occasion for his exhibition of them.

Mill confirms such analysis, at least indirectly, in his comments on conventional marriages in *The Subjection of Women*. Numerous readers have responded to Mill's invitation to read this work as if it were an exercise in autobiography: "One can, to an almost laughable degree, infer what a man's wife is like, from his opinions about women in general" (21:278).[19] He indirectly repeats that invitation at the end of the work when he compares the lot of women to that of a young boy under his father's rule or when he asks his readers to pity a woman cut off from the profession she would like to pursue by evoking the "feeling of a wasted life" experienced by the "numbers of men" forced to do jobs they would never have chosen for themselves (21:340). Mill is speaking from his own experience here. He explains the terrible cost of social bondage and political powerlessness: "An active and energetic mind, if denied liberty, will seek power: refused the command of itself, it will assert its personality by attempting to control others. To allow to any human beings no existence of their own but what depends on others, is giving far too high a premium on bending others to their purposes. Where liberty cannot be hoped for, and power can, power becomes the grand object of human desire" (21:338). One can easily see Harriet Mill, with her desire to dominate and humiliate her husband, behind this description, a conclusion confirmed indirectly by Charlotte Brontë's guess that the author of the "Enfranchisement of Women" was a "woman who longed for power" because she "had never felt affection" (15:629n). Such a woman, Mill suggests, satisfies her lust for power by destroying a man's ambitions, and this passage, which nicely illustrates the relation between fictional characters like Rosamond Vincy and Tertius Lydgate, reveals the link between the Mills' supposedly exalted spiritual union and more conventional bonds. When Mill points in *The Subjection* to the potentially ominous effects of the increased time that husband and wife spend in each other's company, he comments again on his own situation, "It is not with impunity that the superior in intellect shuts himself up with an inferior, and elects that inferior as his chosen, and sole completely intimate, associate." The gender roles linked to this idea of superior and inferior are wholly conventional here: "Even a really superior *man* . . . insensibly imbibes the modes of feeling, and of looking at things, which belong to a more vulgar and a more limited mind than *his own*" (21:335, emphasis added). The personal relevance of these conventional stereotypes is clear. Harriet Mill's mind was "more limited" than John Stuart Mill's, and the disadvantages of allowing it to dominate cannot be ignored.

One of Mill's letters seems to comment with even more specificity on his own condition. Agreeing with Herbert Spencer that it might have been as appropriate to have written a *Supremacy of Women* as the book he had actually written on their subjection, Mill contended that the "best men" are the ones "worst tyrannized over" because their wives' "illegitimate power" has greater influence than "legitimate freedom" would grant them and because the "most generous men shrink from exacting justice" from their wives in deference to "their weakness" (17:1614). One passage from *The Subjection of Women* elucidates the professional implications for the man involved in such a struggle with illegitimate power. A husband cannot "differ in his opinion from the mass" because he cannot risk sacrificing the welfare of his family to his principles. Too often, as well, wives, because they are excluded from the world of affairs and know nothing of that world, have become the "auxiliar[ies] of the common public opinion": "Whoever has a wife and children has given hostages to Mrs. Grundy" (21:331–32). Mill was speaking here, I would argue, from personal experience. Because Harriet Taylor set herself in opposition to "general society" and saw herself as too good for its purposes, she set Mill in opposition to it as well. Because his relation to her convinced Mill to overestimate the power of Mrs. Grundy and to find his work outside areas where Mrs. Grundy could rule, Harriet Taylor turned him into a hostage to conventional opinion.[20] Not from theory or from observations alone could Mill have described with such clarity and force the domestic rage for power in the otherwise powerless wife. Every tongue-lashing to which Harriet Mill treated him—and there is plenty of evidence that such was her habitual response both to his clumsy efforts to manage practical affairs and to his most graceful manipulations of personalities and polemical issues—every tirade of criticism was proof of her inability to accept the disabilities of being a woman in Victorian England, and Mill's reasoned and principled objections to the subjection of women may indeed have reflected his uneasiness with the subjections to which her disenfranchisement exposed him.

I am suggesting, then, that one aspect of Mill's personal experience, his relation to Harriet Taylor, had both positive and negative effects on his status as a commentator on social and political issues. She was largely responsible for confirming him in that role. His life with her provided the energy and occasion for what I take to be the quite extraordinary psychological acuity in a work like *The Subjection of Women*. But her presence and, later, her memory were also responsible for attitudes and opinions that rendered Mill powerless in the arena of practical politics in his own time, a point to which I return later in this chapter. What places his relation to her under such suspicion, however, is the way in which it follows the pattern of Mill's relation to his father. Others have recognized the emotional implications of this pattern.[21] I would suggest its vocational implications. James Mill placed John Mill in the India House; Harriet Mill kept him there. If for no other reason, he continued in his bureaucratic position so that he could meet the financial responsibilities that marriage imposed. In 1837 Mill could imagine "obliging all connected with me to alter their style of living and go (as the vulgar phrase is) down in the world" (12: 346), but Harriet Mill was not one to have easily acquiesced in such a plan. And the India House, like Harriet Mill, became a fact in his life that proved his continued subjection to external forces, that blinded him to the extent of his personal involvement in them, yet gave him a vantage point from which to recognize in some cases or to register unconsciously in others the profound effects of such pressures.

In the *Autobiography* Mill is as careful to defend his role in the East India Company as he is to defend his relation with Harriet Taylor. It taught him the practical implications of theory, the art of compromise, and the patience to wait for the time when change is possible. Mill refused to acknowledge any conflict between his avocation as a writer and his employment as a bureaucrat. Both James Mill and John Stuart Mill believed, along with Walter Scott, that "literature and philosophy" should not be an individual's "means of livelihood"—that one's "subsistence" should be won from the "common vocations," and "higher themes" should be pursued in "leisure hours." [22] John Mill, like Trollope in his comments on his position at the Post Office, emphasized the freedom that his position granted him. In a letter in 1862 to a man who hoped to make a name in philosophy, Mill warned against taking up writing as a full-time career: "combining two occupations makes each of them, as I have found in my own experience, a rest from the other" (15:793–94). Mill seems to have been suggesting that such a bifurcation of attention creates two different capacities that can be devoted to two different kinds of work in ways that promote achievement in both rather than diminish it in either. Other witnesses offer other perspectives. To explain why he could not continue working at the General Board of Health under Edwin Chadwick, Alexander Bain pointed to Mill's experience—the "severe strain" of a conflict between office and writing was, he felt, inevitable. Trollope's superior at the Post Office was furious to read an article in which Trollope claimed to earn his living by his pen,[23] and Trollope, unlike Mill, did his writing in the early morning before he arrived at the office. Mill himself is the best witness against his sanguine later comments on his employ in the East India Company. His earlier attempts to popularize the notion that the learned class should be supported by the state prove how uneasy he was, at least in the 1830s, with the mechanical drudgery that his hours there entailed.

When one considers the enormous output of work that Mill did in the Examiner's Office—he carefully kept a ledger of the 1700 dispatches that he wrote (30:240)—a conflict between his two occupations might seem unavoidable. George Mill, who had worked at the India House with John Mill, deplored his brother's continued employ there.

In the letter to Harriet Mill that so angered his brother, George wondered "what changes your union will make in your mode of life": "It would give me the greatest pleasure to hear that J. was free of the tether that binds *him* to the City & *you* to the neighborhood of London. Twenty-five years at the I. House, believe me, is as much as any man can well bear" (14:73n). In a passage that may have enraged Mill as much as George's questions about Harriet Mill's principles, George blamed Mill's presence at the India House on his too "generous" terms with his publishers. Although George Mill underestimated the number of years that his brother had already spent at the India House, and John Mill would, in the event, spend thirty-five years there before resigning on a pension of £1500 a year in 1858, George had, more justly perhaps than he knew, good reason to hope that his brother could break the "tether" that bound him to the East India Company.

Alexander Bain made the same lament. He regretted that both John Mill and his father could not have been relieved of their duties: "If the two Mills had been wholly exempted from official work, I have little doubt that all the speculative portions of Logic, Psychology, Politics, and Political Economy would have been put forward at least a generation." Bain was speaking as a contemporary witness who had a professional interest in the relation between mind and body as well as experience as a civil servant, and he offered a striking account of the physical cost that the Mills extorted from themselves by their efforts. Their dual careers "brought upon themselves premature exhaustion, and vitiated their theories of life by shaping them under the perverting influence of shattered frames."[24] Bain's language here is strong, but it should be: Mill's official work at the India House had a "perverting influence" not only because it frustrated his political ambitions and kept him from his speculative work—Grote, Bain noted, was wise enough to retire from his banking house for twelve years so he could write without interruption his *History of Greece*—but because it limited the kind of thinking Mill could do.

Most commentators, of course, tell the story differently by emphasizing that the East India Company offered Mill a good and secure income in return for very little sustained work.[25] Even Bain explains that Mill probably gave to official business no more than three hours of the six that he was required to spend at the India House. Visitors were free to come to Mill's office, and even after the other clerks were told to eat breakfast before their duties started at 10 A.M., Mill, in honor of his philosophic eminence and spartan appetites, was allowed to have his egg and toast after getting to the office and before getting down to the day's work. The freedom and lack of work at the India House were legendary, and Mill's output of writing done there—and not in his leisure hours—attests to the truth behind the legend. Letter after letter in the *Collected Works* is headed "India House"—the letter of October 1831 to John Sterling is so headed, and it, Mill later joked, could have filled a quarto volume (12:100). The *Logic* was written at the India House, as well as *The Principles of Political Economy*. The last five of Plato's dialogues translated by Mill are on East India Company paper. The 1825 speech on "Cooperation" is on the back of an East India Company document (26:308). Seventeen of the surviving manuscripts of the debating speeches from the 1820s reveal a similar provenance (27:673–78). Even the *Early Draft* of the *Autobiography* is "apparently" written on the paper "used in the East India Company" (1:xix). Though the editors of the Toronto *Collected Works* do not speculate on this subject, I wonder if the three scribes who copied *A System of Logic* were clerks working under Mill at the office—good help probably being no easier to come by, if less expensive, at that time than it is now. Because Mill defined his writing as a contribution to the public good, he could justify his use of either the paper or the time that might otherwise be devoted to the service of the East India Company as he avoided recognizing the obvious implications of what was, after all, at the time simply standard practice.

Mill was unforgivingly rigorous in his attacks on jobbery in government. The misuse for private interest of one's public trust moved him at times to heights of inventive and splenetic rhetoric that make some of his comments on the jobbery of the Post Office or of Tory members of Parliament sound almost like Dickens on the Circumlocution Office. Particularly in the newspaper articles of the 1830s when the interest in reform focused not only on questions of franchise but on governmental administration, Mill let loose on those who take a salary in return for little or no effort. Sinecures are, he is convinced, the worst aspect of bad government. He is particularly outraged by the monopolistic "privilege of franking newspapers" for fees that "come out the pockets of the people" to fatten the purses of the postal clerks (23:

643). He congratulates Lord Brougham for his law reforms because they have abolished "legal sinecures, which yielded immense incomes to sons, nephews, and grandchildren of Chancellors and Judges" and because they have dammed up "the golden streams which flowed into the strong boxes of these lucky foster-children of the nation" (23: 623). That "connexions"—a term he always renders sarcastic by enclosing it in quotation marks—should lead to lucrative employment of "incapables" is something that Mill cannot countenance (23:618). Yet he refuses to see that his relation to James Mill was the source of his position in the East India Company, just as he later used his own connections to provide for his younger brother George Grote Mill, though in announcing George's new position, he does acknowledge it as a personal favor to himself: "George is now working under me in the India House to which he has been appointed by the Directors in a way very kind & agreeable to me" (13:629). In due course, another brother, James Bentham Mill, followed both John and George into the service of the East India Company.

In fact, in construing his father's initial appointment to the India House and in describing his own rise to the position of Examiner, Mill indulges in a Bounderby-like insistence on unaided effort, an insistence that reveals his refusal to see the role played by "connexions" in either career. According to the *Autobiography,* James Mill's authorship of *The History of British India* was the only reason for his appointment to his post as an assistant in the Office of the Examiner. John Stuart Mill sees it as a somewhat surprising proof of disinterested good sense on the part of the Directors that his father was singled out for such a position when, in fact, he had not been wholly uncritical of the East India Company in his history. In fact, as James Mill's letters reveal, his appointment was the result of his friendship with powerful members of the Board, members who had known him and had been on the lookout for his interest before the publication of the *History* in 1817. Similarly, John Mill "very much staggered" Bain one day by announcing that his father had supported himself and his family in London before 1819 solely by writing, when Bain knew that the Mill family had lived off advances, later repaid, from Francis Place. Bain was always struck by how little John Mill knew about his father, and the son filled out his ignorance with the myth of the self-made man to enhance not only his father's stature but his own.[26] If he had had to admit how much his father owed to others, he might have had to acknowledge that the independence on which he prided himself was also fallacious.

Both Mills spent their careers decrying "sinister interests"—the interests of money and rank that were, they affirmed, directly opposed to the public good. John Mill's account of Bentham's career reveals the centrality of this idea to his goals of social improvement. Bentham identified the root of the evils of his day when he first recognized how thoroughly the professional self-interest of lawyers obscured their judgment. Mill himself never stopped pointing out that an individual's investment in a profession or a class is a "perverting influence," to use Bain's term: "Where there is identity of position and pursuits, there will also be identity of partialities, passions, and prejudices" (10:107). But it is easier to see the mote in another's eye than the beam in one's own. Mill was, he said, consistently a "radical and a democrat" because the "predominance" of the "noble and the rich," the "great demoralizing agency in the country," made public interests always give way to private; the popular respect for riches remained the "chief passport to power" (1:177,179). In one particularly forceful passage in his earlier long letter to John Sterling, Mill scornfully outlined as he mocked the effects of "practical Toryism": "Practical Toryism simply means, being *in,* and availing yourself of your comfortable position *inside* the vehicle without minding the poor devils who are freezing *outside.* To be a Tory means either to be a place-hunter and jobber or else to think that (as Turgot expressed it) tout va bien, parce que tout va bien pour eux; to be one qui ayant leur lit bien fait, ne veulent pas qu'on le remue" (12:83). Mill slipped into French, the language of his earlier revolutionary aims, to castigate those who derived comfort from society as it was presently constituted—the jobber in the coach, the jobber lying in the tidy bed—because they could not see that their comfort was the result of others' discomfort. He saw them as people who "must be driven" out of their refuges of privilege. What he did not see, of course, was his own modest place in the vehicle. Ironically, he penned this attack on jobbery in the letter to Sterling that is headed "From the 20th Oct to the 22d. India House. 1831" (12:74). For three days he had used his employ to decry the institutions that supported it. If "riches" were the root of all evil in English society, Mill was participating in that evil by working for an institution originally founded and perpetuated for the purpose of commercial gain. At this time, in 1831 before the East India Company had lost its part in trade in the reorganization of 1833, Mill and, more significantly, his father were lending their authority to the company by being in its employ.

In fact, Mill refuses to see the contradictions in his situation, and he continued to define himself as a "disinterested" commentator on institutions in which he supposedly had no investment. Indeed, "disinterested" is for Mill the highest praise one can offer a thinker, the most salient reason why one should trust a commentator. Newman and the Puseyites, for instance, deserve praise for their "disinterestedness" (24:814). Similarly, Mill was furious with Scott for having "misunderstood" the Girondins and "cruelly perverted" their motives: they were, he says in rhapsodic defense, "the purest and most disinterested body of men, considered as a party, who ever figured in history" (20:98–99). Mill joined George Grote in his defense of Cleon and the demagogues of Athens because they were "essentially opposition speakers" whose "hostile criticism" was virtually the only "check" against the "rich and the great, who had by far the largest share of personal influence" and not because they were championing their own interests (25:1160). Mill, perhaps inevitably, is seeing Athens in the glass of mid-Victorian England, but he is less forgivably able to see disinterestedness whenever he sees policies and principles of which he approves. The Girondins were trying to protect their own interests as well as France's. Newman admitted that the Oxford Movement was fueled by the participants' desire to release the church from the "tyranny of the State" so that they could control it themselves.[27] And no political group—Tories, Whigs, or demagogues—remains in opposition simply to insure the honesty of the party in power: the point of the criticism voiced by the opposition is to regain leadership and institute its own policies. No political stance is as simple as Mill seems to have wanted it to be, and no professional position, even if one conceives of it as simply a way to earn a living, is without its "partialities, passions, and prejudices."

Nor was there anything simple about the role of disinterested critic that Mill was trying to play, and he seems to have viewed figures like the demagogues and Girondins in idealized terms so that he could ignore the ambiguities of his own position. All these figures stood in opposition to reigning power, and that was the role that Mill cherished for himself. When he stood for Parliament a second time in 1868, he insisted on "absolute purity of principle in electioneering, and perfect independence on the part of the candidates" (16:1531). The one way to insure such purity was always to identify oneself as someone on the outside of the vehicle of state, and Mill continually defined himself as an adherent of the party in opposition so that he could insure his disinterestedness.[28] The pleasure Mill took in speaking from the opposition is evident in his early habit of reading books and "argu[ing every] point" with the author (1:15) or in his recognition that he wrote most effectively when he was treating a subject "controversially" (12: 160). Originally, the Philosophic Radicals were brought together by "their uncompromising profession of opposition" to received opinions (1:103), and Mill found that role so useful that he several times congratulated the Whigs for having been thrown out of office because their criticism of the party in power could accomplish more than their actions could when they were in office. After his first year in Parliament himself, Mill again found the role so congenial that he became a party in opposition to his own party and served as the critical voice denouncing the shortcomings of the Liberals. Mill tried to prove the value of disinterested opposition to prevailing forms of power and authority in whatever form he found it, but in his own case the pose is as much a fiction as it was in the reconstructions of historical figures whose virtue he was so interested to defend.

Whatever Mill's contentions about the usefulness of his official work to his theoretical concerns, his connection to the East India Company rendered his position as a theorist irreconcilably anomalous, just as the institution itself was, as Macaulay recognized, a "very strange . . . anomaly."[29] India House was a no-man's-land between theory and practice, between governmental dependency and professional independence—as an institution, it was neither commerce nor state. Mill's description of it in the *Autobiography* as a "branch of the government of India under the Crown" reveals the ambiguities that had existed since the late eighteenth century when "dual control" of India had become law (1:249): Is the government Indian or British? In what way is this "branch" of government "under" the Crown? Whose interests are paramount here? Who rules? The employees of the India House were neither private citizens nor government employees, neither professionals nor wage-slaves, neither leisured gentlemen nor quill-driving hacks. The office that harbored Charles Lamb and Thomas Love Peacock could, at times, seem less an office than a club for eccentrics.

Victorians, of course, were used to a certain amount of vocational vagueness and fluidity. There is something even typical about John Chapman's positions as titular editor of the *Westminster Review,* physician, inventor, and quack or about John Sterling's roles as clergyman, poet, and plantation manager. The drive toward the demarcation and professionalization of particular occupations increased slowly throughout the period, only exerting its full effects in the 1870s and 1880s.[30] Yet the indefiniteness of Mill's position was both particularly obvious and particularly poignant. Despite Mill's contention that his thirty-five years of "functions administratives" did not constitute a role in government (16:1047), Mill was both in the public pay and not so, both a functionary of government and not so. He tried to comport himself as if the two vocations he adopted—East India Company official and writer in opposition—were not related to each other, as if in his denunciations of "sinister interests," he was practicing no left-handedness of his own. But that, of course, was not so. The silver inkstand that Mill's colleagues gave him on his retirement from the East India Company embodies the anomalies of his situation. Although he perhaps had not actually seen this fanciful tribute before he expressed his anger at the gesture, the object itself epitomizes the absurdities to which his dual roles could force him. In bas-relief along an oblong "casket" is carved a copy of Raphael's *School of Athens,* depicting Aristotle and Plato, Apollo and Minerva (15:570n): the heroic embodiments of philosophy and its divine sponsors appear together in the grandiose service to the pen and ink that represented the slavery of the writer at the India House.

The philosopher driving or being driven in the chariot of imperial and commercial interests is certainly the image that Mill created whenever he treated Indian issues, particularly when he did so, not in his official capacity as an employee of the East India Company, but as a disinterested commentator on topical questions. In 1823, just weeks before he was appointed to the India House, he wrote, no doubt at the insistence of his father, a paper for *The Globe and Traveller* in which he defended East India sugar against its West Indian competitors; he objected strenuously to the "personal interest and *nothing more*" of those defending West Indian trade and to the motives of the "interested

Minister" who was pursuing his own gain; Mill voices these denunciations without, of course, hinting at his own "interest" in the question at hand (22:30). As the editor of the *London and Westminster Review,* he corrected a contributor who had criticized the Company by turning to his father as an authority: the Company had steadily "discountenanced" the "sinister interests" of its *"servants* in India": "See my father's history, *passim.* I believe the E.I.C. to have been, & I know it to be now, what my father represented it, the government which of all others (except perhaps the U.S. of America) wishes to do, & does, most for the people under its sway, & the *protector* of the natives of India against the avarice & domineering spirit of rapacious European adventurers" (17:1983). Here the East India Company is the equivalent of a national government; its rule can be compared with the treatment that the United States accorded its own indigenous Indian population, and Mill refuses to recognize the shortcomings of either system of management. Other European adventurers have raped India, but the Company has protected it, as if its own trading interests were not identical to those of other, more obvious malefactors. Indeed, Mill even cited the East India Company as the ideal model of the Saint-Simonian form of government, "a sort of joint-stock management of the entire productive resources of the nation" (23:678), omitting, of course, to mention the possibility that Britain's colonial rule of India had not originated in the selfless British intention to bring prosperity to the inhabitants of India, but rather in the desire to produce wealth for shareholders thousands of miles away.

Twenty years after the death of James Mill, the authority of the East India Company was threatened as it had been in 1833, and John Stuart Mill defended it as his father had done against those who would strip it of its monopolistic powers. His views on how the institution should be reformed suggest that he was keenly aware of the need to protect the interests of theorists, if not his own personal interests, in whatever form the new government of India would take. In an article in the *Morning Chronicle,* in which he is identified only as "a correspondent," he defends the "double government" of India by citing instances from "the glorious pages in the recent history of the Court of Directors" (25:1191). There is, of course, no mention in this article of his own work in the service of those directors. Mill further advises that the Court of Directors could be improved if its members were elected, not as at present from a list prepared by its current participants, but by a constituency of all those interested in matters Indian—stockholders, former employees of the company, former residents of India. The Court of Directors would then become a "sort of Parliament of India." Finally, in a move similar to his championship of Hare's plan for the representation of minorities or his advocacy of proportional voting in which the educated will have more votes than the ignorant, Mill suggests that a "certain number of seats" be filled by elections among the Court of Directors of "men too diffident, or too dignified, or too little desirous of office, to stand a popular election" (25:1193). If one asks whom the elite electorate might choose to bring among its numbers, the answer seems unavoidable. John Stuart Mill was perhaps too "dignified," as he later proved, to canvass actively for such an office, but not "too little desirous" of a seat even in a "sort of Parliament." As it happened, when he was offered a place on the newly constituted council after the dissolution of the Company, he declined: to have accepted the offer would have been to move too obviously inside the government he was more comfortable opposing.

Paradoxically, Mill's official statements in defense of the East India Company are a good deal more candid and less self-interested than those he made as an anonymous newspaper writer. As the Examiner of Indian Correspondence, second in command at the home office of the Company, Mill was called upon to draft the responses of the Court of Directors to its impending demise as an administrative body. One such document, *Memorandum of the Improvements in the Administration of India during the Last Thirty Years,* is a narrative of the "progressive improvement" wrought in the government of India (30:93), but its writer frequently admits that such changes have been the result of hard practical experience involving significant mistakes and misjudgments. In fact, Mill adopts a scientific metaphor that quite accurately establishes the relation between the British rule of India and its inhabitants: in trying to develop effective ways of governing 150 million people halfway around the globe, the East India Company has performed "experiments" on them. India has been a laboratory; its indigenous populations have served as guinea pigs so that their British rulers could become adept in the science of government.

This metaphor, according to Mill's account, explains the emergence of the Company's financial, agricultural, social, and political policies.

At times, the writer notes, "the experiment succeeded"; at others, "the experiment failed" (30:112,149). In one instance, the handling of the "numerous hill tribes in various parts of India," the policies being given trial "had been failures, sometimes almost disasters, but [they] had laid the foundation of that knowledge of our power, which enabled subsequent conciliatory measures to have their full effect." The report concludes that the East India Company cannot be criticized for not having accomplished more because it "has had all its knowledge to acquire, by a slow process of study and experience, and often by a succession of failures (generally, however, leading to ultimate success)" (30:153,155). Such a tone was, of course, justified and even required by the fact that the most infamous failure of the Company, the Indian Mutiny of 1857, had initiated the move to abolish the body held responsible for it. Although this official admission of failure balanced against a parenthetical "ultimate success" is still an idealization of the history of British control over India, it is a more qualified and realistic assessment than those that Mill allowed himself when he spoke in his private capacity as a theorist proposing the East India Company as a model of ideal government.

Even after the demise of the Company as a semigovernmental agency and his own retirement from it, Mill's unofficial views on the subject became no clearer.[31] His *Considerations of Representative Government* (1861) opens with a discussion of the most general principles of political science. "All speculations concerning forms of government bear the impress . . . of two conflicting theories respecting political institutions," theories based on analogies either to machines or to plants (19:374). After offering the reader a universalizing schema that illuminates "all speculation" at all times and a second set of general principles—permanence and progression—he asks his reader to join him in making a "rational choice" of the kind of government best suited to a particular nation at a particular time, warning, as he offers the invitation, that the "instructed" can offer guidance on this question because they are themselves less guided by their "personal position than by reason" (19:382). Mill's own disqualification as a guide, however, is revealed by the shape of his argument: the discussion that begins in such general terms narrows down to a point of genuinely self-serving specificity. The final pages of his *Considerations* turn to the British rule of India. Mill, the forward-looking reformer who scorns

Comte's visions of renewal based on traditional religious and social notions or F. D. Maurice's attempts to look back to the past of the English universities as a model for what they can become—Mill himself adopts such a backward view of the East India Company.

In the last pages of *Representative Government,* the East India Company emerges as the source of the "true theory of the government of a semi-barbarous dependency by a civilized country" (19:577). In particular, he notes that the old, discarded system protected against the worst sort of jobbery: "This great security for honest bestowal of patronage existed in rare perfection, under the mixed government of the Crown and the East India Company" (19:576). What Mill fears most is that the "personal partialities" of the new Viceroy of India will "warp" the appointments he makes so that he will be surrounded by the incompetent men from "certain families." Even if one grants, as I will, the great difference between Mill's clerkship in the India House and the extraordinarily lucrative postings in India to which he refers here, it is hard not to see Mill's *Considerations* as evidence of a "warp" in his thinking. All the lofty and universal principles that lead Mill to his defense of representative government come down, in the last sentence of this work, to a lament over the loss of the East India Company: only "far wider political conceptions than merely English or European practice can supply" will allow Britain to avoid turning Mill's powerless advocacy of the Company, "this speculative result," into the "only remaining fruit of our ascendancy in India" (19:577). Mill's 1858 *Memorandum* deals with the imperfections of the practical processes by which the government of India had developed; when he treats abstract principles in his *Considerations of Representative Government,* the East India Company becomes the ideal fruit of an ideal ascendancy.

This conjunction between a "speculative result" and the nourishment it will provide in the future became, indeed, the hallmark of Mill's thinking, the almost inevitable result of his definition of himself as a marginal figure of theory in a culture devoted to business and to practice. Throughout the 1830s when Mill might still have joined the ranks of the "practicals," he assumed continuously that the new age was dawning then and there. Every time the French people rose in revolt, Mill's hopes rose with them. Such naive enthusiasm was, as he points out in the *Autobiography,* a common mistake, but the frequency with which Mill thought "we had had our revolution" is striking (1:180n).

Both church and state, as he told Sterling in 1831, were done for. Once Mill had accepted his role as a writer and thinker, such overly eager anticipations ceased. Diderot had declared a century before that the future is the paradise of the philosopher, and in Mill's case it seems clear that as his career went on, he had to set in the more and more distant future the time when his ideas would become reality. Once Mill defined himself as a theorist, he had to define his goal as attainable only in a future after his death, for any changes that he might propose that could be accomplished in his lifetime would have to be accomplished by someone else.

This relation between the theorist powerless in the present and reforms possible only in the future seems to have led, for Mill, to an extreme exaggeration of its premises. He seems to have begun to champion more and more unpopular causes—women's suffrage and property reform—because the ones he had earlier supported but later rejected, the ballot and salaries for legislators, might actually have been accomplished, and that outcome would indeed have proved his impotence. As early as 1825, Mill had claimed that the unpopular cause is the most sincerely held cause because there is no chance for its success (26:287), but he seems to have elevated into a positive cult the concept of success in the future and failure in the present. Such thinking informed his decision to publish his *Considerations of Representative Government*. He wanted, he told Henry Taylor, to propose a "true ideal" for some future time "whenever the movement for organic change recovers strength," but he did not want to speed up the preparations for such a time, "rather to moderate than to encourage eagerness for immediate and premature changes of a fundamental character." In this letter, which closes with a reference to the "few years of life and health" left to Mill (15:731–32), the pattern is clear: he was ready to counsel delay—ripeness is all—because after his death no one could claim that he had not picked the fruit of reform. He scoffed at the overweening egotism of Comte, who thought he could see his ideals realized in his own lifetime, but Mill could not see that the best way to insure that they will not be so realized is to assume that they cannot be—exactly the point that he made in his 1828 speech on "Perfectibility."

Mill recognized that he consciously chose principles that had no chance of succeeding, though he may not have known why he did so.

As he said in 1865, "When one goes in, not for an object immediately attainable, but for a principle, we ought to go the whole length of it." His "opinions" on women's suffrage and the representation of minorities prevented him, he admitted, from "co-operat[ing] with any organised movement for reform that we may have any chance of seeing at present." In this context, he referred quite self-consciously to his isolation, if not to his powerlessness: "I think that I can probably do more good as an isolated thinker" (16:1013–14). In 1837 Mill quoted Coleridge's praise of the thinker "so far before his contemporaries as to be . . . dwarfed in the distance" (6:354), but Mill refused to see that such farsightedness might make of the thinker a figure dwarfed both in the past that his present would become and in the future in which he hoped to take his rightful place.

By the last full year of his life, Mill was suggesting that his "anticipations of the future" made it impossible to "contribute something in a more direct form than I have yet done towards rendering the great new questions which are rising up respecting life & society a little less difficult to our successors." His contribution could be no more "direct," he claimed, because one can recognize change only once it has taken place (17:1873). The reasoning here is entirely contradictory and self-defeating. The thinker cannot encourage change until it has happened. Mill recorded a similar, touching recognition of the frailty of depending on the future as a justification of a lifetime of efforts in its service when he wrote the last entry in his 1854 diary. Fearing that he would die before the year was out, he fantasized about the better times that were to come, times in which "all our diseases" could be cured, when the world would be a "fit place to live in, after the death of most of those by whose exertions it will have been made so." Clearly including himself among the dead and defeated reformers, he closed his diary, "It is to be hoped that those who live in those days will look back with sympathy to their known and unknown benefactors" (27: 668). In this, his private version of the "Elegy Written in a Country Churchyard," Mill was asking for posterity's sympathy both for those whose good works had found fitting memorials and for those whose efforts would remain unsung. The frustration he felt in 1854 about the "mere preparatory trifles" he had written identifies the category to which he would have assigned himself.

The seat in Parliament that Mill won in 1865 offered him, of course, a way of avoiding such self-fulfilling prophecies of defeat. Once in the House of Commons, he was, indeed, the philosopher turned man-of-business. He was the figure who reconciled theory and practice, the figure he could only imagine in 1831; as one of his supporters said, he was a "great practical philosopher" (28:19). Contradicting his earlier statements on the subject, he appealed to the voters by using his thirty-five years in the India House to prove that he knew the "actual business of government" (28:20). In his comments on his parliamentary career, he even slipped into metaphors of military and heroic endeavor that recall his earliest reading of ancient history: the House of Commons was a "field of battle," and there Mill planned to marshal his forces, followers like Thomas Hughes and Henry Fawcett (16:1132). In fact, however, once he did win a seat in Parliament—almost, as his supporters had reason to lament, in spite of his efforts to lose the election—he used his place not as a vehicle to accomplish reforms within reach, but to champion causes so unpopular that they had no chance of success. As he said in 1867, "I look upon the House of Commons not as a place where important practical improvements can be effected by anything I can do there, but as an elevated Tribune or Chair from which to preach larger issues than can at present be realised" (13:1234). By then, his stance as the philosopher in opposition, the voice calling in the wilderness, had become so accustomed that it was hard for him to imagine any other alternatives for himself. Unlike the student in Mill's famous aphorism on education—"A pupil from whom nothing is ever demanded which he cannot do, never does all he can" (1:35)—the member of Parliament who never tries to do what he can, can never be blamed for what he does not do. It was easier to blame the times for being unready for his ideas than to admit that he lacked the courage to change the attitudes of the times and win acceptance for the more moderately unpopular ideas that might have prevailed in his lifetime.

There is no more stunning representation of the handicaps faced by the speculative thinker wed to the future than the women's clothes in which Mill was dressed on eight separate occasions by the cartoonists for the conservative comic newspaper *Judy*. Once he made the long speech of 1867 in defense of his motion to grant women the vote, his most engaged and passionate attempt to rescue women from the disabilities he shared with them, he was branded as something less than a man. During that speech—parts of which were greeted with laughter and dissenting groans of *"Oh! Oh!"*—Mill claimed that a "silent domestic revolution" had taken place: husbands and wives now lived lives of such isolated and constant intimacy that only the existence of "manly women" would make it possible for there to be "manly men" (28:155–56). Such ideas identified him clearly as a womanly man. One of his fellow M.P.s responded to his proposal with the fear that women would soon be soldiers and generals; others raised questions about whether married women would have the right to vote. Mill's vague dismissals of these questions suggest that he had not thought out the implications of his motion before making it. But he did not have to think that far ahead—he knew there was no chance that the motion would pass—and the surprisingly large number of members who supported it did so, I think, because they knew it would fail. In his speech on that "silent domestic revolution," Mill was simply using the domestic isolation that he and Harriet Mill had shared as the condition necessitating reforms that could not possibly be achieved. Whether he championed such impossible goals out of loyalty to her or out of a desire to avoid testing his ability to effect practical measures, an ability he did not exercise until late in life, one cannot know.

Yet one point seems clear: Mill's advocacy of women's rights, a principle for which he claimed to have stood from the earliest years of his career, simply took to its logical conclusion the gender stereotypes to which his career responded and from which emerged his self-definition as a theorist. *Judy,* for all her crude humor, seemed to recognize this fact. The first cartoon in which Mill is made to don bun and bow, skirt and parasol, published in a notice of parliamentary affairs only two months after his major speech on the enfranchisement of women, links the impotence of the "anti-misogynist philosopher" with that of the group for whom he speaks (figure 1). The "powerful aid" of "the LADY'S MILL" has achieved nothing: "both his theory and his advocacy have proved a signal failure." But how can the philosopher be expected to "soil his delicate feet" on the hustings or "drag [women's] chaste garments through the mud of 'public meetings'"? Over the next year the cartoons became nastier and more explicit. By the spring of 1868, Mill frequently appeared in the pages of *Judy* as Gladstone's sweetheart. Conservative maneuvering had effectively set both men on the sidelines, where they were free to attend a popular play appropriately entitled *No Thoroughfare* because there was no work

FIGURE 1.

"The LADY'S MILL" parades his appropriately "non-virile
garments" for the amusement of the readers of *Judy*
(24 July 1867). Courtesy of The Newberry Library, Chicago.

of government left for them to do (figure 2). Again, in this instance,
theory and effeminacy are linked. Gladstone, in the monologue that
accompanies the cartoon, consoles the homely virgin by his side:

> There is no choice, dear Miss, you see:
> So all your sweet philosophy
> You must exert, you know! . . .
> Nay, do not cry, my lovely MILL!

Once Mill lost his seat in 1868, *Judy* was quite content to offer another
cartoon, this time one in which "Miss Mill Joins the Ladies" in the

FIGURE 2.

Gladstone and "Miss M——ll," his timid sweetheart, confront a conservative obstacle on their way to see the popular play *No Thoroughfare* (*Judy*, 25 March 1868). Courtesy of The Newberry Library, Chicago.

drawing room while the real men have brandy and cigars in the dining room.[32]

The man who came to embrace his subjection to a time and place for which he was unfitted used the same image of mechanism to describe the effect on him of the three relations that gave rise to and prolonged this subservience: his father, his wife, and his office. The education in which his father had trained him to function as a disciple of Bentham and of himself had made Mill a "mere reasoning machine" or, as he put it in the first draft of that phrase, "a dry, hard logical machine" (1:111,110). His work at the India House had made him "merely one wheel in a machine, the whole of which had to work together" (1:87). Harriet Taylor reduced him further. She, not he, was "the type of Intellect": someone who "can both think, & impress the thought on others—& can both judge what must be done, & do it. As for me, nothing but the division of labour could make me useful. . . . I am but fit to be one wheel in an engine not to be the self moving engine itself—a real majestic intellect, not to say moral nature, like yours, I can only look up to & admire" (14:43). Mill reveals how seriously he took this metaphor in his 1832 essay "On Genius," "You do not look upon man as having the perfection of his nature, when he attains the perfection of a wheel's or a pulley's nature, to go well as part of some vast machine, being in himself nothing" (1:329). There are, Mill suggests, people who are "self moving engines," people who, in line with his definition of character in *On Liberty*, have "desires and impulses" of their own (18:264). His father and Harriet Taylor were two such people, but he was not one of them.

Such a conclusion was, of course, the result of "the unintentional teaching of institutions and social relations" whose power Mill recognized by the middle of his career. He had indeed been shaped by the institution for which he worked and the social relations of the family into which he had been born and the family into which he had married. These forces had formed a character on the margins and in division against itself. Mill played the role of the speculative thinker, but he continued to admire, almost beyond the bounds of reason, the great man of action. He invested all his hopes in the future, but tried to insure that he would never behold its dawning—to use Macaulay's figure, Mill was ready to mount the hill only if he could keep the sun from rising. Mill idolized the woman who held him back and denigrated the father who had done his best, according to his lights, to set his son on his way. Appropriately, one of Mill's great heroes was Demosthenes: "His life was an incessant struggle against the fatality of the time, and the weaknesses of his countrymen. And though he failed in his object, and perished with the last breath of freedom for which he had lived, he has been rewarded by that immortal fame, which, as he reminded the Athenians in the most celebrated passage of his greatest oration, is not deserved only by the successful" (11:312). This sentiment is the one, as I have pointed out, that Joanna Baillie cribbed from Demosthenes in the last words of her play *Constantine Paleologus*, the play that so inspired Mill as a boy that he took to writing tragedies. If Mill did not achieve the glorious apotheosis of failure envisioned by Demosthenes, even his most unsympathetic contemporaries saw his career as a story of more humble, but more substantial successes, in part because he functioned so effectively as their conscience. It is, perhaps, a tribute to the grandeur of his ambitions that even such an achievement fell short of the standards he set for himself.

Part 2

The Science
of Character

By one of those odd patterns created by chance, 1858 was the year in which Mill, for good or for ill, was released from both the work and the wife who had, until then, to a great degree defined his career. Although Mill had planned to work for the East India Company until 1866, the generous pension granted him in 1858 would have made it difficult for him to bemoan the demise of the company; clearly he welcomed the liberty for sustained writing that the end of his work there offered him. When Harriet Mill died shortly after his retirement, there was no question in his mind that his loss was irreparable: "The spring of my life is broken" (15:574). Yet that event might have been more important than even his retirement in allowing him to take up the theoretical work that he had wanted to do. Among the subjects he had long hoped to study was the science he called ethology, the investigation into the relation between the formation of character and its circumstances. In 1854 Mill had outlined in a letter to Harriet Mill the essays that he proposed to write as an accompaniment to the autobiography he had already begun to draft, and he listed first an essay on "Differences of character (nation, race, age, sex, temperament)." Significantly, he identified it as the subject that "I could do most to by myself" (14:152), but she advised him to write instead an essay on religion, and he agreed. Perhaps it is not surprising, then, that he did not attempt to undertake directly the study of character during Harriet Mill's lifetime. In any case, after 1858 Mill had no reason to delay pursuing the theoretical task that he had defined as uniquely suited to his gifts.

Mill's plans for ethology emerged in the last book of his *System of Logic*. In the late 1830s, Mill conceived of this treatise as the work of theory that would justify his choice of words over deeds. He thought it would do so in the same way that he had earlier justified Bentham, by revealing the future practical benefits of the work of the closet-student, and his conception of ethology was central to this goal. Moreover, by invoking Saint-Simonian ideas on the oscillations between organic and critical periods, Mill defined his own age as a time suited only to the pursuit of theory, and he used this historical scheme to explain his own exclusion from more active, practical endeavors. As Mill said in one account he gave of the *Logic*, "The mental regeneration of Europe must precede its social regeneration." The most one could hope to do was to find the "course which must be taken by the present great transitional movement of opinion & society." His work would advance this cause by "straightening & strengthening the intellects which have this great work to do" (13:563–64). In his *System of Logic,* Mill was ready to admit, not as a matter of personal defeat, but as a result of temporal necessity, that the "one thing to be *done* [is] to *know* the nature and properties of many things" (7:4).

The *Logic,* therefore, celebrates the value of such knowledge and its indispensability to practice. Because logic, as Mill conceives it, is the "science of science," "nearly the whole, not only of science, but of human conduct, is amenable to [its] authority" (7:9). An understanding of sound methods of investigation would allow logic to extend its authority to the subject of human society; and in Book VI, the last book of the treatise, Mill envisions the benefits of a "Science of Human Nature" that will approach his ideal of the physical sciences in its precision and, therefore, provide a basis for the arts of education and government. In particular, Mill stresses the importance of the field that he treats in Chapter V of Book VI, "Of Ethology, or the Science of the Formation of Character." At the end of the *Logic,* Mill looks forward confidently to a "sociological system" raised to the level of a science: "When this time shall come, no important branch of human affairs will be any longer abandoned to empiricism [loose inductions] and unscientific surmise" (8:930). The *Logic* was to contribute to the progress of enlightenment that would banish the ignorance and superstition of customary thinking on the subjects that Mill held most dear. Yet the program that he sets out in the last book of the *Logic* is not simply a blueprint for the future "intellects" who will do "this great work"; in its conception of ethology, it is, quite specifically, the research agenda that Mill set for himself. The *Logic* was not only the record of his decade-long dedication to the science of investigation; it provided the outline, basis, and promise of the "great work" that he himself hoped to accomplish in the coming years.

As early as 1832, Mill was pointing out the difficulties involved in any comprehensive and thorough "investigation" of "the formation of character" (23:415), and fifteen years after the publication of his *System of Logic,* after Harriet Mill had died, that work had not yet been done, and the prospects for future success were not encouraging. As late as 1859, Mill was telling Alexander Bain that although he did not feel "sufficiently prepared" to write a book on ethology, although he now envisioned that his efforts would take "the form of Essays," he still imagined that such work was possible and that he might be the one to do it (15:645). The facts were to prove him wrong. After the publication of the *Principles of Political Economy*, Mill produced no other treatise comparable to it or to the *Logic* and certainly no work dedicated specifically to the subject of ethology. Indeed, by the time Mill wrote his inaugural address for St. Andrews in 1867, he had given up the term *ethology* and substituted for it the more common term *education*, "whatever helps to shape the human being," even the "indirect effects" of government, laws, industrial arts, social convention, and physical circumstances (21:217). Having failed to gain popular or even academic acceptance for his neologism, Mill deferred to more conventional usage even as he insisted on the importance of the issues that his earlier conception of ethology had raised.

Yet Mill's own implicit admission of defeat in his St. Andrews address should not deflect attention from the importance of ethology to either the studies of character he did undertake or to the character that he himself displayed in his writings. The following chapters gauge that importance by addressing the development of Mill's interest in ethology in his early writings, the argument for its inauguration that he put forth in the last book of his *System of Logic*, and his mature treatments of ethological issues in the newspaper writings devoted to questions of practice and in the theoretical discussions he ostensibly devoted to other subjects. In these works Mill seems to have understood how to put to good account even his lack of success in the theoretical investigation of character. Ethology proves to be, I claim, a potent method of argument in *The Subjection of Women* precisely because it can offer only negative evidence on the question at hand. Finally, in the second chapter of this section, Mill is asked to present himself as a test case for ethological analysis. His unremittingly pained questions about his intellectual stature, his defensive attempts to claim and to deny his own originality reveal the qualities in his character that demand to be explained in ethological terms. An analysis of how these intellectual issues pertain to his social and political theory in *On Liberty* clearly delineates the sources of the formation of Mill's character. If this analysis comes to conclusions about Mill's character that he would not have endorsed, they are, at least, the conclusions reached by following in the directions that he himself charted for the study of ethology.

Three

Ethology as Politics

The Character of Marginal Groups

       In conceiving of ethology as a new field of inquiry that he would establish single-handedly, Mill was resorting to one of the most effective ways in which nineteenth-century writers characteristically defended themselves against the marginality inherent in their careers: by setting as their goal works of epic ambition, they defined the writer as hero. As Carlyle pointed out in his lecture on the subject, "the Hero as *Man of Letters*" was a "singular" and "anomalous" creature of recent birth. By defining the world in which such a creature lived as one ruled preeminently by ideas, the writer could attribute to the "life of the mind" not only practical significance but indisputable centrality. By conceiving of a Herculean labor of either imagination or investigation, the writer could claim a dominant position among those Shelley labeled the "unacknowledged legislators of the World." Coleridge had set the pattern for such an endeavor by prophesying that he would write a "great Work on the *Logos*, Divine and Human, on which I have set my Heart and hope to ground my ultimate reputation." To such a work, the *Biographia Literaria* would be a mere preface.[1] Like Wordsworth's plans for *The Recluse,* a cathedral in which the *Prelude* would be an ante-chapel, Coleridge's hopes remained unfulfilled. In Wordsworth's case, however, the great work was already inscribed in the *Prelude* that prophesied it. Victorian writers, whose aims are parodied in a fictional character like Casaubon, held steadfastly to this form of self-justification. George Grote's twelve-volume *History of Greece* is an example of epic accomplishment. As Carlyle became progressively more isolated from his contemporaries, he engaged in writing *The History of Frederick the Great,* the monumental work that would grant him the title of the "hero as a man of letters." Mill hoped to gain similar place in the pantheon of thinkers whose thoughts, he believed, shaped the world in which they lived.

Accordingly, at the end of his *System of Logic* Mill declares the existence of a new science. Like any other explorer into terra incognita, he stakes his claim to this particular territory by naming it: the science will be called *ethology,* its subject the creation of human character.[2] Earlier in his *Logic,* Mill had already displayed the epic scope of his interests: the discussions range over the physical and moral sciences to cover language, linguistics, geometry, astronomy, mathematics, physics, physiology, anatomy, chemistry, sociology, politics, and even the arts of government and education. The only subjects missing are those now commonly labeled *art:* literature, poetry, music, painting, subjects that Mill later classed in *Principles of Political Economy* as varieties of "unproductive labour" (2:50–51). Yet Mill wanted to do more than evaluate the state of knowledge in the various "productive" fields of inquiry that he surveyed in the *Logic.* He wanted to add one more field to the tally, a field that he would create and establish as indispensable to human improvement. In the last book of the *Logic,* then, Mill was testing his own abilities and the methods of science in preparation for the future endeavor that he envisioned as his magnum opus.

Although Mill's desire to explore that subject fully and declare it his own remained unsatisfied throughout his career, he did undertake analyses that may be labeled ethological because they treat character in relation to the formative circumstances from which it issues. The ethological investigation in which he engaged in his mature years was consistently concerned with the nature of marginal groups. Ethology stood, for Mill, at the intersection of politics and psychology, but it turned out to be a science more easily practiced on others than on oneself. Such analysis became, for Mill, a way of establishing both his power over such groups and his identification with them. To understand why that was so, one must examine first the preliminary exercises in ethology in which he engaged in his early essays and newspaper articles and then his presentation of the science itself in his *System of Logic*. If Mill's early hopes for a science of character were much too sanguine, his later practice turned that would-be science into a powerful rhetorical tool that allowed him to compose his most telling challenges to the customary thinking of his contemporaries.

ETHOLOGY CONCEIVED

Before the publication of the *Logic* in 1843, Mill had long been interested in what he sometimes called "mental chemistry" (8:854). Such a science would explain, not individual mental acts, but the "formation of character" as a result of the circumstances and conditions that determined the nature of the individual. Mill used this phrase consistently whenever he pointed out the shortcomings of Bentham and Comte, the two thinkers from whom, besides his father, he had learned most. In his early "Remarks on Bentham's Philosophy" (1833), Mill suggests that Bentham failed as an "analyst of human nature" precisely because he lacked "insight into the formation of character" (10:8). By 1848 when Mill leveled the same charge against Comte, the phrase was elaborated in a way that suggests scientific inquiry: Comte was "resolutely ignorant of the laws of the formation of character" (13:739). Such "laws" did exist and were known, despite Comte's willful ignorance. This subject was, as Mill conceived it, central both to his early political ambitions and to his later faith in the social improvement that would be achieved long after his death. Without the knowledge of character that only ethology could provide, one could not undertake to change social circumstances in a way that would create the kinds of character that one valued most. For all the practicality that Mill attributes to his "idea" of Bentham in the famous essay of 1838, for all the respect that he grants Comte for his conception of society as the proper object of scientific inquiry, on the subject of human character the philosopher of Queen Square was too fully the counterpart of the wild visionary of the Religion of Humanity: both thinkers thought they knew character without recognizing that such knowledge constituted a science beyond their ken.

This gap in the theories of Comte and Bentham, a lack that Mill defined as fatal to any practice based on those theories, opened up a space in which Mill could pursue the subject they ignored. For a thinker as concerned as Mill was to establish his authority on the basis of the originality and influence of his ideas—a point I treat at length in the next chapter—such an opening was crucial. An interest in the formation of character was, as well, a way of both acknowledging his father's achievements and moving beyond them. John Mill followed the lead of James Mill in attempting to formulate the few, simple principles, the "constant laws" that regulate what he calls in the *Logic* "complex uniformities" (7:316), but James Mill's province was the individual mental act; John Mill's new field would be predicated on the one explored by his father and, in particular, on the principles of associationism that James Mill set out in his *Analysis of the Phenomena of the Human Mind*. Although John Stuart Mill claims at the opening of his *System of Logic* that "the science of science" is a "common ground" shared by "partisans" of both experientialist and intuitionist schools of thought (7:14), Mill's essential adherence to associationism is evident long before Book VI, which is, in fact, a partisan polemic in defense of its principles. Ethology, then, seemed to offer the perfect balance between Mill's training and his quite understandable desire for intellectual independence.

Mill began to stake out his claim to the subject of the formation of character at the very beginning of his career as a writer. In his earliest newspaper essays, in which he treats questions of law reform and religious oaths just as Bentham treats them or puffs his father's essays in his own anonymous notices,[3] the young Mill asks questions about character that seem to unite his early taste for history and poetry with his reformist goals in a way that sets him apart from both these early mentors. The rhetoric of these newspaper writings does not attain a tone of authority until late 1828, but as early as 1823 the callow youth of seventeen is decrying those "indolent and superficial reasoners [who] would willingly arrest the inquiring mind in the search after those hidden causes by which the human character is formed," those intuitionists who trace an individual's depravity to a "bad disposition" or "constitution." There is something slightly comic—and appealing—

about so young a writer explaining the "melancholy interest" that "we feel" in "looking back upon the events of [a criminal's] life, and tracing the various circumstances which, by their conspiring influence, formed his mind to guilt" (22:77). There is, as well, something quixotic about his insistence that he can cut to the "original root" of criminal behavior and demonstrate how certain "habits and practices"—in this case, those attendant upon gambling—"infallibly bring about a radical corruption of character." Yet even this early article emphasizes the lessons that Mill would point out to his contemporaries throughout his career: the fallacy of "representing as *natural* that which is merely *habitual*" (22:78), and the need for government policy to change habits and, therefore, to transform what is mistakenly thought of as an individual's "nature."

By 1838 when Mill wrote a review article on Alfred de Vigny for the *London and Westminster Review,* his interest in character was less immediately related to issues of education and government, and he was striving for, even straining toward, a systematic approach to the subject. The bravado of the earlier article is still evident: the first sentence of the essay declares "the French mind" (as if there were only one such mind) "the most active national mind in Europe at the present moment" (1:465), but Mill is trying to achieve some subtlety of analysis by establishing a taxonomy that will explain the individual human beings who compose its categories. In fact, this essay demonstrates Mill's desire to treat character in the same way that one treats the specimens collected in botany, the only science that Mill himself practiced.[4] He quickly loses sight of the specimen in question, the poet Vigny, as he tries at the opening of the essay to place him first in the category of the Royalist or Carlist "element" in France, an "element" subsumed in the larger category of those individuals "trained up in opinions and feelings opposed to those of the age" (1:466), and then finally in the binary classification of writers as either "Royalist" ("Conservative") or "Radical" ("Liberal") (1:467). Mill then imagines the effect of revolution on any "poet of conservative sympathies"; in this "ideal portraiture" he finds both "the genuine lineaments of Alfred de Vigny" and those "more or less" of the "greater part of the Royalist literature of young France" (1:469–70).

That all these preparatory categories are both insufficient and irrelevant, Mill proves by admitting that Vigny's work exhibited such features only after the Revolution of 1830 and then by indulging in a translation of long passages of *Cinq-Mars,* a novel that Vigny wrote before 1830. (Mill seems later to have recognized the inconsistency in his approach; when he edited this essay for inclusion in his 1859 *Dissertations and Discussions,* the passages from the novel disappeared.) Even in the summary of *Cinq-Mars* that remains, the categories tend to overwhelm the instances they are meant to illuminate. Readers in France are compared to readers in England, just as, in the opening of the essay, the "real interests" of the English are contrasted to the passions of the French (1:466). Even when Mill does reach the subject of Vigny's work after 1830—and the date itself is, of course, yet another form of classification—he develops a more encompassing taxonomy for various forms of conservative literature: "Conservatism triumphant, Conservatism militant, Conservatism vanquished." Mill fills these categories with names—Racine, Voltaire, Rousseau in the first, Chateaubriand at the "head" of the second, with Vigny as the epitome of the third. Mill begins a sketch of Vigny's "state of mind," not by naming the poet or by focusing on his individual experience, but by referring to his third category: "This," Mill concludes, "is the character which pervades the two principal of M. de Vigny's works" (1:487).

Yet even this categorization is not enough to explain Vigny's character, and Mill feels compelled to account for the Frenchman's writings by using vocational distinctions as yet another form of classification. Vigny served as a soldier and a poet. These two professions share a common characteristic that returns Mill to his first category, that of the mind out of place in its times: "The soldier, and the poet, appear to M. de Vigny alike misplaced, alike ill at ease, in the present condition of human life" (1:488). Mill then draws a long character sketch of the soldier—a fit subject for "the artist and the philosopher"—as that "type of human nature" has been created by its "circumstances." Here categories define types and seem to engender more types and more categories. Both the agent of the analysis and the subject of the analysis are types: "the soldier" is exposed to the scrutiny of "the artist and the philosopher," Vigny being, of course, the artist, and Mill, the philosopher. Before offering accounts of the various stories that reveal Vigny's understanding of both soldiers and poets, Mill offers one more category: "M. de Vigny has ideas worthy of the consideration of him who is yet to come—the statesman who has care and leisure for plans of social amelioration unconnected with party contests and the cry of the hour" (1:489). This apocalyptic reference to Mill's own social goals and their unnamed future agent suggests, in a subdued but moving way, the relation between Mill's interest in character and his hopes for reform.

As an exercise in ethological analysis, the essay on Vigny, written shortly before Mill drafted Book VI of the *Logic,* reveals the difficulties that he had to confront in attempting to confer scientific status on the study of human character. These difficulties involved both data and methods. In an 1835 essay Mill had explained that a valid moral philosophy could not be constructed without "clear and comprehensive views of education and human culture," and his comments on the problems inherent in developing such views relate directly to the issues raised by ethology. The "materials" for such analysis—Mill does not call it a "science" here—are "abundant" but incomplete and unsystematic. Such materials are not to be found in the work of philosophers, but "on the one hand, from actual observers of mankind; on the other, from those autobiographers, and from those poets or novelists, who have spoken out unreservedly, from their own experience, any true human feeling." Although Mill estimates that it will be a "labour for successive generations" to gather and supplement these materials (10:56), this earlier comment explains why he would have been drawn to the work of a French poet and novelist as the source of the data he needed.[5]

The difference between Vigny's methods of presenting "true human feeling" and Mill's methods of analysis are also instructive. Mill explains that Vigny's powers as a creative artist allow him to create a portrait of the soldier as a philosopher, a "noble character, unfolding to us the process of its own formation; not so much telling us, as making us see, how one circumstance disabused it of false objects of esteem and admiration, how another revealed to it the true." This character, Captain Renaud, is, for Mill, a kind of associationist hero; every circumstance, trial, or temptation he has undergone has left "the impressions it was fitted to leave on a thoughtful and sensitive mind" (1:492). Yet Mill's recourse to categorization testifies to his scientific interest in character as a phenomenon of "complex uniformities" that can be first classified and then analyzed in terms of cause and effect.

Mill wants to study, as his focus on Captain Renaud reveals, the process that allows certain specific circumstances to form certain kinds of characters. Yet the multiplicity of types and the proliferating classifications into which individuals, in turn, are subsumed suggest a rigid compartmentalization of cause and effect. The complex taxonomic framework that Mill brings to his reading of Vigny may be a way for Mill to reach an ethological analysis, but it does not seem to provide a basis for it. Underlying the implicit contrast between Vigny's practice as an artist and Mill's more scientific approach may be Mill's recognition that he himself is not capable of delineating the process whereby conditions create character, although, as the essay proves, he is eminently able to pay tribute to another writer's achievement, albeit his unconscious achievement, in that field.

The essay on Vigny is, then, an example of Mill's early unsystematic attempts to apply the kind of systematic analysis of phenomena for which he had called in the earlier portions of the *Logic* that he had already written. A year after the essay on Vigny was published, Mill was drafting the book of *A System of Logic* in which he would propose ethology as a science of character. The simple method of relentless classifying in this essay, however, does not even hint at the methodological tangles in which Mill involved himself once he tried to analyze ethology itself in Chapter V of Book VI. As numerous commentators have suggested, one of the features that made Mill's work popular is the clarity of his expositions. In fact, Mill's expository skills often allow him to slip over difficulties and inconsistencies that any less skillful writer would be forced to confront. The chapter on ethology is, however, a major exception to this rule. The exposition trips and stumbles, variations in tone from brash certainty to meek insinuation seem misplaced and uncoordinated, and the organization of the argument proceeds in a fashion that can be described as simply backwards. Other masterful and authoritative expositions in the *Logic* suggest that the problem has its origins, not in the immaturity of the writer—Mill had been publishing his work in periodicals and newspapers for twenty years before his first book appeared—but in his unacknowledged uncertainties about his subject.

At the beginning of the decade that ended in the writing of Book VI, Mill offered a prophetic commentary on the problems he later faced in trying to describe ethology. He set out, in his essay "On the Definition of Political Economy," the distinction between the "chronological" and the "didactic order" in the treatment of a science. In the chronological order—the process by which the science is actually conceived, elaborated, and established—its definition must come last, and its so-called "first principles," which actually emerge only late in its development, are initially "made out" with "mistiness" rather than with clarity. As Mill explains, the wall of a city is erected after the city is built, "not [as] a receptacle for such edifices as might afterwards spring up." In the didactic order, however—in the process whereby an established science is taught—clear and distinct definitions must be presented first if the student is to learn about the subject efficiently and accurately. Scientific investigation may actually proceed successfully with quite messy preliminary distinctions and definitions, but the exposition of a sophisticated science requires a "high . . . degree of analysis and abstraction" and rigor (4:309–11). Mill's analysis of the status of political economy, a subject in which he includes what he will later define in his *System of Logic* as a separate Science of Society, seems to contain an apology for and explanation of the kind of exposition he later offers on the subject of ethology: "At a very early stage in the study of [a] science, anything more accurate would be useless and therefore pedantic. In merely initiatory definition, scientific precision is not required" (4:313). Yet Mill makes it difficult to apply this perspective to his exposition of ethology in the *Logic*. He treats the subject as if he were employing a didactic order when, in fact, he himself in his understanding of ethology is very much in the first stages of its chronological order. Chapter V presents a challenge because Mill refuses to treat ethology as what it is, an emerging science; rather, he assumes that it is what he wants it to be, a fully established science.

Almost two-thirds of the way into Chapter V of Book VI, Mill announces triumphantly:

A science is thus formed, to which I would propose to give the name of Ethology, or the Science of Character; from ἦθος [*ethos*], a word more nearly corresponding to the term "character" as I here use it, than any other word in the same language. The name is perhaps etymologically applicable to the entire science of our mental and moral nature; but if, as is usual and convenient, we employ the name Psychology for the science of the elementary laws of mind, Ethology will serve for the ulterior science which determines the kind of character produced in conformity to those general laws, by any set of circumstances, physical and moral. According to this definition, Ethology is the science which corresponds to the art of education; in the widest sense of the term, including the formation of national or collective character as well as individual. (8:869)

After the tortuous route through the part of the chapter that precedes this declaration, the reader may be excused for finding in the writer who declares, "A science is thus formed . . ." something less than the power and certainty with which the God of Genesis commands, "Let there be light." Despite his hesitation over the etymological applicability of the term *ethology*, Mill seems not at all hesitant about the nature of the science that it constitutes; it is a necessary and valuable addition to the "circle of human knowledge" that he defines near the end of the *Logic* as the "sociological system" through which "human knowledge" will be made "complete" (8:930). This confidence seems somewhat surprising in view of the earlier gingerly touch evident in his title for Chapter III of Book VI, "That There is, or May Be, a Science of Human Nature." Shortly after his definition of ethology, Mill does concede that this science has been conceptualized, but not realized: it "is still to be created" (8:872–73). In the remainder of the chapter devoted to ethology and even in the passage just quoted, there are some lingering doubts. The way in which Mill here switches tenses, alternating between present and future, suggests that his assertion may be tentative: "Ethology will serve," but it "is a science." The definition itself comes late in the chapter, long after its title and a reliance on Mill's usually direct modes of exposition have created the expectation that such a definition is imminent. In the following chapter on social science, Mill goes to work by simply announcing his subject, "the science of man in society," and then by defining its purview, "the actions of collective masses of mankind" and "the various phenomena which constitute social life" (8:875). Perhaps the "initiatory" work that Comte had done in the field of sociology made it possible for Mill to apply to it the "didactic order" appropriate to the teaching of an established science. The route to the definition of ethology in Chapter V is a good deal more circuitous. Indeed, the conceptual and rhetorical contortions that precede and follow this announcement late in the chapter reflect the difficulties Mill tried to overcome by refusing to acknowledge them.

Buried in the middle of the chapter, midway in the discussion of a method that Mill rejects as inapplicable to his endeavor, is, perhaps, an indirect recognition of its central problem. When he explains that observation cannot establish the laws of the formation of character, he admits that character itself is too elusive a subject for scientific study:

> Consider the difficulty of the very first step—of ascertaining what actually is the character of the individual, in each particular case that we examine. There is hardly any person living, concerning some essential part of whose character there are not differences of opinion even among his intimate acquaintances: and a single action, or conduct continued only for a short time, goes a very little way towards ascertaining it. We can only make our observations in a rough way, and *en masse;* not attempting to ascertain in any given instance, what character has been formed, and still less by what causes; but only observing in what state of previous circumstances it is found that certain marked mental qualities or deficiencies *oftenest* exist. (8:866)

If the object under examination is the character of a specific individual, if that object cannot be apprehended because, as Mill points out, it is defined only by the opinions of those who observe it, if character is the individual's *nature* as that term is defined in the essay on "Nature," then it is pointless to try to determine the causes that have created an indeterminate outcome. If the inquirer persists, the inquiry must proceed "in a rough way" by having recourse to large numbers of instances. This solution, however, seems only to compound the problem by multiplying the number of cases in which the various opinions about even "marked mental qualities" may find play. Undeterred by such considerations, however, Mill goes on to define the phenomenon under analysis, not as the formation of the character of the individual, but as the formation of the distinctive characteristics of the group. One can achieve, he claims, at least a "comparative result" if one discerns a "particular mental characteristic" in a "given number" of "indiscriminately" chosen French or Italian or English citizens (8:866).

In a footnote, Mill enlarges on this idea of "collective instances." Perhaps he felt the need to remove this speculation from the main body of the text because it stands in ambiguous relation to the subject of character. One can speak, Mill asserts, of the "qualities displayed by the collective body" when it acts as a body: when a nation, for instance, elevates an opinion to the status accorded to "popular maxims," when it admires "the character of . . . persons or writings," or when it develops laws or institutions. "But even here," Mill admits, "there is a large margin of doubt and uncertainty" (8:867n). This note, which begins by holding out the hope of determining the character of large groups of people, is appended to the admission that "there is hardly one current opinion respecting the characters of nations, classes, or descriptions of persons, which is universally acknowledged as indisputable" (8:867). Not surprisingly, then, many of Mill's later commentators have assumed that he envisions ethology as a science that will treat "national character," although he clearly conceives of that subject as a division "carved out of the general body of the social science," and he does not discuss it until four chapters after the definition of ethology (8:904–5). He calls the examination of the formation of the features of a people in a given age or nation "Political Ethology," presumably because national character or the character of a particular historical group is largely developed through the workings of their "institutions or social arrangements." This distinction, which Mill himself continually blurs, is crucial. Ethology, the science of individual character, is a science based on psychology, and associationist laws are, for Mill, the basis of psychology. The "truths" of political ethology "can be but the results and exemplification" of the "Science of Ethology," a science that, Mill admits here in the context of his discussion of political ethology, is in its "infant state" (8:905). The human sciences, as he envisions them, are built up in a hierarchical fashion on the basis of associationism; without ethology, which is erected on the foundation of psychology, there can be no basis for sociology, the science of which political ethology is a specialized part.

Even, therefore, Mill's indirect attempt to define the phenomenon that ethology proposes to analyze seems to involve insuperable obstacles to analysis. The complications and the difficulties only increase in Chapter V when Mill treats what I take to be the main subject of the chapter, the problem of method, a problem that he begins to treat even before he has discovered that it is his main subject. The chapter opens with a reference to the "laws of mind" outlined in the previous chapter, the associationist principles that ideas have their source in sensation, that ideas are linked together by such laws as similarity or simultaneity. Mill immediately announces that the "truths of common experience" must be the "results or consequences" of such general laws (8:861). This approach involves him in an indirect discussion of method, and his need for indirection is not hard to understand once the difficulties inherent in the issue emerge from his discussion of it.

As Mill tries to define the scientific status of the "truths of common experience" gained from "observation of life," he must refer to his earlier treatments of induction. He applies the term "Empirical Law" to that "practical knowledge of mankind" constituted by "familiar maxims, . . . collected *à posteriori* from observation of life": "An Empirical Law (as it will be remembered) is an uniformity, whether of succession or coexistence, which holds true in all instances within our limits of observation, but is not of a nature to afford any assurance that it would hold beyond those limits." An empirical law falls short, therefore, of scientific certainty, and the knowledge of human life derived from observation must not be confused with the "ultimate laws of human action"; for those, one must look to associationism (8:861). Empirical laws are "casual," not causal: they are scientific only to the limited extent to which they account for a phenomenon by pointing out its causes under given conditions. An empirical law is entirely circumstantial: it has predictive value only if applied to a case in which all the circumstances remain the same as those in the original case in which its action was first observed. In the following section of the chapter, Mill undermines even this certainty by explaining that such empirical laws are, in the case of human nature, merely "approximate generalizations." Because both human beings and the circumstances in which they are situated are so complex, "open to continuous and complex modifications," any statements regarding the "feelings and actions of mankind" are liable to falsification by the exceptions too often created by the "peculiarities of circumstances" (8:863–64).

Mill seems in the earlier section that precedes this qualification to be setting out the methodological problem inherent in pursuing a science of character without actually admitting that there is a problem. As the chapter proceeds, his argument reveals further grounds for discomfort. Earlier in his *System of Logic,* he has confidently explained that although all science is inductive, inquiry moves from particular instances to general laws by two methods, either deductive or experimental. Science explains "cases of a new kind" either through the "old inductions" called deductions or through experiments that will lead to "new inductions." Each science aspires to the condition of purely deductive inquiry: once enough experiments have been performed or enough observations have been collected, it is possible to construct the basic laws that will explain all new cases (7:219). The science composed of "the fewest and the simplest" laws is, therefore, the most sophisticated, the most advanced (7:218).[6] Hence, Mill's respect for what he took to be the fully established and stunningly simple science of psychology called associationism.

As soon as Mill reaches his discussion of a science of human character, however, the goal epitomized by the laws of association becomes both impossible and irrelevant—although he refuses to admit that fact. Instead, he recapitulates his arguments on empirical laws, the statements that cannot aspire to such clarity and simplicity, but he does not admit that he is outlining the current state of knowledge about human nature in an attempt to envision the scientific status it might ultimately achieve. Not surprisingly, Mill resorts to simple assertion before facing that problem. Granting the great diversity of both particular characters and their circumstances, Mill insists that there is still uniformity in the laws that form character: "It is possible to determine . . . how any given mode of feeling and conduct, compatible with the general laws (physical and mental) of human nature, has been, or may be, formed. In other words, mankind have not one universal character, but there exist universal laws of the Formation of Character" (8:864).

This assertion seems to give Mill the assurance he needs to face directly the central problem of the chapter, the problem of method. He immediately discounts either experiment or its more casual cousin, observation, as the source of such laws. No one can or would raise an entire generation of human beings simply to examine how their characters are formed. Mill's squeamishness about subjecting individuals to experimentation may reflect his own experience as an experiment. But even if such experiments were ethical, the factors involved would be too numerous and too subtle to be accurately recorded. "Simple observation" offers no better hope of success. Because observation is limited to a specific number of cases, it can yield only empirical laws. In this context Mill raises the problem with which I began, the problem of describing any given character in ways that will win general acceptance. Here Mill seems to involve himself in contradictions and confusions from which there is no escape. The first sections of the chapter refer to "familiar maxims," the "common wisdom of common life," as the knowledge of human nature that needs to be tested against the "really scientific truths" constituted by causal laws (8:861, 864,862), but in his footnote on groups, "current popular maxims" become the evidence of "the character of a nation [as it] is shown in its acts as a nation" (8:867n): popular wisdom serves as both the raw data and the analytical conclusions of the science of ethology, the science that, at this point in the chapter, has yet to be defined. Such common maxims are, as well, the fallacies that Mill has worked so hard to debunk. The maxim about the unsuitability of the philosopher for business is only one example of the errors of customary thinking to which Mill has devoted the entire preceding book of his *System of Logic*.

Method emerges as fundamental and fundamentally problematic in the section of the chapter in which Mill finally does reach his definition of ethology. Because neither experiment nor observation can support this science, "we are driven perforce," he notes, to deduction. Mill, characteristically, tries to make a virtue of even this necessity: deduction would be the "most perfect" form of investigation even if it were not the only form available. "The laws of the formation of character are, in short, derivative laws, resulting from the general laws of mind; and are to be obtained by deducing them from those general laws." In this paragraph, just before that in which ethology is named, such derivative laws are useful only to "explain and account for" the approximate generalizations that have already been developed (8:869). Once the new science appears in the next paragraph, Mill immediately limits its title to the label *science:* in particular cases, such laws have no predictive value. But that, Mill tries to suggest, is irrelevant: "We must remember that a degree of knowledge far short of the power of actual prediction, is often of much practical value." Ethology, then, is a highly imperfect science, yet a nonetheless secure basis for art or practice. It cannot predict outcomes; it can indicate tendencies. That the possibility of creating such a science is demanded by Mill's political goals as a reformer is evident: "When the circumstances of an individual or of a nation are in any considerable degree under our control, we may, by our knowledge of tendencies, be enabled to shape those circumstances in a manner much more favourable to the ends we desire, than the shape which they would of themselves assume. This is the limit of our power; but within this limit the power is a most important one" (8:869–70). Because Mill needs a science to authorize his belief that a change in character is possible through changes in institutions and relations, he invents one.

That this invention is more the result of sleight of hand than proof of substantial achievement, the final paragraph of this section testifies. The paragraph is a kind of argumentative pretzel, with assertion and hesitation alternating constantly as the premises newly set out double back on the ones previously established. It is, for that reason, worth quoting entire:

> This science of Ethology may be called the Exact Science of Human Nature; for its truths are not, like the empirical laws which depend on them, approximate generalizations, but real laws. It is, however, (as in all cases of complex phenomena) necessary to the exactness of the propositions, that they should be hypothetical only, and affirm tendencies, not facts. They must not assert that something will always, or certainly, happen; but only that such and such will be the effect of a given cause, so far as it operates uncounteracted. It is a scientific proposition, that bodily strength tends to make men courageous; not that it always makes them so: that an interest on one side of a question tends to bias the judgment; not that it invariably does so: that experience tends to give wisdom; not that such is always its effect. These propositions, being assertive only of tendencies, are not the less universally true because the tendencies may be frustrated. (8:870)

This "Exact Science" issues in "real laws," but its propositions are merely "hypothetical" indications of "tendencies, not facts." The examples that Mill offers of the findings possible in ethology are even more telling: strength breeds courage, interest creates bias, experience yields wisdom. The conclusions that Mill presents as the current fruit of his grand project are no more than the "familiar maxims" or "common wisdom" that he has introduced at the beginning of the chapter as the rude, untested state of knowledge about human nature before the establishment of ethology as a science. Mill's readers may, at this point, feel somewhat cheated. He has asked for a great deal of patient effort if one is to follow his complicated and difficult arguments, and all one has to show for such labor is the promise of a science whose findings will be equivalent to the old saws of folk wisdom.

In his rhetorical approach, Mill seems to have tried to cover over the difficulties involved in conceiving of a science of human character, but that approach serves only to highlight them. If he had simply admitted that he stood at an early stage in the "chronological order" of the science, if he had tried to prove that such a science ought to exist, that it would have practical implications that would justify any amount of speculative effort, he could have avoided many of the argumentative contortions typical of this chapter. Mill, in fact, goes on in the chapter to equate ethology with other deductive sciences "such as mechanics, astronomy, optics, acoustics," and to equate its propositions with *axiomata media,* the middle principles of "the science of mind" (8:871,870). This leads to a digression—presented, however, as a "logical remark"—on Bacon's methods of investigation and the praise he has unjustly been accorded for denouncing all deductive reasoning. Mill is not ready to frame "any unbending rule" about the direction in which general laws can be formed. Since he holds that all reasoning is inductive, from particulars to particulars, his refusal to be rigidly prescriptive about the methods of scientific inquiry seems reasonable and justified. At this point in his argument, Mill appears to be proceeding in a straightforward and logical fashion: he stresses that deductions from general laws must be constantly verified by comparison to empirical laws, which themselves express the "points of agreement which have been found among many instances" (8:870–72). But even this clarification creates problems. Mill's exposition in this digression, like his treatment of ethology, is too much a matter of the tail wagging the dog: the entire history of science and the status of Bacon, a major figure in that history, must be reconsidered so that ethology can take its place as a field of viable scientific inquiry. I am not suggesting that Mill's account of Bacon is itself suspect. He makes the same cogent claims about Bacon's role as a "false prophet" on the "nature of philosophical discovery" in an article published in 1832, but there the claims, because they do not fulfill such an obviously self-serving function, carry more authority (23:414). Here, however, the context of the digression, the fact that it is a digression called forth by the need to defend the science that he has had difficulty defining casts further doubt on ethology.

What, then, is the status of ethology as Mill envisioned it in 1843 when his *System of Logic* appeared? What can it accomplish? Are both its processes and its conclusions limited to those empirical laws, those bits of folk wisdom that figure so prominently in Chapter V in Book VI of the *Logic*? The clearest statement about what ethology might achieve appears in the middle of this chapter when Mill discusses the generally recognized differences in the characters exhibited by the French and English or by men and women. He suggests that such differences—"peculiarities," he calls them—may result from "diversities" in institutions, climate, customs, education, and such physical factors as "bodily strength and nervous susceptibility." If, Mill argues, one can link general and empirical laws, the results of reasoning by observation and by deduction, "we need be under no difficulty in judging how far [such differences] may be expected to be permanent, or by what circumstances they would be modified or destroyed" (8:868). This is a large claim indeed. Mill affirms that it is possible to know which characteristics of a group are inherent—"permanent" and "congenital predispositions" (8:873), as he calls them elsewhere—and which characteristics are transitory, the result of circumstances that can be changed and that, being changed, will change character. Mill repeats this point at the end of the chapter when he identifies the practical implications of the "consilience" or affiliation of theory and observation: ethology can create a hierarchy of the "effects" that it is "desirable to produce or to prevent" and, therefore, become the basis for the "corresponding Art" of "practical education" (8:874).

ETHOLOGY APPLIED

Although Mill never wrote a theoretical treatise on ethology, during the mid-1840s and into the 1850s and the 1860s, he worked to put into practice the claims he made for it in his *System of Logic*. In particular, the *Principles of Political Economy* and the long series of articles on Ireland in the *Morning Chronicle* treated the issues raised in the *Logic,* and other later works such as *The Subjection of Women* continued the project. A consistent definition of ethology emerges from these essays as well as consistent proof that the science became, for Mill, less a powerful tool of inquiry than a powerful mode of persuasion. Ethology, as his practice of it in the two decades after the publication of *A System of Logic* reveals, is more intimately related to sociology than to psychology, more useful in dealing with groups than with individuals. Mill himself concedes that point at the end of the chapter on ethology in the *Logic* when he notes that the study of "mankind in the average, or *en masse*" renders secondary the issues that ethology is not ready to resolve: "the natural differences of individual minds, and the physical circumstances on which they may be dependent" (8:873). The word *individual* was added to this passage in the 1851 edition of the *Logic,* and this minor revision suggests that the work that Mill had done in the 1840s had convinced him that ethology must, at least for the present, deal with groups, not individuals.

Whenever Mill chose a subject for sustained ethological analysis during the last three decades of his career, he invariably chose groups remarkable for their common status as marginal, dispossessed, or disenfranchised: the geographically and politically marginal Irish, the socially and economically disadvantaged working classes, and the politically and professionally dispossessed group constituted by all women, in England and Ireland, in all classes. Such choices again reveal the political nature of the inquiry. These were the groups whose circumstances were most in need of change. Mill's analyses of such groups are exercises in Political Ethology, not simply because, as he defined that term, they deal with groups of people, but because they study character as a way to determine how legislation can alleviate the disadvantages created by the subjection of these groups to the power that others have over them.

Mill's comments on middle-class, male-dominated, English commercial society emerge, by contrast, only apropos of some other topic. Mill's analysis of the English is fairly specific; he remarks on the provincialism that allows ignorance of French thought and French politics and French history, the toadying of the English classes to their betters, the stultifying narrowness of English manners and morals, and the rampant commercialism that saps energy for all pursuits and values other than the monetary and the material. Such comments, however, and the consistent portrait of English national shortcomings that they draw are usually elicited by more sustained discussions of topics not English, not middle-class, and not male. This point is particularly true of the comments that Mill makes in his *Autobiography;* to defend his unconventional relation to Harriet Taylor, Mill must attack and dismiss the social conventions of middle-class life. Even in *On Liberty*, Mill's most direct and sustained indictment of English society, his criticism emerges in the context of his conception of an ideal society that would not be marked by its present shortcomings. The early newspaper writings that deal with English life are no more directly ethological. Ethology, the science whose laws will guide the reformer's methods, is to be practiced on the dispossessed.

In the case of the Irish, the pressure of events led Mill to undertake the analysis of the condition of the powerless so that he could speak as their champion and, he hoped, change the conditions that threatened their annihilation. Alexander Bain, who saw Mill in the summer of 1844, remarked that Mill "evidently" was "dropping the scheme of a work on Ethology and drifting to the Political Economy project."[7] Bain seems to have ignored how much of Mill's work on political economy in his *Principles,* published four years later, is actually ethology masquerading as economics, but the potato famine in Ireland allowed Mill to "drift" back to ethology in the long series of forty-three leading articles that he wrote for the *Morning Chronicle* between October 1846 and January 1847. In his *Autobiography,* Mill insists that he responded in print to the situation in Ireland because the crisis there gave him "a chance of gaining attention" (1:243), but I suspect he would have taken advantage sooner or later of an even less obvious opportunity so that he could use Ireland in the same way that James Mill had used India: Ireland, for John Mill, was not a test case, a chance to prove the validity of his principles; rather, the condition of its peasants was a specific example of the ethological principles he already held inviolate.

The series on Ireland in the *Morning Chronicle* was the occasion for the insight I have already pointed to as Mill's most acute perception on the relation between character and circumstance, the insight that reveals most about his own experience as a son, husband, and wage-earner: "What shapes the character is not what is purposely taught, so much as the unintentional teaching of institutions and social relations." Mill makes this assertion as he argues for "economical means" endowed with a "moral efficacy" as the only feasible way in which to alleviate the "economical evils of Ireland." He is convinced that a "new moral atmosphere" will "correct everything in [the peasant's] national character which needs correction." The passage in which Mill makes his claims about the unintentional teaching he hopes to eradicate offers a sense of both his rhetoric in this series and the passion with which he argues his points:

> Without a change in the people, the most beneficent change in their mere outward circumstances would not last a generation. You will never change the people unless you make themselves the instruments, by opening to them an opportunity to work out for themselves all the other changes. You will never change the people but by changing the external motives which act on them, and shape their way of life from the cradle to the grave. Much has been said of popular education: but education does not mean schools and school books; these are most valuable, but only as preparations and as auxiliaries. The real effective education of a people is given them by the circumstances by which they are surrounded. The laws are the great schoolmaster, as the ancient statesmen and philosophers well knew, and it is time we should again learn the lesson. What shapes the character is not what is purposely taught, so much as the unintentional teaching of institutions and social relations. It is of little use inculcating industry, prudence, and obedience to law, if every thing which the peasant, throughout life, sees and hears, tells him, in much more intelligible language than yours, that he has nothing to gain by industry or prudence, and everything to lose by submitting to the law. Nothing that you can *say* will alter the state of his mind, only something that you can *do*. Make it his interest to be industrious and prudent, and engage his interest on the side of the law. And if you have inveterate habits of the contrary description to overcome, there is the more need of presenting the motives which tend to correct those habits in the shape in which they will be most intense and palpable. (24:955)

Mill has, of course, reverted to his usual distinction between words and deeds, privileging the latter over the former, yet basing his calls for action on clear-sighted theory. Economic legislation becomes a form of education; law molds character by involving individuals in the processes that will transform the character of the group. That such articles constitute a course of instruction for their readers Mill underlines by speaking to "you," not by invoking as he does elsewhere the "we" that joins reader and writer to display the hegemony they share. Here the writer is distinct from the reader: he uses the lessons of theory to tell "you," the agent, what has to be done. In an 1834 article on a motion to repeal the Act of Union, Mill had described the condition of Ireland as almost beyond repair: the Irish were a "people whose national character has run wild" (6:218). In 1846, however, Mill was confident that his understanding of the relation between institutions and character would provide both a cogent explanation of the reasons for the crisis and a solution to it.

Mill's analysis of the condition of the Irish peasantry is, therefore, clear, simple, and straightforward—almost, as some of his contemporary critics pointed out, too much so. His perspective on the problem is unremittingly English rather than Irish. The population of that other island is being decimated by famine, but England, according to Mill, is reaping the whirlwind: "The whole fruits of centuries of oppression and neglect are coming home to us in a single year" (24: 997). The source of this crisis is not the failure of the crops in a given year, but the long-standing abuses inherent in the cottier-tenant system. Irish peasants have no reason to work hard because everything they earn, beyond that required to support the most miserable level of subsistence, is confiscated as rent. Because they can never pay all the exorbitant rent they owe their landlords, they can never look forward to any earnings as their own. Because they have no assurance that they will occupy the same bit of land from year to year, they have no reason to improve either the land or their methods of cultivation. Because the peasants live in despair, because they can have no hope for the future, they breed like animals, without sense of responsibility or purpose.

Mill does not mince words when it comes to describing the Irish national character created by such conditions. He treats Ireland entirely in terms of its peasants and landlords, and he focuses almost exclusively on the former. The Irish are "already pauperized"—indolent, miserable, reckless (24:1007), but not "so by nature" (24:891). The nurture of English misgovernment has created this monster of surpassing moral and economic deficiencies. "The grand fundamental

defects in the character and habits of the Irish peasant are want of industry and want of providence." The lawlessness with which the Irish
are charged, evident in the violence of the Whiteboys, Mill dismisses
as a temporary response to their "desperate situation" (24:955–56).
Here Mill is confidently identifying the characteristics of a monolithic
national identity as either relatively transitory, created by the peculiarities of the times, or more deeply ingrained by centuries of subjection to an arbitrary and debilitating system of cottier-tenancy. No Irish
characteristic to which he is willing to point reveals an inherent Irish
nature. There is, indeed, according to Mill, no such phenomenon as
Irish character. Under different circumstances, the Irish could be and
would be anything but what they are.

This point emerges most explicitly when Mill defends the measure
that he thinks will eradicate the ill effects of long-term subjection:
peasant proprietorship. Mill proposes that waste lands in Ireland be
drained at public expense and then parceled out to the cottiers so
that they would become proprietors. Property is the one factor capable
of transforming Irish national character totally: revising a quotation
from an English traveler in France, an observer who had to admit, despite his prejudices against small properties, that ownership promotes
industry, Mill claims that tendencies in the current character of the
peasant are reversible. Indeed, circumstances not only form character;
they constitute character:

> Of all tillers of soil, the cottier is the one who has least to gain
> by any voluntary exertion; the small proprietor has most. That
> the one should be the idlest and the other the most diligent of
> all peasants, actual or possible, is but the natural result of their
> circumstances. Put each in the situation of the other, and their
> characters will be reversed. Give the Irishman "the secure posses-
> sion of a bleak rock" or a turf bog, and he too "will turn it into a
> garden." He will be as easily induced as his kindred Celts across
> the Channel, to "convey earth in buckets" to form a soil on the
> terraced side of a hill, if the hill-side when terraced and the soil
> when laid down are to be his own. (24:958)

This passage is remarkable both for the certainty of its tone—there is
no question about the beneficial effects of property on even the most
demoralized Irish peasant—and for the fact that Mill seems to have

discovered a "nature" he is ready to see as inherent. The French and Irish, as "kindred Celts," have a shared racial identity. Here, Mill specifically uses race as a factor, which he elsewhere generally downplays, to equalize the variables that might distinguish the French peasant from the Irish peasant. Because both share the same racial constitution, it can be only their differing economic circumstances that account for the different levels of industry and foresight that they display.

In other leading articles on the same subject, Mill extends the applicability of his belief in the power of ownership not just to all kinds of Celts, but to all races, at all times, and in all nations. Ownership creates in the owner "industry, prudence, and economy" (24:900). This is a law "which never fails" (24:897). This is the lesson to be learned by studying peasants in France, Switzerland, Norway, the Rhineland, and even India. This is the lesson to be learned by remembering the example of the "ancient English" class of yeomanry that disappeared with the Tudors or by reading Wordsworth's accounts of the peasants who lived in the Lake District, "a perfect republic of shepherds and agriculturalists, proprietors, for the most part, of the lands which they occupied and cultivated" (24:940–41). As early as 1831 in his series on "The Spirit of the Age," Mill distinguished between basic approaches to the study of society: the inductive approach of those who, like Macaulay, see different cultures as distinct entities that share no common features; and the deductive approach of those who, like James Mill, depend on "what they term the universal principles of human nature" (22:256) and therefore are blind to the diversities of character at different times and in different places. Both approaches, Mill argued throughout his career, are invalid. Yet in treating property as the cure-all for the situation in Ireland on the basis of so comprehensive a gathering of historical and contemporary examples as Mill adduces, he comes perilously close to erring in the direction of his father's shortcomings. Mill had been particularly severe on Bentham's limitations on this score: "How could [Bentham] whose mind contained so few and so poor types of individual character, rise to that higher generalization" of "national character"? Without that "higher" knowledge, any speculation on the efficacy of social institutions is an "absurdity" (10:99). But in Mill's own theorizing, the peasant proprietor is simply such an unvarying type, *the* peasant, so abstract a formulation, that a particular institution will have the same effect on the peasant character no matter how geographical or climatic or historical factors may vary.

Such reductive and formulaic thinking explains, perhaps, Mill's sanguine forecasts about the speed with which the medicine of ownership will cure Irish ills, although he is signally silent about how the Irish are to feed themselves before their waste lands can be reclaimed, before those lands yield their first crops. Mill imagines that the character of the children of those granted land will be wholly transformed from that of their parents before they owned land: "The generation born and brought up in the new circumstances would be a new people" (24:1004). He does not seem to calculate, as he does elsewhere, that habits are the growth of long training, that new habits take even longer to inculcate than those they displace. The peasants originally granted ownership, he seems to assume, will be models for their children, but he does not explain how they themselves will learn to be upstanding, industrious, provident, and sexually restrained. The land will simply make them so—as if a magic wand had been waved over their heads.

Yet this single-mindedness, this unquestioning assurance is exactly what allows Mill to speak to this issue with such genuine passion and authority. He knows what he knows, and he knows he is right. His scorn for those who champion other proposals is pitiless. Those who suggest that the Irish should emigrate are simply and foolishly arguing that a people barely civilized themselves should set off as the missionaries of civilization to those too utterly barbaric to recognize that the Irish are little better than savages. Those who want to see the Poor Law extended to Ireland are as wrongheaded as those who would give brandy to a drunk or arsenic to the victim of poisoning; they are like those who would cut off a "limb because it is paralysed, or [put] out an eye because it has a cataract" (24:1007). The rhetorical power of these essays is equalled only by passages in an essay such as "Nature" or in sections of *The Subjection of Women*. Mill takes every advantage of his capacity for plain speaking. In his article "The Proposed Irish Poor Law" that followed shortly after the series of leaders and extends their premises, anger joins certainty to create outrage. The moment to reclaim the waste lands of Ireland is passing, and Mill looks forward to a time when poor-law funds will be depleted and "we shall be forced to begin treating the Irish people as moral agents, influenced by motives, and who must be acted on by a system of moral government, and not as creatures whom we can feed like pigs or turkeys, and prevent as easily from straying out of the bounds of the stye or poultry yard" (24:1072–73). Broad jokes about Irish laziness and Irish profligacy and Irish fecundity are a staple of Victorian literature—even the drunken Irish nursemaid who tries to pass herself off as an English gentlewoman in *Villette* was the creation of the daughter of an Irishman—but Mill refuses to disguise as simply comic the effects of the improvident English government of Ireland. Mill knows how the English see the Irish, as dumb domestic animals penned within the confines of their squalid little island, and he confronts that prejudice directly. Ethology, if it does not reveal the specific ingredients and determinants of an illusive and indistinct Irish character, does cut to the bone of certain unattractive English characteristics.

Although Mill labeled as a failure his series on Ireland in the *Morning Chronicle*—he wrote Bain that he had "little hope left" after the ministry had adopted none of his proposals—he felt ready to return to his work on political economy because he had taught others how to do the work he had left undone: he claimed to have "indoctrinated the *Chronicle* writers" on the subject of Ireland (13:707). Yet Mill's *Principles of Political Economy* is, in its treatment of the working classes, as much an exercise in ethology as the articles on Ireland. As soon in Book I, for instance, as Mill discusses "greater energy of labour" as a cause of productiveness, he raises ethological issues about the effects of climate or military discipline on character (Chapter viii, sec. 3). If the point of investigating character on a scientific basis is to isolate the conditions that need to be changed, political economy for Mill has the same goal within a more limited range of conditions. In Book II, Mill asks what is for him simply a rhetorical question: "Can political economy do nothing but only object to everything, and demonstrate that nothing can be done?" Mill's *Principles of Political Economy* testifies, throughout, his certainty that such is not the case, that the so-called dismal science need not be either "melancholy" or "thankless" (2:367). Some of Mill's analysis, the writing of which was interrupted while he wrote his series on Ireland for the *Morning Chronicle,* recalls that series. Offering five-acre plots divided from common lands to create a "class of small proprietors" will function as an "inducement to prudence and economy pervading the whole labouring population." Even better would be granting five-acre plots to some laborers and ten-acre plots to others—such inequality being yet another inducement to labor (2:377). Because Mill is dealing in his *Principles* with some populations that are not white or European, he can be even more blunt than he has been about the supposedly Christian Irish: "To civilize a savage, he must be inspired with new wants and desires, even if not of a very elevated kind." Desires create energy, and energy yields improvement. Even a debased motive like the love of finery can work wonders, therefore, on the freed slaves of Jamaica and Demerara (2:104). Mill would not have suggested that the ownership of property that was to civilize the Irish was equivalent to a string of glass beads, but the principles in both instances are the same. People will work when they have something for which to work.

Mill's discussions of working-class issues in the *Principles*, however, reveal more clearly than do the articles on Ireland the difficulties that he faced in pursuing his interest in ethology, difficulties that would eventually prove how far his goals eluded his grasp. The revisions that Mill made in the seven editions of this treatise demonstrate that the conclusions he reached were more tentative, more completely contingent on unforeseen and unpredictable circumstances than he would have liked to admit. At the end of Chapter xiii in Book II, Mill proposes the use of public money to encourage the emigration of large numbers of young agricultural workers. In 1865 he felt compelled to add a new concluding paragraph to that discussion so that he could admit that improvements in transportation and communication had rendered the recommended governmental action unnecessary: workers could now learn about far-distant opportunities that they could reach with relative ease, and their own efforts would relieve the pressure on population without government action (2:378). This single example highlights the major problem Mill faced in his ethological studies: he could see how certain causes had created a national character that he could recognize and describe—the Irish worker was lazy and improvident; the English worker was energetic and improvident—and he could see what kinds of characters he wanted to create out of the material they offered to the legislator's art, but discovering the process that would effect that transformation was beyond the scope of ethology.

In response to this difficulty, Mill often presents not one, but two or more ways in which the character of a group may be altered. In his advocacy of population control as a way to raise wages, he proposes abstinence both before and after marriage. How to encourage abstinence is, however, the real problem that requires a knowledge of the relation between character and circumstance. First, Mill suggests public opinion, peer pressure, as the answer: if workers learn that having too many children depresses wages—and here Mill seems to be advocating a campaign of public announcements or a course of popular education—then "the expectation of being disliked or despised" will diminish sexual activity. Mill then proposes that the granting of "the rights of citizenship" to women would have the same effect, but the argument becomes quite murky here. The power to vote would presumably allow women to keep their men out of their beds. This idea is explained, in part, later in the *Principles* when Mill suggests that offering women the freedom to choose various "industrial occupations" instead of what he has earlier called the "intolerable domestic drudgery" of raising children would cause a "great diminution" in population (2:371–73; 3:765–66). But this argument itself is no more satisfying. If working-class women have fewer children or no children, then they will be free to choose other occupations; but such a condition presumes continual sexual self-restraint, not by women alone but by men as well. Achieving that end would clearly be more difficult than conceiving of it as desirable.

In fact, the discussion of population control in the *Principles* testifies not simply to the difficulties inherent in an analysis that requires constant attention to a myriad of contributing factors, but to the way in which public and personal considerations conspire to defeat Mill's intentions. The discussion is almost ludicrously limited by its reticence on sexual matters. In this sense, Mill participates in the conventions that disable his analysis—conventions that landed him in jail in 1823 for having distributed birth-control literature and conventions that nearly destroyed Harriet Martineau's career when she published her fictionalized treatment of population control in her *Illustrations of Political Economy.*[8] Mill begins his argument in Book II by decrying the terrible cost in human misery exacted by the "scrupulosity of speech" that makes it impossible to recognize the effects of sexual activity. Two paragraphs after he calls for an end to the "spurious delicacy" with which this subject is treated (2:368), he is quoting the French text of Sismondi's *Nouveaux principes* to enforce the idea of voluntary celibacy as a solution to the population problem, as if the foreign language would serve as a kind of barrier to those unable to read it. Significantly, the People's Edition of the *Principles* (1865) offers translations of such passages. Only as the discussion proceeds and only by indirection does it become clear that Mill sees abstinence as the only solution. When he comments that "the most disgusting" of the "barbarisms which law and morals have not yet ceased to sanction" is "that any human being should be permitted to consider himself as having a *right* to the person of another" (2:372), it finally becomes clear that the alternatives that Mill has in mind involve either having sex or not having sex, but not the possibility of sexual activity without the birth of children as its inevitable result.

In framing alternatives that deny the use of birth control, Mill is, of course, revealing his personal inclinations and disinclinations. Sexual appetite is an "animal instinct" that, according to Mill, must eventually be extirpated if civilization is to advance (3:766). More important still is his belief that members of the laboring classes do have choices, that they can make decisions about how they want to live and about how to achieve what they want. As I have stressed, the need to reconcile choice and necessity was the central problem that Mill tried to solve in every area of inquiry he undertook. On the question of population control, however, the question of choice creates argumentative tangles reminiscent of those in the chapter on ethology in the *Logic*. Mill is irate that the number of one's children should not be seen as a matter of choice: "The idea, in this country, never seems to enter any one's mind that having or not having a family, or the number of which it shall consist, is amenable to their own control. One would imagine that children are rained down upon married people, direct from heaven, without their being art or part in the matter" (2:369). But as soon as Mill outlines his argument for abstinence, choice magically disappears as a good that must be granted a member of the laboring classes, and coercion, in one form or another, becomes the way in which Mill's choice for them will be imposed on them.

The extent to which Mill is willing to take such coercive measures is remarkable. First, as I have noted, he invokes the power of public opinion as a way of lowering the birth rate; once that power proves itself effective, however, Mill advises that "the moral obligation against bringing children into the world who are a burthen to the community" should become a "legal one." Although Mill does not specify what kind of "legal sanction" he proposes for the "recalcitrant minorities" who continue to have too many children—should they be fined? imprisoned?—his conviction that such behavior deserves punishment is clear (2:372). Considering that abstinence is the only means that Mill is willing to countenance to achieve a reduced birth rate, one can only say that his proposal seems extraordinarily high-handed as well as impractical. Choice is a good only when it involves the choice Mill would make for himself: if he had the power to do so, he would render illegal sexual activity even between consenting adults too poor to maintain their children—if, of course, a woman could be found degraded enough to consent, a possibility that he sees as highly unlikely. Only when working-class character reflects Mill's disgust with the body and its functions will it be the kind of character that is worth creating.

Mill's ethological examinations into the conditions of working-class character are, like so many other less scientific treatments of the subject, not so much an opportunity to understand the conditions of those unlike oneself as they are a chance to parade one's own prejudices and presuppositions. It is hard not to see a relation between Mill's insistence on abstinence as a form of population control and his repulsion at the spectacle of working-class appetites and their untoward results. In a series of articles in the *Morning Chronicle* and the *Daily News* from the late 1840s into the mid-1850s, Mill denounces the assaults by working-class men upon women, children, and animals, and such men are labeled at one point the "baser" or "brutal part of the populace" (25:1186). Although Mill notes in his list of articles that many of these short notices were "joint productions" with Harriet Mill—"Very little of this was mine"[9]—Mill sympathized enough with her horror at working-class brutality to submit the articles as his own. If workers had fewer children, if wages rose and conditions improved, such atrocities would occur less frequently. Mill clearly saw sexual activity of any sort as a form of brutality, the exertion of the physical force of the stronger over the weaker. For men, it involved an "odious" customary right that he explicitly abdicated for himself in his statement on his intended marriage to Harriet Taylor when he promised not to exert any "power or control" over her "person, property, and freedom of action" (21:99).

Early in his career as a journalist, Mill had attacked the "littleness of mind which caste-distinctions engender" and the gentleman's "assumption of superiority" over the poor (23:653). He had explained that the "higher classes" have "no title" to "legislate for the morals of the people": "All the judgments of our higher classes respecting the working people . . . though clothed . . . with the disguise of morality and conscience, originate in some interest or some fear relating not to those whom they persuade themselves that they are concerned for, but to the higher classes themselves" (6:213). Mill's treatment of working-class issues in his *Principles* stands indicted on precisely the charges that he uses to convict others. When, for instance, Mill advocates educating the workers in order to inculcate "moral trustworthiness," he quotes an "intelligent and experienced" Swiss manufacturer whose ambition for what he calls "better educated workmen" is simply a desire to transform them into less well remunerated copies of middle-class employees. According to this Swiss observer, educated workers have "superior moral habits." They are sober. Their amusements are "rational and refined." They are admitted to "better society" because they are "respectful" of it. They read, "cultivate music," and go sightseeing (2:109). Most of all, however, their habits of economy protect their own purses and "the stock of their master." In parroting the middle classes, the working classes would protect the interests of the middle classes, upholding middle-class values by adopting them and paying proper respect to the property and profits of their betters.

Mill's Swiss authority, whose evidence appeared as an appendix to a report of the Poor Law Commissioners, goes on to say that if "uneducated English workmen [are] released from the bonds of iron discipline in which they have been restrained by their employers in England," they become unmanageable because they "do not understand their position." Workers, like slaves and women, need to know their place. Mill probably found this appendix particularly interesting from an ethological point of view because it compared the national character of workers from Italy, France, Switzerland, and Germany. That he continued to agree with its conclusions is clear from the two celebrated sentences that he added to its analysis in the 1852 edition of the *Principles:* "As soon as any idea of equality enters the mind of an uneducated English working man, his head is turned by it. When he ceases to be servile, he becomes insolent." Mill presents this idea as an observation born out of experience (2:109). It is one of those empirical laws that he found central to a science of character. But it suggests one of the factors that make such a science impossible: his statement reveals less about the circumstances that shape the character of the group being studied than it does about the way in which social prejudice shapes the conclusions of such a study and disguises moral judgments as psychological principles.

In the earlier article in which Mill denies "the higher classes" the right to legislate for the people—a right that he grants himself *in posse* throughout his *Principles of Political Economy*—he complains that the "higher" do not "know enough of [or] feel enough" with the people (6:213). Just such ignorance of the marginal groups that he studied explains both Mill's choice of his subjects and the inherent limitations of his inquiries. His sense of his own marginal status as a theorist in an age devoted to practice allowed him to feel with the dispossessed groups he studied. Such sympathy was, I think, a primary motive, the source of much of the energy behind such investigations. But the pain of such marginality also motivated the desire to speak for and to represent the values of the dominant culture with which Mill felt so ambiguously allied. His view of the workers is the manufacturer's view, the perspective of the individual who makes use of people he does not know to achieve his own ends. After all, the Irish and the working classes were groups about whom Mill had little first-hand knowledge.

In this sense, Mill's forays into ethology are open to the same strictures commonly raised against James Mill's *History of British India:* he simply did not know what he was talking about. In the preface to his history, James Mill treats this disability as an added capacity for the work he has undertaken. With some bravado, he claims that his never having been in India and his ignorance of oriental languages are not disqualifications—Tacitus, after all, had never been to Germany, and he had been able to write an "exquisite account of the manners of the Germans." James Mill claims further that "whatever is worth seeing or hearing in India, can be expressed in writing"—that is, in the English language—and that the "closet in England" well stocked with books affords more knowledge of India than a journey to India itself.[10] For all the doubtful logic of this argument—an argument remarkable for its insistence on the reduction of all experience to its written form— James Mill's larger point deserves at least attention, if not acceptance: he argues that the distance between England and India allows the English student of India the sense of perspective, the "expansive view" of the unseen subject, that closer acquaintance would deny. All those messy details and nuances would only get in the way.

Such considerations certainly explain John Stuart Mill's choice of subjects for ethological investigation. Achieving the clarity engendered by a distanced perspective is more likely in cases about which one knows few of the particulars. In the writing that Mill did on the Irish and the laboring classes, his confidence in the generalizations he propounds is striking. The experience of all historical generations in all nations comes down to a law that can be formulated with algebraic precision: without "experience of lawful rule [and] reverence for the law . . . no people can be any thing but, according to their physical temperament, savages or slaves" (6:217). By the time Mill came to the third major group that he treated to ethological analysis, when he wrote *The Subjection of Women* in the early 1860s, that confidence, however, had been eroded precisely because he recognized his ignorance about this group as a disqualification for his study of it. By acknowledging how little one can know about the members of a marginal group, simply because they are marginal, Mill was able, paradoxically, both to enforce his ethological principles more energetically and to suggest the impossibility of ethology as a science.

One of the central points in *The Subjection of Women* involves the inexplicability of its subject. Mill maintains—not, like Freud, that women's desires are simply incomprehensible—but that their subjection makes it impossible either to know what their character now is or to predict what it could be. At first, Mill claims that such specific ignorance is simply part and parcel of the wider "unspeakable ignorance and inattention of mankind in respect to the influences which form human character." Clearly, Mill's interests and ambitions have not changed since the 1840s: such a statement sounds very much like his call in *A System of Logic* for a science of character. But he repeats the point again and again, each time focusing more specifically on the issues of gender differences and their implications. The "present state of society" renders futile any attempt to "obtain complete and correct knowledge" on the "natural differences" between men and women. To supply this deficiency, Mill calls for the "analytic study" of the "laws of the influence of circumstances on character," although he does not give that study the name he invented for it; rather, he calls it the "most important department of psychology." Soon he is declaring that it is not possible to determine if there are inherent differences between the genders. The problem is not, like that treated in the *Logic,* a problem of method, but a lack of data. Medical research has yielded some information on physical differences, but doctors, Mill laments, are not psychologists; on the subject of mental differences, "their observations are of no more worth than those of common men." Men do not know women because women either do not know themselves or avoid communicating what they do know. Harking back to his associationist emphasis on the observation of self and others that is necessary to psychological analysis, Mill asserts that "the mental characteristics of women" constitute "a subject on which nothing final can be known, so long as those who alone can really know it, women themselves, have given little testimony, and that little, mostly suborned. . . . The greater part of what women write about women is mere sycophancy to men." Men, as members of the group with power and education and resources, are clearly the ones most suited to undertake the ethological analysis of women, but any given man can know only a few women and those few only from the perspective created by his "amatory" relations with them. His knowledge of them is necessarily "wretchedly imperfect and superficial" (21:277–79).

Not surprisingly, then, the issue on which Mill speaks with greater certainty than on any other in this essay is the effect of women's subjection, not on women, but on men. Mill is fairly confident when he suggests that women, under their present circumstances, are more practical than men, more attuned to the concrete, "the actual facts of nature," than to the abstract (21:306). But he expatiates with great passion on the way in which the subjection of women "pervert[s] the whole manner of existence of the man, both as an individual and as a social being." In the passage in which he treats this subject, Mill uses exhortations, rhetorical questions, and a long series of balanced antitheses to drive home his point:

> Think what it is to a boy, to grow up to manhood in the belief that without any merit or any exertion of his own, though he may be the most frivolous and empty or the most ignorant and stolid of mankind, by the mere fact of being born a male he is by right the superior of all and every one of an entire half of the human race:

including probably some whose real superiority to himself he has daily or hourly occasion to feel; but even if in his whole conduct he habitually follows a woman's guidance, still, if he is a fool, he thinks that of course she is not, and cannot be, equal in ability and judgment to himself; and if he is not a fool, he does worse—he sees that she is superior to him, and believes that, notwithstanding her superiority, he is entitled to command and she is bound to obey. What must be the effect on his character, of this lesson? (21:324)

Whenever Mill resorts to such rhetorical tactics, to the full artillery of his argumentative weapons, he signals the intensity of his conviction and his commitment. As Stefan Collini acutely argues, Mill "wrote to convince, and where he could not convince, to convict" (21:xiv). In this particular passage, Mill implies that those men who do not accept his point are convicted on two counts: one, of not recognizing their condition in his depiction of it; and two, of not freeing others from the subjection that has made such men the monsters of false superiority that they have become.

Mill uses exactly the same tactics in his 1867 speech on extending the franchise to women. Speaking to a group of men, his fellows in the House of Commons, he appeals, in good Benthamite fashion, to their interests, and he focuses on the ill effects they will suffer if women are not granted social and political equality. If men live in constant intimacy with women trivialized by their disabilities, they too will become trivial. Similarly, in the conclusion to *The Subjection of Women,* Mill points out the "lesson" that men need to learn about their "fellow creatures" based on what they know about themselves. Whenever he appeals to them to change the circumstances that cause such suffering to women, he does so entirely in terms of the analogies he draws between women's experience and the kinds of subjection that men have experienced—as boys, as wage-earners forced to do uncongenial work, as old men burdened by the inactivity of retirement (21:337–40). Only by drawing attention to male experience does Mill attempt to create sympathy for the unremitting effects of female subordination. If judged on its rhetorical approach alone, *The Subjection of Women* is, then, very much an address by a man to an audience of men. Like a speech on the floor of the House of Commons, it can be overheard by women, but it is not directed toward them. *The Subjection* proceeds by adducing the marginality that individual men have experienced at one time or another, but, in effect, that tactic puts women, once more, on the margins of its discourse. To do so, however, is not merely to reproduce the cultural conditions that are being opposed; rather, it is to understand quite accurately how those cultural conditions may provide the rhetorical strategems capable of encouraging motives for change.

The Subjection of Women, in fact, reveals so frequently Mill's rhetorical tact, his interest in finding a way to win a hearing for his unpalatable message, that it may be perilous to base any conclusions about Mill's larger ethological project on this text alone. On the one hand, his reluctance to speculate on how women might differ from men if women lived under different circumstances simply emphasizes how completely circumstances determine the character of a group, so completely, in fact, that their effects cannot be calculated. On the other hand, Mill simply may be holding his peace on a subject that instilled a great deal of irrational fear in both women and men. Many dreaded a world in which women would refuse to have children and refuse to run households. Others—"lovers of fun," Mill calls them—portrayed the effects of equality by drawing ludicrous pictures of young girls sitting as members in the House of Commons (21:339). In fact, the short-lived comic newspaper *Banter* had said of Mill, "He'd make, if he could get his will, / Full many a *'Polly'*-tician!" The one effect of emancipation that Mill describes at any length is the communion between equals that marriage will become in such a new world. *The Subjection* may simply be an example of *economy,* "the cautious dispensation of the truth," against charges of which Newman defended himself in the *Apologia* by noting that even Jesus advised his followers, "Cast not your pearls before swine." [11] In the conservative context of his own culture, Mill may well have decided not to reveal all that might be said on the subject of female emancipation. He may not be telling actual falsehoods here, but practicing the "reserve" that he had counseled Comte to use in his attempts to gain the attention of the timidly conventional English audience.

Yet one point is clear. If *The Subjection of Women* is evaluated by the standards for ethological investigation set out in the *Logic,* it falls short of the mark. There Mill specifically uses the case of the differences between men and women to claim that empirical laws can be verified by the "more general laws" of psychology to determine with "no difficulty" which traits are inherent, which open to modification (8:868). That claim, whether from reasons of conviction or in response to the rhetorical exigencies of the occasion, is no longer tenable in *The Subjection*. Ethology can point out what cannot be known; it cannot discover what is unknown.

As early as 1843 Mill had identified women as a proper subject for ethological investigation. Writing to Comte to dispute the biological essentialism of the French thinker's view of women, Mill attributed the lack of progress in the science he called "Ethologie" to the reigning idealist tendencies of the day (13:604). Yet there are other, more obvious reasons that Mill did not do the great work in ethology that he set as his task at the end of *A System of Logic*.[12] When he began to engage in political ethology, he depended so thoroughly on clichés and stereotypes as to render his analysis a perpetuation of prejudice rather than an investigation of its sources. Because he was so attuned to the conventional attitudes by which he was surrounded, his writings on national character are an encyclopedia of racial and national slurs, and he frequently confirms rather than challenges them. The "indolence" of North American Indians is, according to Mill, "proverbial" (2:103). It is a matter of "public notoriety" that the Irish cannot be expected to pay their debts—any respectable tradesman will admit as much (23:397). In his essay on Bentham, Mill extols the virtues of such customary, popular wisdom. It embodies, he claims, "the whole unanalysed experience of the human race." If this "collective mind," freed from the peculiarities of individual experience, "does not penetrate below the surface, . . . it sees all the surface" (10:90–91).

What Mill needed was a scientific method that would allow him to analyze such "unanalysed experience." The brief note on Mill's ethology that Bain offers in his work *On the Study of Character* implies that such a science of character cannot be established in the absence of an accepted system of classification.[13] Among the methods of analysis that Mill did not choose to employ was statistics. Another, which he also rejected, was physiology. As early as 1843, Comte took Mill to task for not having paid attention to the findings of physiology (13:605). Later,

Bain often lamented that Mill could not be interested in what Bain and another physiological psychologist, George Henry Lewes, called the "physical basis of mind." In a letter of 1853 to Harriet Mill, Mill explained that he was reading a "thick book" on physiology, a subject "so closely connected with the subjects of mind & feeling that there is always a chance of something practically useful turning up" (14:111). He confessed, however, that the evening before he had simply fallen asleep over the book he deemed so relevant to his interests. He repeatedly recognized that associationism lacked any convincing account of the function of the nerves and that the "chief imperfections" in his father's *Analysis* all resulted from its inability to treat the relation between "Ideas & states of the nerves" (16:1333). It is the central problem that Mill discusses in his chapter on psychology in *A System of Logic,* the chapter that prepares the way for the discussion of ethology. It is clear that Mill could not make progress in ethology without solving such anterior problems. All that he can affirm on this subject is protected by a tentative double negative: "It is certain that the natural differences [between individuals] are often not unconnected with diversities in their organic constitutions" (8:857). Mill was, once again, either before his time or behind the times: the formation of character would not have been considered a subject of scientific inquiry in an earlier period. At a later date, it would become the subject of experimental psychology,[14] the science that Mill thought inconceivable on ethical grounds, or of statistics as a branch of sociology.

Associationism itself proved to be, in Mill's hands, a remarkably weak tool of analysis and inquiry, although that fact may say more about the limitations of experientialist psychology than about the capacities of its loyal adherent. Whenever Mill tries to explain the formation of character in associationist terms, his arguments deal in either contradictions or obfuscations. His account of his crisis in the *Autobiography* offers many instances of such an outcome, as I have already suggested. At other times, Mill treats the sources of character as simply inexplicable. He attributes Bentham's ability to recognize the law as a realm of profitable "fraud" to his "moral sensibility and self-reliance," and Mill wonders why "thousands of educated young men" failed to see what was so obvious once it was recognized and revealed by Bentham. Yet Mill cannot begin to answer that question, and his phrasing of it demonstrates that he has tried: he cannot point to the circumstances that distinguished Bentham from those "thousands" who have "successively been placed in Bentham's position and with Bentham's opportunities" (10:81).

The failures of analysis to which associationism often led are nowhere more obvious than in the instances in which Mill tries to explain how strengths of character are formed. In his comment at the end of his translation and condensation of *The Gorgias,* Mill points out that Plato's call for others to follow virtue will appeal only to those who have already heeded it: "Plato, when he argues about [virtue], argues for the most part inconclusively." Because Mill conceives that virtue is communicated by feelings, not reason, he uses the kind of language that calls into question his associationist principles: the "love of virtue" is "caught by inspiration or sympathy." As if to prove that he is speaking of the ancient vatic form of inspiration that can be conveyed only by the movement of air, he notes that poets "breathe [feelings] into us" by "clothing" them in "beautiful forms" (11:150). Although this particular essay was published at the time when Mill most openly questioned his father's ideas, it conveys exactly the kind of confusion that Mill exhibited later in his career whenever he treated such questions. In his 1867 inaugural address as rector of St. Andrews, he claimed that "elevation of sentiment" is a virtue that "spreads . . . contagiously from teacher to pupil" (21:248). It was easier to account for the love of virtue as if it were a disease than as a moral strength that had its source in positive associations.

Ultimately, Mill's associationism was more important as the source of foregone conclusions than as a repository of methods suited to the study of character. His use of the phrase *formation of character* is almost invariably consistent. Instead of using the more neutral term *development,* which might attribute some of the energy and motives behind the process to the individual undergoing it, Mill continued to portray the individual as the passive object of a process it could not alter or direct. Yet because Mill could not accept the conclusion inherent in such associationist principles, he tried to use ethology as a way to grant to the individual the opportunity for choice and the power of will that associationism denies. The Irish do not have to remain the lazy, improvident, ill-educated savages that their conditions have made them. The laboring classes can rise above their appetites and choose a life of self-restraint and self-improvement. Women do not always have to remain merely weak, sycophantic witnesses to male power. If nothing else, Mill's unwritten ethology allowed him to recognize and perhaps encouraged his contemporaries to see with him that none of the characteristics customarily accepted by society as the inalterable nature of a group was immune to change.

Yet the fact that ethology remained a blank space that Mill failed to fill is the result, I think, of his sense that his efforts in this area would only confirm the determinism he so vehemently and so consistently rejected. Mill's treatment òf George Grote's work on Greek history is particularly instructive in this regard. In an article of 1846 on the first volumes of Grote's *History of Greece*, the longest passage that Mill cites and the one with which he approvingly concludes his review claims that physical factors like climate and geography were the source of Greek civilization. By 1853, Mill's analysis had moved away from consideration of such circumstances to focus instead on human institutions as the source of national character. "The intellectual and moral pre-eminence" of Athens "was wholly the fruit of Athenian institutions" and, particularly, the fruit of the institution of democracy (11:324). Mill is equally certain about the source of such institutions, but his analysis is framed in a way that totally defeats the attempt to trace character to the circumstances that presumably formed it: "For the peculiar and excellent organization of her own democracy, Athens was indebted to a succession of eminent men." If one asks what factors create a great man such as Solon, the answer definitively rejects the question: Solon is "the first capital prize that Athens drew in the dispensations of the Destinies" (11:326). The only way to account for Solon's appearance in Athens is to invoke ancient superstitions about fate and its gifts. All George Grote's careful analysis of the relation between national character and social institutions simply serves as support for Mill's need to believe that great men are above circumstances, that they are empowered to act and to lead others by mysterious forces to which no associationist analysis is relevant.

When Mill accused Bentham of not rising above the "accidental peculiarities of his individual modes of thought" to recognize the truths enshrined in the collective wisdom of the "collective mind" (10: 90–91), he was prophesying the source of his own failure to do the work of theory he thought himself suited to do. Neither the obsessive classifications of the essay on Vigny nor the elaborate method of observation and verification outlined in his *System of Logic* would allow Mill to proceed in the development of a science that could call into question the power of great men to determine the circumstances that formed the character of those they ruled. Although this need, resulting from both the circumstances in which James Mill had raised his son and the indoctrination in the psychological system to which he had been subjected, impeded Mill's progress in his attempts to study character, those circumstances were themselves the source of his preoccupation with character. Although an intellectual endeavor that grows out of an emotional need may indeed lead to impressive theoretical analysis, in Mill's case it yielded instead the impressive energy of his often trenchant pleas that his contemporaries recognize their politically motivated blindnesses to the conditions in which characters are formed. If Mill told his readers anything worth knowing, it was that the poor, the marginalized, need not be always "with us." Despite the fact that he might have wanted the poor—Irish peasants and workers and women—to be more like "us" than "with us," Mill's calls for changes in their circumstances were rhetorically powerful efforts of opposition.

Influence and Authority

The Ethology of the Individual

When George Grote heard from Mill that he was planning to analyze Sir William Hamilton's philosophical doctrines, Grote rejoiced that his friend was revisiting those realms of theory that he had abandoned to treat the social and political issues that dominate *On Liberty, Considerations of Representative Government,* and even *Utilitarianism.* Grote hoped "that you may one of these days revert to those higher speculative and logical subjects with which [Hamilton] busies himself." In the event, Grote was able to tell Mill that *An Examination of Sir William Hamilton's Philosophy* (1865) "completely answered my expectations," containing as it did "valuable expansions" of ideas in *A System of Logic* and "contributions to the most obscure and recondite expositions of Psychological Science."[1] Grote clearly saw the *Examination* as a continuation of the *Logic,* particularly in the areas of psychological investigation, and if it is not the work in ethology that Mill had envisioned, it is, at least, a compelling demonstration of the issues involved in the formation of the individual's character. The *Examination* contains important passages on the questions of freedom and necessity as well as Mill's famous statement of defiance to conventional religious belief, "I will call no being good, who is not what I mean when I apply that epithet to my fellow-creatures; and if such a being can sentence me to hell for not so calling him, to hell I will go" (9:103). But in the present context, the contents of the *Examination* are less relevant than the impulses that Mill revealed in writing it and the light they shed on the formation of his character.

In his early letter on the subject to Comte, Mill defined ethology as a study specifically limited to "la formation du caractère moral et intellectuel" (13:604). In the material I discuss first in this chapter—the *Examination,* along with portions of the *Autobiography,* and *A System of Logic*—Mill treats intellectual issues of influence and authority as if they could be divorced from social, physical, and even moral considerations. In his *Principles of Political Economy,* he differentiates between influence and authority as forms of political power by suggesting that the former encourages certain actions, while the latter enforces them (3:937). Yet when Mill uses these terms to analyze intellectual relations—for instance, when one thinker influences the work of another—their implications are less obviously distinct. Typically, thinkers prove their claims to authority through the influence they exert over other people. In such a case, however, the relation is no less a matter of power than it is when a government enforces its laws on its citizens. Because Mill believed so firmly in the primacy of ideas as motivations, he assumed that the most potent of the circumstances that create character is the influence exerted on it by ideas and by those individuals whose ideas establish their authority. As he puts it in *Considerations of Representative Government,* "speculative thought" is one basis of "social power": "It is what men think, that determines how they act" (19:382). Indeed, the intellectual power that Mill attributes to ideas has its analogy both in the social power that he locates in public opinion or in the political power that he identifies with the laws of the state.

In the entire corpus of his work, Mill unwittingly offers himself as an example of the intellectual formation of the individual. Because he is not often concerned with the social effects of one's familial circumstances or the emotional effects of one's physical conditions, the priority that he grants ideas over other formative factors tends to isolate intellectual development in an illuminating way. Limited to one faculty, more the material for analysis than analysis itself, Mill's comments on this subject do reveal what he learned about intellectual development over the course of a life devoted to ideas. In *Eustace Conway,* one of Maurice's characters complains that disillusioned Benthamites usually become "intellectual all-in-all's."[2] Although that label is hardly adequate to describe Mill's work, it does characterize the limits within which he attempted to portray his own development. Yet if Mill's intellectual concerns are subjected to the kind of ethological analysis that he applied to the characters of disenfranchised groups, the experiment proceeds to some firm conclusions that he would have wanted to reject: for every instance in which Mill disclaims his desire for intellectual power, he attempts only the more energetically to exert it; for every claim about the relative autonomy of the individual, he more forcefully displays his own subjection to his times, his teachers, and his circumstances. For every attempt to treat ideas as if they existed in isolation, he demonstrates their implication in complex networks of social and psychological issues. Mill's disinclination to recognize what he himself continually proves paradoxically allows him to create in *On Liberty* an argument that persuades by so deeply burying its assumptions about freedom and authority that it seems to reverse them. In order to gauge the political argument of that work, however, one must first examine the intellectual issues that provided, for Mill, its crucial counterpart.

INTELLECTUAL STATURE

The *Examination of Sir William Hamilton's Philosophy* raises a number of troubling questions. Why did Mill choose to use Hamilton's work as the example of the intuitionist theories he found, as he says in the *Autobiography,* so inimical to sound practice? Why did Mill write about Hamilton at such length and with such engagement and even ferocity? As Alan Ryan convincingly argues, Hamilton, a liberal many of whose convictions Mill shared, was simply not a well-chosen target. Mill first intended to write a review article on Hamilton's *Lectures on Metaphysics and Logic* (1859–60), the notes of the lectures that Hamilton had delivered, with very few alterations, since he was named Professor of Logic and Metaphysics at the University of Edinburgh in

1837.[3] When Mark Pattison came to review the book that issued from Mill's more modest plan, he recognized this original intention behind the massive treatise it had become. Pattison called the *Examination* "an article, indeed of gigantic proportions," and after complimenting Mill on the "Christian gentleness" with which he treated Hamilton, Pattison caught exactly the extent and spirit of the task of demolition that Mill had undertaken: Mill had achieved the "absolute annihilation of all Sir W. Hamilton's doctrines, opinions, of all he has written and taught. Nor of himself only, but all his followers, pupils, copyists, are involved in the common ruin." Mill had simply erased Hamilton, destroying his claims to authority and rendering his influence nonexistent. Comparing Hamilton's philosophy after Mill's attack to a coastline of desolate sandhills, Pattison likens Mill to a mongoose: "Like the ichneumon disposing of a snake, the critic begins with the head, and passes every joint in his victim's body between his teeth, deliberately crunching each bone separately."[4] That image accurately conveys the slow, thoughtful, and thorough dismemberment of Hamilton's work that proceeds in the *Examination*.

But if the mongoose has its reasons for crunching the snake, why did Mill devour Hamilton? The answer, I think, is simple: Hamilton had authority. Again as Alan Ryan points out, Mill and Hamilton were "the two people in Britain whose names might occur to a philosophically educated foreigner who was asked to name a British thinker of any distinction" (9:xiv). More importantly, Hamilton's authority put in question Mill's influence. In annihilating Hamilton's stature, Mill revealed how very important to him his own stature was. Mill both longed for intellectual preeminence and hoped to conceal the longing. He wanted to declare his authority over Hamilton's, but he could not acknowledge that goal or use any direct means to achieve it. He could not be honest about his motives, but his attempts to disguise them simply draw attention to the unacknowledged pressures to which he was responding.

Mill's work on Hamilton partakes of the more openly combative tone that Mill gave to his writings after the death of Harriet Mill, after the end of the seclusion and isolation that marriage to her entailed. The martial spirit with which Mill invested this intellectual exercise emerges in his preface to the third edition, written between the parliamentary session of 1866 and that of 1867, a fact that may account for some, if not all, of the combative language in which he describes his motives.[5] Mill begins by demurring, "In former writings I have perhaps seemed to go in search of objectors," but in defending the *Examination,* the case, he claims, is "far different": "A host of writers, whose mode of philosophic thought was either directly or indirectly implicated in the criticisms made by this volume on Sir W. Hamilton, have taken up arms against it, and fought as *pro aris et focis.*" Mill claims innocently that he cannot "leave these attacks unanswered" without turning traitor to the principles of a lifetime (9:ciii), but his account of the writing of the *Examination* in the *Autobiography* suggests that encouraging such counterassaults was exactly what he had been looking for in the publication of its first edition: after declaring in no uncertain terms that "intuitional metaphysics" is "one of the chief hindrances to the rational treatment of great social questions and one of the greatest stumbling blocks to human improvement," Mill describes his state of mind before writing the *Examination:* "I had for some time felt that the mere contrast of the two philosophies was not enough, that there ought to be a hand-to-hand fight between them." The language of military engagement continues: Sir William Hamilton was, to Mill, the obvious choice as a point of attack because he was "the great fortress of the intuitional philosophy in this country" (1:270). Yet the fact that Hamilton had died by the time Mill staged his attack makes such an explanation seem disingenuous. In his "Introductory Remark" to the *Examination,* Mill tries to explain that he could not have fought Hamilton until after he died because so much of his substantial work was published posthumously. "We have now all that is to be had," Mill notes (9:3). Perhaps Hamilton's demise actually contributed one of the motivations for the assault launched in the *Examination.* Because Hamilton's *Lectures on Metaphysics and Logic* were published only after his death, Mill may have feared that Hamilton's reputation would gain from the simple authority inevitably accorded the dead.

Yet the monument erected by Hamilton's writings witnesses, not to his power, but to his incompetence, and Mill spends many long chapters both proving this point and proving that it is not worth proving. Sir William Hamilton emerges from the *Examination* as the oddest sort of antagonist: a highly learned writer, but one so confused and confusing that Mill must often attack, not the ideas he opposed, but the fuzziness of thinking that prevented any clear ideas from emerging. The complaints about Hamilton's dull-wittedness become more evident as the *Examination* continues in its relentless course: "It is strange, but characteristic, that Sir W. Hamilton cannot be depended on for remembering, in one part of his speculations, the best things which he has said in another" (9:281). Mill is clearly so pained by his ability to expose the weaknesses of Hamilton's arguments that at one point he even suggests "a way out of [the] difficulty" created by Hamilton's fuzzy thinking, "though it has not been pointed out by Sir W. Hamilton, and is hardly compatible with some of his opinions" (9:363). The medicine that Mill proposes for Hamilton's ailments seems only to make the disease worse.

Furthermore, the target continues to shift throughout the *Examination*. Its full title betrays Mill's difficulties in defining his subject: *An Examination of Sir William Hamilton's Philosophy and of the Principal Philosophical Questions Discussed in His Writings*. First, Hamilton is treated as the chief example of intuitionist thought; then he is displaced because Mill proves that he is not a competent spokesperson for his own ideas. By the opening of Chapter VIII, Mill is asserting, "For the future, therefore, we shall be concerned less with Sir W. Hamilton's philosophy as such, than with the general mode of thought to which it belongs." In the next sentence, however, Mill contradicts himself again: "We shall be engaged in criticizing doctrines common to him with many other thinkers; but in doing so we shall take his writings as text-books, and deal with the opinions chiefly in the form in which he presented them." Because Hamilton has "the great advantage of coming last" (9:109), he can serve as the most cogent representative of his school of thought, but even that assertion does not stand the test of exposition for long in the *Examination*. In an attempt to rectify the problem created by Hamilton's incompetence, Mill adds Henry Mansel as a target, partly because Mansel could write clearly and therefore serves as a more easily sighted target, partly because "he very often fights a better battle against adversaries" (9:262). Once the work has taken a detour so that it can attack Mansel, the pupil, rather than Hamilton, the teacher, Mill seems to recognize that the detour has led him to his best target, but even that decision is soon reversed.

In fact, the organization of the *Examination* becomes more wayward as it proceeds.[6] Various theories that seem to have no connection to intuitionism must be discussed in the interests of offering a comprehensive survey of Hamilton's thought. That motive leads to a discussion of his work on logic and to a consideration of the "ultimate principles" of his thought. By Chapter XXVII, Mill has decided to attack Hamilton's evaluation of the benefits offered by the study of mathematics, and he can do so only by acknowledging that the topic is not relevant: "Though there is no direct connexion between this and his metaphysical opinions, it affords the most express evidence we have of those fatal *lacunae* in the circle of his knowledge, which unfitted him for taking a comprehensive or even an accurate view of the processes of the human mind in the establishment of truth" (9:470). Yet to make it seem that he has not attacked a straw man, Mill must constantly praise Hamilton's "acuteness," a quality that might make him a worthy target. As soon as Hamilton is credited with such a quality, it again evanesces when Mill points out another instance of Hamilton's obtuseness. That something more than the reputation of one highly esteemed but befuddled thinker is at stake here is clear at the end of Chapter XXIII when Mill quotes at length, one after another, no fewer than thirteen authorities from Aristotle to Du Hamel whose theories disagree with Hamilton's. By this point Mill is accusing Hamilton of misleading the ignorant, playing fast and loose with scientific terminology, and even "embezzling" words from English, Latin, and Greek (9:413–16). Intellectual dispute has become moral attack.

Only in the last third of the *Examination* does it become clear why Hamilton, not Mansel or Ward, was the object of the extraordinary controversial energy that Mill poured into this work. Only in Chapter XXII, "Of Sir William Hamilton's Supposed Improvements in Formal Logic," does it become clear that Hamilton had won his "European celebrity" (9:1) in the only field of inquiry in which Mill believed his own work to be undeniably preeminent and indisputably original. Mill quotes Hamilton's own dismissal of "all previous logicians, 'with the doubtful exception of Aristotle'" (9:385), and he quotes at length the conclusion of a work by Thomas Spencer Baynes, one of Hamilton's pupils, who describes the "true joy" and patriotic pride that all English citizens must feel because Hamilton has made his discoveries "in our own country." Baynes's *Essay on the New Analytic of Logical Forms* ends on a crescendo of fatuous praise for the author's teacher:

We rejoice to know that one has at length arisen, able to recognise and complete the plan of the mighty builder, Aristotle,—to lay the top-stone on that fabric, the foundations of which were laid more than two thousand years ago, by the master-hand of the Stagirite, which, after the labours of many generations of workmen, who have from time to time built up one part here and taken down another there—remains substantially as he left it; but which, when finished, shall be seen to be an edifice of wondrous beauty, harmony, and completeness. (9:386)

The penultimate paragraph of the *Essay*, which Mill does not quote, makes the same point by invoking an imperial version of the language of military conquest that Mill uses about his own work in the 1860s. According to Baynes, Hamilton rules over the "entire region of formal thought, conquering and to conquer"; and he inaugurates "the golden age of simplicity and order" by "dethroning the potentates" who have "long there exercised a usurped authority."[7]

Not only does Baynes erase Mill by erasing all logicians between the two great minds of Aristotle and Hamilton, but he does so in a work published in 1850 and based on notes taken "while attending SIR WILLIAM HAMILTON'S class in 1845–6," years when anyone lecturing on logic would have had plenty of opportunity to read and therefore to cite Mill's *System of Logic*. Baynes never once mentions Mill's work. To add insult to injury, Baynes appends to his essay a long historical survey of all the writers on logic whose works are worthy of notice. Most of the authorities he cites are seventeenth-century writers, but he does refer to "a recent Oxford writer" when he cites the 1848 edition of *Moberly's Lectures on Logic*. Baynes discourses on the "wonder amounting to marvel" that writers of such "real ability" should have left so much territory for Hamilton to conquer. This "wonder" becomes explicable only, according to Baynes, if one grants the "weight of authority" that has blinded such thinkers.[8]

Mill never directly betrays the fact that such studied ignorance or implicit denial of his own work might have affected the *Examination* in any way. In the four chapters on logic, he mentions his *System of Logic* only three times—once in a note, once by name in the text, and once by implication in the text (9:369n, 390, 416). When Mill does refer to his own *System of Logic*, he does so to point out a distinction that

Hamilton has ignored, that "the syllogism is not the form in which we necessarily reason, but a test of reasoning" (9:390). Only in the last section of Chapter XXIII, the last chapter that deals with this issue, does Mill treat directly the formulation on which he based his own claim to originality. If it is not read in the context provided by *A System of Logic,* the reasoning in this passage is somewhat hard to follow. Mill refers to the "admitted truth" that a syllogism is a *petitio principii,* that its conclusion can contain no assertions not already obvious in its premise. Hamilton reveals his dullness by agreeing that this "admitted truth" is "unrefuted, if not unrefutable." He then compounds his error by suggesting that this truth can be disproved by simply rewriting a syllogism so that the conclusion precedes the premise. Mill can resort only to sarcasm: "One might almost imagine that a little irony had been intended here." Surely Hamilton must be joking. Mill then goes on to outline his own attempt to refute this objection by referring to the theory that a syllogism is the "mere interpretation of the record of a previous process" of inference, not a process of inference itself. He does so in an indirect reference to the *Logic:* "This theory, and the grounds of it, having been fully stated in another work, need not be further noticed here" (9:416). He also does not explain that he himself argues that a premise merely contains the conclusion drawn from previous inductions, not the basis of independent deductions. Mill seems to imply that he does not need to refer by name to his book because it is so well known; had Hamilton been able to understand it, he could have avoided the ludicrous procedure of treating the order of the assertions in a syllogism as if that order were not crucial to any efficacy the syllogism might have as a test of reasoning.

Hamilton, however, has done more than simply ignore what Mill had accomplished in the field of logic. In his thirtieth lecture on logic, on which Mill comments that "nothing could be more meagre, trite, and indefinite," Hamilton claims that in the sciences there is "little to be done by the force of individual intellects" (9:368), thereby dismissing all those who set themselves the object of discovery in even the physical sciences, a claim that Mill would not have accepted in any field. This point becomes central again when Mill comments on Hamilton's handling of the topic of sorites, argument through a chain of incomplete syllogisms:

If Sir W. Hamilton had found in any other writer such a misuse of logical language as he is here guilty of, he would have roundly accused him of total ignorance of logical writers. Since it cannot be imputed to any such cause in himself, I can only ascribe it to the passion which appears to have seized him, in the later years of his life, for finding more and more new discoveries to be made in Syllogistic Logic. If he had transported his ardour for originality into the other departments of the science, in which there was so great an unexhausted field for discovery, he might have enlarged the bounds of philosophy to a much greater extent, than I am afraid he will now be found to have done. (9:411)

Here the subtext is not hard to read: Hamilton, who has dismissed the possibility of making original discoveries, must have been struck by some aberrant passion of old age to think that he could make discoveries in the field of logic in which Mill himself had made the only discovery that mattered. The "ardour for originality" here is as much Mill's as it is Hamilton's.

By focusing in both general and specific ways on the intellectual issues of central import to Mill, Hamilton had made himself a target almost impossible to resist. Yet Mill's response is, I think, even more personal than such considerations suggest. The relation between Hamilton and his student Baynes, as it emerges in Baynes's *Essay*, parodies the relation between James Mill and his student, John Stuart Mill, and it does so in ways that highlight the links between questions of authority, originality, and pedagogy. Baynes's essay was written in a competition that Hamilton sponsored to elicit expositions of his own ideas. Baynes won this prize, and Mill, who is normally quite cavalier about giving subtitles or even full titles in his footnotes, makes sure that he cites the whole title of Baynes's work, *An Essay on the New Analytic of Logical Forms, being that which gained the prize proposed by Sir William Hamilton in the year 1846 for the best exposition of the new Doctrine propounded in his Lectures. With an Historical Appendix* (9:385–86n). The work is prefaced by "Sir William Hamilton's Requirements for the Essay," and it concludes with a "Note by Sir W. Hamilton." This sycophantic display of the relation between teacher and student, the complete abasement and dependence of the latter proved by the student's putting of the teacher's ideas into writing, is simply a more extreme example of the relation typical of John Stuart Mill's training in political economy, logic, and, most particularly, associationism. His first published essay, like Baynes's, was an elaboration and defense of his teacher's ideas. If later on Mill had decided to publish as a separate volume the notes that he appended to James Mill's *Analysis,* a plan he did consider adopting, those notes would have become, even more clearly, the equivalent, in Mill's intellectual development, of Baynes's *Essay.*

Imitative writing had, as I have stressed, an important role in John Mill's education and in his development of his identification of his character and his writing. Baynes's *Essay* exhibits the perils of such a process: the only authority that Baynes can claim must rest on his status as Hamilton's student. Baynes stresses, in fact, that he does not know very much about his subject—a fact that his silence about Mill's work certainly seems to prove. To Baynes, this disqualification does not seem to matter, however, since taking notes on Hamilton's lectures grants him vicariously the authority of his teacher. If Baynes had known more about logic, Mill might have commented, he would not have been so sanguine about Hamilton's importance. To Mill, who was both a more intelligent, more learned student of a better teacher and a writer more able to question himself and his knowledge, such a direct line of authorization was never quite so reassuring. By granting the teacher authority, the student implicitly denies his or her own originality. As soon as the student demonstrates such independence, the teacher loses a measure of his or her authority over the student, although most good teachers are glad to do so.

To the link between authority and pedagogy so obvious in Baynes's *Essay* is added, in the case of the two Mills, the much stronger and more highly charged bond between authority and paternity. Baynes might well have found the preeminence he granted to Hamilton more unsettling if Hamilton had been his father. Mill often referred to the power granted by tradition to the father when he treated political theories based on the analogy between the state and the family: monarchy seems "natural" because it is "framed on the model of the paternal, which is anterior to society itself, and, as [its supporters] contend, the most natural authority of all" (21:269). Although Mill characteristically objected to such lines of argument, he had to recognize their force. Paternal power could only be increased, as well, when the father in question was a writer. The Latin term for authority (*auctoritas*) evolved from the same root (*auctor*) that stands behind *author* and *authorize*.[9] James Mill is defined by his work as a writer; as his son famously put it, "I was born in London, on the 20th of May 1806, and was the eldest son of James Mill, the author of *The History of British India*" (1:5). Numerous commentators have noted the remarkable double act of engendering to which this sentence points, the child at the beginning of the sentence being rendered equivalent to the book at its end. Yet the link is quite conventional and conventionally Christian. God authored the world and therefore rules it, a conjunction that Mill points to in the *Autobiography* when he grants God the titles of "Author and Governor" (1:47). St. Augustine extends this link to Christ and to the act of authorship when he defines the Son as one who holds power by virtue of God's authorship of him and by virtue of the Son's authorship of the Gospels. In *Paradise Lost,* Milton wryly parodies these relations when Sin addresses her father, Satan:

> Thou art my Father, thou my Author, thou
> My being gav'st me; whom should I obey
> But thee, whom follow? (2:864–66)

Such a customary imperative that the child follow the father or that the student follow the teacher inevitably conflicts with the desire for independence, cast in intellectual terms as the desire for originality.

That such issues were important to Mill, he admits only indirectly in the *Autobiography*. On the surface, that work seems intended to prove that John Stuart Mill contentedly played the roles only of son, student, and follower. He is most anxious, however, to prove that his father was a thinker exhibiting both independence and originality. James Mill, whom history is happy to treat as Bentham's lieutenant and a lesser thinker than his son, is the figure in the *Autobiography* to whom the issues of authority and influence are most directly related. The entry in John Mill's diary of 1854 casts in terms of influence his dismay over "the oblivion in which my father has fallen" in the eighteen years after his death: "He had no little influence on opinion while he lived, most of the reforms which are so much boasted of may be traced mainly to him," but not even his name was known among those who had reached maturity after 1836 (27:642). If one of the declared motives behind the writing of the *Autobiography* was John Mill's desire to repay his intellectual debts, another unstated and closely related motive was the equally obvious desire to give publicity to his father's name and to raise it from oblivion.[10]

The *Autobiography* continually exhibits that second motive as if to prove that Mill's view of his father was wholly positive and unambivalent. In Chapter VI, in the panegyric for his father's intellectual gifts that is occasioned by the need to record his death, Mill's claims for James Mill are unequivocal. He is "one of the most original thinkers of his time" and "quite as much the head and leader of the intellectual radicals in England, as Voltaire was of the *philosophes* in France." Over and over again on behalf of his father, Mill demonstrates the anxiety of influence. James Mill was "anything but Bentham's mere follower and disciple." While Mill concedes that his father's ultimate achievement cannot equal Bentham's, he claims that in the "power of influencing by mere force of mind and character," James Mill was succeeded by "no equal among men" and by only "one among women" (1:213). Earlier, in Chapter IV, Mill carefully elucidates the workings of such power. Bentham may have influenced others by his writings, but James Mill "exercised a far greater personal ascendancy" through his conversation. The crucial test of authority for Mill is whether one has disciples. Bentham, according to this measure, had no authority: it is "simply ridiculous" to think that he was "surrounded by a band of disciples who received their opinions from his lips." On this score, James Mill holds sway. The "supposed school" of Benthamites actually, his son remarks, "had no other existence than what was constituted by the fact, that my father's writings and conversation drew round him a certain number of young men." This judgment, in fact, is borne out by numerous contemporary accounts: even a novel like *Eustace Conway* treats James Mill as the spokesperson for the Utilitarians in the same way that Wordsworth is the chief of the Romantic poets.[11] John Mill then paints a portrait of his father as a "most lively and amusing companion," a portrait that most readers of the earlier chapters of the *Autobiography* may have trouble crediting. Mill, however, insists that his father's personal qualities, as well as his originality, fitted him for the role of intellectual master. His "exalted public spirit," his ability to establish himself as the final judge of another's worth, his courage, and his confidence in reason and progress—all these qualities made natural and almost inevitable the ascendancy that "gave the distinguishing character to Benthamic or utilitarian propagandism" (1:103,105).

James Mill himself had testified to the significance of such power when he declared in one of his essays, "The grand object of human desire is a command over the wills of other men."[12] In an act of filial piety, his son pays homage to his father in the lengthy and detailed evidence that he gives of James Mill's ascendancy. Through this topic are introduced a number of figures who might otherwise not appear in the *Autobiography*: Charles Austin, Eyton Tooke, John Black, Charles Buller, and, in a forgivable bit of filial name-dropping, "Strutt, afterwards Lord Belper, and the present Lord Romilly, with whose eminent father, Sir Samuel, my father had of old been on terms of friendship" (1:105). On this topic, John Mill indulges a verbal inventiveness that, except in the case of his mental crisis, is unusual indeed in the *Autobiography*. James Mill's opinions "flowed from him in a continued stream" and into different "channels." Influence of this sort has a ripple effect. James Mill "forms" his son's mind, and his son in turn acts as his father's agent and exercises "considerable influence . . . over various young men who became, in their turn, propagandists." Influence is also like electric current "received and transmitted" through "various other persons" (1:105). James Mill is a "great centre of light" or the element that gives "colour and character" to the thought of the other Philosophic Radicals (1:107). James Mill's opinions at times "fell singly scattered" like seed on fertile ground (1:105).

The last of these metaphors, in which ideas appear as seed, is ultimately the most significant. In Mill's earlier essays, Bentham and Coleridge may be the "two great seminal minds of England in their age" (10:77), but in the *Autobiography* they are accorded no such status. James Mill is the one who proves his influence by the seed he plants. The use of this metaphor in the *Autobiography* depends, I think, on the famous distinction that Socrates draws between "written discourse" and the "real and living discourse," the speech, "of the person who understands the subject" at hand. The distinction, mentioned in the *Examination*, appears at full length in the *Phaedrus*, one of the Platonic dialogues that Mill published in the 1830s. Writing, Socrates points out, is seed that may be planted at the wrong season or on barren ground; seed that is meant to bear fruit of "what is just, and noble, and good" should not, therefore, be sown "with a pen and black liquid." It is "far better" that "any one, employing the dialectical art, and find-ing a mind which affords a suitable soil, sows and plants therein, with knowledge, discourses which can defend themselves and him who sows them, and which are not barren, but in their turn bear seed, from whence other discourses being reared up in other minds, can make their truths immortal" (11:91). If James Mill's written discourse, his essays and books, have fallen on barren ground, as his son's diary entry in 1854 suggests, then his influence can be established only by defining it as the warm seed of talk that falls on the ready ground of his listeners' minds. That is precisely how James Mill appears in the *Autobiography* and how he is distinguished from Bentham: "The influ-ence which Bentham exercised was by his writings," but James Mill's conversation spread the seed of his thought and, further, "warmed into life and activity every germ of similar virtue that existed in the minds he came in contact with" (1:105).

This metaphor, naturally enough, is used most strikingly in the case of James Mill's ascendancy over his son. As a very young boy lis-tening to very sophisticated topics, John Mill often heard from his father ideas beyond his comprehension; but they "left seed behind, which germinated in due season" (1:25). Throughout the *Autobiog-raphy*, Mill's account is faithful to the implications of this metaphor. James Mill's is the seminal mind; John Mill's is the one that bears the impress of his father's originality. Careful to defend his father from a charge of belatedness in relation to Bentham, he is careless of his own reputation on this score. Some minds, like James Mill's, are genuinely creative; others, like his son's, simply pass on and share the bounty they have received. Comments on his father's "personal ascendancy" and originality are usually preceded or followed by admissions of "my own inferiority" (1:213).

The same process in which the father's authority is explicitly de-fended while the son's is ignored or denied appears in the *Examination*, a text that illuminates and is illuminated by Mill's earlier tactics in the *Autobiography*. Although Mill's own works are relegated to the foot-notes or to indirect references in the *Examination*, Mill cites chapter and verse when it comes to James Mill's writings, quoting his father at length in the body of the text. Such quotations certainly seem defen-sive: Hamilton enjoys the "European celebrity" that ought to belong to other, better thinkers, and Hamilton nowhere proves that point more forcefully than when he quotes James Mill and then ignores his arguments. John Stuart Mill objects with particular force to Hamilton's blindness to the importance of his father's treatment of the "law of Inseparable Association," the law that explains the apparent indistinguishability of the ideas that have been frequently experienced together. To James Mill, his son declares, "more than to any other thinker, mankind are indebted for recalling the attention of philosophers to this law." John Mill then quotes a long passage from the *Analysis,* a passage that remained unappended in the revised edition of 1869 (1:90–94), which he prefaces by taking Hamilton to task for discussing "a theory of so wide a scope and such large consequences" in a "bye corner of his work, incidentally to one of the smallest questions therein discussed" (9:252).

If Hamilton has made a "disparaging reflection of Mr. Mill's philosophy in general," as John Stuart Mill accuses him of doing, he is paid back in full measure: "Sir W. Hamilton's authority can have little weight against the doctrine which accounts for the more complex parts of our mental constitution by the laws of association, when it is so evident that he rejected the doctrine . . . having taken for granted that it did not deserve examination" (9:255). The authority for Mill's rejection of Hamilton is, of course, that he has thoroughly "examined" Hamilton's ideas, but even more viscerally, that Hamilton has rejected Mill's father's ideas. Mill had earlier gotten himself into a nasty tangle with the editor of the *Edinburgh Review* over his father's reputation when there appeared in its pages a review containing Bentham's criticisms of James Mill. John Mill accused the editor of disloyalty to an old friend and forced him finally to print, in a highly unusual move, the clarification that John Mill had written. Although Mill claimed that "the most honest self examination" did not reveal that he had exhibited "any oversusceptibility" on this occasion (13:600), both the *Examination* and the *Autobiography* reveal how excessive such touchiness could be.

Yet the *Autobiography*—more indirectly and, for that reason, perhaps more forcefully—also evidences Mill's abiding concern to establish his own originality and authority. He so constantly disclaims a right to these powers that his anxiety cannot but surface. Mill's uncertainty about his power to initiate and to lead is evident in the inconsistencies of his account of where, when, how, and whether he emerged as an original thinker. At one point Mill claims that articles published in 1826 contained "original thinking," but he immediately undercuts that claim with a qualification: "as far as that name can be applied to old ideas in new forms and connexions" (1:123). Later he suggests that his "real inauguration as an original and independent thinker" came before 1829 during the informal morning study sessions in which he and his friends tenaciously discussed every detail of political economy, logic, and psychology (1:127). On matters of influence, he is equally evasive or uncertain. His earliest association with his peers in the Utilitarian Society, which he himself founded, allowed him to be "for some time a sort of leader" and exert "considerable influence" over other youths. As soon as he makes this assertion, however, Mill compromises it. He influenced none of the members of the Utilitarian Society who became his "intimate companions—no one of whom was in any sense of the word a disciple, but all of them independent thinkers on their own basis" (1:83). In other words, anyone worth influencing was beyond the reach of Mill's suasion. Similar qualifications undercut his status in the account he gives of his journalistic efforts in the *London and Westminster Review* and elsewhere. From 1832 to 1839, he had sown both sorts of seed, using "personal influence" and his writings to rouse life in the Philosophic Radicals (1:205). But Mill, by his own account, labored in vain. Only his championship of Lord Durham's ideas on Canadian self-government and his praise of Carlyle's *French Revolution* had any effect. In the latter case, he undercuts his efforts by admitting that anybody who had "expressed the same opinion at the same precise time . . . would have produced the same effect" (1:225)— exactly the terms that James Mill had used to dismiss Luther's agency in the Reformation.

The power to create and the power to lead, qualities so excessively granted his father, are precisely those which Mill denies himself even as he exhibits his longing to claim them. "I thought for myself almost from the first," Mill explains (1:33), but he serves throughout as the chief witness against this assertion. Although he declares, "Mine . . . was not an education of cram," the amount of time he spent "diting" his father's ideas made of the son, at least temporarily, more the "mere parroter" than he liked to admit (1:35).[13] In one of his frequent attacks on the narrowness of English emotional and intellectual life, Mill claims that its debilitating limitations "reduce" the English "as spiritual beings, to a kind of negative existence" (1:61). In the portrait that he paints of himself in the *Autobiography*, if not elsewhere, that reduction might well apply to his own existence. His difficulty asserting his own influence and originality stem from his inability to believe that he has the mind and the will either to be original or to attract followers. Despite his assertions to the contrary, Mill's *Autobiography* portrays his education as one whose methods inevitably made the achievement of one's own influence and authority insuperably difficult.

In other contexts, Mill proved himself acutely aware of the contemporary controversy over pedagogical methods, and the comments he made outside the *Autobiography*, when he was not discussing his own education, explain the defensiveness with which he treats these issues there. In a notice written in 1837 about several works published by the Society for the Diffusion of Useful Knowledge, Mill refers to the "two methods" of teaching "as remote from each other as light from darkness"—"the system of *cram*" and "the system of cultivating mental *power*." Cram involves stuffing a child's memory with words that have no meaning, and Mill attacks in particular the "climax" of this method, the system advocated by the French mathematician Joseph Jacotot. This method "surpasses all former specimens of the *cram* method in this, that former cram-doctors crammed an unfortunate child's memory with abstract propositions [without] meaning; but Jacotot . . . actually makes the unfortunate creature get by rote not only the propositions, but the reasons too!" (24:786–87). Subjects of former methods of cram were at least spared having to memorize the reasoning behind ideas they could not possibly understand; new, improved methods of cram double the burden.

This passage quite accurately evaluates and damns the method by which, for instance, James Mill first introduced the subject of logic to his son. In the second of the two distinct references to physical setting in the *Autobiography*, Mill recounts the moment at which his father first broached this all-important subject:

> I well remember how, and in what particular walk, in the neighbourhood of Bagshot Heath . . . [my father] first attempted by questions to make me think on the subject, and frame some conception of what constituted the utility of the syllogistic logic, and when I had failed in this, to make me understand it by explana-

tions. The explanations did not make the matter at all clear to me at the time; but they were not therefore useless; they remained as a nucleus for my observations and reflections to crystallize upon; the import of his general remarks being interpreted to me, by the particular instances which came under my notice afterwards. (1:21,23)

James Mill's educational practices, his parody of the Socratic method, are even more potentially debilitating than Jacotot's. The student is not asked to repeat orally an explanation he cannot understand; rather, he must silently review it until he is able to comprehend it; he becomes his own taskmaster as well as his own slave. The student must accept the validity of the teacher's ideas and mold later thought and experience to the form they impose. The teacher's incomprehensible explanation becomes the "nucleus," the annoying grain of sand around which the pupil will develop the pearl of wisdom. The power in this form of education is all on the side of the teacher. One wonders why James Mill persisted if his motives did not involve proving his intellectual superiority at his son's expense. John Mill, however, refuses to see the procedure in this light. The statements he makes to prove his independence prove instead his utter dependence: although "anything which could be found out by thinking, I was never told, until I had exhausted my efforts to find it out for myself. . . . my recollection of such matters is almost wholly of failures, hardly ever of success" (1:35). How could it be otherwise? Repeated failures to solve a problem on one's own can lead only to a sense of impotence.[14]

In view of the way in which Mill was first introduced to the subject of logic, it is not surprising that the question of originality became both the subject and the goal of his treatise on logic. As he explains in the *Autobiography*, "I . . . puzzled myself, like others before me, with the great paradox of the discovery of new truths by general reasoning." Mill is not original even in the questions he asks about originality. If the conclusions of the syllogism are already implied in its premise, how "could [it] be a new truth"? When Mill felt able to answer this question, he felt capable of "produc[ing] a work on Logic, of some originality and value," but the process of arriving at the answer was itself derivative: Mill says he simply extended Dugald Stewart's ideas on axioms by applying them to "all general propositions." This point is highlighted by the composition history of the *Logic* that Mill offers in the *Autobiography*. For five years, he explains, work on the *Logic* was halted: "I had come to the end of my tether." Significantly, Mill hoped to escape this impasse by reading "any book which seemed to promise light on the subject" (1:189,191). A book did indeed offer Mill the light he was looking for, but he is careful to say that Whewell's *History of the Inductive Sciences,* on which he depended so heavily, was misguided in its "philosophy," but "the materials were there, for my own thoughts to work upon" (1:215).

Competing impulses to claim and to deny the originality of his ideas and, therefore, his authority conflict throughout Mill's *Logic.* In all eight editions that were published in his lifetime, an obvious instance of such impulses in the preface remained untouched. In the first sentence Mill demurs, "This book makes no pretence of giving to the world a new theory of the intellectual operations," but he immediately qualifies that point. The ability to organize ideas, to cement and harmonize and disentangle different positions "require[s] a considerable amount of original speculation" (7:cxi). Such concerns and the inevitable contradictions they involve appear throughout the text. In a note in Chapter V of Book II, Mill draws attention to the similarity of his thinking to that of Sir John Herschel's article on Whewell. Mill defends the "whole chapter" he is writing by saying it was composed "before I had seen the article, (the greater part, indeed, before it was published)," as if he needs the facts offered by publication dates to support his veracity, and then he makes such scrupulosity seem irrelevant: "It is not my object to occupy the reader's attention with a matter so unimportant as the degree of originality which may or may not belong to any portion of my own speculations" (7:248n). In fact, the questions raised in this note were so clearly the reverse of "unimportant" that Mill retained it in later editions, merely changing its location in the chapter to give it more prominence.

Such defensive self-contradictions appear throughout Mill's works. The prefatory remarks to *Principles of Political Economy, On Liberty,* and *Essays on Some Unsettled Questions of Political Economy* all parade Mill's anxiety about influence. In his *Considerations of Representative Government,* he even accuses himself of having cribbed his material from his own earlier works: readers of his previous books, he cautions, will find nothing new here (19:373). In his early essay "On Genius," an essay whose ideas he later disavowed, Mill even went so far as to claim that knowing anything beyond what is "immediately obvious to the senses" is an act of originality (1:332). But these issues were more pertinent to the writing of the *Logic* than to any other of his works because it was Mill's first book, because it was written during the last years of his father's life and published after his death as a kind of declaration of independence, because it was the product of Mill's thought before Harriet Taylor joined him in their "joint productions," and because it was, in fact, so highly derivative a work.

As the defensive note on Comte that Mill added in the last section drafted for the *Autobiography* in 1869–70 proves, the *Logic* was widely enough judged to be derivative as to make Mill quite uncomfortable: "The amount of these obligations [to Comte] is far less than has sometimes been asserted" (1:255n). Mill himself cites one of those assertions in a note added in 1867 to the *Examination* when he corrects a critic's "mistakes" regarding Mill's debt to Comte: "A short list would exhaust the chapters, and even the pages, which contain" thought indebted to Comte (9:216–17n). In the *Autobiography,* Mill defends himself against this charge by referring the reader back to one of its earlier sections, saying that he has already outlined his debt to Comte even as he recapitulates that outline: "It is only in the concluding Book, on the Logic of the Moral Sciences, that I owe to him any radical improvement in my conception of the application of logical methods. This improvement I have stated and characterized in a former part of the present Memoir" (1:255n). In the "former part," written first in the 1850s, a rather different story is told of the "radical improvement" that Comte's *Cours de philosophie positive* offered the *Logic.* There Mill, as usual, very carefully compares the composition history of his book and the publication dates of the various volumes of Comte's major work. After Mill had drafted two-thirds of the *Logic,* he read the two volumes of the *Cours* that had then been published. Before this time, Mill had arrived at his analysis of induction; Comte had nothing to offer to this analysis because he remained oblivious to the importance of "the exact definition of the conditions of proof." Although Comte provided an "essential service" in Mill's rewriting of the draft he had finished and in his writing of "some of the parts which still remained to be thought out," Mill emphasizes his disagreement with Comte on "social subjects." Mill does admit that Comte's Inverse

Deductive Method was "entirely new" to him and that without Comte, "I might not soon (if ever) have arrived at it" (1:217,219), but he counters that admission of indebtedness with a long digression on Comte's later work, his *Système de politique positive*, to which, since it was not published until 1851–54, Mill could not possibly be indebted in the work on logic completed in 1841. In the *Système*, Comte propounded social thought "truly alarming to think of": "the completest system of spiritual and temporal despotism, which ever yet emanated from a human brain, unless possibly that of Ignatius Loyola" (1:221). With that bit of conventional anti-Catholic prejudice, Mill puts so much distance between himself and Comte that the readers of his later note may be excused if they have not properly gauged the "radical improvement" that the French thinker is supposed to have made in Mill's thought. Indeed, the inverse deductive method is, as Mill acknowledged, the basis of all he hoped to achieve in the science of society and, particularly, in the creation of ethology. And to Comte Mill owed that method.

If Mill was so cagily defensive and even deceptive when it came to sources he was willing to acknowledge, he may have been even more misleading about those sources he did not acknowledge. Such is, I think, the case. Take, for instance, his treatment of his reading of Herschel's *Preliminary Discourse on the Study of Natural Philosophy* (1831). In the *Autobiography*, Mill explains that he had read Herschel's work several years before Whewell's but with "little profit." In the *Early Draft*, however, Mill notes parenthetically that he "even reviewed" the book in which he "found little help" (1:216)—that he thought it worthy of such attention suggests perhaps a larger role for this source than Mill is willing to admit. Reading Whewell's *History of the Inductive Sciences* leads Mill back to Herschel, according to the account in the *Autobiography*, "and I was able to measure the progress my mind had made, by the great help I now found in this work" (1:217). Mill attributes the active power to his mind, not to any "seeds" that Herschel's work might earlier have sown. A look at the review Mill wrote of Herschel's book in 1831 reveals how great a debt he is later willing to overlook. The excited tone in which the young reviewer speaks of Herschel's plans to use science as a model for other modes of inquiry and of his claims about the need to develop a philosophy of philosophy are equaled in the record of Mill's intellectual development only by his account in the *Autobiography* of his reading of Dumont's Bentham. Mill writes as if, in reading Herschel, he had found his vocation. He quotes a "noble passage" in which Herschel prophesies that progress in the physical conditions of human life may "impress something of the well weighted and progressive character of science on the more complicated conduct of our social and moral relations": "Great and noble ends are to be achieved, by which the conditions of the whole species should be permanently bettered" (22:286–87). In the context of Mill's failed political ambitions, the context that I find crucial to all his intellectual endeavors, one can hardly avoid seeing why Herschel's commitment to philosophy as a source of social improvement would be so inspiring to Mill in the early 1830s, why it would reconcile theory and practice and therefore serve as an authorization of the writing of the *Logic*. But the *Autobiography* refuses Herschel that role: his work, when read in 1831, offered Mill "little help." Exactly seven months after the publication of the review on Herschel, Mill was writing at length to John Sterling about the "only thing" he was "really fit for"—the science of investigation—and he quotes F. D. Maurice on the centrality of method to all inquiry. Mill then announces his plans to write a "treatise" on logic (12:78–79), but there is no more in this letter than there is in the *Autobiography* about Herschel's contribution to this development in Mill's intellectual ambitions, a contribution to which Mill's review of Herschel itself attests.

Other such instances could be adduced, but I will allow myself only one, perhaps the most significant. At the end of the *Logic*, as I have stressed, Mill sets out a program of research in the social sciences, a program that defined what he and other thinkers like himself would try to accomplish in the future. James Mill's *Analysis of the Phenomena of the Human Mind* ends, more concisely, in exactly the same way. After lecturing his contemporaries on their debased and improper use of the word *theory*, after claiming that he has established "the THEORY of the Human Mind" as far as the "imperfection" of his execution will allow, James Mill outlines the work yet to be done:

> If, however, the *Theoretical,* or Expository part of the Doctrine of the Human Mind were perfected; another great branch, the *Practical* (which, to be rationally founded, must be founded on the Theoretical) would still remain. This subject, it appears, might be conveniently treated in three Books:

I. The Book of Logic; containing the Practical Rules for conducting the mind in its search after Truth:

II. The Book of Ethics; or the Book of Rules for regulating the actions of human beings, so as to deduce from them the greatest amount of good, both to the actor himself, and to his fellow-creatures at large:

III. The Book of Education; or the Book of Rules, for training the Individual to the greatest excellence of his nature; that is, to the highest possible state of efficiency (ability and will included), as cause of good to himself, and to his species.

THE END

(Analysis 2:403)

Here, in miniature, is an outline of the work that James Mill's son would undertake. Although James Mill distributes the labels "theoretical" and "practical" in ways that his son would not, although he does not envision an intermediate science between psychology and sociology or even use the latter term, in some ways this program is a more accurate forecast of John Mill's work than the list of subjects that he and Harriet Mill drew up in the mid-1850s. The Book of Logic is, of course, the *System of Logic*. Indeed, many of the topics treated in the *Logic* are those treated in the *Analysis*—language, classification, relative terms, belief, consciousness. The Book of Ethics foretells the writing of the *Principles of Political Economy, On Liberty, Considerations of Representative Government, Utilitarianism,* and *The Subjection of Women,* all of which deal with the ethical implications of the social or political or economic issues they treat. The Book of Education that James Mill envisioned corresponds to his son's unwritten ethology. By the 1860s, as I have noted, Mill had stopped using the word *ethology* altogether, having substituted for it the more widely accepted term *education*. The research agenda that James Mill published in 1829 was, therefore, remarkably prescient. John Stuart Mill was not only prepared by his father to do the work he did; James Mill also defined that work, just as he defined his son's professional status by putting him at his desk in the India House.

That outcome is not, however, the story of his life as Mill tells it in the *Autobiography*. He focuses on the limitations of James Mill's thought as relentlessly if not as wittily as Macaulay had done, claiming in fact that understanding why his father's "method of philosophizing in politics" was not "legitimate" laid the foundation for the work in Book VI of the *Logic* (1:167,169). Earlier, writing as a youth not yet out of his teens, John Mill could acknowledge, as openly as anonymous publication in the *Westminster Review* would allow, that he had "no higher ambition than that of treading in [the] steps" of "Mr. Mill, the historian of British India" (21:4,4n). As he matured, the role of the dutiful follower in paternal footsteps became one he could not acknowledge publicly. By contrast, James Mill, as a mature writer in his own right, with his magnum opus already behind him, was quite comfortable in admitting that on a particular subject he along with all others "who proceed in this road, . . . can do little else than travel in [Bentham's] steps."[15] James Mill was freed from the need to feel any jealousy about his own originality and authority by his belief in the "inessentiality" of the particular agent doing the work whose time had come. John Stuart Mill could not confront such issues with either disinterest or equanimity. His desire to claim the authority that he attributed to his father, the authority that his father rarely pursued as an end in itself, impresses itself on his writings and particularly on the *Autobiography*, the record of his writings. He expresses his jealous regard for his own status by defending his father's, but belittles his father's contributions to his own intellectual career.

In the *Autobiography*, similar considerations account for the extraordinary influence and authority that Mill grants to Harriet Mill. As in his account of his professional dilemmas, his treatment of her is a screen behind which his genuinely obsessive self-regard in intellectual matters can both conceal and exhibit itself. Because Mill and his wife were "two persons [who had] their thoughts and speculations completely in common," he argues, "it is of little consequence in respect to the question of originality which of them holds the pen." In fact, Mill claims both originality and influence only in his wife's name. "The most valuable ideas" of his writings "originated with her," and their value is measured precisely in terms of their influence: her ideas have been "most fruitful of important results" and have won the "success and reputation of the works themselves" (1:251). Mill attributes to her the ability to see the relation between "the exigencies of human society" and his own more abstract philosophical concerns. In this respect he is eminently "her pupil" (1:257). As such, his role is, of course, the one he played as a young boy making notes on his father's lectures on political economy or recounting in his own words what he had read: he is "an interpreter of original thinkers, and mediator between them and the public." Yet when he says that he "had always a humble opinion of my own powers as an original thinker," he adds a qualification that turns humility into something like pridefulness: his work is not original "except in abstract science (logic, metaphysics, and the theoretic principles of political economy and politics)" (1:251). In how many fields, one wants to ask, does Mill have to grant himself originality before he becomes "an original thinker"?

Mill's account of his intellectual relation to Harriet Mill goes on to undercut even such indirect assertions of incipient self-satisfaction. His manysidedness, the basis of his claim to intellectual usefulness, appears in this account as a lack of conviction or rigor: he is a kind of philosophical jellyfish, amorphous enough to conform to the shape of any new doctrine that reaches him; Harriet Mill, on the contrary, is the voice of authority constantly warning him against his own weakness of will and lack of determination. She "render[s him] bolder" in his thinking and keeps him to the straight and narrow of radical and democratic thought (1:257). "Her steadying influence," Mill claims, "often protected" him from allowing new ideas to usurp the place of the old (1:259). The image of Harriet Mill that emerges here is not at all attractive; ironically, Mill himself may have done as much to damage her reputation as her detractors have been able to do. If James Mill appears in the *Autobiography* as the teacher cruelly proving his own worth by humiliating his defenseless pupil, Harriet Mill is the thin-lipped schoolmarm ready to dampen any new intellectual enthusiasm by slapping the wrist of her young scholar so that she can maintain for him his ideological purity. Authority and influence, powers combined in Harriet Mill's ascendancy, can go no further.

Or do they extend even this far? Significantly, Mill does not attribute his belief in the equality of women to Harriet Mill. He seems to find demeaning the assumption that this was a lesson "learnt from her." Rather, his attitudes, fully developed in all their theoretical implications before he met her, were "the originating cause of the interest she felt in me" (1:253n). Mill further undercuts the preeminence he has granted Harriet Mill in this section of the *Autobiography* by ceding the same power to her daughter, Helen Taylor. Like his wife, Mill's stepdaughter is granted all the motive force in a partnership in which she initiates both thought and action; once again, Mill simply carries out the orders or conveys the ideas she originates. Subject to her suggestion, he writes *The Subjection of Women;* she urges him to speak out on the American Civil War when his dissent against English sympathies with the South is most needed. In commenting on the "great power of original thought" that Mill recognizes in the woman who wanted only to be an actress, he concludes, "Whoever, either now or hereafter, may think of me and of the work I have done, must never forget that it is the product not of one intellect and conscience but of three, the least considerable of whom, and above all the least original, is the one whose name is attached to it" (1:264–65). Such a claim is so excessive that it might be depended upon to elicit disbelief. It makes sense only as a private message of gratitude from Mill to his stepdaughter for her self-sacrifice in coming to serve as his housekeeper and helpmate after the death of her mother. Despite the note in Mill's hand on the manuscript of the *Autobiography,* "To be published without alterations and omissions" (1:2), Mill may simply have expected Helen Taylor to excise such comments before publishing the work, over which he had given her complete control. In fact, in the first edition (1873), as the result of Alexander Bain's almost frantic pleadings, Helen Taylor did delete most of the passages that refer to her, and just such an effect was achieved, although she replaced them with rows of asterisks to tantalize the reader's curiosity.

Yet if Mill had expected these passages to reach a wider audience than their first reader, Helen Taylor, there are other, more obvious ways in which he evidences for one last time his desire not to cede all authority to those around him. Indeed, in the first edition the two long footnotes clarifying and qualifying Mill's indebtedness, first to Harriet Mill and then to Comte, appear on facing pages. The battle that Mill waged for and against his intellectual stature is played out in type, and the body of the text is reduced to six lines on one page and half a sheet on the next so that there is space for Mill's excessive counterclaims.[16] The footnote on Harriet Mill, in particular, constitutes the strong undercurrent that runs against the tidal wave of adulation that he lavishes on her intellectual prowess. Mill's role as the agent of others' thoughts, as translator or propagandist, is paramount in this section of the *Autobiography.* He explains his efforts to popularize Hare's voting scheme, Bain's studies of psychology, and Austin's work on jurisprudence. But his more limited, though patent attempts to defend his own originality suggest how important the issue is to him. By attributing his thought to Harriet Mill or, even less plausibly, to Helen Taylor, he remains the passive receptor envisioned by associationist theory even as his defensive footnotes and the qualifications in them question the influences on his intellectual life that he is willing to acknowledge.

THE INTELLECTUAL SUBJECTION
OF *ON LIBERTY*

In the first long footnote in the *Autobiography*, in which Mill distracts attention from his debt to Comte by holding him out as a "monumental warning" of the dangers involved in losing "sight" of the "value of Liberty and of Individuality," Mill restores his focus in the next paragraph with an awkward and uncharacteristic rhetorical signpost, "To return to myself" (1:221). The argument, however, has been about Mill himself all along. For him, questions of intellectual priority and indebtedness were related to the larger social and political issues of liberty and individuality, and nowhere is that fact more central than in the work in which he treats those larger issues directly, *On Liberty*. Not surprisingly, Mill's account of the intellectual stature that he exhibited in writing *On Liberty* is the most contradictory and self-defeating in the *Autobiography*. Mill explains that the volume, uncharacteristically focusing as it does on one idea, has no claim to originality except "that which every thoughtful mind gives to its own mode of conceiving and expressing truths which are common property" (1:260).[17] Mill seems here to be back in the realm of the essay "On Genius," where everything is original and, therefore, nothing can be. Yet here, in the context of the discussion of a book that Mill attributes more "emphatically" than any other to Harriet Mill's "mode of thinking," such a qualification is telling (1:259). Does he mean to suggest that Harriet Mill is not actually any more capable of originating ideas than he is? In dedicating *On Liberty* to Harriet Mill, he claims that it has been revised by her "in a very insufficient degree" (18:216). In the *Autobiography*, however, her meticulous revisions are so extensive that the book "surpasses, as a mere specimen of composition," any other work with Mill's name on it (1:259). Is her function, then, as Jack Stillinger proves in his examination of the *Autobiography,* a "mere" matter of editorial tinkering?

The puzzles proliferate as the discussion continues. Mill lists many of those whose ideas on individualism have preceded the publication of *On Liberty*—Pestalozzi, Wilhelm von Humboldt, "a whole school of German authors," Goethe, William Maccall, and Josiah Warren. (Carlyle with his *Sartor Resartus* might well be represented here, but he is not.) Mill then justifies not having mentioned any of these thinkers but one in the text of his own work because he makes no claim that it is either an original contribution to or a history of the subject. Then his desire for priority surfaces again: "It is hardly necessary here to remark that there are abundant differences in detail, between the conception of the doctrine by any of the predecessors I have mentioned, and that set forth in the book" (1:260–61). Such wavering between submission to and rejection of his own belatedness recalls Mill's earlier, inconsistent account of his emergence as an independent thinker. Such wavering might also suggest that the devotion to liberty and individuality propounded in Mill's "kind of philosophic text-book of a single truth" (1:259) is not quite so single-minded as he claims. That, I will argue, is precisely the case.

By examining the basis for the liberty that Mill wishes to grant the individual in *On Liberty,* it is possible to understand not only the nature of the social and political authority that he saw as valid and beneficial, but also the nature of his intellectual debt to those teachers whose influence over him he most wanted to ignore. *On Liberty* might have been as appropriately entitled *On Authority* or, even more specifically still, *On the Influence of Authority.* Mill, however, wanted to emphasize the values he apparently cherished rather than the dangers to them posed by modern society. As it turns out, I think, Mill argues covertly for authority and so completely redefines liberty as to make it unrecognizable by any common or traditional standards. When he does so, he exhibits his subjection not only to his times but to his first teachers.

For all the display of the predecessors of *On Liberty* that Mill makes in the *Autobiography,* he does not mention the two most significant, Jeremy Bentham and James Mill. Indeed, *On Liberty* is often seen as the work in which John Mill most thoroughly repudiates his Utilitarian inheritance, in which he is least willing to follow in the footsteps of either Bentham or his father.[18] But just as John Mill held that indirect teaching is the most effective, *On Liberty* demonstrates that Mill's unacknowledged sources made the greatest impress on his thought. In the *Autobiography* when Mill wants to evaluate his debt to Bentham, he focuses on Bentham's desire to apply scientific methods of classification to social and legal problems—the "vast mental domain" that Dumont's Bentham opened up for Mill involved the "scientific classification [of] the great and complex subjects of Punishable Acts" (1:69). Yet Mill says nothing directly in the *Autobiography* about the panopticon, Bentham's plan for a penitentiary that would as effectively compartmentalize the human beings undergoing punishment as his taxonomies would classify punishable acts. It is this scheme, I think, that is, of all Bentham's ideas, the one most relevant to *On Liberty*.

Bentham's panopticon, for which he has regained a certain notoriety through Michel Foucault's treatment of it as the epitome of modern society in *Discipline and Punish,* involved an architecture of segregation and subjection.[19] Elaborating on Sir Samuel Bentham's "simple idea in architecture," Jeremy Bentham envisions a building, shaped like a wheel, that would house around its rim story after story of cells in which its inmates would be confined and exposed for constant surveillance by the unseen keeper in a central "inspector's lodge." As the inmates became habituated to the surveillance that at any time might or might not be trained upon them, they would, so Bentham thought, begin to surveille themselves, and the disciplinary structure of the building would become a mechanism to promote self-discipline. In the *Panopticon; or, The Inspection House* (1791), Bentham emphasizes certain features of the system that Foucault ignores.[20] In the plate on which the well-known elevation of the building appears (figure 3a), there is another drawing of three panoptic structures on one plot of ground (figure 3b). They are joined by a common exercise yard where prisoners are to be separated by moral categories: quiet old offenders as opposed to daring old offenders, dissolute females as opposed to decent females. All these areas and buildings are connected by covered and, therefore, secret passageways. Each cell in a panopticon Bentham imagines as connected to the inspector's lodge by separate speaking tubes; the cells are connected to each other by an indoor water supply and an indoor plumbing system with a sort of rudimentary toilet in each cell. In the second postscript to the *Panopticon,* in which Ben-

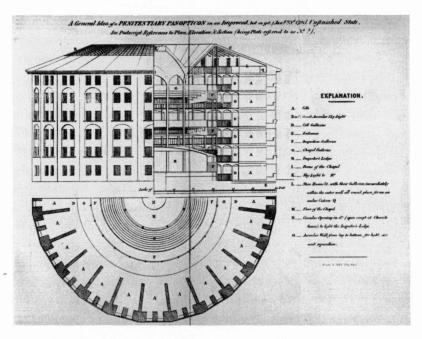

FIGURE 3.

Two Views of Bentham's Panopticon: (a) Elevation: A designates the cells;
F, the inspection galleries; and H, the inspector's lodge.

tham outlines the management of the system, he stresses the utility
of "limited association," whereby a small number of prisoners in each
cell will be responsible for each other: "so many comrades, so many
inspectors" (164).

The record of Mill's reading strongly suggests that he knew Bentham's *Panopticon*, but the record of Mill's writing would not seem to
prove that it had caught his attention in any significant way.[21] In his
newspaper account of Bentham's death, Mill refers in a perfunctory
way to the *Panopticon* as "an admirable work on prison discipline"
(23:473), thereby ignoring what was for Bentham the work's chief
value, the fact that this structure could be adapted to serve as the
model for factories, schools, hospitals, reformatories, insane asylums,
as well as prisons. In an earlier newspaper article on the treadmill,
published when Mill was only seventeen, five or six months after he
entered the India House, Mill demonstrated his understanding of
one of Bentham's panoptical principles: punishment must be "visible

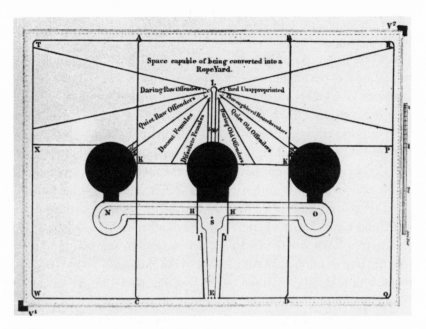

(b) Three panoptical structures joined by an exercise yard. (Bentham, *Works*, ed. John Bowring [1843], vol. 4). Courtesy of the Northwestern University Library.

to every eye." "Reformatory discipline," which involves substituting "useful habits" for "pernicious," the writer goes on, must be separated entirely from punishment. In an extraordinary and extraordinarily erroneous instance of anxiety for James Mill's originality, his son then refers the reader James Mill's article on prisons, "Prisons and Prison Discipline," in which, John Mill claims, the distinction between punishment and reformation is formulated for the first time (22:69–70). James Mill, however, clearly acknowledges both at the end and at the beginning of the *Encyclopædia Britannica* article cited by his son that his work simply condenses and recapitulates Bentham's work: there is "not . . . an idea that did not originate with Mr. Bentham." While ignoring Bentham's influence on James Mill, the young Mill tries to elevate his father as an authority. Yet even after the cooling of relations between Bentham and James Mill, Bentham praised the elder Mill as a "sincere trumpeter of Panopticon."[22] Unlike his father, however, John Stuart Mill seems not to have been as enthusiastic about using India, for instance, as a laboratory in which to test the virtues of the inspection house or "elaboratory."

Yet Mill's silence on the subject is not, after all, so surprising. The educational experiment to which James Mill had subjected his son was a private and lonely version of the panopticon. Although it involved only two people, father and son, it also involved the two principles most important to the functioning of this disciplinary mode: segregation and surveillance. The son was kept separate from other boys his age—otherwise, he might have learned the methods and rationale of revolt against parental authority—and seated as he was at his father's desk, he passed hour after hour in fear of his father's scrutiny. The son could never know when his father would raise his head from his eleven-year labor on *The History of British India* to see what and how well the boy was doing. In his account of his education in the *Autobiography,* Mill is clearly mystified by the fact that his father, so obviously "one of the most impatient of men" (1:9), should have allowed himself to suffer the constant interruptions occasioned by the son seated at his side. Mill attributes the arrangement to the lack of Greek/English dictionaries at the time—James Mill served as a living depository of instant translations—but the two, master and pupil, had to be in the same room, even at the same table, so that the inspection principle could be put into practice. Reprimand and examination were linked together as equally constant and equally inevitable. The writing that the son produced, the writing that became the measure of his character, was the typical result of the panoptical principles embodied in his education: the output of the system must be constantly measured so that individuals will function as efficiently as possible in the production of whatever good or goods the structure serves to produce.

Sir Samuel Bentham, in fact, had first thought of his "simple idea" of panoptic architecture when he visited the Royal Military School in Paris and observed the two rows of partitioned sleeping quarters exposed to the master's supervision as he walked down the center of the room (63), and the last letter in the original series of letters in which Jeremy Bentham outlines the "inspection principle" is a *jeu d'esprit,* as he calls it (40), in which he imagines erecting schools in accordance with this principle. Championing the thoroughgoing application of the old saw that "children cannot be too much under the master's eye" (63), Bentham dismisses any objections to his idea of partitioning students from each other and subjecting them to constant supervision. Here he gives up the advantages offered by "limited association" in favor of insuring each student's absolute solitude. Such a plan will not, he claims, cause the student too much discomfort; it will not deprive the student by removing him or her from the society of peers in which the "business of maturity [is] rehearsed in miniature"; it will not weaken the student's energy; it will not "construct . . . a set of *machines* under the similitude of *men*." Any of these "mighty fine" objections, Bentham counters, is worth nothing beside the happiness of the student created by such a system: "Call them soldiers, call them monks, call them machines: so they were but happy ones, I should not care" (63–64). The feared outcomes of the inspection principle as the basis of a pedagogical system, objections which Bentham so easily casts aside, were, of course, precisely the untoward effects of the education that Mill outlines in the *Early Draft* of his *Autobiography*. The child depicted in the passages deleted from that draft is all that any opponent of Bentham's system might have feared: he is uncomfortable, unenergetic, lonely—a machine, and an unhappy machine at that.

Although Mill recorded the pain caused by his father's unyielding severity, he also acknowledged that the system had worked extraordinarily well, perhaps better than its subject ever recognized. Over the years, the father's watchful eye and his intellectual measuring of his son's progress became an internal principle so habitual as to be unconscious. Equating one's character with what one had produced became, for Mill, axiomatic. Unlike many other Victorians whose lifework yielded a staggering volume of writing, Mill as an adult never found self-discipline lacking. He needed no servant to call him to his writing desk or bring him his morning cup of coffee, as did even Trollope, no external call to effort and endeavor like the printer's boy standing at Thackeray's door. No superintending authority had to call Mill to his duty. He simply saw it and did it in one seemingly automatic motion of will and achievement. Defining his duty, choosing the work he had to do, might, as I have suggested, involve insoluble difficulties, but determining that a duty must be fulfilled, that work must be done—that first step never posed a problem for Mill. Bentham saw nothing wrong in giving "such herculean and ineludible strength to the gripe of power" granted to the teacher (63), and John Mill's herculean power over himself is, if not a happy result, at least the efficient benefit of being trained as a "mere reasoning machine" (1:111). The habit of diligent effort had been so deeply ingrained in him that it might easily have been mistaken for his nature.

On Liberty, Mill's hymn of praise to the power of individuality, is the work that seems least sympathetic to Bentham's desire for social control and security,[23] least interested in subjecting others to the constant inspection to which Mill's father had subjected him. Mill's description of the potential of each individual sets aside his father's mechanistic and atomistic psychology for metaphors characteristic of Romantic poetry: "Human nature," Mill states categorically, "is not a machine to be built after a model, and set to do exactly the work prescribed for it, but a tree, which requires to grow and develope itself on all sides, according to the tendency of the inward forces which make it a living thing" (18:263). All the tag lines of Mill's essay—"doing as we like," "pursuing our own good in our own way" (18:226)—along with its famous dictum "Over himself, over his own body and mind, the individual is sovereign" (18:224) suggest that Mill in the midpoint of his career had moved into diametrical opposition to the thinking of both Bentham and his father. Indeed, the end of the last sentence of *On Liberty* seems to use Bentham's terms to disparage Bentham's goals: "A State which dwarfs its men, in order that they may be more docile instruments in its hands even for beneficial purposes . . . will find that with small men no great thing can really be accomplished; and that the perfection of machinery to which it has sacrificed everything, will in the end avail it nothing, for want of the vital power which, in order that the machine might work more smoothly, it has preferred to banish" (18:310). The power of the state to drain all vitality from its inhabitants partakes of the nightmare vision of the carceral society so forcefully evoked by Foucault from the example of Bentham's panopticon. The careful balancing of antithetical terms—men/instruments, "perfection of machinery"/"vital power," everything/nothing—suggests that Mill is dealing with mutually exclusive alternatives. One can choose to be human or mechanical, everything or nothing, but one cannot be both.

The language of *On Liberty* seems specifically calculated to repudiate the inspection principle and the inspection house. Throughout the work Mill uses metaphors that evoke Bentham's "admirable work on prison discipline." He deplores the ease with which the "moral police" of society encroach on individual liberty (18:284). Like Foucault, he sees the prison as the chief metaphor for modern society. The "social intolerance" that deprives eccentric individuals of the chance to earn a living "might as well imprison" them (18:241). He uses the older language of unreformed prisons when he speaks of individuals "fettered" (18:220)—both Bentham and James Mill exulted in the fact that the walls of the panoptic cell would make irons and chains completely unnecessary. Yet Mill more forcefully uses panoptic terms when he describes individuals "cramped" and compressed into "the small number of moulds which society provides" (18:242,267). The authority commonly granted to public opinion is imaged forth with particular effect in the panoptical terms of segregation and supervision: "In our times, from the highest class of society down to the lowest, every one lives as under the eye of a hostile and dreaded censorship" (18:264). Public opinion, custom, habit all man the central tower in this panoptical society so that there is no privacy; what concerns only the "individual and the family" is rigorously controlled by "social tyranny." Mill particularly evokes Bentham's panopticon when he suggests that the end result of such "social control" is that it exercises its power unnoticed and unquestioned. Religious creeds become external authorities that do "nothing for the mind or heart, except standing sentinel over them to keep them vacant" (18:248). The effect of this discipline, which Bentham saw as profoundly beneficial, becomes for Mill most injurious when it becomes habitual: a "universal illusion" in which "custom" is not only "a second nature, but is continually mistaken for the first" (18:220). Such "illusions" have no place in Mill's conception of a society in which individuals are allowed to develop and prosper according to their own needs and desires.

Or do they? Far from being banished from Mill's vision of society, panopticism so deeply informs and pervades his thinking that it seems invisible when its control over that vision is most effective and extensive. The reputed inconsistency of Mill's ideas in *On Liberty* is, I would argue, so remarkably consistent that he conceives of both the problem he describes and the solution he offers in terms of the inspection principle. The source of this contradiction, more apparent than real, is the striking congruity between Bentham's panoptic architecture and the psychological model at the center of *On Liberty*.

In one of the playful fancies in which Bentham envisions the educational uses of the inspection house or "elaboratory," he imagines how useful it would be as a site for experimentation, "a rare field for discovery in *metaphysics*," by which he means, as John Mill always did in his use of the word, psychology. These amusing schemes make Foucault's depiction of the carceral society look positively innocent by comparison. Bentham imagines the uses that the panopticon would serve if a "set of children had been consigned [to it] from their birth." He elaborates on this chilling fancy. The King of Egypt who wanted to discover "the lost original of language" could do so with a panopticon. Boys and girls could be separated from each other for sixteen or eighteen years, and researchers could see "at the end of that period . . . what the language of love would be." Helvetius could put the subjects of his "experiment" under "circumstances exactly similar" and judge the effect. Bentham even imagines a panoptical school for girls that would be the perfect source of indisputably intact and, therefore, highly marriageable virgins. He suggests that such experimentation even on a "small scale" would furnish an "appendix to *Hartley upon Man*" (64–65), and he points, in this comment, to associationism as the source of his own panoptical notions and to associationism as the link between those notions and the work of his intellectual grandson, John Stuart Mill.

The associationism central to Mill's plans and projects for a science of society was, as much as his education, a matter of panoptical structure. Bentham's concept of an inspection house simply externalized, on an institutional scale, a psychology in which each individual is a panopticon in which lower mental functions are kept in line by the superintendence of the higher functions. In his *Analysis of the Phenomena of the Human Mind,* James Mill emphasizes the hierarchical structure of his associationism and thereby distinguishes it from earlier versions like that of Helvetius in which all thought is reduced to sensation. In the panoptical version of associationism to which both Mills adhered, each lower or simpler level is subsumed in and raised to a higher and more complex level. Each of the three "grand classes" builds progressively on the previous class: ideas are formed from sensation, and trains of ideas from single ideas (*Analysis* 2:1). Each new state encompasses the last: memory is more complex than imagination and therefore "has in it all that Imagination has" and "something more" (*Analysis* 1:328). As in Bentham's inspection principle, command and control are the effects desired. James Mill concludes his discussion of the will by praising those who "have certain leading ideas, called purposes, so established, as to maintain a control over both their Ideas and their actions." He conceives that the "most perfect work" of education has been done when "the grand schemes of felicity are formed into the leading and governing ideas" so that the individual becomes "to the greatest degree, the source of utility to others, and of happiness to himself" (*Analysis* 2:378).

Although James Mill was less interested in classification than Bentham, and Bentham was less interested in psychology than the elder Mill, John Stuart Mill's comments on associationism revealed the extent of his debt to both these thinkers. Although he worked hard to deny the deterministic implications of associationism, he never demonstrated any uneasiness with its emphasis on self-control. In his annotations of his father's *Analysis,* the notes in which he most often takes his father to task involve James Mill's desire to simplify his classifications or to reduce their significance by claiming, for instance, that classes are simply an economical way of handling the multiplicity of names with which consciousness is confronted. Mill supported Alexander Bain's attempts to systematize associationism through a taxonomical approach; Mill saw Bain's desire to construct a "Natural History of the Feelings" as a step in the direction of the ethological studies he hoped to pursue.[24] By championing classificatory refinements in his father's already panoptical conception of psychology or by praising Bain's efforts, Mill was implicitly recognizing the value of Bentham's methods as they might be applied to the study of psychology.

In *On Liberty* Mill finds the solution to the tyranny of society over the individual in the same panoptical model in which he describes that tyranny; the fact that he does so proves the power of the model both to inform an argument and to disguise its effect. At different points in this work, Mill offers a fairly complete if disjointed image of his social and political ideal, and that "ideal," as he once calls it (18:278), is, on both the level of the individual and of the social whole, an associationist construct. In such a society, the consciousness of the individual would be a perfectly self-regulated panopticon, and society itself would be the aggregate of such individual units, separated from each other to perform their distinct functions and kept separate by their respect for each other's individuality, but brought together under the gaze of a centralized supervisory power.

Mill posits the individual as a discrete panoptical structure in his chapter "On Individuality." Strength of character depends on having all levels of associationist consciousness, the lowest as well as the highest, "desires and impulses" as well as will and intentions (18:264). Mill imagines the perfection of human development, the "ideal perfection of human nature" as he calls it in the next chapter (18:278), as the condition in which "desires and impulses" are "properly balanced" by "beliefs and restraints" so that an individual can keep "strong" impulses "under the government of a strong will." The individual is then free to "employ all his faculties"—observation, reasoning and judgment, activity, discrimination, firmness and self-control—and the opportunity to make choices "exercises" all these faculties (18:262–63). If such perfection were attained, it would no longer be necessary to "enforce" responsibility because "the conscience of the agent himself [will] step into the vacant judgment seat" (18:225) or into the inspector's lodge, as Bentham would have put it. Because individuals in this society can be guided by "conviction and persuasion," what they freely choose to do will necessarily benefit society. Genius will flourish because each individual will be free to develop the highest degree of energy under the highest degree of self-control.

This cultivation of human potential and human diversity will create, Mill claims, both the few capable of leading and the many ready to be led. Originality will be granted the status that its intellectual preeminence deserves. The "highly gifted and instructed" leader will "point out the way"—he cannot compel others to follow—and the average citizen will "respond internally to wise and noble things, and be led to them with his eyes open" (18:269). In Bentham's terms, the average person will have so internalized the goals and aims of those above, in this case the educationally superior, that those goals will seem to be his or her own. To Mill, such individuals are neither docile nor passive. He claims that such a system makes each individual an active participant in it. "When there is more life in the units there is more in the mass which is composed of them" (18:266), but the result is the same: the well-regulated machine is the one in which units function so automatically that they seem to be in charge of its action. In such a society, liberty and discipline would not be, as Mill claims they are now, "standing antagonisms," but different words for the same phenomenon (18:254).

Mill suggests that these individual panopticons can be joined together in a social structure that mimics their internal organization when he tries, in his final chapter on "Applications," to imagine the kind of government that would allow the greatest freedom for individual development. As he says earlier, political parties at present defined by their exclusive allegiance to progress or to order should "enlarge" their "mental grasp" and comprehend both (18:253). A government run by such parties must be the reverse of one dominated by a centralized bureaucracy that absorbs into itself all the best minds of society. Rather, Mill finds his model in the local administrations of the New England states because they combine "the greatest dissemination of power consistent with efficiency" and "the greatest possible centralization of information, and diffusion of it from the centre." As Mill further elaborates the characteristics of this model, he suggests how thoroughly it depends on the principles of segregation and supervision, principles that he did not need to go as far as New England to discover: he advises a "very minute division among separate officers . . . of all business which is not better left to the persons directly interested" and "in each department of local affairs, a central superintendence." "This central organ should have a right to know all that is done, and its special duty should be that of making the knowledge acquired in one place available for others. Emancipated from the petty prejudices and narrow views of a locality by its elevated position and comprehensive sphere of observation, its advice would naturally carry much authority." Local officials would be "left to their own judgment" to decide whether to follow that authority, "the central administrative authority only watching over their execution" of the laws (18:309). Yet, as might be expected of its superior panoptical survey and its centralization of information, such authority is its own argument for informed acceptance. Such a system of government depends, not on its own energy, but on the energy that it "aids and stimulates" in those it, quite literally, oversees (18:310). There is no need for fetters or for action on the part of the government itself. Citizens themselves do what the government, like the keeper in the inspector's lodge, expects them to do. The model of the panopticon, for which Bentham had such high and diverse hopes, seems to have found its fullest and perhaps most influential embodiment in Mill's *On Liberty.*

By focusing on the single issue of liberty—or, as I have suggested, on the definition of authority as liberty—Mill emphasizes the associationist basis of his political and social thought. Elsewhere in his writings, scattered, less formulaic statements suggest that he adhered to such doctrine consistently throughout his career. Education, for Mill is simply a way of training the individual in habits that subordinate the impulses to the will. "Will is the child of desire, and passes out of the dominion of its parent only to come under that of habit" (10:239). In his *System of Logic,* Mill quotes his own essay on Coleridge to define education as a *"restraining discipline"* (8:921). In an early essay on Ireland, Mill points out that because England is a nation of educated citizens, it is "a country [that] could go on almost without any government at all." This quite extraordinary claim, published in 1834, amidst the uproar over the New Poor Law, which was proposed and supported by the Utilitarians who recognized the need for governmental action, is based on the idea that the English, unlike the Irish, are self-governing: "Opinion and conscience and habit [do in England] much more for the ends of government than government itself" (6:218). Mill's 1836 article on "Civilization" identifies the same shortcomings of English character that Mill deplores in *On Liberty:* the enervation of character typical of the English proves that education has not done its work properly. There Mill engages in a lengthy ethological analysis of the effect of a "high state of civilization" upon character (18:124). The fear of the physical pain that is so rarely experienced in such a state destroys the capacity for "the heroic." A "moral effeminacy, an inaptitude for every kind of struggle" prevents the creation of a "great character" (18:131). Mill counsels Cultivation as a counterpoise to Civilization (18:143)—precisely the kind of cultivation of individual character that he advises in *On Liberty.*

The atomism of Mill's political thought, so disturbing in *On Liberty,* is also equally characteristic, equally consistent. He cannot imagine that when numbers of individuals come together to form a group, the resulting whole can be anything other than or function in any way other than as the sum of its parts. In his posthumously published "Chapters on Socialism," he imagines a "new order of society" in which new "motives to action" arise from groups that are the size of a village or a town, "the entire country . . . the multiplication of such self-acting units" (5:737). In *On Liberty* each individual is a "self-acting unit," but Mill cannot see that putting such units together creates a "new order" that can be understood only in new terms. Mill saw such atomistic social thinking as the inevitable result of democratic organization. Commenting on Tocqueville's analysis of the way that democracy forces individuals to "retire" into the privacy of self-interested concerns, he describes the organization of society as it is envisioned in *On Liberty:* "The members of a democratic community are like the sands of the seashore, each very minute, and no one adhering to any other" (18:182). In the essay on Bentham, Mill complains that "Bentham's idea of the world is that of a collection of persons pursuing each his separate interest or pleasure," and Mill suggests that this "world" can be made a place fit to live only through "self-education; the training, by the human being himself, of his affections and his will" (10:97–98). Twenty years before the publication of *On Liberty,* Mill had outlined the program it embodies. He simply improved the social organization that Bentham had conceived by combining it with a system of education based on his father's psychological theories: Jeremy Bentham and James Mill join to become the sum of their ideas, John Stuart Mill.

On Liberty proves, then, the point that Mill himself made at a very early age: "early impressions," the irresistible hold of early impressions, can, indeed, determine the "whole life of the man" (26:411). The more Mill tried to escape his training, the more that training informed his thought. Even when he tried to imagine an escape from the carceral society epitomized by Benthamite ideals of control, he could do so only in the terms that it provided and only in a way that would tighten its grasp on the individual. But such a formulation does not explain all that is genuinely anomalous about *On Liberty,* specifically the fact that Mill uses the language of panopticism to express his ideas and, presumably, to encourage their acceptance. The last chapter of the *Principles of Political Economy,* for instance, "Of the Grounds and Limits of *Laisser-Faire* or Non-Interference Principle," offers the same social analysis, supported by discussions of the same topics organized in the same order as those in *On Liberty.* Mill deals with influence and authority, and he attributes progress to "originality of mind and individuality of character" (3:940). Mill first treats the distinction between public and private realms, determines what authority functions within those realms and the extent to which it does so, examines the "large exceptions to *laisser-faire*" (3:947), and ends with a discussion of education and the New Poor Law. Mill does not describe these issues, however, in panoptical terms. His frequent use of the proverbial reference to "the master's eye" in the *Principles* is specifically limited to the relation between workers and their supervising employers. In the earlier work, Mill does not speak of a liberty that involves submission to an internal authority, but of the uses of authority to encourage liberty: the result may be the same, but the rhetorical effect is vastly different.

The striking similarity of the arguments and the dissimilarity of rhetorical approaches in the last chapter of the *Principles* and in the essay *On Liberty*, separated as they are by little more than a decade— less, if one calculates by the dates of composition and not by publication dates—can be attributed to some of the personal issues I have focused on earlier: between the publication of the two works, Mill had married Harriet Taylor, although their union did not change his ideas as much as it ratified his inability to be the agent who would put those ideas into practice. In *On Liberty* the focus on the future, on improvements to be achieved long after Mill's death, is much sharper, for that reason, than it is at the end of the *Principles*. In the earlier work, Mill defines general principles that can account for different kinds and levels of civilization: there he looks to the past, present, and future to find his examples and to define their relevance. *On Liberty* looks almost exclusively to the future, to a "stage of intellectual advancement which at present seems at an incalculable distance" (18: 252).[25] In the *Principles,* Mill cannot say that governments should not take on certain tasks more effectively undertaken by individuals; as he says in the penultimate paragraph of that treatise, under certain conditions in which the citizens are not as civilized as the government—in colonial administration, for instance—governmental action is the only hope for moving citizens to a level of civilization at which such action is unnecessary. *On Liberty* imagines a society that has reached a level of civilization at which the powers of government can be and should be restrained because its citizens are self-restrained.

The difference between the two works is also, of course, the difference between a work of theory meant for a learned audience and a treatment of an idea for a popular audience, a treatment that will have its effect only if it is convincing and appealing. The *Principles,* like the *Logic,* is a "book" (2:xci; 7:cxi); *On Liberty* is an "Essay," published in the smaller format that Mill used for his other essay *The Subjection of Women,* a fact that is announced in the first sentence of both works (18:217; 21:261). That difference, I think, accounts for the fact that in *On Liberty* Mill engages in rhetorical approaches that can be described as evasive, if not deceptive. The attempts to dominate in *On Liberty* masquerade as attempts to conciliate. Central to this rhetorical sleight-of-hand is the fact that Mill's focus on the future, his description of what his ideal society would be like if each individual were indeed a self-regulating panopticon, is cast as if he were talking about the present. "The incalculable distance" between the present noisy collision of ideas and a future in which truth emerges unchallenged is, in the rhetoric of *On Liberty,* merely an apparent distance. Mill speaks of the present as if it were a future in which all his ideals have been realized. He acknowledges as much—at least about the dangers he envisions—when he says in the *Autobiography* that his contemporaries labeled as "chimerical" his negative analysis of contemporary life in *On Liberty* because they did not recognize that he treated there "tendencies," not existing conditions (1:259). Macaulay, for instance, accused Mill of crying "Fire!" during Noah's flood.[26] Yet the words *tendency* and *inclination* appear so frequently in *On Liberty* that Mill's annoyance at being misunderstood is understandable.

In that sense, the underlying basis of Mill's conception of English life in *On Liberty* resembles the assumptions that he identified as the basis of Tocqueville's work on America. Comments on the first part of *Democracy in America* in Mill's 1840 review provide an admirably acute and prescient analysis of the rhetorical problem in his own later essay: "The despotism complained of was, at that time, politically at least, an evil in apprehension more than in sufferance; and [Tocqueville] was uneasy rather at the total absence of security against the tyranny of the majority, than at the frequency of its actual exertion" (18:176). Later, Mill claimed that events had justified Tocqueville's fears, and Mill clearly uses the same approach in *On Liberty:* because he is convinced that present tendencies will have dangerous results, he treats those results as if they were present evils so that he can heighten his rhetorical power over his audience, an audience, he assumes, that might never recognize the dangers of such evils if they were portrayed merely as "tendencies."

Similarly, but even more strikingly, Mill imagines the solution to those problems that have yet to bear their most noxious fruits as if the solution had already been found and put into practice, as if people were already living well-regulated lives in submission to the internal authority of the will and to the external authority of the learned and the noble. In treating his readers as if they can be "led with their eyes open," Mill hopes to lead them with their eyes closed to the rhetorical manipulations he himself is employing. The paradox at the heart of *On Liberty* is, moreover, comparable to the Christian paradox that sub-mission to God insures the freedom of the believer, but Mill's method of presenting his message is exactly the opposite of the way in which the good news has been openly celebrated from the New Testament on. In *Eustace Conway*—a novel whose action Maurice casts entirely in terms of a conflict between freedom and necessity, thought and action—the hero, who begins as a Necessitarian, learns from an Angli-can priest that "we are not free unless living in subjection to the law that made us so." In *The Friend*, Coleridge counsels that "an energy of continued self-conquest" yields "a free and yet absolute government in our own spirits."[27] Mill's similar associationist faith is never so boldly stated. Most revealing, of course, is the fact that when his rhetoric is most manipulative, it is most Benthamite. Mill's language, at least, exhibits the power of the panopticon not only to control but to per-suade. In his mature work for a popular audience, Mill returned to the Benthamite principles that had fallen into such disrepute in the 1830s and, he feared, had fallen into oblivion by the 1850s. The irony of Mill's use of those terms to enforce a liberty based on authority is almost too obvious to mention.

As Mill himself, however, said when arguing against the ballot, "Dis-guise in all forms is a badge of slavery" (19:337), and *On Liberty* dis-guises not only the source of its social thought—so much for that plethora of German thinkers Mill points to in the *Autobiography*—but even its subject, its purview, and the applicability of its lessons. The deceptive qualities of Mill's rhetoric are in themselves a mark of the marginality that he attributes to his role. As early as 1832, he an-nounced in print that "whoever . . . wishes to produce much immediate effect upon the English public, must bring forward every idea upon its own independent grounds, and must . . . take pains to conceal that it is . . . part of a *system*" (23:445). Mill counseled such concealment particularly when he discussed English squeamishness about systematic thought with French thinkers interested in exporting their ideas.[28] Similarly, Mill quoted with great approbation Grote's analysis of political debate in Greece: those orators speaking for the dominant ideas of their times could eschew rhetoric and present their points "as plain, downright, honest sense and patriotism." Their opponents, those marginal thinkers who found themselves defined by their stance as the opposition, had to resort to "collateral argument, circumlocution, and more or less of manoeuvre" (25:1128). *On Liberty* exhibits maneuver throughout: speaking to a largely Christian audience, Mill uses Marcus Aurelius's persecution of Christians and the death of Jesus on the cross as his principal examples of the ill effects of intolerance.[29] In fact, in some of its rhetorical effects, *On Liberty* capitulates to the popular prejudices against Utilitarianism even as Mill tries to use conventional rhetoric to make palatable a Utilitarian system.

One of Mill's contemporary reviewers, a writer for the *National Review,* was clearly puzzled by the tone of the work, by the contrast between the subject of *On Liberty* and the stature of its author: "It might almost, indeed, have come from the prison-cell of some persecuted thinker bent on making one last protest against the growing tyranny of the public mind, though conscious that his appeal will be in vain,— instead of from the pen of a writer who has perhaps exercised more influence over the formation of the philosophical and social principles of cultivated Englishmen than any other man of his generation."[30] The image of the prison-cell is, I think, doubly apt. In evoking Bentham's panopticon, it describes the kind of mentality that informs both the problem Mill outlines and the solution he recommends. But it also suggests that the subjection deplored in *On Liberty* involves something other than the tyranny of opinion and the abstract fate of individual liberties. In the last analysis, I think, *On Liberty* responds less to Mill's observation of a danger in his society than to his own sense of the limitations of the role he had chosen as the lonely voice of reason drowned out by the cacophony of Victorian materialistic culture. His continual outcries against the power of opinion, custom, and habit, the power to silence those whose unpopular ideas might indeed reform and regenerate the society that oppresses them, say as much about his self-imposed limitations as about those he found imposed upon him by others.

The writing of *On Liberty* was ultimately, I think, for Mill a declaration of an endlessly deferred independence, a potential liberation from the responsibilities that James Mill and Bentham had imposed on him to a society that he could not control or seem to affect. In this essay he imagines a world in which the voice of the critic would no longer be needed, in which the arduous burden of opposition would be lifted and the challenge of finding the courage required for dissent would not have to be met. If society could become all that John Stuart Mill envisioned for it, there would be no need for John Stuart Mill. That time would not come soon; it was, as he says of another of his hopes in *On Liberty*, "a stage of intellectual advancement which at present times seems at an incalculable distance." But by imagining a future in which the rich diversity of human potential would already be realized, he was imagining his own escape from his present circumstances as a man committed to declaring new truths to a public he thought he had to trick into listening to him. Perhaps that, after all, was the liberty for which Mill genuinely longed.

If examined in ethological terms, then, as a demonstration of the role of influence and authority in the formation of character, *On Liberty* embodies the laws of necessity, the inevitable results and unavoidable outcomes, that Mill hoped such a science would disprove. On the obsessive question of his independence as a thinker, his stature as a man with a claim to authority on the basis of his original ideas, *On Liberty* points toward a negative conclusion. Indeed, as Mill's career proceeded, he developed a kind of reciprocal touchiness on the question of influence: if he could not countenance the idea that Comte had made him the thinker he was, Mill could no more accept the fact that his writings had exerted a profound and determining influence on the minds of other thinkers. In a footnote added to the *Examination of Sir William Hamilton's Philosophy* in 1867, the work that presents influence as pernicious when wielded by a man of dull wit like Hamilton, Mill is careful to defend his own disciples against the charge of being his disciples. He takes one critic to task for concluding "without any warrant" that Alexander Bain has " 'elaborated into a minute system the general statements scattered throughout Mr. Mill's *Logic*'"; the same critic "in another passage refers to [Bain] and to Mr. Herbert Spencer (Mr. Herbert Spencer!) as merely following out an investigation indicated by me." The exclamation point nicely captures Mill's amused disbelief and his rejection of such lines of influence. He goes on, citing Coleridge's idea that a man may get his water from his own spring as well as from a hole in "another man's cistern," using Coleridge as an authority to deny Comte's influence over himself (9:216n). As the editors of Mill's *Autobiography* remark, one of the many missing pieces in his account of his life is a record of his own disciples: "As young men gathered round him—Bain, Cairnes, Fawcett, Morley, even Spencer—it was his influence on them that mattered, not theirs on him. And that tale he does not choose to tell" (1:xvi). Why he refuses to define his influence on others is, I hope, by now apparent. Because Mill was so susceptible to charges of being influenced—both because he was so thoroughly influenced and because he wanted so much not to be—he could not bear to subject to the same doubts the men whose minds he respected. After all, they were the men who had listened to him. Such empathy arose from Mill's highly imaginative capacity to see in others conditions that he did not want to acknowledge in himself and to treat others on the basis of those conditions with a tenderness and consideration that he did not allow himself. As the following chapters demonstrate, his ability to do so was a fundamental quality in his character and in his character as a writer.

Part 3

The Art of Character

To claim that Mill worked as an artist of character is, of course, a proposition at which he would himself have demurred. In writing to Thomas Carlyle in 1833, Mill emphatically denied that he possessed any imaginative or intuitive gifts: "I am not in the least a poet, in any sense." Carlyle was, according to Mill, the "Poet and Artist"; Mill himself, the "Logician in Ordinary," the servant who can explicate the "higher truths" made available by his master's "intuitive" powers (12:162–63). Later in his career when Mill was less willing to grant that the "truths" of art are more exalted than those of science, he might have dismissed the title of the artist as a belletristic decoration beneath the dignity of the role he actually sought to fulfill as a theoretician. Yet as a writer, particularly as a writer whose work was often devoted to the evaluation of the ideas and achievements of his contemporaries, he put into practice and therefore tested the theories about character that he elaborated elsewhere.

Art was, for Mill, the preeminent agent in the realm of practice, the realm in which decisions are made about the "effects" to be achieved through action, and it provides *"rules, or directions for conduct"* (4:338,312). I am not here suggesting, however, that Mill himself directly engaged in such a political art. That function he conceived to be the role of the governor or legislator. The nature of his art as a writer can be defined more accurately by looking at a notice of a new German periodical that he wrote for the *Examiner* in 1834. Most of the notice is devoted to a lengthy quotation from the prospectus to the periodical. In it Mill claims to have found a "notion" of the role of the literary critic "so remote from the vulgar one" that he "could not refuse ourselves the pleasure of translating it." Within that "notion" is defined as well the role of the art, specifically of the literature, that the critic analyzes. According to Mill's translation, the writer for *Deutsches Leben, Kunst, und Poesie* denounces "empty prattle on the beautiful and the not-beautiful" in favor of aesthetic criticism that treats literature as a form of self-expression:

> We seek in the writer, above all, the man. How *he*, in and for himself, figures himself to us from his writings, we shall endeavour to unfold; and when we have pictured to ourselves the man, we shall next inquire what phasis, if any, of German life, he and his existence are the reflexion of; in what manner the age, and

his individual circumstances, have influenced the formation of his character as a man and as a writer; or, on the other hand, what influence he himself has exercised on the age and on his circumstances; and, in this perpetual reference to actual life, many political leanings may possibly evince themselves, not, we conceive, without cause. This political tendency we shall least of all be able to avoid, if we likewise endeavour to show what the writer did *not* become, in consequence of the wretchedness of his times; and how often the fairest flowers of the German mind have, by the pressure of circumstances, been snapped off, or prevented from duly unfolding themselves. For it is not the greatness of many of our writers which ought to astonish us, but often that it was possible for them to attain any greatness whatever. (23:748–49)

One can immediately see why Mill should have been so struck by a project in the kind of literary criticism to which he had exposed the work of Junius Redivivus a year earlier. Moreover, this lengthy passage, the only one from the new periodical that Mill chooses to quote, reveals his sometimes obsessive interest in failure, failure that can be traced to its "political" source in the "pressure of circumstances" and the "wretchedness" of one's time, and this concern, as I finally argue, is central to his art. Yet this passage is most remarkable for its revelation of the extent to which Mill defines writing as an autobiographical activity: the critic reads the work of the writer to discover there, "above all, the man" and the lineaments of the historical period of which the writer's characteristics are the "reflexion." The following analysis of Mill's critical essays on the political and social thought of his contemporaries as well as the subsequent examination of specific chapters of his *Autobiography* both confirm the supposition to which this early review points: for Mill, writing, even the least ostensibly "literary" writing, becomes an art in which he "figures" his own character, not so much, however, to reveal the "political tendency" of such a figuration as to deny it.

Yet precisely because Mill did not think of himself as a literary artist, particularly not as an autobiographical artist, his work provides a telling example of the autobiographical basis of writing and of some of the more difficult issues that theories of autobiography have broached. In fact, my analysis of Mill's work becomes the occasion here for a reconsideration of the issues raised, not only by his *Autobiography*, but by the fictional and nonfictional Victorian autobiographies with which I find it shares so many characteristics. Even Mill's critical essays, by embodying an imaginative process that he elsewhere calls assimilation, reveal the specular nature of writing, the way in which the object that the writer attempts to analyze becomes a mirror that represents the face of the beholder as fully as the object that the writer purports to behold. In the last chapter of this study, Mill's *Autobiography* invites an analysis of the referentiality of the genre of which it is an example. Specifically, the quality of his account of his political career makes it difficult not to ask questions about its reliability, questions that can be answered only by investigating the complex relation between the narrator's achievements or lack thereof and his earlier aspirations. If, as I argue, Mill did indeed use his writing to surmount the limitations and dissatisfactions of his experience, he was able to do so because his writing, whether dealing directly with himself or with others, allowed him to fashion anew the character that his experience had written for him.

Specular Reflections

When Mill had published his "complete . . . demolition of a brother-philosopher," as he shamefacedly called his *Examination of Sir William Hamilton's Philosophy* (15:902), he turned immediately to evaluate the work of another brother, this time the French thinker Auguste Comte. In this instance the "demolition" was almost as thorough as it had been in the case of Hamilton. After praising the Frenchman's early work in the first part of *Auguste Comte and Positivism* (1865), Mill turns to "The Later Speculations of M. Comte," and he tries to keep his temper as he reveals the monstrous effects of the unbridled self-confidence of a mind both cut off from others and disinclined to self-examination. Mill patiently outlines Comte's views on an ideal society in which humanity or the Grand Etre will be worshipped through rituals more ornate and according to doctrines more dogmatic than those of the Roman Catholic Church. Comte's propensity to make fetishes of his positivistic beliefs led him to argue that humankind should worship not only itself but "the Fatality on which reposes the whole aggregate of our existence," an idea that Mill had spent a career trying to invalidate. Not until after Mill has communicated the following details of this philosophic folly does he cry "uncle"—"We cannot go on any longer with this." According to Comte, writes Mill:

We should conceive of this Fatality as having a fixed seat, and that seat must be considered to be Space, which should be conceived as possessing feeling, but not activity or intelligence. And in our abstract speculations we should imagine all our conceptions as located in free Space. Our images of all sorts, down to our geometrical diagrams, and even our ciphers and algebraic symbols, should always be figured to ourselves as written in space, and not on paper or any other material substance. M. Comte adds that they should be conceived as green on white ground.

We cannot go on any longer with this. (10:364–65)

In the original periodical version in which this passage was published, Mill is actually a bit more blunt, confessing that he cannot "go on any longer with this trash" (10:365n).

The source of Mill's anger is not hard to discover. Comte's conception, at least as Mill presents it, is clearly ridiculous, riddled with contradictions and adolescent inanities about the circumambient fate that space is figured to represent. The idea of green figures on an immaterial ground is, in particular, the absurdity beyond which Mill cannot go for the simple reason that it calls into question the basis of his own work: for Mill, the materiality of writing, its embalmment of thought in black figures on white paper, is a way of insuring that his ideas will last long enough to be read by thinkers capable of putting his theories into practice. For the same reason, Mill earlier labels as a "crime" Comte's plan to subject all books to a "systematic holocaust" when society reaches that stage of perfection at which neither discussion nor learning is necessary to the inhabitants of an authoritarian state ruled by the Spiritual Power (10:357). Mill's disgust, presented as the result of a disinterested and "fair examination" of Comte's thought (10:316), clearly had its personal sources: Mill's conception of his work was threatened both by the idea of making bonfires out of the libraries in which his own books might be held and by Comte's certainty that society would be regenerated as he envisioned it within his own lifetime.

At the end of *Auguste Comte and Positivism*, Mill tries to regain his balance by paying tribute to Comte's insights. In particular, Mill singles out the analogy that Comte drew between mathematics and physics, calling it an "assimilation [that] throws a flood of light on both conceptions" (10:365). Shortly thereafter, Mill refers to the fact that Comte considered Descartes and Leibnitz to have been his "principal precursors," the thinkers to whom he bore the "nearest resemblance." Agreeing on the grounds that all three thinkers were capable of profound thought as well as great folly, Mill concludes, "We think the assimilation just" (10:367). When Mill uses the term *assimilation* to describe the similarities between thinkers or between fields of inquiry, he is pointing up a central quality in his own thought. His mature evaluation of Comte—his attempt to put some distance between himself and the philosopher whose early work he still found admirable and useful—resulted, of course, from his desire to prove that he himself had not so thoroughly "assimilated" Comte's thought as to have had none of his own. Although *Auguste Comte and Positivism* reveals more overtly than the *Examination* Mill's defensiveness anxiety about influence, his use of the term *assimilation* in it points to other, potentially more productive processes. It suggests the act of recognizing resemblances—Comte saw his likeness to Descartes and Leibnitz—but also the act of making one phenomenon resemble another. Just as the word may imply influence when one thinker assimilates or is nourished by the thought of another—as in the case of the "pemican" Mill hoped his writing might become—so it suggests the mental capacity to see as similar dissimilar entities.

The word *assimilation* and the complex process to which it refers appear at crucial points in Mill's work when his analysis of another thinker brings him face to face with qualities in his own experience that would otherwise remain unacknowledged. Repeatedly in his career, Mill was impelled to examine those of his contemporaries or predecessors whose work raised the central issues of his own thought and career. Such analysis served the purpose of both disguise and revelation. By focusing attention on such qualities, Mill revealed the significance they held for him; by attributing them to others rather than to himself, he protected himself from the often harsh and unflattering self-evaluation that more overt treatment would have made explicit. In this sense, Mill worked as an artist whose subject was character, his own character, but whose medium was the lives of his contemporaries. By writing about others, he could read his own features in that writing. Criticism, the act of representing and interpreting another's character, then becomes for Mill an act of self-recognition and even self-construction. Such acts offer opportunities both to face the facts about one's limitations and, at least in writing about them, to transcend them. In the final analysis, I think, Mill's most important depictions of character allowed him the kind of imaginative escape from his circumstances that he could not otherwise attain. As an artist rather than as a scientist, Mill was able to master, at least in conception, the forces over which he had so little control.

In two instances from his writings in the 1830s, Mill uses the term *assimilation* to explain the educative power of hero-worship, and he does so in a way that elucidates the potentially liberating effects of the process. In his "Remarks on Bentham's Philosophy" (1833), he defined, through a characteristic reference to ancient superstitions, the action of the heroic mind on the unheroic observer: "It is by a sort of sympathetic contagion, or inspiration, that a noble soul assimilates other minds to itself." This process turns out to be more a matter of reciprocal response than it at first appears. Figures of extraordinary virtue can liken others to themselves only if they have faith that they can make "others feel what [they] feel," but those being exposed to the "contagion" of virtue must have the capacity to recognize that "firm, unwavering confidence" and respond to it (10:16). Mill elaborates on this idea in the essay "Civilization" (1836): Great minds can be formed only if examples of other great minds "circulate" through their thoughts and feelings and "become assimilated, . . . part and parcel" of themselves (18:145). By conceiving of this process in the directly physical terms that recall his definition of his character in terms of his writing, Mill suggests the power that this idea holds for him. The "great mind" must become one with that of the aspirant so that the virtue of the former "circulates" like blood through the latter. Yet such a desire to become consubstantial with the "virtuous soul" may devolve into simple wish fulfillment. The process of assimilation, therefore, has two possible outcomes: one may become a hero or merely imagine that one has attained heroic stature.

The emotional investment and the potential for imaginative reward that such a process involves offer yet another way of evaluating the *Autobiography* in the larger context of Mill's work as a whole. Indeed, the character sketches that he drew in his earlier critical essays provide, I think, the most appropriate introduction to his practice as an autobiographer. In fact, the specular nature of these essays, with their covert acts of self-construction, illuminates Mill's treatment of those relatively few acquaintances or colleagues who join him in the pages of the *Autobiography*. As an artist of character, he outlines a more conclusive ethology than he proposed as an analyst of character. But he also demonstrates that one's writing, one's analytic use of one's experience, can be a way of transforming experience. If character is the blank page on which experience writes—to revert, once again, to Locke's formulation—writing is a way of revising what experience has written. Writing is a way of rewriting character. The length to which such revisions extend in the *Autobiography* is the subject of the final chapter of this study. Before proceeding to that demonstration, however, it is necessary to examine the theory that underlies and the practice that points toward such culminations in Mill's art of character.

MIRRORING THE LIFE OF THOUGHT

Mill's imaginative capacities are qualities whose existence is often mentioned but whose full significance is rarely gauged. In his *Autobiography*, he does not tell his readers that he was an amateur composer, that he could spend hours at the piano, entranced by the melodies he was creating. In a gathering of friends, as he read the passage from *Sartor Resartus* in which Carlyle describes George Fox wrestling with his vocation as a prophet, Mill's voice "tremble[d] with excitement." At the nadir of his famous crisis, he experienced a particularly imaginative version of his anxieties about originality: he was "seriously tormented by the thought of the exhaustibility of musical combinations" (1:149). At other times, his worries were fanciful to an extreme: he admitted that he "could get into the state of being unable to bear the impossibility of flying to the moon" (14:249). Such susceptibilities cost Mill greatly; they go a good way to account both for his attraction to the imagined gifts of Harriet Taylor and for his exaggeration of the slights to her that alienated him from his family.[1] Yet such creative capacities were firmly grounded in Mill's theories about the nature of perception, theories that gave form and direction to the imaginative energy with which he was so clearly endowed.

Mill's imaginative practice was founded on what he called the "relativity" of human knowledge, a phrase, as he suggests, that can encompass so many shades of meaning as to be either "full of important consequences" or so "thin and unsubstantial" as to be meaningless. Mill rejected, in particular, Sir William Hamilton's conception of such relativity as the relation "between the thing known and the mind knowing" (9:5), the reality of neither things nor minds being, according to Mill, capable of proof. He did accept the term *relativity* as it expresses the fact that "we only know anything, by knowing it as distinguished from something else; . . . two objects are the smallest number to constitute consciousness; . . . a thing is only seen to be what it is, by contrast with what it is not" (9:4). In the *Logic* and in his footnotes to James Mill's *Analysis,* Mill seems interested in this fact only as it applies to relative terms; naming the father implies the existence of a child, naming the brother implies his sibling (31:182), and James Mill treats such relative terms as merely convenient and efficient modes of speech. Yet when John Mill refers as he does in the *Examination* to Alexander Bain as the chief of the "highest authorities" who sanction the understanding of the term *relativity* that he himself accepts, Mill suggests that the relation in question is more than a simple convenience. Bain's footnote to this chapter of the *Analysis* argues that James Mill is pointing to "the fundamental fact of the consciousness [that] all consciousness, all sensation, all knowledge must be of *doubles*": "Any single thing is unknowable by us; its relative opposite is part of its very existence." Every named object contains its "correlative" or "negative" (*Analysis* 2:12n). Here Bain elaborates on and specifies points that Mill makes in both *A System of Logic* and the *Examination.* One does not know one thing simply in relation to another, as Mill argues in the *Examination,* but by contrast to its opposite. The two objects that are known must be each other's "negative" and not merely different phenomena.

Mill's practice as a theoretician bears out Bain's claims that any two items must be each other's "relative opposite" if either is to be comprehended. In the *Principles of Political Economy,* Mill finds particularly instructive the condition of slaves as opposed to the condition of peasant proprietors. The two groups are "extreme opposites of each other," inverse images because in each case, capital, labor, and land (the material used in production) are owned by one person; in the case of the slave, by the owner of the slave; in the case of the peasant, by the peasant himself. Whereas peasant proprietors are "the most uncontrolled arbiters of their own lot," slaves are the least so (2:252). These opposed types are significant because, between them, they define the extremes of the thoroughgoing categorization of production that Mill is constructing. Similarly, in his essay "Civilization," Mill begins to define the term *civilization* by evoking its contrary, "rudeness or barbarism" (18:120). He cannot educe one without the other, and the definition by opposition so characteristic of Mill's thought reveals the centrality of such differentiations; without them, he cannot develop the larger categories that comprehend them. This method is, as Mill said, a traditional approach among logicians, who treat "things which are farthest from one another in the same kind" (10:120). It provides a key, as well, to Mill's prose style, whose chief rhetorical characteristic is the balanced antithesis. Such oppositions offer Mill the kind of "commanding view" that, he claimed, using one of Bentham's terms, makes a subject *"cognosible"* (21:56).

When Mill examines the characters of individual human beings, his approach emphasizes even more forcefully the need to understand one individual through his or her opposite or opposing type. The companion essays on Bentham and Coleridge are simply the best-known instances of what is, for Mill, an inescapable method of analysis. At times, this method seems to be the result of an impulse beyond his control. "Bentham" (1838) opens with a statement that establishes a similarity between the "two great seminal minds" of Bentham and Coleridge, and Mill then disavows a desire to compare the two because such a comparison is not possible "unless there were first formed a complete judgment of each" (10:77). But Mill goes on to compare them as types of the "Progressive" and the "Conservative" mind as if to prove that he cannot understand either mind without placing it in relation to its "relative opposite." By the time Mill wrote the essay on Coleridge (1840), he was ready to admit that "it is hardly possible to speak of Coleridge . . . without reverting to Bentham: they are connected by two of the closest bonds of association—of resemblance and contrast" (10:120). Resemblance and contrast are, of course, among the primary relations that the associationist conceives to be the basis of consciousness, and Mill's conviction of the relativity of knowledge is clearly grounded in the associationist laws he accepts as fundamental.

Such oppositions provide the framework for Mill's analysis of character. I have already pointed to the obsessive categorization in his essay on Vigny: those categories, of course, are constructed as "relative opposites"—the conservative writer as opposed to the radical, Vigny as opposed to Tocqueville. Similar contrasts proliferate throughout Mill's work. "Thoughts on Poetry and Its Varieties" (1833) yields a distinction between Wordsworth and Shelley, just as Chapter V of the *Autobiography* contrasts Wordsworth and Byron, and one of Mill's accounts of a journey to the Lakes sets Wordsworth against Southey, the many-sided poet as opposed to the "one-sided" poet (12:81–83). Mill's initial description of the French radical Armand Carrel appears in the context of his opposite, Cavaignac (12:196–97). The poor figure that George Grote cuts as leader of the Philosophic Radicals is countered by the success that James Mill might have had in that role. John Austin is the thinker who unties intellectual knots, but his work can be understood only in relation to that of Bentham, the thinker who cuts knots (21:167–68).

Often in his early letters, Mill himself served as one of the two characters who constituted the oppositions that he continually evoked, and this fact has important implications for Mill's later practice as an autobiographer. Carlyle was told that he played the poet to Mill's logician (12:163). Admiring Wordsworth's "extreme comprehensiveness and philosophic spirit," Mill admitted that he longed to be his companion: "We should be like two travellers pursuing the same course on the opposite banks of a river" (12:81). He used a similarly concrete image to define his relation to John Sterling, to whom Mill said, "I know no person who possesses more, of what I have not, than yourself" (12:29). Their minds, by 1833, were like planets that have "passed that point in their respective orbits where they approximate most" (12:168). Here the term *approximate* carries some of the nuances of *assimilate*. The two men, in their very differences, evidence similarities to each other that reveal more about each other than the analysis of each alone would demonstrate. More importantly, if objects of perception can be known only when they are each other's "double," to use Bain's term, then Mill's use of himself as one of the two characters being compared suggests that the process of perception makes known or *"cognosible"* not only its ostensible object—Carlyle or Wordsworth or Sterling—but the source and subject of the perception, Mill himself.

Mill's most elaborate explanation of this process occurs in a letter of 1832, presumably to William Bridges Adams, the Junius Redivivus whose work Mill twice reviewed in 1833. Mill told Adams that he looked forward to meeting him, not because he imagined that *"equality"* was to be the bond of association between them—"nothing can be so little interesting to a man as his own double"—but because he conceived the relation to be one of *"reciprocal superiority"*: "just that difference in character" between the two men would make them "highly valuable" to each other. That the assimilation envisioned in this letter is the union of opposites Mill proved by drawing a comparison that may, indeed, have startled his correspondent: "We are almost as much the natural complement of one another as man and woman are" (12:123–24). In fact, the term that Mill used in this private context, *reciprocal superiority,* became his description of the ideal marriage as he defined it later in *The Subjection of Women* (21:336). Like the other relative terms that James Mill cites in his *Analysis,* the terms *man* and *woman* or *husband* and *wife* are mutually defining; neither one can exist before or without the other. Clearly, assimilation is less a process that unveils the distinctions between individuals than a complex series of reflections that dissimilar but mutually dependent characters cast on each other. Mill told the man he had not even met, "Our intimacy is its own reward" (12:124), and he might more specifically have noted that the fruit of such intimacy is the self-definition of the individuals who enjoy it.

In Mill's published work, such explicit contrasts between himself and another are less frequent, though the "reward" of the implicit unions may be more palpable. Often, Mill or Mill's "idea" of himself, as he labeled his portrait of Bentham, serves as the unstated contrast that opens out into proliferating images of difference, similarity, and reversal. Such, I think, is the case of Mill's evaluation of Comte in *Auguste Comte and Positivism.* As my analysis of *On Liberty* suggests, Mill shared more with the authoritarian prophet of the Religion of Humanity than he cared to admit. In fact, the society envisioned by Comte, the *"liberticide"* (14:294), is the mirror image of the ideal that Mill sketches. Certain qualities in Comte are, similarly, the reverse of those in Mill. Comte looks to the past and bases his new world on traditional forms and attitudes; Mill looks to the future for new forms as yet unimagined. Comte ignores psychology; Mill makes it the basis of social science. Comte values the practical Romans; Mill, the theoretical Greeks. Comte urges the "submission and obedience" of the individual to the state, the wife to the husband, and, most importantly, of the intellect to the feelings (10:352). Mill champions the sovereignty of the individual, the equality of husband and wife, and, most importantly, the predominance of reason over feelings. Comte's deification of feeling clearly threatens the rational basis of both Mill's thought and his reformist goals, and Mill carefully refutes Comte's denigration of reason by comparing feelings to the steam that provides the "motive power" to a ship: "To say that men's intellectual beliefs do not determine their conduct, is like saying that the ship is moved by the steam and not by the steersman." Ideas, the "will" and "knowledge" of human agents, direct and inaugurate all actions, including all great social changes such as the Reformation and the revolutions in England and in France. Like the idiocy of thinking that one's propositions float free as green figures in white space, believing that "the world is governed or overthrown by feelings, to which ideas serve only as guides" is simply foolish (10:316–17).

Yet if analyzing Comte is, for Mill, like looking in a mirror in which all his own features are seen in reverse, it is also a way of covertly acknowledging the resemblance between the two faces. Mill's representation of Comte invites such a conclusion as it avoids formulating it overtly. Characteristics that Comte shares with Mill can be evaluated with more equanimity and justice because they are presented as Comte's, not as Mill's. This is particularly true of their ambitions for a science of society. Both thinkers base their expectations on a feature that they share with Bentham, a profound faith in classification as a method of inquiry that grants both knowledge and power; and they use classifications as a way to arrange the various sciences into a hierarchical system that must, they argue, yield a science of sociology. But in this instance Mill can be more candid about Comte's failures than he can be about his own: Comte merely pointed to the space that such a science should occupy; he has not "created" it so much as "advanced" its creation (10:327). Similarly, Mill contends in the case of Comte, as he did for other thinkers like Hamilton and Leibnitz, that the entire body of a thinker's writings must be considered before that work can be understood, but he also argues in Comte's case for a perspective that he sets aside as irrelevant in his own: a knowledge of certain facts in Comte's "personal history" is "almost indispensable to an apprehension of the characteristic difference" between his early and later writings (10:329).

Mill feels compelled to obtrude Comte's biography on the criticism of his thought when he discusses the French thinker's abstention in "later life" from "all reading" except that of a "few favourite poets" on the grounds of maintaining a "hygiène cérébrale." Although such a "complete concentration of the intellect upon its own thoughts" may have its advantages, the conclusions resulting from such concentration are "merely provisional" because they have not been tested against or modified by the work of other thinkers (10:330). The emphasis on Comte's intellectual isolation comments, more forcefully than Mill would have recognized, on his own "concentration on [his] own thoughts." Such isolation was, of course, typical of his years of intimacy and marriage with Harriet Taylor Mill; ironically, she was particularly strident in her attempts to isolate Mill from the pernicious influence of Comte. Yet even after her death when Mill rejoined the world both socially and politically, he remained remarkably impervious to the intellectual trends around him. He could not understand, as I have suggested, the wider implications of the physiological investigations into psychology being undertaken at the time. He could not see the significance of Darwin's development hypothesis, though it might have offered a telling perspective on the subject of ethology. Similarly, Mill's attempts to carry on an intellectual dialogue with Herbert Spencer were almost comic. Even when Spencer's formidable eccentricity is taken into account, one can only conclude that Mill was signally obtuse when it came to the differences that divided them: Spencer would explain the point of contention, Mill would publish an account of their essential agreement, Spencer would protest, and Mill would respond simply to prove once more that he could not understand the distinction that seemed crucial to his colleague. As Mill acknowledged on one occasion, "It is evident that I have again a misapprehension of your opinion to confess and correct" (16:1110). Mill made a great virtue of his openness to new ideas, his willingness to learn from every book he read.[2] The relative stability and consistency of his thought from the 1850s on, however, suggest that he was in some ways as impervious to new challenges and new information as Comte was.

The second point of Comte's "personal history" that Mill finds inescapably relevant is the "moral regeneration" that Comte underwent as a result of his relation to Clotilde de Vaux, the "angélique influence" with whom Comte shared one year of "pure" and "passionate enjoyment" before her death (10:331). Mill's evaluation of this liaison—which one approaches, as Alan Ryan so justly notes, with a certain trepidation because it so closely resembles Mill's relation to his "own precious darling angel," Harriet Mill (14:225)—is remarkably fair and evenhanded.[3] Mill can be just in assessing the advantages and disadvantages of Comte's relation to Clotilde de Vaux simply because it is not his own relation to Harriet Mill. In Mill's account, Clotilde de Vaux is a slightly qualified French version of Harriet Taylor: "uniting everything which is morally with much that is intellectually admirable" (10:331), she has on Comte an effect like that which Mill attributes to his wife in the *Autobiography*. Both women open the eyes of their men to the emotional and practical ramifications of the regenerative systems they are engaged in constructing. Both men lose these paragons, and both men publicize their grief over their losses, as Comte does in the dedication of his *Système de politique positive* (1851) and as Mill does in his dedication of *On Liberty*. Just as Harriet Mill becomes in the *Autobiography* a proof of Mill's faith in the "internal culture of the individual" (1:147), Comte reveres the memory of his beloved as the "type of his conception of the sympathetic culture proper for all human beings" (10:331). According to Mill, she converted a man who was "purely, and almost rudely, scientific and intellectual," even in his ardor for human improvement, into a man surpassingly "sentimental." In each case, the thinker insists that his love has been "pure," above all "animal appetites" (1:236). Accordingly, Mill declares the memory of Harriet Mill a "religion" (1:251), and Comte, in addressing his dead saint, claims that he performs acts of daily worship "devant ton autel domestique."[4]

In this section of *Auguste Comte*, with its emphasis on the import of the dedication of the *Système*, Mill seems to be offering a mirror image of his own personal history. Although he credits Clotilde de Vaux with the "improved feelings" that Comte displays in his later writings, Mill laments that she was not as capable of amending Comte's intellectual faults (10:332). It is, conversely, Harriet Mill's influence on Mill's feelings that ought to be deplored. Despite Mill's insistence in the *Autobiography* that she epitomized the moral benefits of rich and powerful feelings, Harriet Mill often undercut Mill's more generous and tolerant impulses when she tried to confine him within her own intense, sometimes paranoid, but always narrow emotions. When Mill wanted to give up his portion of his mother's inheritance either to one widowed sister who needed it or to another who had "behaved decently well" to him and his wife, Harriet Mill objected (14:220, 223). In writing to her husband about his earlier relations with Comte, she explicitly complained of the "generous defect in your mind . . . your liability to take an over large *measure* of people"; her role was to counsel the "more needful than pleasant" process of "drawing in afterwards" to save Mill from his too precipitate association with those who did not meet her standards (Hayek, 115).[5] Harriet Mill may not have improved Mill's thought, but she too often encouraged him to deny the sometimes impulsive expansiveness of his emotions. In turn, if Mill's analysis of the relation in *Auguste Comte and Positivism* covertly acknowledges some of the untoward effects of Harriet Mill's influence over himself, its relative generosity may also reflect his own hopes that the relation had, indeed, offered him enough to offset its costs.

Yet if Mill's account of Comte is a refracted self-portrait, it epitomizes the complications inherent in such representations. Like the "flood of light" cast on the disciplines that Comte compares, this assimilation of Mill and Comte places them in a mutually defining relation to each other. Here the double meaning of *assimilation* again becomes pertinent: Comte's attitudes seem to have influenced Mill's; therefore, the image of Comte's character that constitutes Mill's as its "relative opposite" issues from both the subject and object of the act of perception that creates it. Mill's specular vision of Comte defines the qualities of the seer as fully as it does the qualities of the seen. This formulation is particularly revealing in the case of Comte's relation to his human angel because his published accounts of that relation predate both Mill's writing of the *Early Draft* and his later public accounts of his relation to Harriet Mill. The extraordinary "Dédicace" in the first volume of Comte's *Système* may, in fact, have determined the content of Mill's public statements about Harriet Mill and, therefore, the form of the assimilation that defines their dissimilar, but comparable experiences. Throughout the "Dédicace," Comte is careful to attribute to Clotilde de Vaux only "des plus hautes facultés de l'esprit féminin" (iv). He parcels out the great work of regenerating the human race between the opposed functions of masculine intellect and feminine feeling. Addressing his saint, he declares the former to be his province, the later hers. Both abilities are required, but both ultimately prove what Comte calls in his preface "l'ascendant nécessaire du coeur sur l'esprit" (5). When he credits his beloved with having completed his philosophic system by teaching him "la juste prépondérance des affections domestiques dans l'ensemble du véritable essor moral," he specifies that her contribution, her "participation réelle et puissante," is nonetheless "indirecte et involuntaire" (v–vi). In their letters during the 1840s, Mill and Comte had engaged in a frank and extended debate about women, and Comte's depiction of Clotilde de Vaux must have struck Mill as the final proof of the folly of Comte's essentialist position.

Instead, therefore, of insisting that Harriet Mill epitomized the perfection of female "nature," as if there were such a thing, Mill insists that she had the capacity, if not the opportunity, to develop into a "great orator" or a ruler as well as a poet or an artist (1:195). Her part in his work, he claims, was not confined to the conventional role of the muse, the role that Comte's angel, according to his account, so timidly and modestly fulfilled. Rather, Harriet Mill had engendered the thinking in Mill's best work in unison with him. In the dedication to *On Liberty*, she appears as "in part [its] author" (18:216). Her role had been as thoroughly theoretical and central as Clotilde de Vaux's was emotional and ancillary. As Mill specifies in his comments on the author of the "Enfranchisement of Women," "if mankind continue to improve, their spiritual history for ages to come will be the progressive working out of her *thoughts,* and realization of her *conceptions*" (21:394; emphasis added). In effect, then, Mill's stress on Harriet Mill's intellectual capacities may owe less to her mental prowess than to Mill's need to refute Comte's essentialist diminution of Clotilde de Vaux's and his concomitant elevation of feeling over reason. Yet such an opposition of Mill's own experience of female virtue to Comte's would not have struck him as necessary unless, in his reading of the *Système*, he had seen himself reflected in Comte's portrait of his own mental development. Both the *Autobiography* and *Auguste Comte and Positivism* proclaim the centrality of this assimilation.

Such a process, in which critical analysis of another thinker's work becomes a hall of mirrors that create the various images of the analyst's own visage, characterizes not only Mill's later career, a time when he was, reasonably enough, trying to sum up and evaluate the work he had done, but also his earlier writing. A similarly unstated contrast between Mill and John Roebuck determines what can and cannot be said about Roebuck in the character sketch in the *Autobiography*, a sketch that is, as I have suggested, as self-serving as it is self-protective. The same is true of Mill's essay on Coleridge, written relatively early in his career when he was solidifying his commitment to theory and still repining over his exclusion from the world of practice. As the disinterested appraisal that it purports to be, "Coleridge" offers a very odd analysis. The editors of Mill's *Autobiography*, in reference to another of its telling omissions, ask, "Where then is Coleridge?" (1:xviii), but if that question is an appropriate response to Mill's written life, it is even more pertinent to the essay that bears Coleridge's name. Fully halfway through the essay Mill apologizes for not having reached his subject, yet the "long, though most compressed, dissertation on the Continental philosophy" to which he has devoted so many pages is not introduction enough (10:141). Mill goes on to offer a lengthy sketch of the state of English philosophy before Coleridge's arrival on the scene. As in the essay on Vigny, which preceded "Coleridge" by three years, Mill continually defers the treatment of the avowed subject of his analysis so that he can erect a framework of oppositions—this time between conservatives and liberals, between idealists and experientialists—oppositions that will, presumably, explain the subject.

The Coleridge who does emerge in the last and shortest section of the essay is a proto-Mill, a prophetic incarnation of the thinker that Mill hopes he will become once he has combined the "partial truths" of the schools of thought he has been describing. Appropriately enough, in an essay written for publication in the *London and Westminster Review*, Mill declines to treat Coleridge's thought "in all its aspects"; rather, Coleridge appears only "with relation to Reformers, and especially to Benthamites." He is, Mill argues, their "brother Reformer" (10:146). Mill has prepared his readers for this outcome by suggesting earlier that in the reaction of one school against the other, improvement occurs when the "oscillation," the distance between the two, diminishes with each cycle (10:125). The essay on Coleridge attempts to prove that the distance is less than any of Mill's contemporaries would have thought. Every one of Coleridge's ideas that the writer is willing to share with his readers is one of his own convictions—state support for the clerisy, land as a trust held for the benefit of all members of the community, the preeminence of ideas, the utility of reason even in the realm of religion. Moreover, Coleridge's leading political idea, his contrast between the interests of Permanence and of Progression, simply recapitulates the contrast between conservative and liberal philosophies to which Mill has devoted so much space. In admitting that he has neither time nor space to deal with Coleridge's moral or religious thought, Mill again doubles back to the beginning of the essay when he quotes Coleridge to establish that errors are actually "half-truths taken as the whole" (10:158). Coleridge comes to mirror the character of the writer of the essay by counseling the kind of reconciliation that the essay itself undertakes. Mill knows that he has not "given any sufficient account of Coleridge," but he hopes that he has proved that a Tory philosopher can be a "better Liberal than Liberals themselves" (10:162–63). What he has proved, in fact, is that he himself is a better conservative than Coleridge himself, but the oppositional structure of the essay, emphasized by the lengthy contrasts with which it opens, protects that realization from surfacing and therefore makes its indirect assertion possible. Coleridge both is and is not the mirror image of the writer of the essay, and its long preamble sets up differences that Mill's perception of Coleridge as a "brother Reformer" serves to efface. It is less to the point to suggest that Mill's comprehension of Coleridge is "faulty" (10:xxx) than to recognize that Mill is not as interested in comprehending Coleridge as he is impelled to use his analysis of the Sage of Highgate for the purposes of self-definition.[6]

According to one of the paradoxes that Oscar Wilde delighted in proposing, criticism is "the purest form of personal expression" and the "only civilized form of autobiography" because it erects its own standards and deals with thought, not action.[7] Many of Mill's critical essays besides "Coleridge" confirm this point: by constituting himself as the implicit contrast to the subject under discussion, Mill reveals the similarities between himself and the subject, and such an assimilation becomes an act of self-construction. The portrait of James Mill in John Mill's preface to his edition of the *Analysis* reveals the extent to which the son compounded his disappointments about his career with the oblivion into which his father's best works had fallen. One of John Mill's review essays on John Austin quotes Austin to express his own longing for a "reading public, numerous, discerning, and *impartial*," an audience that would not only accept but indeed encourage challenging thought (21:58). In different contexts Mill defines both Austin and himself as thinkers adept at the "untying of intellectual knots" (21:168; 1:217); both staked their claims to value on their ability to train others in "the difficult art of precise thought" (21:167). Similarly, Mill's portrait of a Vigny "sadder and wiser" after the Revolution of 1830 evokes, in moving terms, Mill's own condition after 1832; the pain of personal defeat leads to a kind of "impartiality" that is a liberation for the individual who, having lost everything, has nothing left to lose (1:469–70). Even the two review essays on Junius Redivivus, which I discussed at the beginning of this study, exhibit the same pattern. By labeling a writer with whom he shares so much, including his anonymity, as "bold and independent in thought," "manly and pure in purpose" (1:390), Mill not only reflects an admiration for such qualities, but attempts to embody them in himself by recognizing them in another.

What such essays seem to suggest is not, of course, remarkable. They demonstrate the degree to which every act of perception is simply an act of self-perception or, if one wants to use the moral terms so congenial to Victorian thought, the degree to which each mind is inalterably caught in its own egoistical concerns, incapable of moving the candle placed on a horizontal pier glass, as George Eliot figures the problem. Yet the extent to which Mill gives this capacity free play is remarkable in the case of a writer who claims so forcefully that disinterestedness, impartiality, and objectivity provide the only basis on which valid analysis can proceed. Mill's practice as an analyst turns such ideals upside down: his criticism is a matter of assimilation, a definition of his own character through the characters he chooses to examine. Not surprisingly, such a process underlies his practice in the more centrally, but sometimes no less covertly self-reflective qualities of the *Autobiography*.

THE SPECULAR STRUCTURE
OF AUTOBIOGRAPHY

The issues raised by the specular qualities of Mill's critical writings become, not simpler, but more complex when the writing in question is directly autobiographical, particularly as those issues entail an understanding of autobiography as a genre in which self-reflection involves not only the writer's attempt to portray his or her own image, but also the construction of the writer by the image portrayed. If, according to Wilde, criticism is the purest because most direct form of self-expression, autobiography is, in many ways, the least direct, the most impure. To explain the full implications of this point, I need to set Mill's *Autobiography* not only in the context of his other works, but in the larger context of both Victorian autobiographical literature and the theoretical issues raised by autobiography as a genre. Modern commentators have noted that the autobiographer, in choosing himself or herself as the object of observation, cannot directly see the subject that is being written about; as Georges Gusdorf puts it, "interior space is shadowy in its very essence." This recognition would hardly have startled Victorian writers. As George Eliot explains in the first of *The Impressions of Theophrastus Such,* rendering an "account" of one's own "character" is so perilous an undertaking that it may often yield no more than "the blind man knows of his image in a glass."[8] As my examination of Mill's critical essays has claimed, it is easier to depict in the portrait of another the characteristics that one recognizes or would like to be able to recognize as one's own. Quite logically, then, an essay such as "Coleridge" or Mill's treatment of Comte depends on a mutually constitutive process of objectification, and this process epitomizes the complex structure of self-representation characteristic of autobiographical narrative.

To a surprising extent, nineteenth-century authorities in both the intuitionist and experientialist schools of thought agreed on the mutual interdependence of subject and object in the act of perception, even as they disagreed on the reasons that might explain such an interdependence. This conception is central to both Romantic theory and practice, with much of which Mill was familiar and to which his own formulation of the relativity of knowledge is similar. Sheila M. Kearns has argued convincingly that for Coleridge the autobiographical process is firmly based in his conceptions of the nature of consciousness and language. The state of self-consciousness, as Coleridge asserts in his *Logic,* depends upon "a subject which becomes a subject in and by the very act of making itself its own object." In the *Biographia Literaria,* Coleridge's definition of self-consciousness points even more specifically to autobiography: the "perpetual self-duplication of one and the same power into object and subject, which presupposes each other, and can exist only as antithesis."[9] Self-consciousness involves a doubling in which mind is both the power to perceive and the phenomenon being perceived. Without the "antithesis" that results from the bifurcation of consciousness into the subject and object that "presuppose" each other, there is no "one and the same power" of consciousness. The term *self-duplication* precisely describes the aim of autobiography; by qualifying that term with the adjective *perpetual*, Coleridge points to the continuous and continuously repetitive nature of that act. If one argues, as I do, that Mill conceived of himself as one of the "relative opposites" being made known in so many of his acts of critical perception, then Mill's conception of the relativity of knowledge leads to conclusions strikingly similar to Coleridge's claim that subject and object constitute each other in the act of consciousness that creates them. Moreover, Mill's practice as an essayist seems to bear out Coleridge's claims about the "self-duplicating" powers of consciousness. For both Mill and Coleridge, every perception is an autobiographical act.

De Quincey, in his *Confessions of an English Opium Eater,* elucidates the mechanism involved in this process. Describing the most frightening of his opium visions, he speaks of the terrifying power of the mind to "mak[e] itself . . . *objective;* and the sentient organ *project* itself as its own subject."[10] To illustrate that process more vividly, De Quincey creates an image of his opium visions by depicting a composite "imaginary prison" drawn by the artist Piranesi, a "vast Gothic hall" complete with "all sorts of engines and machinery." Situated in this oppressive architecture and "groping" up a staircase is "Piranesi himself." De Quincey asks his reader to scan the drawing he is describing: "Whatever is to become of poor Piranesi, you suppose, at least, that his labours must in some way terminate here. But . . . behold a second flight of stairs still higher: on which again Piranesi is perceived. . . . Again elevate your eye, . . . and again is poor Piranesi busy on his aspiring labours. . . . —With the same power of endless growth and self-reproduction did my architecture proceed in dreams" (106). In describing an "endless growth and self-reproduction," De Quincey, of course, refers to the power that the images in his dreams have to proliferate endlessly, but his obsessive evocation of the repeated images of the artist Piranesi within his own engraving provides a telling figure of what Coleridge calls the "perpetual self-duplication" inherent in consciousness and particularly apparent in autobiography. In De Quincey's view, Piranesi is as much his own subject as his *carceri* are, but in Coleridge's terms, the images in the *carceri* constitute the self-consciousness of the artist who creates them.

Self-duplication, objectification, and assimilation are all terms that point to the particular specular structure through which autobiography as a form of self-writing constitutes the narrator as his or her own object. At this point, one might even want to add to this list of terms the neologism *subjectification:* the process whereby the writer becomes the object that concomitantly constitutes the writer as subject, as the "relative opposite" of the object portrayed in the autobiographical text. Such a definition goes well beyond any simple statement about the referential nature of autobiography: it is not only that autobiographical writers create images of their past selves, but that they create texts that witness to identities that have no existence independent of the texts in which they are created. One form characteristically taken by such a specular structure of subjectification involves the relation between the younger self that the autobiographical narrator evokes and the contemporaries or acquaintances who also people the text. The apparent inevitability with which portraits of others turn into portraits of the narrator demonstrates the full extent of the specularity that defines autobiographical narration.[11] What Bain says of perception is particularly true of the form that self-consciousness takes in autobiography, "all knowledge must be of *doubles*."

In Victorian works, both fictional and nonfictional, the literal image of such a specular structure is the face in the mirror. The individual looks out and sees an uncanny vision that is both here and there, familiar and alien, known and unknown. Frequently in Victorian autobiography, the central character is subjected to such a specular view, a view that comes to represent the author's reduplicative relation to the text. In his *Apologia pro Vita Sua*, Newman uses the figure of the mirror to represent a crucial moment in his movement toward conversion to the Church of Rome: reading church history, he confronts an analogy to the current heresy of Anglicanism, "I saw my face in that mirror, and I was a Monophysite." Later on, in his 1874 "Autobiographical Memoir," Newman turned the structure implicit in this moment into the basis of his autobiographical practice by speaking of himself as "Mr Newman," a figure he can see and therefore describe rather than a figure through whose eyes he sees; as the editor of this document claims, Newman wrote "his own biography, as though the writer and his subject were distinct individuals." Similarly, in opening the second volume of *Praeterita*, Ruskin compares the writing of his autobiography to gazing at his face in a looking glass: the second volume will be "less pleasing" than the first, "for as I look deeper into the mirror, I find myself a more curious person than I had thought." Here the text becomes a mirror that creates a face "more curious" than that which exists without it. Even in a staid account like Darwin's *Autobiography*, the absence of references to literal mirrors is simply an opportunity to provide an imaginatively specular view: Darwin claims to be writing "as if I were a dead man in another world looking back at my own life," as if he were already set apart from himself by the distance that marks the difference between the living and the dead.[12]

Not surprisingly, the most intense instances of such self-consciousness occur in Victorian fiction. Although they are usually prompted by drugs, liquor, dreams, or madness, even the act of reading or the power of memory are stimulants potent enough to evoke moments of specular vision. In the novel by John Sterling that Mill admired, *Arthur Coningsby*, the hero recounts the effect of his early reading of romances in these terms: "I was perpetually surrounded by fantastic mirrors, and felt as if transferred into the distorted portraits of myself which they multiplied around me." As Coningsby matures and his despair deepens, even his travels throughout Europe and the Middle East have this frightening effect: all the nations that Coningsby sees are "reflections of myself, thinking thoughts which are my thoughts, speaking languages I have spoken." In *Villette*, the autobiographical narrator has a conversation with a friend in which the two women reveal the extent of their shared sympathies and attitudes, and she comments, "there are certain things in which we so rarely meet with our double that it seems a miracle when that chance befals."[13] The uncanny quality of such recognition requires some force beyond the usual workings of nature—some "miracle"—to generate it. Lucy Snowe suffers from hypochondria, David Copperfield yields to drink or sexual desire, and suddenly identity is both subject and object, the condition from which autobiography arises.

Such uncanny visions account for much of the suggestive power of autobiography—after all, the genre seems to arise from impulses associated with the fears that myth and folklore seek to assuage—yet they also illuminate the uncanny nature of autobiography itself and the theoretical problems that bedevil the study of it. Like a ghost, autobiography is both real and illusory, both referential and imaginative. Similarly, the characters within autobiographical texts may purport to have existences independent of that of the main character—indeed, in autobiographies like those of Ruskin and Newman, the authors' contemporaries are historical personages—but they function as shadows of the writer and of the younger self figured forth in the text. Because much of the analysis of Victorian autobiography has focused on it as a genre devoted to self-interpretation rather than self-representation, such figures have not been granted the attention they deserve, but their presence and prominence are unmistakable.[14] The more obvious pairs of such "relative opposites" in Victorian fiction include David Copperfield and Uriah Heep or Lucy Snowe and Paulina Home, but equally important within their respective texts are Ruskin's portrait of Charles Eliot Norton as a man as "hopelessly out of gear and place . . . as a runaway star dropped into Purgatory" and the character sketch of St. Alfonso, the man "scrupulous" and "anxious of conscience," that Newman offers at the end of his *Apologia*. Such figures have their Romantic forebears in the "figures of deprivation, maimed men, drowned corpses, blind beggars, children about to die" with whom Wordsworth populates the *Prelude*.[15] Similarly, just as De Quincey projects multiple images of Piranesi into the picture that the artist draws, De Quincey appears in various guises in his account of his past experience, specifically in the figures of the abandoned child and the "lost Pariah woman" (139) of his wretched months in London.

Psychoanalytic theorists like Otto Rank have seen such doubling as proof of a death wish on the part of the writer because of the profound and self-destructive narcissism it involves; the projection of identity can lead to its loss or to the punishment and destruction of that other that constitutes the self. Yet such a conclusion depends on viewing an author's work as a simple reflection of his or her identity, an identity that should, in conditions of health, strive to be whole and independent; any hint of a fragmentation or dispersal of self-concept is, according to such assumptions, both pathological and dangerous. A poststructuralist theory like Jacques Lacan's concept of the mirror stage suggests otherwise: identity, if it is to be apprehended at all, must appear already alienated from its source. Doubled characters function in relation to each other as if they were the infant and the image in the mirror at the mirror stage.[16] According to Lacan, the child beholds a powerful and integral identity that both is and is not his or her own. In autobiographical fiction, structures recalling the mirror stage are particularly apparent. Uriah Heep stands in for David to represent the sexual designs on Agnes that David himself cannot acknowledge. It is not simply that David Copperfield's urges are reflected in those of Uriah Heep: they could not be perceived by David at all if they were only his own. Without the mirror that Uriah provides, David could not acknowledge, even covertly, his feelings for Agnes. His identity is never single, independent, and whole; because it is defined by its specular relation to another character, it is necessarily fragmented, dependent, and dispersed.

Although by the end of the century such assumptions may have led to an annihilation of identity in a work such as Edmund Gosse's *Father and Son,* the process as it appears in mid-century Victorian literature can be both frightening and salutary. The existence of a double can serve to validate the source of the perception from which it issues. As Carlyle indirectly claimed in his "Characteristics" (1829), self-consciousness may indeed be a disease, but the healthy state of unselfconsciousness involves a potentially troubling lack of awareness: the faculty that has no consciousness may, in fact, not exist at all. As Carlyle explicitly states, self-consciousness is both "the symptom" and the "attempt towards cure."[17] Mill makes something of the same point when he claims that Bentham "was a boy to the last"—Bentham experienced no "self-consciousness," no "dejection," and in being so whole and so untouched, Bentham was undeveloped, less than a fully mature human being (10:92). Unlike the process of identification, in which one risks merging with another and thus losing whatever integrity one may pretend to have, autobiographical assimilation offers a doubling of identity. Once the autobiographical subject is granted a consciousness, the ability to perceive an external world—and every memory assumes that ability—the narrative takes for granted the mind that both perceives and is created by the assimilations that it is registering. In effect, the primacy that Locke and Hume grant to memory as the only proof of identity is simply ratified by and embodied in the specular structure of autobiography.

All this, however, may seem fairly remote from Mill and his *Auto-biography.* That text includes no references to Mill's face, much less to his perception of a face in a mirror, and such psychological effects seem far removed indeed from a writer who privileged reason over imagination throughout his career. Endowing external phenomena with one's own characteristics was a practice that Mill recognized as both customary and deplorable. Such perception is, for him, a case of degenerative assimilation: it is a "primitive tendency or instinct of mankind to assimilate all the agencies which they perceive in Nature, to the one of which they are directly conscious, their own voluntary activity." Thus, primitive peoples see "life, consciousness, will" in natural phenomena (10:272). In his *System of Logic*, he treats modern instances of such perception as examples of inaccurate inference. Using the example of a person who says, "I saw my brother" when no brother has appeared, Mill explains away such an aberration as the result of sleep, inattention, nervous disorder, or "waking hallucination" (8:642). The cause he does not name, the cause perhaps that explains his use of this particular example in this passage, is memory, the force that elicits visions of absent brothers, second selves. Mill seemed to dismiss explicitly such uncanny recognitions when he remarked to William Bridges Adams that "nothing can be so little interesting to a man as his own double" (12:123). As usual, however, the phenomenon that Mill set aside as simply uninteresting was, for him, so closely pertinent as to be threatening. Not being able to conceive of having an identity that could be doubled was at some points, for Mill, an urgent problem.

Besides Mill's temperamental indisposition to and theoretical rejection of such displays is the fact that for much of the time in his life that the *Autobiography* covers, he viewed his identity as too thoroughly incorporated in his father's to be capable of even such primitive forms of objectification. If the son was the father's parrot, then it was the father's character that was projected onto the son. Mill himself offers precisely this analysis of his condition. Like other children of "energetic parents," he was "unenergetic" because his father was "energetic for" him (1:39). All motive force is embodied in the parent, not in his mechanical offspring. In a passage from the *Early Draft*, Mill explains that being under the "constant rule of a strong will, certainly is not favourable to strength of will. I was so much accustomed to expect to be told what to do . . . that I acquired a habit of leaving my responsibility as a moral agent to rest on my father, my conscience never speaking to me except by his voice" (1:613). Here is an almost pathological form of identification: the individual speaks not through another, but speaks for another in his own voice. The younger does not assimilate the wisdom of the elder; rather, the elder figure of authority incorporates the younger. Writing to Carlyle in 1834, Mill described one of his essays as the "truest" he had written because it reversed the direction of such assimilations: the essay "*emanated from* me, not, with more or less perfect assimilation, merely *worked* itself *into* me" (12:205). Later, Mill would define *assimilation* quite differently, not as the imposition of someone else's character on his own, but as a process that "throws a flood of light" on the characters being compared. Yet such early comments suggest both how difficult and how important it was for Mill to be able to believe that an essay or a thought could "emanate from" himself.

In fact, if Mill seems at times the least likely of Victorian writers to have chosen to write an autobiography because he was the least convinced of the substantiality and independence of his individuality, his lifelong equation of character and text actually predisposed him to engage in the genre that, by definition, honors that equation. At points within the text as well, Mill objectifies the autobiographical narrator that he has become in ways that recall Victorian fictional autobiographies or a work like Newman's *Apologia*. Particularly in Chapter V of the *Autobiography*, Mill completely reverses the process that the dominance of his father has entailed: here, incorporation yields to the subjectification of consciousness, the process whereby the subject becomes a subject by being its own object. Like Lucy Snowe's illness or De Quincey's drugs, Mill's breakdown leads to a new form of self-constitution. For at least the space of one chapter, Mill can imagine that he has experienced an identity that has the power to impose itself on the world around it, to be refracted in a process that both questions its integrity and testifies to its existence.

As one might expect in the written life of a "bookish man," Mill's reading—in this case, his reading of Marmontel's *Memoirs*—provides the crucial episode in the development of this awareness. Earlier passages in the chapter prepare the way for this event. Mill has experienced as a symptom of his malaise an intense self-consciousness from which he can find no relief. He cannot elude the sense that he is dead weight, mechanism. Yet even his famous question and its negative answer are cast in the form of a doubled identity that may point to the vitality inherent in this disorder: "It occurred to me to put the question directly to myself, 'Suppose that all your objects in life were realized; that all the changes in institutions and opinions which you are looking forward to, could be completely effected at this very instant: would this be a great joy and happiness to you?' And an irrepressible self-consciousness distinctly answered, 'No!' " (1:139). Mill engages in a dialogue between "me" and "myself," a dialogue that is itself proof of an "irrepressible self-consciousness." Mill here issues from the boyhood that Bentham never escaped. The "dry heavy dejection," the desire for annihilation, first lifts when Mill reads an account of Marmontel's response to his father's death: Mill is particularly moved by "the sudden inspiration by which [Marmontel], then a mere boy, felt and made [his family] feel that he would be everything to them—would supply the place of all that they had lost." The barely suppressed expression of Mill's desire to be free of his own father is here so obvious as to need no comment. More significant, however, is the immediate result of the death of Marmontel's father: the son tells his family not only that he will take his father's place, but also that he will fill that place completely. To his declaration, the family unquestioningly accedes: Marmontel's mother presses her son to her bosom, and the rest, brothers and sisters, aunts and grandmother, fall in worship to their knees. Mill, of course, does not mention these details in the *Autobiography*, though he says he was moved to tears by his "vivid conception of the scene and its feelings" (1:145), nor does he note that Marmontel claims to have removed himself from this scene so that he could go to sleep in the only bed available, his father's.

Yet for all the cheerful triumph of oedipal instincts on display in the *Memoirs*—and Mill is clearly blind to the almost comic overtones of Marmontel's self-dramatization [18]—surely the effect on Mill of his reading of the first book of Marmontel's life was more cumulative than the account in the *Autobiography* suggests. Marmontel pictures his childhood as a feast of tenderness. The dominance of a reserved father who, like James Mill, had earmarked his son for an uncongenial trade beneath his sense of his dignity, is wholly offset by the loving devotion of a refined, educated, and spiritually elevated mother. A kind of modern-day St. Monica, Marmontel's mother is all that James

Mill's wife is not: she is the predominant figure in Marmontel's *Memoirs*, just as Mill's mother is the predominantly absent figure in the *Autobiography*. Moreover, the story of Marmontel's life, as he tells it, involves his adoption, one after another, of willing and able father figures. It advertises the importance of that relation even in its title, *Mémoires d'un père:* the man who has had so many good fathers is now himself one. The most important of these surrogate parents is Voltaire, whose status among the *philosophes,* of course, John Mill accords his own father among the Philosophic Radicals. Marmontel's account serves as a flattering reflection for Mill not only because it grants the son a place in the family, but also because it charts an easy transition from the role of son to the role of father, a transition that Mill, in his childlessness, never made. Marmontel's *Memoirs* seem almost preternaturally suited to function as a textual mirror for an identity undergoing a late reversion to Lacan's mirror stage. Perhaps no other account of a father's death could have answered so responsively to the needs that Mill defines in the *Autobiography* as his own at this time of crisis.[19]

This signal instance of objectification becomes typical of the imaginative mode that dominates Chapter V. Soon Mill is explaining, "I felt that the flaw in my life, must be a flaw in life itself." This "egotistical" mode of perception, as Mill calls it, may be unhealthy—like the effect of liquor or drugs, it grants a character too great or too unrestrained a power—but it does prove that character's existence: if my life is disordered, then the entire world is disordered (1:149). In the midst of his crisis, Mill demonstrates that his consciousness, in the throes of an emergence into self-consciousness, is more than willing to recognize its own case in those of others. Byron's poetry is of no help to Mill because the "poet's state of mind was too like my own" (1:151). Wordsworth, on the other hand, offers consolation for precisely the same reason: "he too had had similar experience to mine" (1:153).

This process of objectification and assimilation reaches its climax in Chapter V in Mill's account of his relations with John Sterling, a passage that, unlike the account of Roebuck, escaped deletion at a later stage in the composition of the *Autobiography*. Two earlier accounts of Sterling's life, the memoir published by Julius Hare (1848) and the biography by Carlyle (1851), had excluded anything more than a mere mention of a relationship that was important to both Mill and Sterling.

The centrality of Sterling's characterization in Chapter V was, moreover, something like an act of apostasy to the "religion" of Harriet Mill's memory: she had, in fact, been adamant in her opposition to any publication of the letters that the two men had exchanged. To her mind, Sterling was simply Mill's "*evident* inferior" (Hayek, 158). Yet Mill persisted in his plans to include Sterling in this section of the *Autobiography*, perhaps as a gesture toward the biography of Sterling that he had once contemplated writing. Like Carlyle, Mill evokes the exemplary qualities of Sterling's career. In the penultimate paragraph of *The Life of John Sterling*, Carlyle presents his subject as a figure suited to encourage a process of subjectification in his readers: "In Sterling's Writings and Actions, were they capable of being well read, we consider that there is for all true hearts, and especially for young noble seekers, and strivers towards what is highest, a mirror in which some shadow of themselves and of their immeasurably complex arena will profitably present itself."[20] In many respects, the Sterling of Mill's *Autobiography* serves as the same kind of reduplicating "mirror" that Mill later saw in Comte. In Sterling Mill finds more than "some shadow" of his character and his circumstances.

At first, it seems that Mill will outline yet another relation between seminal and disseminating minds. Like Mill himself in his relation to his father, John Sterling is the "orator," the voice of the thoughts "almost entirely formed for him by Maurice," the "thinker" (1:159). Mill goes on to set up a more extensive chain of influence from Coleridge to Maurice to Sterling, a chain of influence that is very much like the one that ran from Bentham through James Mill to John Mill. Like earlier patterns so rigorously established in the first four chapters of the *Autobiography*, such configurations involve the dominance of one character over another: honor is accorded only to the originating mind, a criterion that sets at nought such characters as Grote and Black and John Mill and, now, Sterling. But suddenly this pattern disappears, and in its place emerges the image of Sterling, not as a figure incorporated into another's authority, but as an object of analysis in which John Mill's ideals express themselves:

> With Sterling I soon became very intimate, and was more attached
> to him than I have ever been to any other man. He was indeed
> one of the most loveable of men. His frank, cordial, affectionate

and expansive character; a love of truth alike conspicuous in the highest things and the humblest; a generous and ardent nature which threw itself with impetuosity into the opinions it adopted, but was as eager to do justice to the doctrines and the men it was opposed to, as to make war on what it thought their errors; and an equal devotion to the two cardinal points of Liberty and Duty, formed a combination of qualities as attractive to me, as to all others who knew him as well as I did. With his open mind and heart, he found no difficulty in joining hands with me across the gulf which as yet divided our opinions. (1:161,163)

Mill goes on to say that Sterling had feared that Mill was simply a "'made' or manufactured man, having had a certain impress of opinion stamped on me which I could only reproduce" (1:163). Mill, of course, has had precisely this fear about Sterling's relation to Maurice, and both men are pleased to discover their errors.

Mill's portrait of Sterling is a description of the character that Mill would become if he could lose all those impulses to closeness and reticence that he attributes to his father's training of him. Sterling is "attractive" to Mill because he is the image of his ideals, just as the character of Paulina is to Lucy Snowe in *Villette;* Mill and Brontë use exactly the same term and the same tone to describe these two characters and the affectionate intimacy that the young Mill and Lucy enjoy with their doubles. As Sterling has told Carlyle and as Mill repeats in the *Autobiography,* when Sterling and John Mill met, it was a meeting of "brothers" (1:163). Mill deleted a passage from the *Early Draft* that calls such amiability into question by referring to "a violent and unfair attack" that Sterling had made on Mill's political philosophy (1:162). In the *Autobiography,* what remains of the friendship reveals only the similarities of the two men. Sterling is the brother who is able to "outgrow the dominion which Maurice and Coleridge had once exercised over his intellect."

The fact that Sterling had died before Mill first drafted his written life allows Mill the freedom to idealize their relation. Sterling's is the "ever progressive" mind, which starts out "as wide apart" from Mill's opinions "as the poles," but approaches identity with Mill: "if he had lived, and had health and vigour to prosecute his ever assiduous self-culture, there is no knowing how much further this *spontaneous assimilation* might have proceeded" (1:163; emphasis added). In this instance, the assimilation of the two men to each other seems almost uncaused: it is neither simply the effect of Mill's perception of Sterling nor proof of an unequal contest between them for intellectual supremacy. Sterling is the figure who will never go on to prove his intellectual dependence on his teachers and who does prove, through Mill's friendship with him, that Mill himself is similarly liberated. Like Hallam for the speaker of *In Memoriam* or like Helen Burns for Jane Eyre, Sterling constitutes an ideal that transcends the usual mortal fears because he cannot be touched by change or decline: because he is dead, because he has died young, he is wholly a figure of promise, never a source of disappointment or disillusion. As Carlyle put it in his *Life of John Sterling,* the man who died young is "bright, ever-young in the memory of others that must grow old" (267). Just as Mill sees Sterling as having approached "assimilation" with him, Mill in his *Autobiography* can assimilate himself to Sterling. Writing this passage in the *Autobiography* offers the opportunities that death or, more importantly, life denies; through his depiction of Sterling's character, Mill rewrites his own.

Such rewriting takes a tacit form in Mill's silence about the qualities of Sterling's experience, like those of Comte's, that correspond most closely to his own. Sterling had told his son in 1844, "hardly—I suppose were ever two creatures more unlike than [Mill] & I" (12:29n), but their careers, their places in the "complex arena" of Victorian culture, were remarkably similar inverse images of each other. Both men saw themselves as mediators between opposed systems of thought: as Mill tried to reconcile the goals of Utilitarian philosophy with the individual's need for "an internal culture" of the feelings, Sterling tried to reconcile the claims of religion and the values of art. Both were rewarded for their efforts by being labeled renegades by their early mentors. Carlyle served a comparable function in both their developments. Just as Mill's Utilitarian associates took as proof of his "muddled" thinking his eagerness to enlist Carlyle as a writer for the *London Review,* Sterling's more conventionally religious colleagues construed his tendencies toward agnosticism as Carlyle's doing. Shifting his attention to the German higher critics from the Coleridge whose disciple Maurice was, Sterling drove a wedge between himself and Maurice. His brief career as a clergyman at Herstmonceux was followed by a deconversion remarkably similar in its effects to the crisis that Mill accounts in the *Autobiography*. In some ways, Sterling could have been describing himself when he delineated Mill's position to Caroline Fox: "He has made the sacrifice of being the undoubted leader of a powerful party for the higher glory of being a private in the army of Truth, ready to storm any of the strong places of False-hood, even if defended by his late adherents" (Fox, 179). In the 1840s when Mill's plans for a magnum opus on ethology still seemed viable, Sterling hoped to write a major work on theology. In the end, Sterling had to admit the failure of his attempts at publication; *The Election,* he told Mill, gave "no offence" because "nobody [read] it at all": "May you be more fortunate in this and in all things."[21] Mill was, of course, more fortunate than Sterling in such matters, but Mill's sense of his own relative failure must have found confirmation in the clear image of Sterling's defeated ambitions.

In the long run, however, Sterling's ambitions for a life of action most clearly evoke Mill as his "relative opposite," an extreme "in the same kind." Although Carlyle claimed that Sterling's "faculties were of the active, not of the passive or contemplative sort," *The Life of John Sterling* continually stresses that its subject's "bewilderments," his repeated failures to match his ambitions with achievement, reflect "everywhere . . . the colour of the element he lived in" (6, 267–68). In his account of his friend's life, Mill never mentions Sterling's part in the Cambridge Apostles' disastrous attempts to foment revolution in Spain. Not only did Sterling convince his cousin, Captain Robert Boyd, to fund the undertaking; Sterling served as the "financial man-ager" for the expedition that led to the execution of General Torrijos and Boyd along with the Spaniards who accompanied them to Spain in 1831. At just the time that Mill gave up any hope of a political career, Sterling reached a similar conclusion: in 1832, he declared that he had become totally disillusioned about his plans to use his role as the manager of his mother's plantation on St. Vincent as a way of putting his theories about reform into practice; from then on, he claimed, he wanted only to "keep clear of public life." Despite this studied dis-tance from practical involvement in political issues, his zeal for public questions remained strong, and many of his positions were also Mill's. Indeed, his passionate outbursts against the government's handling of Ireland sound very much like Mill's later articles in the *Morning*

Chronicle: "Stagnant misery would not move them a jot. But they do not like their own machinery to be clogged by living bones and flesh getting into it."[22] The life of writing to which Sterling in his ill health devoted his last years was, like Mill's, a second-best alternative to a life dedicated to the action that would have saved such "living bones and flesh" from the governmental ineptitudes that devoured them. In the *Autobiography,* Mill turns the defeated Sterling of Carlyle's *Life* into a figure of promise whose glorious achievements were cut off only by his mortality, never by his own incapacities or by the weight upon him of the times in which he lived.

Such specular visions, such mirrors as Marmontel and Sterling provide are, of course, figments of the imagination, figures who exist in the fictions that the mind creates to console itself for what actuality withholds. Chapter V of the *Autobiography* exists in this realm, but that fact does not negate the satisfactions that this mode of perception can offer. Rather, it reaffirms them. As Mill told Roebuck in one of their arguments over Wordsworth's poetry, the "imaginative emotion which an idea when vividly conceived excites in us, is not an illusion but a fact, as real as any of [its] other qualities" (1:157). That Mill chooses to record this remark in the part of the *Autobiography* that illustrates its force suggests, perhaps, that he might have understood the sources of such imaginative satisfactions. In Chapter V, Mill can at least conceive of the possibility that his character is powerful enough to throw its reflections upon the world beyond it, to make impressions on others as impressions have been made on him. For as long as he is writing Chapter V, Mill can allow such objectifications to prove the autonomy and strength potential in his character as that character is written into the text of his *Autobiography.*

Inevitably, in Chapter VI, "Commencement of the Most Valuable Friendship of My Life," this process again reverses itself, and James Mill, the dominant figure of the first four chapters, is replaced by Harriet Mill. Yet that substitution allows Mill a freedom in his representation of himself that his account of his father's domination has not permitted. Although Comte had used the word *assimilation* in his account of his relation to Clotilde de Vaux—"Puisse cette solonnelle assimilation à l'ensemble de mon existence révéler dignement ta supériorité méconnue!"—he clearly saw the process as one in which he proved his own priority and superiority over the woman he loved by incorporating her virtues and giving them a place in "les plus lointains souvenirs de l'humanité reconnaissante" (xx–xxi). For Mill, however, offering an account of his relation to Harriet Mill is an occasion for employing both the forms that assimilation takes in his work. She is Mill's double, the object who defines him as subject, as well as the over-powering identity to whom Mill subjects himself. Mill's representation of her is, therefore, both a proof of his dependence and a declaration of his independence.[23]

Harriet Mill in the *Autobiography* is, first and foremost, proof that character can be its own creation. Mill's character is formed by edu-cation and experience; Harriet Mill's is not the sport of circumstance, but the product of her own "moral intuition" (1:621). She proves, as John Sterling does in breaking away from Maurice, the autonomy of the individual. Hers is a character of "intuitive intelligence" (1:193) and "sympathy" that "grew and unfolded itself" like a plant follow-ing the dictates of its own nature (1:253). Earlier James Mill has been granted the power to "warm" into life the "germs" of virtue in others; here Harriet Mill is granted the power to perform that operation on her own being. She is an inhabitant of another world, the only figure in the *Autobiography* who does not and need not prove the validity of asso-ciationist psychology. She conforms to the ideal implied by use of the term *character* in *On Liberty:* she has desires and impulses of her own, and they are not presented as the outcome of her past experience. Her power is unaccountable, innate, unquestioned, and unquestionable.

Harriet Mill, the embodied disproof of Mill's associationist fears, becomes, then, the "presiding principle" of his "mental progress" (1:199).[24] Mill creates yet another image of his intellectual dependence when he uses the term *assimilation* in relation to Harriet Taylor: "The greatest part of my mental growth," he writes, "consisted in the as-similation of [the] truths" that she had revealed to him (1:253). As Mill grasps John Sterling's hand across an abyss, so his progress goes "hand in hand" with hers (1:237). In short, Mill's work is "not the work of one mind, but of the fusion of two" (1:199). The character that seemed to be emerging into independence in Chapter V has now be-come identified with another so thoroughly that their "fusion" admits of no distinctions between them. Mill is once again in the realm where other authorities rule, where other voices give rise to the ideas that he transmits into the body of print. Once again Mill serves as another's amanuensis. In the short section appended to the original conclusion of the *Early Draft* in 1861, Mill codifies this complete identification: Harriet Mill, now dead, is both a religion and a standard by which to evaluate all one's efforts: "My objects in life are solely those which were hers" (1:251). Harriet Mill, in dying, has taken into the grave with her any potential for change, expansion, and progress that Mill might otherwise have attributed to himself.

The representation of Harriet Mill, then, seems simply to involve Mill in the same kind of assimilative process that James Mill's education of him had entailed: Mill is incorporated into the identity of his stronger, more willful, more energetic partner. Yet Harriet Mill plays a double role in the *Autobiography*. She is both an ideal endowed with qualities that Mill found lacking in himself and, by virtue of his ability to recognize and value those qualities, she is also the occasion for Mill's assertion of them as his own.[25] By identifying Harriet Mill as the source of the most far-reaching conclusions that he published under his own name, Mill allows himself to define their value in a way that, if they appeared as simply his own, could only seem grossly egotistical. This process recalls the doubling implicit in the semifictional and semiautobiographical form in which Carlyle proclaims his ideas in *Sartor Resartus:* because the Editor is praising Carlyle's thought as it appears disguised as the work of the German philosopher Teufels-dröckh, Carlyle can both glorify and question his own thought without appearing to do so. Similarly, Mill is protecting his ideas from too harsh an evaluation at the hands of his contemporaries by providing them with a rationale for dismissing such ideas: they are, after all, only the formulations of an uneducated, untrained woman. At the same time, Mill is freeing himself to exaggerate and to idealize their value.

This reading of the representation of Harriet Mill in the *Autobiography* is supported by Alexander Bain's chilling description of her: "She had a knack of repeating prettily what J.S.M. said and . . . he told her it was wonderful." Another witness recalled that Harriet Mill once "had repeated" for an hour "what afterwards turned out to be an article Mill had just finished for the *Edinburgh*."[26] The record beyond the *Autobiography* suggests the same conclusion that the assimilation at work within it implies: Harriet Mill was less the overmastering intellect of the relation than the figure assimilated into the role that John Mill had played for his father. So much for the marriage of "reciprocal superiority" that Mill envisioned in *The Subjection of Women*. Harriet Mill became the perfect blank slate; on her mind Mill could write his opinions; on her character as he wrote it in the *Autobiography*, he could inscribe the qualities he had hoped and failed to embody in himself.

More chilling than even Bain's dismissal of Harriet Taylor Mill is the way in which the *Autobiography* conceives of her as a cipher whose character Mill is free to elaborate as he wishes. Throughout the *Autobiography*, she is virtually nameless. She is once called "Mrs. Taylor" (1:193). Throughout Chapter VII, she is "my wife." In other instances, Mill resorts to circumlocutions that invariably draw attention to their unnecessary awkwardness: Harriet Taylor Mill is, like Clotilde de Vaux, "one whom the world had no opportunity of knowing" (1:5), "the incomparable friend" identified only by reference to "her first husband, Mr. Taylor" (1:237), or "her whom I had lost" (1:261). Mill's refusal to name "my wife" results in long paragraphs in which she appears only as "she" and "her" so that her abstract virtues and her unindividuated potential come to outweigh any sense of her personality. In the long paragraphs that open Chapter VI, she is, quite literally, a "being of these qualities" (1:197). In the famous passages in which Mill measures her against James Mill, Shelley, and Carlyle so that she can emerge their superior, Harriet Mill is conjured up only by hyperbolic elliptical expressions, never by name.

In conferring on his "wife" and "lady" such a studied lack of personal identity, Mill was, of course, avoiding one assimilation that would have been more awkward than his circumlocutions. Any reference to "Mrs. Mill" or "Harriet Mill" might have compounded Mrs. John Mill (Harriet Taylor Mill, née Hardy) with Mrs. James Mill (Harriet Mill, née Burrow). The two Mrs. Mills were, indeed, as far removed from each other as Victorian wives could be: the kind but simple woman who "drudged" for her children when James Mill's resources were too meager to afford household help (1:612) could not be more unlike the delicate, would-be bluestocking who clearly thought that her children lived for her convenience, not she for theirs. Yet the two are, of course, their "relative opposites" in their relations to the Mills who married them. Much as John Mill tried to defy convention and overturn Victorian stereotypes in his paean to Harriet Taylor's intellectual prowess, his picture of her in the *Autobiography* has simply confirmed her ancillary role in his career.

Yet Mill's desire to avoid any confusing identifications of his mother with his wife sprang, perhaps, from a desire to avoid another possible assimilation, the identification of himself with his mother, an identification from which her absence in the *Autobiography* defends him. Francis Place's description of Harriet Burrow Mill, "poor thing she had no mind in her body,"[27] is too similar to complaints that James Mill made about his son, the complaints recorded by that son in the *Early Draft*, not to suggest that she may have been excluded from the *Autobiography* because Mill could have too easily assimilated his identity with hers. Surely his mother's constant humiliation by James Mill was the source of some of the lessons that John Mill learned about the subjection of women, just as his own subjection to his father taught him to analyze that condition through analogies to the child's uneasy dependence on the parent. Yet to acknowledge such a bond between his mother and himself would have been itself too painful a humiliation. For such reasons, I think, the woman who had been "dear Mammy" to her son (13:392) simply disappeared when the *Early Draft* became the *Autobiography*.

In fact, the energy that Mill devoted to locating and describing and analyzing his "relative opposites" in his letters, in his critical essays, and in both the *Early Draft* and the *Autobiography* proves how crucial it was for him to engage in a specular structure of vision that would confirm its source. Twice in passages from her 1840 journal, Caroline Fox quoted Mill's comments on the assimilative process that was central to his writing. On one occasion, he evaluated the process in moral terms that ultimately celebrate the pleasures of egoism: speaking of "the great share of self-love . . . in our appreciation of the talents of others," he exclaimed how "delightful" it is to "see the gigantic shadow of ourselves, to recognize every point in our own self-consciousness, but infinitely magnified" (105). Earlier, Caroline Fox quotes him as saying, "There is an exquisite delight in meeting with something in the ideas of others answering to anything in your own self-consciousness" (70). Such "delight," as Coleridge's theories of consciousness might suggest, is particularly sweet to the individual who fears that there is no shadow, certainly no "gigantic shadow," to be cast by his own character.

Harriet Taylor Mill seems to have confirmed, rather than eased, such fears. Imagining once that she would be disappointed with him after a long separation in 1855, Mill shared his anxiety with her, noting that he did not think he had changed, but meekly adding, as if to confirm a point they had often discussed, "I know how deficient I am in self consciousness & self observation" (14:476). During an early crisis in their long relationship, Harriet Taylor had complained, "The most horrible feeling I ever know is when for moments the fear comes over me that *nothing* which you say of yourself is to be absolutely relied on—that you are not sure even of your strongest feelings" (Hayek, 48). Such a criticism, understandable as it is from a woman who was risking her reputation and her marriage to respond to Mill's "feelings," nevertheless recalls James Mill's thorough critiques of his son's faults and the grown son's recognition that at fourteen he had had no sense of his identity or capacities: "I did not estimate myself at all" (1:37). If Mill had remembered Harriet Mill's accusations, as his comments in 1855 suggest that he did, no wonder he turned to Comte and Coleridge and Sterling, even to Marmontel and Roebuck, so that he could "become a subject" by writing their characters into a text in which he emerges as his "own object." Like the figure of Piranesi that De Quincey locates in the artist's engravings, Mill posits himself within the specular structure of autobiography to prove that he has a character about which he can be self-conscious. Yet even such a demonstration was not defense enough against the questions about his character implied by the continual faultfinding of, first, James Mill and, then, Harriet Taylor. Only a radical revision of character as it was written in the *Autobiography* could answer the doubts that such voices had raised.

Six

Revisions in the Life of Thought

The opening of the last and seventh chapter of Mill's *Autobiography* flatly advertises the irrelevance of the content that it introduces:

> From this time, what is worth relating of my life will come into a very small compass; for I have no further mental changes to tell of, but only, as I hope, a continued mental progress; which does not admit of a consecutive history, and the results of which, if real, will be best found in my writings. I shall therefore greatly abridge the chronicle of my subsequent years. (1:229)

Here Mill casts doubt on the entire autobiographical project that has brought the reader to this point. When he adds the parenthetical expressions "as I hope" and "if real" to the statement of the "continued mental progress" that he experienced in "subsequent years," he seems to call into question every assertion he has already made about his intellectual career. If Mill does not know that his progress is "real," if he can only "hope" that it is so, what is the reader to think? This paragraph seems an appropriately inept beginning for Chapter VII, which brings together sections of the *Early Draft* written in the 1850s along with the portions completed in 1861 and 1869–70. The chapter covers a hodgepodge of topics and seems, like its first paragraph, to be at cross-purposes with its stated intentions. There are eleven headings under the dates that constitute its title in the first edition of 1873, and the first of these, now elevated to the status of a chapter title in the Toronto edition, is unprepossessing to say the least. Here Mill promises to offer a "General View of the Remainder of My Life." "General View" is, of course, bad enough. Narrative will disappear in favor of a perspective on events, and this "view" will be both abstract and superficial, a forecast that might cause even the most interested reader to quail. But the word "remainder" is worse yet. In this chapter, the reader will be treated to the tag ends of a life, the leftovers, an autobiographical version of a second-day dinner, the loose ends that an editorial Boffin might dutifully cart off to the dustheap. At this point, the reader may take heart at Mill's promise that he will now "greatly abridge" the telling of his story.

In fact, however, Chapter VII goes on to belie every belittling dismissal and apology that its first paragraph puts forth.[1] The "very small compass" that Mill projects as sufficient to cover his life from 1840 on actually involves more space than that taken up by the chapter that includes his account of his famous crisis. Chapter VII also contains, not merely a record of "mental progress," but an account of a significant "mental change," his evolution from a democrat into a socialist. Once Mill no longer viewed private property as the essential fact of all legislation, he accomplished, in political terms at least, the transformation that seemed most stunning and most threatening to his contemporaries. Mill charts this evolution by discussing the differences between the first and third editions of *The Principles of Political Economy* (1848, 1852); the changes in his thinking were great enough to cause him to cancel whole passages in the first and second editions and replace them with his "more advanced opinion" in the third (1:241). Although Mill claims to be eschewing "consecutive history" in Chapter VII, that is precisely what the chapter offers. It even achieves some coherence by treating, with almost equal attention, the subjects of influence and authority, Harriet Mill's influence on Mill's writings and the authority, along with the seat in the House of Commons, that such writings won for him.

Moreover, Mill's dismissal of Chapter VII directs attention from the part of his written life that, in many respects, testifies more forcefully than others to the impulses that he has attempted to suppress in the earlier chapters. Even more centrally than in Chapter V, the material in this final chapter depends on an assimilative process in which Mill constitutes himself as a subject by seeing himself in terms of those objects, those contemporaries and predecessors, who are his "relative opposites." The specular structure that defines the perception of the young Mill who is represented in Chapter V dominates the consciousness of the much older narrator of Chapter VII, and it does so without the earlier disadvantages that its elicitation by a condition of crisis has entailed. Mill's account of the "remainder" of his life gives him the opportunity to do even more effectively what he achieves through the assimilations of Chapter V; it is a *tabula rasa* on which his character can be written and his experience revised.

In conceiving of the writing of his *Autobiography* as an opportunity to undertake such wholesale revisions, however, Mill confronts and makes his readers confront the problematic referentiality of the medium in which he is working.[2] Unlike Newman, who adduces in the *Apologia* diary notes, letters, and passages from his previous works to document his claims about his past, Mill bases his account primarily on his own word, the words of the text that he is composing—counting, as I think he does, on his almost universally acknowledged reputation for probity to stand as witness to the authenticity of this document. Yet if autobiography partakes of the uncanny because it is both patently illusory and purportedly real, if its declared basis in fact is central to the kinds of character that can be constituted in its pages, Chapter VII of Mill's *Autobiography* offers proof of the complexity of these issues.

More obviously specular, more obviously illusory than any other part of the text, this chapter is at the same time the part of the *Autobiography* that deals with Mill's public role in a way that can be most directly either confirmed or challenged by other sources. If in some ways the chapter demonstrates an even greater lack of self-consciousness than Chapter V, it nonetheless represents Mill as an artist of his own character, an artist who knows what he wants and how, at least in the writing of his life, he can achieve what he wants. In the final chapter, Mill revisits his "juvenile aspirations," his longings for a life of action, not only to prove their power over him, but to satisfy them. Moreover, to achieve this end he must ignore the historical circumstances against which he has always chafed. When Mill quoted in 1834 the assertion that a writer must be seen in relation to "the age, and his individual circumstances," he tacitly agreed that such analysis explains why so many of the "fairest flowers" of intellect necessarily meet with failure rather than success. In Chapter VII Mill ignores "the wretchedness of his [own] times" (23:749), the pressures that the "spirit of the age" have exerted upon him, so that he can rewrite his actions in the heroic mold that has hitherto been inappropriate to them. In the long run, I would argue, the art of character to which Mill devotes the last chapter of his *Autobiography* is itself the source of his most unquestionable achievements.

THE PARLIAMENTARY CAREER

At the climax of Chapter VII appears Mill's account of his brief parliamentary career from 1865 to 1868, when he served as M.P. for Westminster during the debates over the Second Reform Bill. If sitting in the House of Commons was something less than the "transcendant glory" he had once imagined a legislative career to be (1:67), he seems determined to tell the story as if it had completely fulfilled his earlier and long-unrealized dreams. In particular, Mill's desire for a life of heroic action, so long suppressed by the career chosen for him and by the wife he chose, underlies his account of his role as a member of Parliament. Until 1865 the writer who had, as a boy, aspired "to the character of a democratic champion" (1:65) has had no opportunity to match those aspirations with their fulfillment in deeds. Mill has been speaking of his life as "purely literary" until he is asked to stand for Parliament in 1865. Now the cog in the machine has a chance to prove that he is a motive force. The man excluded from direct participation in the first reform movement now has an opportunity to test his ideas against the challenges of a second reform movement. His more active and engaged relation to events in the realm of politics makes unnecessary the figurative representation of himself as the man engaged in a "hand-to-hand fight" with the dead writer, Sir William Hamilton (1:270). Significantly, Mill does not compromise the unqualified masculinity of such political pursuits by mentioning in his account of them either Harriet Mill or Helen Taylor. Their absence from this account, even as figures of inspiration or ambition, simply highlights the manliness inherent in the language of military engagement that is typical here. Once more, Mill is employing those cultural assumptions that equate women with thought or feeling and men with action so that he can elevate his own status on the standards they provide.

The *Autobiography* even changes its character as Mill reports the changes in his sense of himself that his election entails. He speaks of his service in Parliament—to use David Copperfield's terms—as if he were the hero of at least this portion of his life. At times the *Autobiography* begins to read like a novel in which the narrator recounts an exhilarating tale of integrity, force of character, and victory over circumstance. The John Stuart Mill who is represented in these pages of the *Autobiography* is single-minded, dedicated, and determined. He acts only in accordance with his own best principles. When asked to stand for a seat in Parliament, he responds with rigid and unconventional conditions, refusing to contribute to his election expenses, refusing to campaign, refusing to hide his unpopular stands on important issues. Mill takes some pleasure in reporting that a "well known literary man, who was also a man of society," at the time claimed "the Almighty himself" could not be elected under such conditions. Perhaps there was no hope for God in such a situation, but Mill is indeed elected, despite the fact that he also refuses to flatter working-class supporters by recanting an earlier statement about their habitual lying. Mill notes that the laboring classes favor those who treat them with "complete straightforwardness" (1:274), and he approaches this part of his story with precisely such a strategy. Passages of impersonal commentary, cast in the third person and dealing with the responsibilities of "the candidate," yield to a first-person account of Mill's actions on the hustings. He is clearly proud of the integrity of his methods. Besides leading as it did to his election, the campaign, in which he finally agreed to take a minor role, has allowed him "to scatter [his] political opinions" as his father had set out similar seed. By winning Mill new readers, the election increases the "presumable influence" of his writings (1:275).

The first two paragraphs that follow Mill's announcement of his election to Parliament—an event "as much to my own surprise as to that of anyone else"—mingle bold self-assertion with the self-effacement characteristic of earlier sections of the *Autobiography*. Mill claims that he spoke before the House on occasions that he would not have chosen "if my leading object had been parliamentary influence." Eschewing influence as his goal, he "reserves" himself for "work which no others were likely to do" in championing causes such as the abolition of capital punishment and the institution of universal suffrage (1:275). He does, as well, the work that others set him to do, particularly on the issue of municipal government in London: "I was the organ of an active and intelligent body of persons outside [the House of Commons], with whom and not with me the scheme originated" (1:276). Mill, so accustomed to marginality and to inactivity, seems to have had difficulty adjusting to a new role that might involve neither. Later reflection has made him realize that his decision to withhold his participation in the "great party questions" was ill-advised (1:277). Although he offers the usual excuse that the times were not ready for his ideas, he wavers on this issue as much as he has wavered earlier in the *Autobiography* on the question of his originality. Opinions that seemed in 1866 and 1867 to be "whims" on Mill's part have since, barely two or three years later, made such "great progress" that "what was undertaken as a moral and social duty" at the time has now become the source of "personal success" (1:276). Even the silence that followed a particularly unpopular speech on the Irish question, a silence that allowed others to believe that Mill "had turned out a failure," only increases the success of his subsequent speech in the first debate on the Second Reform Bill. Even his stature as a writer is enhanced by his performance on the floor of the House. With obvious self-satisfaction, Mill explains that a passage he had earlier written to explain the stupidity of the Conservative party, a passage that has been quoted by the Conservatives to humiliate him, has become a badge of dishonor that they are forced to wear "for a considerable time afterwards" (1:277). (The speech he made on this occasion was indeed, according to the account in the press, a deeply satisfying transformation of a potentially weak defense into a witty offensive maneuver.) In this context, Mill confronts directly the issues that indirectly affect much of his written life. Here, his writings gain power only because he is now a man of action. Deeds, finally, take priority over words.

As this section of the *Autobiography* reveals, Mill clearly wanted to see his parliamentary role as the capstone of his career, the realization of his earliest ambitions, and the proof of his autonomy. Significantly, Mill never once, as far as the public record reveals, quoted James

Mill on the floor of the House of Commons.[3] John Mill had arrived in Parliament on the strength of his own efforts, and he needed no authority other than that offered by his own writings to support his points. But the seat in Parliament that Mill had won in 1865 he lost in 1868. Not only that, the role of Gladstone, the leader for whom he had had such hopes, had been usurped by the Conservative Disraeli, and the Second Reform Bill, a Conservative achievement, prepared the way for an election that excluded from Parliament the candidates whom Mill most admired. In closing the *Autobiography*, therefore, with the loss of his place in Parliament, he has to confront the harsh reality that again limits and questions his influence and his authority. Mill, however, uses the assimilative power of autobiographical re-creation to turn what might be the occasion for narrative self-flagellation into an opportunity for self-glorification.

In the last few pages of the *Autobiography*, Mill demonstrates the extent to which he, as narrator, is willing to rewrite his own experience through the treatment of another individual's character. Here the medium of such revision is Charles Bradlaugh, the fellow candidate who supported working-class interests and to whose campaign Mill had contributed £10. Mill offers several reasons for his own defeat— the animosity of the Tories, the indifference of his fellow Liberals— but most of all, he focuses on the untoward effects of his support of Bradlaugh. Mill does so, however, only after he has already described his defeat and after he has distracted attention from his parliamentary career by recounting the events that belong to the period after it, his republication of James Mill's *Analysis* and Helen Taylor's contributions to the founding of the National Society for Women's Suffrage. By deferring his description of Bradlaugh until the end of the *Autobiography*, Mill suggests that the contribution he gave Bradlaugh was the most important factor in his defeat. By granting it such a rhetorically powerful position as the last in a series of causes, Mill offers it pride of place in his sense of his own career.

The thumbnail sketch of Bradlaugh with which the *Autobiography* closes—if one discounts its perfunctory last paragraph—reasserts the claims that Mill has earlier made in his own name, claims that the electors for Westminster have so rudely ignored. Bradlaugh, a "man of ability," is supported by the working classes. He is a democrat who puts principle above demagoguery by opposing "the prevailing opinion of the democratic party" on crucial issues. His "anti-religious opinions," unlike Mill's only in Bradlaugh's "intemperate" expression of them, should not disqualify him for office. Mill sets forth in Bradlaugh's case a general argument that he could well apply to his own circumstances: "Men of this sort, who while sharing the democratic feelings of the working classes, judged political questions for themselves 'and had courage to assert their individual convictions against popular opposition, were needed, as it seemed to me, in Parliament." Mill's status in this sentence as "me," as the object of a preposition in a parenthetical expression, here asserts as it attempts to disguise his personal investment in this issue. In the *Autobiography* Mill fails to say that Bradlaugh lost the election. It is enough to have said already that Mill, one of the "men of this sort," does not win at the polls. "The utmost possible use, both fair and unfair," of Mill's contribution to Bradlaugh, along with the Tories' usually "unscrupulous" use of their funds, defeats Mill (1:289). In his account, however, he presents this personal failure in the objectifying terms that provide their own consolation. In praising Bradlaugh, Mill argues that both he and the man he supported should have been returned to Parliament.

In the *Autobiography* Mill chooses to ignore the issues that made Bradlaugh's candidacy for Northampton a matter of intense national debate. Like his earlier treatments of his wife, Mill's handling of Bradlaugh erases all individualizing characteristics so that his fellow candidate emerges simply as an only slightly compromised version of the idealized type of the working-class candidate. In fact, Bradlaugh was notorious for both his radical opinions and his provocative advocacy of them. In the 1868 *Cornhill* articles that became *Culture and Anarchy*, Matthew Arnold repeatedly invokes Bradlaugh's name, along with that of the trade-union official George Odger, as the epitome of the mindless working-class revolutionary: "Mr. Bradlaugh, the iconoclast, . . . seems to be almost for baptizing us all in blood and fire into his new social dispensation." Ever since 1860 Bradlaugh had been publishing his opinions under the pseudonym of Iconoclast in the *National Reformer*, the newspaper whose editorship he assumed in 1866. That name attached as well to his role in the career he made for himself as a lecturer devoted to the spread of the secularist movement and to his position as the first president of the National Secular Society, which he founded in 1866. The *National Reformer* was anathema, not only to

Conservatives and members of the established church, but to many pious Liberals and Radicals as well. Early in 1868, Bradlaugh had reprinted in his newspaper the infamous parable of "The Fanatical Monkeys," which pictures God as "a great big monkey sitting upstairs [with] his all-seeing eyes upon you." The *Saturday Review* responded predictably to "this atrocious blasphemy": "Such filthy ribaldry as we have from a sense of duty picked off Bradlaugh's dunghill is simply revolting, odious, and nauseating to the natural sense of shame possessed by a savage" or, one presumes, by a monkey or even by a worker. As repellent as Bradlaugh's irreligion were his republicanism and his neo-Malthusian advocacy of contraception. His 1861 pamphlet on birth control parades his offensive ideas even in its title, *Jesus, Shelley, and Malthus: or Pious Poverty and Heterodox Happiness;* and its content compounds such an unholy conjunction of religion and political economy by recommending a work that touts the salutary benefits of giving free play to one's sexual drives while abstaining from marriage, George R. Drysdale's *Elements of Social Science* (anon., 1854). Even the radical M.P. John Bright, not a man to be cowed by the threat of adverse publicity, refused to support Bradlaugh's bid for election. And Bradlaugh himself confessed that it was "scarcely wonderful" that he had lost the election of 1868.[4]

None of these issues surfaces in Mill's *Autobiography* except in the sanitized reference to Bradlaugh's "intemperate" expression of his unpopular opinions. In defending the principle of electing working-class representatives to Parliament after he had acted on such a principle, Mill simply ignores the distinctions between himself and Bradlaugh, between the respected political philosopher and the noisy publicist, so that the two can be assimilated as parallel cases. Such an approach allows both men to be vindicated against the prejudices of an obtuse electorate.

Mill's more immediate response to this defeat, as he recorded it at the time in letters to friends and supporters, clearly set a greater distance between himself and Bradlaugh. Before the election, Mill was careful to explain that he had offered his assistance to Bradlaugh only on the condition that he plan to stand for Parliament in an election in which he would not oppose any of Gladstone's supporters (16:1433). To Mill's chagrin, Bradlaugh contested Northampton and challenged a Liberal incumbent, Lord Henley. Yet Mill stood firm. A man who holds "original opinions," he claimed, is worth even a "good average liberal" of rank like Lord Henley (16:1435). Mill evidenced his understanding of the difficulty of his situation by resorting to alternate pleading, a ploy that, according to Helen Taylor, sullied his reputation as "an open truthful man." After seeing the letter to his election committee that was published in the *Daily News,* she berated him for the "mean and wretched subterfuges" that he had employed to palliate Bradlaugh's atheism. Shortly after the election, Mill was less sure of the justice of Bradlaugh's cause. Though he shared a number of unpopular views with Bradlaugh, particularly on the need for the representation of women and minorities, Mill pleaded ignorance on the actual extent of those similarities: "How far Mr B. supports any of these opinions in the same manner and on the same grounds that I shd do myself I have not watched his career sufficiently closely to know. I do know that he supports some of them very differently from the way I think right" (16:1501). Twice Mill explained that he would not have "volunteered" to support Bradlaugh, but did so only when asked (16:1501,1522). Mill spoke of his relation to Bradlaugh as that of combatants on the same side in the same battle. The union that should bind them is not that of their principles, but of their disinterestedness: "We want now to establish a bond of union . . . between all disinterested men. They ought all to stand by one another, whatever their opinions, on this ground, & on this ground alone" (16:1501). Most significantly, Mill cautioned his correspondents against identifying the former member from Westminster with the man to whom he had merely given £10. Writing to an elector who had objected to his support of Bradlaugh, Mill declared, "I beg to say that in the first place to wish for a man's success as a parl^y candidate is not to identify oneself with him" (16:1522).[5] Just such an identification is, however, the way in which Mill consoles himself for having lost the election when he comes to write about it in the *Autobiography.*

In fact, Mill's parliamentary career was a good deal more problematic than the account in the *Autobiography* acknowledges. Although he does describe his chairing of the privately organized Jamaica Committee and the threats of assassination that his prominent role there brought him, he does not stress the unpopularity of his stand on women's rights or the "tempest in a tea-room" caused by his 1867 meeting inside the House with representatives of the Reform League (an indiscretion for which he apologized on the floor of the House [28: 219])[6] or the hostility of Westminster officials to the plan for municipal reform that he put forth or his support of Edwin Chadwick as a candidate for Kilmarnock in 1868. Yet all these factors were, in combination, crucial to Mill's defeat in Westminster, a traditional Liberal stronghold, during elections that saw Liberal victories in every other metropolitan London district.

Mill's role on the Jamaica Committee was particularly unpopular. Throughout the years of Mill's tenure in Parliament, the most divisive issue of national debate centered on the controversy over the actions of Edward Eyre in Jamaica. In October 1865 after an uprising there—Mill calls it a "brief disturbance," not a "premeditated rebellion" (1:281)—Governor Eyre had instituted martial law and had kept it in force for a full month after the disorder had been put down. The results, which no one on either side of the debate disputed, involved widespread floggings and the deaths of hundreds of blacks, including that of the supposed ringleader, a mulatto planter named George William Gordon, who was summarily executed. Although the government refused to prosecute Eyre for his actions—he was suspended from his post—the peculiarities of English law allowed any interested private citizen to institute proceedings against him. Mill, vowing that he would have Eyre prosecuted for murder "if there was not another man in Parlt to stand by me" (16:1206), was publicly attacked again and again for his apparently vicious vindictiveness toward a man whom the majority saw as a hero, a man whom Mill condemned as guilty even before he had been tried. A contemporary account of the Jamaica case labeled Mill the "master spirit" and "principal promoter" of the "persecution" of Governor Eyre. Four unsuccessful attempts by the Jamaica Committee to bring to trial either Eyre or his subordinates—in March and April, 1867, and February and June, 1868—kept this issue alive in the newspapers and, therefore, in the minds of Mill's constituents. On the day of the election, one prominent elector, Sir Roderick Murchison, claimed to have hit the streets at 8:00 A.M., "I would walk the shoes off my old feet to have the fellow [Mill] turned out after his infamous conduct towards Governor Eyre."[7] As Bradlaugh said of his own loss, it was "scarcely wonderful" that Mill met a similar fate at the polls.

Perhaps equally damaging was Mill's attempt to support the candidacy of Edwin Chadwick, the sanitary reformer and civil servant with whom he had been friends since the 1820s. When Mill wrote a letter praising Chadwick to E. P. Bouverie, the Liberal M.P. of long standing whom Chadwick hoped to unseat, Bouverie published both Mill's letter and his own response in the *Times*. Mill had been rash enough to suggest that any candidate should have the good sense and generosity to "give way" for Chadwick by withdrawing from the contest. Bouverie accused Mill of creating "dissension" among the Liberals and of attempting to "substitut[e] your individual opinion for the free choice of the constituency" (16 October 1868, p. 10). The *Times* relished the adverse publicity for the Liberals that this internecine quarrel involved. On three occasions, editorial leaders mocked Mill for his support of an untried politician and for the inconsistency of his views on political campaigns. Mill clearly thought, the *Times* complained, that it was "the duty of the candidate to interfere with every election but his own." Moreover, Mill's choice of candidates—Bradlaugh and Odger and, now, Chadwick—revealed his lack of judgment; apparently, according to the *Times*, Mill thought that "the world knows nothing of its greatest men" (16 October 1868, p. 6). The writer of this editorial could not have known how close he was cutting to Mill's pained sense of the fate of the unsung hero, but the paper clearly enjoyed and publicized every evidence that Chadwick gave that he was not the great mind that Mill found him to be. It did not matter to the *Times* that the letter to Bouverie in which Mill had praised Chadwick was private, and that Mill had objected after the fact to its publication. The *Times* was willing to acknowledge only that Mill's "gushing effusions" had brought down "ridicule" on his protegé (22 October 1868, p. 7).

Mill's actions in this case were blamed on all sides, even on contradictory bases. Bouverie claimed that Mill was damaging the Liberal party through his disloyalty, while an anonymous letter to the *Times* castigated Mill for complaining that Bouverie's voting record revealed his disloyalty to the party. The writer, who adduces the principles of *On Liberty* to attack that work's author, concludes that if Mill had his way, "Intellectual capacity is to stand for nothing, honest and free judgment are actually forbidden, and submissive obedience is the one thing requisite [in an M.P.]. Of course, that admirable rule does not apply to Mr. Mill, who must be free to do anything he likes" (24 October 1868, p. 3). Convicted on the pages of the *Times* for bad judgment, behavior obviously inconsistent with his declared principles, and a blindness to Chadwick's inferiority, Mill clearly faced significant challenges in his own bid for reelection.

Yet this unsettling episode makes no appearance in the pages of the *Autobiography*, though it certainly explains the lukewarm support of his fellow Liberals, a factor that Mill mentions in its penultimate paragraph. More telling still is his silence about the national climate in which he pursued his often unpopular goals, a national mood that in many ways insured his defeat. Nowhere in Chapter VII does Mill acknowledge that his years in the House of Commons were marked by numerous and varied threats of revolution or that the fear of incipient insurrections led to widespread defensive postures on the part of the middle and upper classes. Mill treats this period as one in which "a spirit of free speculation" reigns (1:247)—so much for the calumny that Bradlaugh's candor won him—although Mill laments that such speculation was still dominated by intuitionist thinking. His treatment of political conflict is particularly abstract and bloodless. When he mentions a gathering of working-class demonstrators, he fails to explain why the government made "military preparations" to prevent it (1:278). When he refers to the conditions in Ireland, he mentions only "the anger against Fenianism" and the "more decided" evidence available of "Irish disaffection" (1:277,279), bloody "disaffection" that was heralded week after week across the pages of the *Times* under the heading "The Fenian Insurrections." Throughout his account of his stand on Ireland, Mill refuses to grant that his defense of Fenian causes might have rendered suspect his own loyalty or, at least, his judgment.

In 1867 and 1868, "riot and murder were the order of the day," as Bernard Semmel concludes when he places the Jamaica case in the historical context that Mill refuses to offer in his own account of his actions. The American Civil War, the Jamaica controversy, the reform demonstrations, trade-union violence, bread riots, and the Fenian uprisings were all issues of the late 1860s that polarized the classes and portended further bloodshed in the future.[8] By October of 1867, the *Saturday Review* was proclaiming, "the war between society and the dangerous classes, or roughs—between order and rapine—has begun" (26 October, p. 526). By February of 1868, the same paper was ready to blame Mill for encouraging such unrest: his pamphlet on

England and Ireland gave comfort to the "anarchists of Europe" who should gratefully "crown [Mill] the most thoroughgoing apostle of Communism in the next convention at Geneva" (29 February, p. 282). Even when one takes into account the rigid conservatism of this particular paper, such attacks reveal the extent of the fear of revolution that Mill simply never mentions in his account of his work in the House of Commons. The writer who had proclaimed so often the need to consider the relation between the individual and his or her historical circumstances simply ignores all such analysis of his own situatedness.

Instead, Mill claims in the *Autobiography* that the election meant little to him, that he was glad to return to his books and his retirement in Avignon; in short, he implies that he lost the election as much as the result of his own inattention as through the irrational and unfounded "personal prejudice" against him created by his support of Bradlaugh and his attempts to bring Governor Eyre to prosecution. Clearly, Mill's parliamentary career was filled with more vicissitudes than he as a youth had been capable of imagining. His treatment of the end of that career reveals how consistently he tried to defend himself against the recognition that his failures might be laid at his own door.

Mill's contemporaries did what they could to uphold the opposite interpretation of events. Predictably, in light of its earlier criticism, the *Saturday Review* found Mill, "in the main, the cause of his own defeat" (21 November 1868, p. 667). Even the most sympathetic observers agreed. Writing to the *Times* to take issue with Mill's account of his defeat, published earlier in the *Revue des deux mondes*, W. T. Malleson, secretary to the committee that had supported Mill, explained that Mill's constituency had been "affronted" because he had acted so obviously in disregard of their interests. Malleson also disputed Mill's claim that his supporters could not have succeeded against the power implicit in Tory organization and Tory money: "Unfortunately, the full wind upon which we had counted to fill our sails fell away under the influence of the Bouverie correspondence and the Bradlaugh subscription" (21 December 1868, p. 5). George Jacob Holyoake, the radical writer and publisher who admired Mill excessively, had to concede that the £10 that Mill gave Bradlaugh "was worth £10,000 to his Tory opponents, and cost Mill's own committee the loss of £3,000." From the spectacle of Mill's defeat, Holyoake drew a lesson unflattering to the "philosopher" he otherwise invariably honored: "To maintain your opinions at your own cost is one thing, but to proclaim them at the cost of others, without regard to time, consent, or circumstance, is quite a different matter."[9] Needless to say, such pointedly critical voices are not heard in the *Autobiography,* nor is Mill interested in eliciting an understanding of the "time" or "circumstance" that validate what his contemporaries had to say about his defeat.

Yet, as much as Mill seems intent in the *Autobiography* on ignoring the obvious difficulties he faced as a novice politician in his parliamentary career, he ignores as assiduously the credit clearly due him for his substantial achievements as a party man. Bruce Kinzer offers a persuasive analysis of Mill's actions in the House of Commons that stresses how carefully he limited his expression of his more outrageously unpopular ideas until after it was clear that Gladstone would not be able to lead the Liberal party to the successful passage of a Liberal reform bill. Once Disraeli had taken over that role for the Conservatives, Mill felt free to say what he thought; he had, for instance, held his peace in the House about Governor Eyre until the fall of the Russell and Gladstone cabinet (28:xli). Such discretion suggests a much higher degree of political awareness and skill than Mill's own account of his legislative activities would grant him. Yet even this perspective reveals his desire for heroic action, undertaken either by himself or by another. To say that Mill was a "good party man" means that he admired and supported Gladstone (28:xxvi) because Gladstone had the potential to be the kind of heroic leader Mill longed to see at the head of government. Similarly, Mill only briefly mentions his successful opposition to the Parks Regulation Bill that would have closed the royal parks as places of public assembly. This was perhaps the most significant work he did in the House of Commons, but Mill does not emphasize this work because he did it as "one of a number of advanced Liberals," not as the lone warrior facing challenges that no one else would face (1:279). Mill was interested in recording only the work he did in opposition to his own party or as a single, autonomous individual. His treatment of the incident that introduces his mention of the Parks Bill, the Hyde Park riots of July 1866, makes that point even more forcefully. Once again, the imaginative assimilations capable of both revealing the limitations he faced and liberating him from them characterize as well as illuminate his account of his time in the House of Commons.

The most dramatic incident of Chapter VII involves Mill's intervention in the reform agitation that came to be known as the Hyde Park riots. On the evening of 23 July 1866, under the auspices of the Reform League, a large mass of demonstrators were turned away from the gates of Hyde Park; as they turned to march toward Trafalgar Square, where the government had agreed they could rally, violence broke out. Contemporary accounts of the ensuing events vary predictably according to the observers' political and class affiliations. Either the park railings gave way under the pressure of the confused retreat, or they were willfully torn down. By some accounts, the crowd, composed mostly of boys and "roughs," was responsible for the injuries that led to a number of hospitalizations. According to other accounts, the crowd, composed throughout of respectable and peaceable workers, was viciously attacked by the overzealous police. There was no agreement about the extent of the damage—the *Times* was particularly exercised over the flowers and shrubs that had been trampled under lower-class heels—but Mill's later analysis of the situation, that "something very serious seemed impending" (1:278), would have been universally accepted.[10]

Looking back on this moment of crisis, Mill confesses that he feels "much satisfaction" over the part that he had played. Three days after the riot, in a meeting with leaders of the Reform League, Mill convinced them to give up plans for a second rally there, plans that had already been announced on placards posted around the park. As he notes, "At this crisis I really believe that I was the means of preventing much mischief." Mill was able to defuse the situation because he had been the spokesperson for the working classes in the House of Commons. The leaders whom Mill here mentions, Edmond Beales and Colonel Dickson, had "already exerted their influence . . . without success," and Mill pointedly makes no reference to Charles Bradlaugh, a prominent member of the executive committee who had frequently counseled nonviolence. Mill alone was able to carry the day by arguing that another meeting in Hyde Park was justified only if the workers could triumph in a revolution that they were convinced was inevitable. "To this argument . . . they at last yielded." In recording his announcement of his success to the Home Secretary, Sir Spencer Walpole, Mill notes proudly, "I shall never forget the depth of his relief or the warmth of his expressions of gratitude" (1:278).

Here Mill finally has the opportunity to display his powers as "a democratic champion," to participate in a struggle between "patricians and plebians." The personal authority attributed earlier in the *Autobiography* to James Mill is outdone by his son in the arena of public affairs in which the father never directly tested his powers. Theory has been set aside, and Mill is now the man of action, and he is filling that role to the admiration and gratitude of his parliamentary audience, not least important among whom is John Stuart Mill himself. "No other person, I believe, had at that moment the necessary influence for restraining the working classes" (1:279). Satisfaction, on the part of both the participant in the event and the narrator who recounts it, is the hallmark of this section of the *Autobiography*. Here self-abnegation and apology, the tones so typical of earlier sections of Mill's written life, cease. Both the event itself and the occasion of its telling encourage his latent powers of self-assertion.

Significantly, the most careful of recent scholarly research has not been able to corroborate Mill's version of his decisive intervention in the Hyde Park crisis.[11] There are reasons for such a silence in the historical record. Mill's political enemies and even those allies disaffected by his championship of unpopular causes may not have wanted to give him the credit he was due in the records they left either in the House of Commons or in their memoirs. But there is also some reason for doubt in this instance. Particularly suspicious is Mill's account of Walpole's grateful response to the announcement that the crisis had passed. On July 26, four days before the scheduled second public meeting in the park, Walpole, in speaking to the House of Commons, acknowledged that he knew nothing about the intentions of the leaders of the Reform League, who had clearly misunderstood Walpole or been misunderstood by him in their conference on the previous day. Mill then took the floor to assure the members that "Mr. Beales and several leading members of the League" had "just" assured him that no meeting would take place on the thirtieth (28:101). Walpole may have conveyed his appreciation by the look on his face or after the debate, but the text of *Hansard's Parliamentary Debates* reports no spoken "expressions of gratitude." Indeed, the official record reveals the painful fact that Mill's announcement was greeted, not with cheers, but with laughter. He tried to explain that the leaders of the Reform League with whom he had just met did not speak for the entire organization because its governing council had not yet convened. This scrupulous qualification to the announcement of his good news clearly struck a number of members as simply comic. Mill was even moved to chastise his audience: "That ribald laugh might well have been-spared" (28:102).[12]

The public record, then, casts some doubt on Mill's account. Indeed, the event may be one of those instances in which he simply conflated similar events occurring at different times.[13] The excessive gratitude toward him that Mill attributes to the Home Secretary is suspiciously similar to those "expressions of gratitude" he recorded as Lord Durham's response to the writing that Mill did on his behalf: "I saved Lord Durham—as he himself, with much feeling, acknowledged to me" (13:426). The advice that Mill claims to have given the members of the Reform League sounds suspiciously like the counsel that he is on record as having given a year later when, in the spring of 1867, the Reform League renewed its efforts to secure permission to meet in Hyde Park, thereby occasioning another crisis. At that time, Mill withdrew his support from the Reform League because he felt its agitation dangerous and unwarranted by the circumstances. He explained his reasoning, using exactly the formula that he says he used in 1866. Responding to the reports of a rally of the Reform League where Bradlaugh and Dickson had asserted their intentions to seize the rights that the government denied them, Mill argued that physical violence is justified only if there is no redress possible within the framework of existing institutions, and "no one will say that any of these justifications for revolution exist in the present case" (16:1248). Three months later Mill had to defend his position that there were indeed situations in which revolution is justified after he made that point in a speech he gave at the National Reform Union (16:1275; 28: 172). The stand that Mill took in 1867, reported in the *Times* (27 May 1867, p. 12), may simply have become so associated in his mind with his actions during 1866 that specific incidents during the two crises became interchangeable. But whatever the status of Mill's version— be it fact or fiction or some amalgamation of the two—it reveals the profundity of his desire to serve as a "democratic champion" even if that meant furthering the people's interests by persuading them not to demonstrate their power. Unlike so many of his associates, he had not been elected to Parliament after the First Reform Bill had been passed. He had not even had a major role, as James Mill had, in the support offered by the Philosophic Radicals outside Parliament. Now, however, in 1866, he could be a "reformer of the world" and prove his competence as a practical politician.

ASSIMILATION AS ACTION

Mill's early reading and the taste for heroic action that it encouraged provided, I think, the sources of the specific role that he casts for himself in his account of the Hyde Park crisis. As a "book-ish" youth, Mill had gathered his most profound impressions from his reading, and long before the 1860s he had found the figure he wished to emulate in Parliament in a book that held the place of holy writ in his agnostic upbringing: Condorcet's *Life of Turgot*. Even in his maturity, this work seemed to Mill "one of the wisest and noblest of lives, delineated by one of the wisest and noblest of men," and it profoundly affected him at the time when he claimed he was a "dry, hard logical machine" (1:115,110). As if to highlight the uniqueness of its place in his education, Mill treats it long after he records reading works like Joanna Baillie's *Constantine Paleologus* and the histories of Tacitus, works that presumably developed his taste for "animated narrative." Turgot provided an example of active political service based on the most unimpeachable of philosophic principles. This biography offered Mill "poetic culture of the most valuable kind" (1:115) because Turgot was, as he said elsewhere, the "most memorable example in modern times of a man who united the spirit of philosophy with the pursuits of active life" (4:335). According to Mill, Turgot's bold reforms as finance minister under Louis XVI might even have stemmed the course of the revolution that followed not long after the king dismissed him from office. Turgot, despite the reverses he suffered, closed the gap, always so troubling to Mill, between theory and practice. Carlyle might counsel his contemporaries to close their Byron and open their Goethe, but Mill, having opened Condorcet's *Life of Turgot* early in his training, would continue for years to read his own life in its pages.

Turgot, in particular, provides the mold into which Mill casts his account of the Hyde Park crisis. The centerpiece, both literally and thematically, of Condorcet's *Life* deals with Turgot's response to the 1775 corn riots. A bad harvest and the resulting rise in the price of bread are used by Turgot's enemies to question his policy of free trade. Turgot and his supporters are publicly attacked as "men employed in wild systems, who wished to govern from the recesses of the *closet* upon speculative principles, and who sacrificed the people to the experiments which they were desirous of making to ascertain the truth of their system." Like Bentham and Coleridge, but more dangerous because he had more power, Turgot is a closet student. Like Mill, who was publicly mocked as the "lost philosopher" out of his element in the House of Commons, Turgot is seen as the theorist defeated by the exigencies of practical politics [14]—until, of course, public welfare is genuinely threatened by agitators who plan to "starve the capital." Someone must be ready, says Condorcet with a flourish, to "check the evil, to save Paris, and perhaps the kingdom": "All the powers of government seemed suspended. M. Turgot [alone] acted" (172–73). Like Sir Spencer Walpole, the Home Secretary whose public tears during the Hyde Park crisis had revealed both his impotence and his frustration, the local authorities in Paris seem paralyzed. As in the later English crisis, the corn riots turn on the question of public assembly: the parliamentary order prohibiting a mass meeting of the people, Condorcet claims, "might have renewed the [earlier] tumult." Turgot, however, stands firm in the face of this threat; unlike Mill, he uses his governmental position to prohibit assembly on pain of death. Like Mill's act of persuasion, however, his decisive intervention insures that no assembly will take place. In both cases, the threatened peace of the capital is maintained. "From this moment," Condorcet concludes triumphantly, "tranquillity was restored." Here the French biographer waxes lyrical: "Virtue and genius had obtained in this moment of crisis the ascendency they necessarily possess when they have an opportunity of displaying all their energy" (173–74). The crisis passes, and Turgot, like Mill receiving the thanks of Walpole, finds his reward in the king's praise: months later when he passes through the area in which the unrest arose, Louis XVI says, "*It is M. Turgot and I only that love the people*" (175).

This comment—and the irony it casts on Turgot's subsequent dismissal when the king could not endure the heat in the kitchen of Turgot's reforms—clearly impressed Mill: he paraphrases the line and comments on it in his 1828 review of Scott's *Life of Napoleon* (20:80). Later on, Mill told John Morley that "in his younger days whenever he was inclined to be discouraged, he was in the habit of turning" to Condorcet's *Turgot*. Just before Mill resumed work on the section of the *Autobiography* that would include his account of the Hyde Park riots, Morley in the *Fortnightly Review* had compared Mill's failure to be returned to Parliament after the passage of the Second Reform Bill to "the dismissal of the great minister of Lewis XVI." In writing Morley to express his appreciation, Mill said, "I never received so gratifying a compliment as the comparison of me to Turgot; it is indeed an honour to me that such an *assimilation* should have occurred to you" (16: 1497; emphasis added). Mill credits Morley with the power to see the similarity between himself and Turgot, but, particularly in his account of the Hyde Park crisis, it is Mill himself who assimilates his character with that of the eighteenth-century Frenchman. Turgot had been the subject of the long and passionate peroration of Mill's 1827 speech on "The Uses of History." There Turgot stands as the preeminent example of the "sublime character" of the philosopher as statesman, the epitome of integrity and self-sacrifice who is derided by his ignorant and self-interested contemporaries as "a visionary and a theorist." In the *Autobiography*, Turgot and Mill become one, to prove that such an attitude merely displays "the presumptuousness and besotted ignorance" of those who hold it (26:397).

Turgot, as a prerevolutionary figure, was, however, both a fully appropriate hero for a man who never had the opportunity to participate in the revolution he longed for and hero who, for precisely that reason, left something to be desired. As usual in the complex imaginative and emotional equations of the *Autobiography*, Mill has it both ways: his assimilation of Turgot to himself allows Mill both to imagine success and to accept defeat. Another, later figure in French revolutionary history, the journalist Armand Carrel, exerts an equally powerful and perhaps more pervasive effect on Mill's treatment of his parliamentary career. Mill erases Carrel's presence from his account of his experience even though the two men had actually met in 1833. Yet that absence, I think, belies Carrel's profound significance as the unacknowledged master spirit of this section of the *Autobiography*.

Mill's adulation of the figures of French history was consistently excessive, a point that John C. Cairns proves repeatedly and convincingly in his introduction to the Toronto edition of Mill's writings on *French History and Historians*. As Cairns notes, Mill found in France "a mirror, the clearest he knew, in which to see what preoccupied him in England" (20:vii); and this general point deserves more specific, personal application.[15] On repeated occasions before the 1850s, Mill had hoped that France would chart a European course toward democracy and that Britain would follow, but even after those hopes faded, figures like Turgot and Carrel could be for Mill a mirror in which he could see reflected the ambitions he had earlier, as a boy and a youth, cherished for himself. Yet he attempts to disguise this unpopular and un-English excess in the *Autobiography* by deleting as a "useless waste of space and time" the details about his imitation of the *philosophes* that he had included in the *Early Draft* (1:111). Even his account of the Girondins as models of the revolutionary future he envisioned for England after visiting France is tepid beside the table-thumping rhetoric of his early review of Scott's *Life of Napoleon*. There, the twenty-two-year-old writer does not "*solicit*" the reader's attention when he provides the evidence of the nobility of the Girondins; rather, he "*demands*" it in the name of all humanity (20:104). The passage is the only one in the review that reveals the relative immaturity of its author. Such "childish" or "boyish" enthusiasm may be displaced from the surface of the mature record of his life, but figures like Turgot, Carrel, and the Girondins formed for Mill a pantheon of revolutionary saints, to whose lives he resorted for justification and explanation. Mill turned to such figures as other, more conventionally reared Victorians would look to Paul, John the Baptist, Isaiah, or Jeremiah.[16] A phrase that Mill uses in his account of the Hyde Park crisis, his reference to "*les grand moyens*" to which he had to resort in his dealings with the Reform League (1:278), suggests that just such a model of French political action was in his mind as he recounted that crisis. Carrel, the historical figure closest in time and in ambition to Mill's own experience, was a particularly powerful figure of self-interpretation, so fully assimilated into the *Autobiography* as not to require mention.

When Mill met Carrel for the first and perhaps only time in 1833, Mill had been struck enough by him to write Carlyle a lengthy account of the Frenchman's character and actions (12:194–97). In 1837, more than a year after Carrel had died senselessly in a duel, Mill published this account as part of his article "Armand Carrel," an article that he said was written "*con amore*" because Carrel was, even more than the Girondins, "the type of a philosophic radical *man of action* in this epoch" (17:1978). Mill exhibits nothing less than hero-worship in this account of Carrel as the man who might have become the Mirabeau or Washington of his era. Mill endows Carrel with his own democratic goals and his own principles on free speech, the toleration of different views, and the rights of the minority against the power of the majority. The future author of *On Liberty* bluntly refuses to believe Désiré Nisard, the source of much of his information on Carrel, when that source claims that Carrel ultimately lost faith in such ideals (20:210). As John Cairns points out, Mill "made of Carrel everything a young liberal should be, even to coming round at the end [of his life] to reflect a touch of the English radical" (20:lxvii). Mill self-consciously notes Carrel's exemplary qualities: "We can learn from the study of him, what we all . . . must be" if reform is to take place because the "true idea" of Carrel is not that of a "literary man, but of a man of action" (20:171). Again Mill resorts to the conventional distinction between thought and action to elevate, as his contemporaries did, deeds above words.

Mill's 1837 assessment of Carrel clearly transforms the French journalist into the ideal man whom Mill had conceived during his recovery from his earlier crisis. Speaking of the ambitions of "all young and ardent Frenchmen" but actually describing his own, Mill calls Carrel "the expression of what in their best moments they would wish to be" (20:212). Carrel is the epitome of both unselfconsciousness and manysidedness. Mill quotes the letter that he wrote to Carlyle in 1833 when he explains that Carrel combines "perfect self-reliance with the most unaffected modesty"; he is "free" of self-consciousness as if he were free of disease (20:202). Carrel can argue any side of a case because he understands all sides better than their adherents. Significantly, Mill wrote this article in the year following his father's death, and his spirited defense of Carrel vicariously defeats the father who threatens to dominate his son even in death. Carrel, the young Mill's second self, is a member of the "new historical school"; he does not judge others "by the rule and square of some immutable theory of mutable things" (20:186). In this passage, Mill makes Carrel sound like Macaulay explaining the shortcomings of the deductive reasoning upon which James Mill based his political philosophy. By stating Carrel's opinions in such a way, Mill identifies Carrel with the younger self whose reading of Macaulay's analysis liberated him in 1829 from the confines of his father's narrowly constructed Utilitarianism. Carrel is, finally, that ideal unreachable among the English: the union of Bentham and Coleridge in a whole human being, a reformer who understands that institutions serve varying purposes at various points in history. Of Carrel, Mill proclaims triumphantly, "He was a human being complete at all points, not a fraction or *frustrum* of one" (20: 213). Mill grants to Carrel the integrity that he questions in himself. The Frenchman's passion and commitment prove him to be, like the individuals of *On Liberty* or like Harriet Mill, "the artist [who] has a character" (20:196).

Carrel, as Mill represents him, comes not only to embody his ideals but also to share with him the circumstances that inevitably limit or preclude the implementation of those ideals. Forced out of public life by the repressive measures that followed the Revolution of 1830, Carrel enacts the compromise that Mill was forced to accept after he began to work for the East India Company. Mill, as editor of the *London and Westminster Review* in the 1830s, was playing something of the role of Carrel the journalist, though Mill was never so deeply and so dangerously embroiled in politics as Carrel was. "Excluded from the region of deeds," Carrel "has still that of words; and words are deeds, and the cause of deeds" (20:172). Even in his depiction of Carrel's subjection to the restrictions imposed upon him by his placement in a particular country at a particular time, Mill rewrites his own diminished status in glorifying terms. Here, words become deeds, more than simply the cause of deeds, though they are that as well.

Carrel, moreover, serves as the medium in which Mill can draw an idealized self-portrait for the simple reason that his death has removed any possibility that such theoretical justifications as the equation of word to deed might have to be tested in practice. Like Sterling, Carrel is a powerfully appealing figure because he has died young, before he could be fully tested. Writing in 1848 at the opening of yet another revolution in France, Mill admitted that his "every second thought has been of Carrel—he who perhaps alone in Europe was qualified to direct such a movement" (13:731–32). By deciding that the only figure equal to the challenges of the times was a man already dead, Mill was offering a graveside tribute to his own revolutionary goals. Fortunately, at least for Carrel's standing in Mill's estimation, Carrel did not live to become humbled by the further disillusionment of Mill's earlier hopes. Circumstances could not besmirch "the noble-ness of [his] character" or cast doubt on his "eminent talents as a political leader" (20:203).

The assimilations that characterize Mill's early depictions of Carrel make it impossible to distinguish the subject from the object of the analysis that Mill undertakes. In the portion of the letter to Carlyle reprinted in the article on Carrel, Mill actually describes the "quiet emphasis" of Carrel's speech by quoting the words that Carlyle had used to characterize the tone of an essay that Mill himself had writ-ten in 1833 (20:201). By invoking that phrase, Mill identifies himself with the younger self who originally evoked it from Carlyle, with the French journalist to whom it is now attributed, and even with Carlyle, the writer who had first used it to praise Mill himself. But the process of assimilation in this article may be even more complex than such an example implies. Mill, who knew Carrel only slightly, may have drawn his portrait of the French journalist in accordance with the out-line of Turgot's character as it appears in Condorcet's *Life*. Mill seems to have attributed to Carrel the qualities in Turgot that he himself wanted to emulate, therefore finding in the editor of the *National* the fulfillment of the promise of an active political life epitomized by the minister of Louis XVI. The characteristics that Condorcet emphasizes are precisely those that appear in "Armand Carrel." The hero-worship of one French thinker for a French politician provides the terms in which an English writer can worship a contemporary figure of French political life. Accordingly, Condorcet's relation to Turgot is recapitu-lated in Mill's relation to Carrel. As the account of the Hyde Park riots allows Mill to play Turgot's role, the writing of "Armand Carrel" offers him a chance to identify, at least briefly, with even Condorcet, the *"last of the philosophes,"* the only one to have participated in the French Revolution.[17]

The adulatory description of the hero of *The Life of Turgot* offers an uncanny prophecy of the principles that Mill would most honor, both in himself and in others. Condorcet sees in his subject a philosophical "wholeness" that raises him almost to the level of "perfection" (377, 380). Like both Carrel and Mill, Turgot is a man interested in all sub-jects, a man who can speak with authority on many and diverse topics, but a man whose primary allegiance is to truth, no matter the im-mediate consequences of his decision to follow wherever it may lead.

Turgot believes that knowledge and the free dissemination of knowledge can only accelerate the progress of humanity toward the social and moral perfection that awaits in the future. Turgot's specific principles, as they are described in Condorcet's *Life,* correspond to those Mill came to espouse: representative government, the equality of the sexes, and the importance of education as the "first duty" of the state (335). Mill, with doubtful justification, attributes the first of these to Carrel. Most importantly, Carrel acts on Turgot's ideals by asserting through his journalistic practice both freedom of speech and freedom of the press. Condorcet enunciates this principle in words that inevitably recall both the author of *On Liberty* and the editor of the *National:* "All truth is useful, and a printed error cannot be dangerous, at least while we have the liberty of attacking it" (337). Turgot, as one of the privileged class who was willing to question privilege, sheds an idealizing light on both Carrel and Mill. Even in this early essay, Mill seems to be entering the hall of mirrors typical of his more directly autobiographical writing. It is impossible to tell whether the figure being drawn represents the subject or the object of the perception that constitutes it: Turgot, Carrel, Mill, and even Condorcet are all assimilated here.

Even though Mill thoroughly revised his essay on Carrel for the 1859 and 1867 editions of his *Dissertations and Discussions,* both revisions being completed shortly before he turned to the *Early Draft* or to the later additions he made to it, Carrel does not appear by name in any extant draft of the *Autobiography.* Yet Carrel is literally absent from the text, as I have suggested, because his figurative presence so thoroughly pervades it. The similarities between Turgot and Carrel that lie below the surface of the 1837 essay become more complex and more complexly interwoven in the *Autobiography,* and they testify to the ultimately inextricable combinations of cause and effect that mark the assimilation of identities in autobiographical narrative. Yet it is possible to demonstrate that Carrel's presence in Mill's written life is most clearly felt at exactly the juncture at which the example of Turgot exerts its fullest pressure—in the account of the Hyde Park crisis.

Carrel, according to Mill in 1837, is "one of the few . . . who seem raised up to turn the balance of events at some trying moment in the history of nations, and to have or to want whom, at critical points, is the salvation or the destruction of an era" (20:169). In the chapter added to the *Logic* for the edition of 1865, the year before the fray in Hyde Park, Mill uses the same formulation to defend the instrumentality of the great man: "A good or a bad counsellor, in a single city at a particular crisis, has affected the whole subsequent fate of the world" (8:941). The inflated rhetoric, which suspends the fate of an era or a world on the action of one person, is that which marks Condorcet's *Life*, Mill's account of his dealings with the Reform League, and Mill's description of the "most trying" test of Carrel's political skill, his handling of the insurrectionary tendencies of the Society of the Rights of Man.

Mill explains in "Armand Carrel" that he "had the good fortune to be present" at the meeting in 1833 of the Society for the Protection of the Liberty of the Press when the integrity of its republicanism was put in question by the members of the Society of the Rights of Man (20:207). This more radical group had called for the adoption by the larger society of their Declaration of the Rights of Man, which they had adopted from Robespierre and had published as a statement of their own revolutionary principles. Mill depicts this challenge as a genuine crisis, hyperbolically calling it the turning point that threatened "every other kind of republicanism" in France and the event that actually raised "the passionate resistance to the democratic movement" and led, after 1835, to the "imprisonment and exile of its most active members" (20:205). At first, Carrel had responded to this challenge with words, using the verbal sword that Othus glorifies in *Constantine Paleologus*. Displaying "though in a bloodless field, the qualities of a consummate general," he had marshaled his skills as a writer and published a series of articles in which he had set a distance between himself and the "objectionable" qualities of the Declaration while still praising the intentions of those who supported it (20:206–7). Yet words were not enough. When Carrel attended the meeting of the Society for the Protection of the Liberty of the Press, he came face to face with the champions of more extreme republicanism. In effect, Carrel played Girondin to their rendition of Robespierre and his followers. In essence, this minor moment in the history of French journalism allows Mill to rewrite the history of the French Revolution. Although "Paris was convulsed with apprehension on the subject" (20:205), Carrel mastered the situation and moderation triumphed, unscathed by the fury of violent radicalism.

The writer of "Armand Carrel" is greatly impressed by the result of this confrontation, and he expresses his admiration in the same words that he will later use to record the gratitude that the Home Secretary expressed to him when he saved London from the rebellious Reform League: "We shall never forget the impression we received of the talents both of Carrel and of the leader of the more extreme party, M. Cavaignac." Mill goes on to contrast the talents of the two men so that Carrel can win the contest between them. Carrel defuses the volatile tension between the two groups assembled at the meeting just as Mill convinces the members of the Reform League not to challenge the government: Carrel takes their point of view, argues their premises to their logical conclusion, and literally convinces them to take his word on what they should do. He shows them the implications of their theories by "plac[ing] himself at their point of view; [laying their ideas] down in more express and bolder terms than they had done themselves" and thus startling men who thought themselves to be more extreme than he (20:207). This is precisely the tactic that Mill claims to have used with the Reform League, the tactic that was criticized in 1867 because it seemed to justify the undertaking of revolutionary measures if such action has a chance of success. So impressed are the members of the Society for the Liberty of the Press that Carrel is chosen to report on the manifesto—to speak for some among those who thought him their opponent—just as Mill is asked by the members of the Reform League to speak at the meeting they held, not in Hyde Park as originally planned, but at the Agricultural Hall, an invitation that Mill uncharacteristically accepted despite his differences with the League on the issue of women's suffrage.

Carrel's guilt by association, the result of his dealings with the Society for the Rights of Man, had exposed him to severe criticism by more conservative onlookers. Again, the parallel between Mill's and Carrel's experiences is clear. As Mill explains in the 1837 essay, Carrel was "publicly calumniated" for his advocacy of republicanism and was charged with having "indirectly instigated" the attempted assassination of the French king by Guiseppe Fieschi, an "atrocity" of which Carrel was wholly innocent (20:207–8). Similarly, the *Saturday Review* had published a particularly harsh criticism of the speech Mill made in the House of Commons on the day after the disturbance in Hyde Park. In that speech, he had chastised the government for its repressive measures, a "job of work" that it would take many years to efface (28:100), and Disraeli had countered by mocking Mill's words as more appropriate to the rabble-rouser in Hyde Park than to a gentleman in the House of Commons. Mill, the politician who, according to the *Saturday Review,* should have been trusted to restore peace because of his "philosophic neutrality," had actually offered the "inflammatory harangue" of a demagogue, the kind of talk that might have brought "brute force" into play.[18]

Carrel and Mill used comparable, writerly strategies to deflect such criticism. In response to the attacks on him and much after the fact, Carrel decided to publish his earlier report on the proposed acceptance of the Declaration of the Rights of Man by the Society for the Protection of the Liberty of the Press. According to Mill, Carrel's report put on paper "his whole mind on the new ideas of social reform considered in reference to practice," and Mill presents it in exactly those terms that he uses to characterize his aspirations for his own writing: it "subsists for any one to read," it puts "his past conduct in its true light," it is a "monument at once of the farsighted intellect of Carrel, and of his admirable skill in expression" (20:207–8). Similarly, Mill explains in the *Autobiography* that he has "entered thus particularly into this matter," the account of his role in the Hyde Park crisis, because Tory and Tory-Liberal journalists have charged him with having been "intemperate and passionate" during "the trials of public life" (1:278–79). In Mill's case, such a written vindication was not a document resurrected from the past to shed a particular light on the past; rather, it was his present rewriting of the past, his revision of his character in accordance with the ideals of political action epitomized by the conduct of his French predecessors. Mill, indeed, could suggest that he had gone one better than even these French models of heroic authority. Turgot had died before the great revolution. Carrel had died uselessly in a duel before the Revolution of 1848. In London, in 1866, John Stuart Mill was, finally, the right man in the right place at the right time. Such a conclusion, however, rests solely on the evidence of the text that Mill creates to represent his experiences during that crisis. Writing becomes the only and imperishable register of character.

Although the lengthy final chapter of the *Autobiography* may be dismissed as irrelevant to the goals that Mill proclaims on the first page of its first chapter, it, like the earlier sections written at earlier times, reveals the power of Mill's youthful ambitions. He has attempted to convince both himself and his readers that those ambitions are the toys of childhood, toys that must be put aside for the more mature, less dramatic satisfactions of a "literary existence." But in the pages of the final chapter in the *Autobiography,* Mill is living a "literary" life in a more literal fashion than he is willing to admit. Writing in his sixties, John Stuart Mill—the saint of rationalism, respected author of the *Logic* and *Principles of Political Economy,* former M.P., Lord Rector of St. Andrews University—this same John Stuart Mill seems to be reverting to a childish identification with the figures who populate his own imagination. The writer whose authorial presence in other works is so often marked by its magisterial calm and assurance is here subjected to his own earlier desires in a way that reveals their continuing significance to him. His treatment of the Hyde Park crisis reveals his unsatisfied need to prove himself, as Turgot and Carrel had done, in the realm of active political life.

That Mill's profound distrust of his own role as a speculative thinker should surface at the end of the *Autobiography* results, at least in part, from the nature of the work he was writing. Autobiography has frequently been described as the narrative equivalent of psychoanalysis,[19] but it is, more specifically, like any powerful imaginative or emotional engagement with one's past, a form of regression. As the writer relives his or her past in the retelling of its crucial events, those impulses proper to infancy, childhood, and adolescence may be resurrected to assert their power over accounts of later events to which they have no direct relation. Just as Tristram Shandy proves that the autobiographical task expands indefinitely because one continues to live as one writes, so past time collapses as the writer looks back on it from the perspective of the present. Events separated by ten years in the living of them may be separated by ten days or ten weeks in the telling. Recent accounts of autobiography have been so scrupulous, and rightly so, in defining the effect of the writer's present attitudes on his or her depiction of the past—the face reflected in the moving water, as Wordsworth's image in the *Prelude* has it—that it is easy to overlook the effect of past events on the equanimity of the mature writer. But autobiographies are, by definition, both incomplete and immature. There is often in these narratives such an unabashed but unconscious display of still unsatisfied needs that one is almost embarrassed for the author, as one might be embarrassed for an adolescent who parades the bleeding heart upon the sleeve. Preoccupations and longings that are deeply buried or less obviously apparent in the author's other works come to dominate and overwhelm more mature impulses once the act of writing an autobiography brings them to the fore.

Such a process evidences itself in a variety of autobiographical narratives. In this sense, the speaker of *In Memoriam* is indeed "an infant crying for the light," and the narrator of Darwin's *Autobiography* is the simple, wide-eyed innocent whom he presents himself to be, a child who expects to find the world exactly as he wants it. The entire structure of *Villette* serves as an elaborate compensation for Lucy Snowe's early losses. The death of David Copperfield's mother, in his retelling of it, not only "cancels" the present and recalls to him an "earlier image" of her; it returns both the speaker and his subject, his younger self, to infancy: "The mother who lay in the grave, was the mother of my infancy: the little creature in her arms, was myself, as I had once been, hushed for ever on her bosom." For the length of its telling, this incident allows both character and narrator—as well, presumably, as the reader—to relive the infantile fantasy of union with an all-accepting, unchanging maternal presence in a warm embrace that defies death. For John Stuart Mill, however, the childish desire was less for union than for escape, less for subsumption into the paternal figure than for the ability to usurp that figure's place. Only a life of political action would satisfy that longing. As Herbert Spencer noted acutely about Mill's defeat in the 1868 election, Mill was "not content to [advance social welfare] by word only; he sought to do it by deed also," and if he had lived, Spencer thought, Mill could have been expected to return to the political stage.[20]

Mill's treatment of his parliamentary career in general and of the Hyde Park crisis in particular reveals his continuing need to write about his experience in ways that rewrite his character. In looking to the past, Mill is able to see again an individual who can play a more heroic role than that his father had played in his life and who can fulfill the ambitions that his earliest reading had impressed upon him. The vocation of reformer, to which the young Mill had looked forward with religious fervor, could be only indirectly undertaken during the thirty-five years of his life that he served as an employee of the

East India Company. The writer who kept adding to and rewriting his account of his life could not but revisit and have revisited upon him the allure of his childish ambitions, and passages in the *Autobiography* testify to their enduring power long after Mill has tried to deny their strength when he records the appeal those ambitions held for him at the age of twelve or fifteen. Whether Mill felt himself infused with the spirits of Turgot and Carrel as he confronted the leaders of the Reform League in 1866, one can never tell; that he felt so inspired when he recounted that confrontation seems clear. The regressive power of autobiographical narration would have been enough to determine this outcome. Once the imaginative re-creation of the past brings to the surface the adolescent fantasy of replacing the parent through heroic action, that fantasy comes to dominate and determine the story being told.

In this sense, then, even Mill's imaginative experience, like his personal and professional experience, was determined for him rather than by him. The writer who equated his own character with his writings would, almost inevitably, write an autobiography. That autobiographical activity, reviving the regressive pains and hopes of childhood, would involve finding its satisfactions, almost inevitably, in the reinscription on his experience of the forms of heroic action that had been impressed upon the writer by his early reading. In trying to escape the trap set by the theory that character is formed by experience, Mill simply demonstrates that the most creative and imaginative gestures of such escape take their form from that experience. Although it would be a mistake to ignore the genuine pride and pleasure that Mill exhibits as he writes the passages that recount his parliamentary career, such pleasure does become identified with and limited by its identification with writing. Such a record may become "monumental" in that it exists for others to witness once it is converted into the permanence of print, but it becomes for the writer an embalmed pleasure, an emotion experienced in the writing and not beyond it, no more an assurance of fulfillment and success in the future than any past activity can be.

In the last analysis, the figures to whom Mill assimilated himself in the *Autobiography* and elsewhere are, without exception, figures of failure. They are men more remarkable for their potential than for their achievement, more significant for the promises they hold out for the future than for the certainty of substantial achievements in the past. Turgot, Carrel, the Girondins, Comte, all join their English counterparts, Coleridge, Sterling, John Austin, and Bradlaugh, to demonstrate in strikingly similar fashion the constriction of individual ambition and talent by historical circumstances and social conditions beyond the individual's control. The reasons for their failure are diverse—death, distraction, drug addiction, popular prejudice, personal disinclination—but the outcome is the same in every case. What could have been accomplished is left undone. The work that could have contributed to the evolution of human institutions toward the improvement they will someday reach, that work remains for future generations to undertake.

Even poor, confused Sir William Hamilton comes to play this role. In the last pages of the *Examination,* Mill laments that a mind so packed with learning has left its proper work undone, and Hamilton emerges as another of Mill's "relative opposites," the "brother philosopher" who, through his "over-anxiety to make safe a foregone conclusion," became "thoroughly his own dupe" (9:492–93). The conclusion that Hamilton was so anxious to protect, the Doctrine of Free-will, is simply another version of the autonomy that Mill himself was so concerned to grant every individual.[21] But Mill cannot rest with such a harsh conclusion, either for himself or for Hamilton. In the last paragraph of the *Examination,* Mill regrets that Hamilton never engaged in the kind of work for which his vast and unparalleled erudition had fitted him, the writing of a history of philosophy, and Mill cannot bring himself to deny to a fellow philosopher an immortal agency even if it must be premised on work that has not been prepared for publication. Mill hopes that Hamilton's "copious common-place books," which "he was known to have left," might be "carefully preserved; that they will, in some form or other, be made accessible to students, and will yet do good service to the future historians of philosophy." Hamilton's notes may actually be, like Mill's books, an intellectual pemican. After his devastating attack on his colleague, Mill can still envision a book that might be written by Hamilton and published after his death so that "future ages" will "rejoice in the fruits of his labours, and . . . celebrate his name" (9:504).

This odd note of tender hope and charity toward Hamilton, whose very bones, as Mark Pattison put it, Mill had delighted to chew, reveals the extent of Mill's ambivalence about the figures of failure who populate his works and reflect his sense of his own career. In the long run, he did not want to defeat Hamilton utterly because Hamilton served too thoroughly to represent his worst fears about his own work. In a similar attempt to explain the relative lack of achievement in a man like John Austin, a man whose precision of thought and openness to the ideas of others Mill found so admirable, he notes that Austin never completed his anticipated work on jurisprudence, but rather left his "literary remains" in "fragmentary" form to serve, like Hamilton's, as a "mine of material for the future." In the last words Mill says about Austin, he draws a portrait of a "naturally enthusiastic character," a man whose admiration for human nobility led him to speak of "the godlike Turgot" (21:204). Just as Austin expresses his character in admiring Turgot and Mill expresses his own in admiring Austin, both Turgot and Austin are assimilated with Mill through their failure to do what they set out to do. According to Condorcet, after Turgot lost his place as minister of finance, he retired into privacy to write a great work in which "truth without restraint" would be presented to "Posterity only" (271), but that great work, like Austin's treatise on jurisprudence or Mill's ethology or Hamilton's history of philosophy, was never written. According to Mill, both he and Turgot practiced what he called the "politics of the future" (1:262), by which he meant, of course, that their ideas looked to the future, that their ideas would determine the course of human improvement. But endlessly deferred achievement may be no achievement at all, and the prominence that Mill gives to such figures in the submerged narrative of professional frustration in the *Autobiography* suggests some awareness of the dilemma he faced: the life that claims value for itself primarily in terms of the practical benefit that will accrue only if its ideas are acted upon has set for itself a goal that can only retreat more distantly into a future that cannot even be glimpsed.

Early in life, Mill jokingly referred to himself as the "person whom I see oftenest and with whom I am most intimate" (12:117). As a good associationist, he took for granted the idea that he did see himself, that he was intimate with what went on in his mind. In fact, I think, his practice as an artist of character comes close to supporting such a claim. As a theorist of character, Mill was self-deceived, even "duped" by himself, to use the harsh word he applied to Sir William Hamilton. He could not finally solve the problems inherent in his associationist thought, and he would not recognize that a verbal feint does not resolve the conflicting claims of freedom and necessity. The assertions of the relative autonomy of the individual that he so frequently makes whenever he discusses the formation of character in his essays or in works like the *Logic, On Liberty,* and *The Subjection of Women*— such assertions are weak objections to facts that Mill cannot face and cannot deny. The changes in character that he envisions in theory as within each individual's reach turn out to be impossible to effect in practice. As Mill's own experience proves, each outcome is not simply determined; it is overdetermined, not the probable outcome of one cause, but the inevitable result of a combination of causes. Yet as an artist of character, as a writer who drew the portraits of so many of his contemporaries, Mill may have achieved an attitude that approaches something like an acceptance of that condition. In assimilating himself to so many varied instances of failure, in seeing the same features in so many of the mirrors that his writing proposed, Mill suggests that his experience and its unsatisfying results are not, after all, unique. For every Mirabeau or Washington, there are countless Carrels.

Taken as a whole, then, as Mill wished it to be taken, his work defines the conditions of his own career as nothing less than universal. Such limitations, such disappointments become the common denominator of all experience. The character that is written in these terms is simply an instance of the limitations inherent in all ambition, in all longing for achievement, authority, and influence. In this sense, therefore, Mill's work constitutes his *Middlemarch* rather than his *Prelude:* a panoramic view of present impossibilities in light of historic aspirations and achievements. Perhaps Mill's plight was unique only in its pitting of a "nature," like Dorothea Brooke's, particularly "ardent, theoretic" against circumstances that denied the revolution that would have tested and perhaps confirmed its strength and its power. Like so many modern Theresas, Mill had no chance to live "a grand life here—now—in England," just as Dorothea has only the opportunity for vicarious participation in "the unhistoric acts" of her husband's less than heroic political career. The "medium" for "ardent deeds" is, as George Eliot puts it, "for ever gone."[22]

In his sketches of Coleridge and Comte, Turgot and Carrel, Hamilton and Austin, Mill, like George Eliot, creates a cast of characters so encompassing as to achieve the illusion of universality, characters who propose the rule of failed ambitions and prove the inability to find an exception to it. By focusing so exclusively on such characters, by giving them such prominence, Mill not only expresses freely his long-cherished desire for heroic action, a desire that remained strong throughout his life; he also approaches a mature recognition of the fact that the ability to have such desires at all is as close as most people ever come to having them satisfied. In the "Finale" that remains implicit in his work, in the energy of his assimilative imagination, Mill balances the desire for an epic life against the recognition of its impossibility. By chronicling his imaginative engagements with the lives of his contemporaries and his predecessors, Mill achieves an art of acceptance that acknowledges the historic inevitability of his own "unhistoric acts."

Afterword

At the opening of his 1873 review of Grote's *Aristotle,*
Mill pays tribute to his lifelong friend and the work he left unfinished
at his death. Here, in one of the last and least graceful passages of
Mill's prose, he equates life with the opportunity to write; its end is to
be regretted only as the end of writing, the cessation of the "goodly
volumes" that have come from the writer's hand. Even a few sentences
from the passage convey the complications involved in Mill's attempts
to mourn Grote's death simply on the basis of the work that will never
be accomplished because of that death:

> Seldom has any literary undertaking given more cause to lament
> the shortness of human life . . . than this work, in its present un-
> finished condition, exhibits. For Mr. Grote's death was not, in the
> ordinary meaning of the word, premature; he lived to the ripe
> age of seventy-six years; but this, his latest production, down to
> the very chapter in which his pen was interrupted by fatal illness,
> shows an undiminished vigour of intellect and perseverance of
> mental industry, which raise sad thoughts of how much good work
> he might still have done, if the merely animal and nutritive organs
> of his bodily frame had been capable of as long a persistency of
> life and health as the properly human organ, the reasoning and
> thinking brain.

Death may stop the heart, but, more importantly, it interrupts the pen.
The body is "merely animal." Its organs function only to nourish what
is "properly human," the power to reason and to think. Mill finally asks
his readers to "rejoice" with him that a work "commenced after the

age of seventy" has yielded at least "two goodly volumes": "let us . . . rather rejoice that so much has been given" (11:475). The faint echo of the conclusion of Wordsworth's "Immortality" ode charts the distance between this cerebral call to celebration and the poet's evocation of the "human heart by which we live." In Mill's view, that heart exists only as the vehicle for the mind, a faculty that writing has converted into a substance that one can hold in one's hands and use to nourish one's brain.

In this passage, Mill is contemplating not only Grote's recent death, but also his own impending demise. As Helen Taylor explains in her brief continuation of the *Autobiography*, Grote's death was one of a series of events, including the serious illnesses of both herself and John Elliot Cairnes, the "friend to whom [Mill] looked as the man best qualified to carry on his own work," that "combined to depress his spirits" so "that there seemed danger of his own health giving way" (1:626–27). He recovered, however, to undertake in 1872 his usual strenuous course of writing, which included the review of Grote's *Aristotle*. The sentimentality of this review, so rare a note in Mill's work, might thus be explained, if not excused, by the supposition that he felt himself to be writing his own obituary. His generosity to Grote's last work, which admittedly displays the age of his friend's mind as well as his tenacity, might be a tenderness toward his own last labors in which, as this passage so remarkably reveals, a hardening of the intellectual arteries is all too apparent.

This passage makes the same point that the sparer ending of the *Autobiography* established when Mill wrote it in 1869–70: after listing what he has written and published since losing his seat in the House of Commons, he notes that he has "commenced the preparation of matter for future books, of which it will be time to speak more particularly if I live to finish them." Life, experience worth recording in an autobiography, is equated only with books that have been completed; autobiography is therefore a rewriting or doubled writing of what has already been written. Without completed works about which to write, there is nothing worth recording: no stages of thought, no composition, no experience either intellectual or emotional. "Here, therefore, for the present, this Memoir may close" (1:290). In the event, the Memoir did indeed close there, but not before witnessing in this last, awkward paragraph, as Mill does in his review of Grote's *Aristotle*, to

Mill's characteristic reduction of his life to his writing and of the time one has lived, not to the marks experience has inscribed on one, but to the marks one has made on the page.

That, according to tradition, was not the last word that Mill had to say on his career as a writer. Deathbed speeches, even if apocryphal, are granted an authority by time and circumstance that is hard to deny, and John Stuart Mill's is no exception. He was reported to have said to Helen Taylor before he died on the morning of 7 May 1873, "You know that I have done my work."[1] Like any assertion, this one contains its opposite: Mill may have been stating a firm conviction, or he may have been voicing a fear that perhaps, after all, he had not done his work. Prefacing the statement with a reference to his stepdaughter's knowledge of his achievement—"*you know* that I have done my work"—is a poignant gesture of childlike uncertainty. Mill seems to have needed a witness, the authority of the one person who, since 1858, had been the companion and observer of his labors. It is hard not to hear the longing for self-justification in this simple line— tell me, it seems to say, that I have accomplished what I set out to do. It bespeaks a profound and characteristically Victorian sense of duty, but it marks the tentative nature of Mill's understanding of his own, individual, and unique duty.

Long after Mill and Carlyle had gone their separate ways, Mill continued to quote the biblical line so favored by Carlyle, "Work . . . [for] the night cometh, when no man can work." Energy, moral earnestness, and the impulse to endeavor were all quite evident in Mill's career. The question for him early in his life was to define the work he should do. Over the course of years, responding to different necessities and pressures, he had adopted the role of theorist and tried to convince himself and others that it was the only one open to him. As Mill says in summing up his activities during the first reformed Parliament, "What I could do by writing, I did" (1:205). The question in 1873 was whether he had done his work or even whether he had discovered what it was. His writing was his work; his writing was his life; but his writings, from the *Logic* to the *Autobiography* to the last words recorded for him, reluctantly but conclusively reveal his ambivalence toward his status as a "bookish man."

Perhaps, however, the way to accord Mill credit for his achievements as a man of action is not to privilege, as the *Autobiography* does, his work as a writer, but to turn to the institutional role he fulfilled as a servant of the East India Company. In that role, the power of historical circumstances to determine the nature and extent of individual effort was perhaps greater than in any other instance in Mill's experience. The changes made in the organization and function of the East India Company near the end of James Mill's life severely limited the ability of its employees at the India House to direct and to determine policy. James Mill, for instance, might support the erection of panoptical prisons in, as Bentham put it, the territory under his "dominion," and Peacock might use his position to promote his interest in steam navigation, but John Mill, through no fault of his own, had no such latitude. Rising to the position of the Examiner in 1856, only two years before the dissolution of the Company, he simply did not have, as one historian puts it, the opportunities that his father had had. Policy was made in India, not in England.[2]

"I had given enough of my life to India," concludes Mill in commenting on his departure from his bureaucratic post (1:249), yet he may have given more than he knew. That contribution, which he tries to render almost invisible in the *Autobiography*, was important simply because it was so unremarkable. For thirty-five years, Mill served as a cog in the machine, functioning as the anonymous, unidentified agent of other wills. If the East India Company was not the model of Saint-Simonian cooperation that Mill hoped it would be, it was, indeed, the model of the professionalization of state that occurred during the nineteenth century. In this sense, James Mill had created, just as Harriet Mill had encouraged and the Company itself had confirmed, precisely the sort of individual required for the work of state. He was, as he called his colleagues in the India House, one of a number of "competent subordinates" (30:53): more than intelligent enough to do his work well, committed to it by his need for a secure income, and clever enough to know that he had to satisfy elsewhere, through other kinds of writing, his impulse to exercise and define his sense of his own individuality.[3]

John Stuart Mill was, then, the Wemmick of colonial administration. On the job, he always defended the Company by referring to the efficiency of its army of nameless clerks: it was a "government of record," a goverment "carried on in writing" (30:71,33). Off duty, he could find satisfaction in imagining the imperishable monuments to his character that his writing might become. Off duty, Mill could indulge cultur-ally nostalgic longings for the heroic exploits of individuals who have blossomed like plants. On the job, he valued those workers who func-tioned silently like the gears in a well-greased machine. Furthermore, in offering what John Morley called Mill's "pontifical authority"[4] to the anonymous professional management of the modern state, Mill may have done his most significant work. Perhaps his own recognition of this fact stands behind the uproar that Mill created when he re-fused to accept the gift of the silver inkstand with which his colleagues at the India House chose to mark the end of his career there. Such administrative work is done well only when it is done without remark, without drawing attention to itself. The nature of such work, as his at-tempted rejection of the inkstand implies, Mill clearly understood, and by understanding what was required of him, he did it supremely well.

Notes

1. Because of the peculiarities of Mill's experience and his attitude toward it—or, as some would say, because of his incapacity for certain kinds of experience—he would have sympathized with recent theoretical arguments that equate self and text. Despite the fact that Mill was not primarily an autobiographical writer, the current emphasis on the etymological origins of the word *autobiography* as "self-life-writing" would have seemed particularly suggestive to him. See, for instance, James Olney, ed., *Autobiography: Essays Theoretical and Critical* (Princeton: Princeton University Press, 1980); Paul Jay, *Being in the Text: Self-Representation from Wordsworth to Roland Barthes* (Ithaca: Cornell University Press, 1984); Avrom Fleishman, *Figures of Autobiography: The Language of Self-Writing in Victorian and Modern England* (Berkeley: University of California Press, 1983). Even more in line with recent poststructuralist theories of the subject was his conviction that character is created from without; for the fullest treatment of this issue in relation to autobiography, see Felicity A. Nussbaum, *The Autobiographical Subject: Gender and Ideology in Eighteenth-Century England* (Baltimore: Johns Hopkins University Press, 1989).

2. Samuel Smiles, *Self-Help* (1859; rev. ed.; New York: Thomas Y. Crowell, n.d.), pp. 396, 406; *Character* (1871; New York: Harper, 1872), p. 18. Nina Auerbach discusses similar passages from Smiles in *Woman and the Demon: The Life of a Victorian Myth* (Cambridge: Harvard University Press, 1982), pp. 193–4. Her more recent work further establishes the publicity of Victorian conceptions of character; see *Private Theatricals: The Lives of the Victorians* (Cambridge: Harvard University Press, 1990).

3. Alexander Bain, *On the Study of Character* (London: Parker, Son, and Bourn, 1861), p. 191. Bain serves in the study as a kind of chorus on Mill's career. He was among John Mill's first biographers (*John Stuart Mill: A Criticism with Personal Recollections* [London: Longmans, Green, 1882]) and James Mill's only biographer (*James Mill: A Biography* [London: Longmans, Green,

1882]). John Mill and Bain met in 1842 but had corresponded since 1839. As Mill's younger colleague, Bain shared many of his interests; although hardly an imaginative man, he had an eminently practical and, I think, often accurate perspective on Mill's career. Bain made his own career as a writer and then as a professor at the University of Aberdeen. He is often credited as the first modern psychologist. For a clear account of his role in the emerging science of psychology, see L. S. Hearnshaw, *A Short History of British Psychology 1840–1940* (London: Methuen, 1964), chap. 1.

4. Thomas Carlyle, *Sartor Resartus*, in *The Works of Thomas Carlyle*, ed. H. D. Traill, Centenary Edition (New York: Charles Scribner's Sons, 1896–1901), 1:164,142. For most Victorians, as Nina Auerbach demonstrates, the ideals of character and womanhood were associated because they both were thought to reveal the link between the human and the divine (*Woman and the Demon*, pp. 189–200). For Mill, women were the quintessential embodiment of character because they are so obviously the creatures of their circumstances.

5. The example of Coleridge comes from Jerome Christensen's *Coleridge's Blessed Machine of Language* (Ithaca: Cornell University Press, 1981), pp. 161–62. John Henry Newman, *The Idea of a University*, ed. Martin J. Svaglic (New York: Holt, Rinehart and Winston, 1960), p. 220. Newman, *Apologia Pro Vita Sua*, ed. David J. DeLaura, Norton Critical Edition (New York: Norton, 1968), p. 136.

6. It would give Mill some satisfaction, however, to know that in the Toronto edition of the *Collected Works*, his writings appear exactly as he had wished: the final version of his thinking serves as the copy text with the "successive strata" clearly visible and intact in the editorial apparatus.

7. For an account of the *Examiner* indexes, see Robson, "Textual Introduction," 22:cv–cvii; a facsimile of the list for 1833 is reprinted on 23:xi. For the more extensive list, see *Bibliography of the Published Writings of John Stuart Mill*, ed. Ney MacMinn, J. R. Hainds, and James McNab McCrimmon (Evanston, Ill.: Northwestern University Press, 1945).

8. Alexander Bain, *Autobiography* (London: Longmans, Green, 1904), pp. 117–22.

9. James Mill, "Education," in W. H. Burston, ed., *James Mill on Education* (Cambridge: Cambridge University Press, 1969), pp. 58, 70, 116.

10. James Mill, qtd. Michael St. John Packe, *The Life of John Stuart Mill* (London: Secker and Warburg, 1954), p. 14. For an analysis of James Mill's associationism and his son's attempt to work within the framework it provided, see Howard C. Warren, *A History of the Association Psychology* (New York: Scribner's, 1921), chaps. 4 and 6.

11. *Analysis of the Phenomena of the Human Mind*, ed. John Stuart Mill (London: Longmans, Green, Reader, and Dyer, 1869), 1:2–3. Hereafter quoted in the text. Mill's notes to this edition are cited from *Collected Works*, vol. 31.

12. Jonathan Loesberg, *Fictions of Consciousness: Mill, Newman, and the Reading of Victorian Prose* (New Brunswick: Rutgers University Press, 1986); Alan

Ryan, *John Stuart Mill* (New York: Pantheon, 1970), p. 130. "Stuart Mill on Mind and Matter: A New Song," *Blackwood's* 99 (1866): 259.

13. Ann P. Robson and John M. Robson, "Private and Public Goals: John Stuart Mill and the *London and Westminster*," in Joel H. Wiener, ed., *Innovators and Preachers: The Role of the Editor in Victorian England* (Westport, Conn.: Greenwood, 1985), pp. 240–42. A codicil in one of Mill's wills left all his copyrights to John Morley to support a periodical "which shall be open to all opinions and shall have all its articles signed" (31:334).

14. See Alan Ryan, *John Stuart Mill*, pp. 87–101; F. E. Sparshott, "Introduction," 11:xlviii.

15. William James, *Principles of Psychology* (1890; Cambridge: Harvard University Press, 1981), 2:959. For commentary on this passage, see Michael Fried, *Realism, Writing, Disfiguration: On Thomas Eakins and Stephen Crane* (Chicago: University of Chicago Press, 1987), p. 143n.

16. R. P. Anschutz, *The Philosophy of John Stuart Mill* (Oxford: Clarendon, 1953), pp. 172–73; Ryan, *John Stuart Mill*, pp. 103–31. Loesberg identifies Mill's "desire for a form of free will within associationism" as the central problem of his thought (*Fictions of Consciousness*, p. 22).

17. William Thomas discusses the *Autobiography* as an associationist tract, "John Stuart Mill and the Uses of Autobiography," *History* 56 (1971): 356; see also Loesberg, *Fictions*, chap. 2; F. Parvin Sharpless, *The Literary Criticism of John Stuart Mill* (The Hague: Mouton, 1967), p. 67. For a good example of the typical conflict of opinion on the success of Mill's attempt to defend himself against determinism in his *Autobiography,* see: Martin Warner, "Philosophical Autobiography: St. Augustine and John Stuart Mill," in A. Phillips Griffiths, ed., *Philosophy and Literature,* Royal Institute of Philosophy Lecture Series 16 (Cambridge: Cambridge University Press, 1984), pp. 189–210; and Andrew Griffin, "The Interior Garden and John Stuart Mill," in U. C. Knoepflmacher and G. B. Tennyson, eds., *Nature and the Victorian Imagination* (Berkeley: University of California Press, 1977), pp. 171–86.

Mill's refusal to question the validity of associationism in Chapter V explains the singularity of his narrative method there. He carefully places not only his account of his crisis in the past tense—that, of course, is the choice that almost all autobiographical narrators make—but he also locates his analysis of the crisis in the past tense, thus avoiding a duty taken seriously by most Victorian autobiographical writers, the duty to offer a mature perspective on and evaluation of the important junctures in their pasts. In recounting the point in his life that is presented as both the most significant and the most dramatic, Mill, who is capable elsewhere of offering his later perspectives on his past, offers none. Literally parenthetical expressions such as "(I thought)" and "(I reflected)" pepper the text to make clear his refusal to examine this experience from a more mature vantage point than that available to a disturbed and confused twenty-year-old. By choosing such an odd way to tell his tale, Mill, I think, protected himself from any obligation he might otherwise have felt to reexamine the very psychological system that he hoped to support through the writing of the *Autobiography*.

18. See William Thomas, "John Stuart Mill and the Uses of Autobiography," pp. 348–49.

19. Locke, *An Essay Concerning Human Understanding* (1690), ed. Peter H. Nidditch (Oxford: Clarendon, 1975), p. 104.

20. Jack Stillinger remarks on this passage and concludes that Mill casts his father here as a "priest-figure" ("Introduction," *Autobiography* [Boston: Houghton Mifflin, 1969], p. xviii).

21. Anna J. Mill usefully analyzes this journal as Mill's first attempt to register in writing his understanding of the significance of William Gilpin's theories of the picturesque ("John Stuart Mill and the Picturesque," *Victorian Studies* 14 [1970]: 151–63). Mill's forthcoming meeting with Wordsworth may have made him more acutely aware of his need to measure himself against such a standard.

22. Charles Kingsley, *His Letters and Memories of His Life* (1877), qtd. in *On Liberty*, ed. David Spitz, Norton Critical Edition (New York: Norton, 1975), p. viii.

CHAPTER ONE: VOCATION

1. Bain, *James Mill*, p. 465.

2. James Mill, "Theory and Practice: A Dialogue," *London and Westminster Review* 3 and 25 (1836): 229–30, 232. A later comment on John Mill's career reveals the more typical attitude of the times when the writer speaks of the "gulf which necessarily separates the man of action from the man of thought" ("Mr. Mill as a Politician," *Saturday Review*, 11 August 1866, p. 167).

3. For a good analysis of Mill's social goals in these terms, see John M. Robson, *The Improvement of Mankind: The Social and Political Thought of John Stuart Mill* (Toronto: University of Toronto Press, 1968), especially pp. 35–48, 66–67.

4. Bain, *James Mill*, pp. 200, 205.

5. See John C. Cairns, "Introduction," 20:lxxxix. Cairns offers a good analysis of Mill's romantic enthusiasm for France; Mill's idealization of the Girondins, for instance, "was an assertion of independence from his father" (20: xxxvii).

6. Joanna Baillie, *Constantine Paleologus; or, The Last of the Caesars* (1804), in *Miscellaneous Plays*, 2d ed. (London: Longman, Hurst, Rees, and Orme, 1805), p. 405. Hereafter cited in the text.

7. Many accounts of Mill's life mention his interest in Parliament, but do not explore its implications. In general, like Alexander Bain, commentators refer to Mill's earlier desire for such public service only when describing the seat he finally won in 1865 (*John Stuart Mill*, 124). Ann P. Robson sees in

Mill's newspaper articles from the 1830s "a hint" that "he saw himself as a possible candidate" (22:lix). Joseph Hamburger, whose *Intellectuals in Politics: John Stuart Mill and the Philosophic Radicals* (New Haven: Yale University Press, 1965) deals most directly with this material, first mentions Mill's interest in a footnote (p. 28, n. 67), though he explains that the Philosophic Radicals "naturally looked forward to careers in Parliament" and that many left the law to enter political life (p. 28). The *Spectator* (9 December 1837, pp. 1164, 1166) listed "Mr. John Mill" as a likely candidate for a Radical cabinet (qtd. Hamburger, p. 176).

8. John Neal, qtd. Hamburger, p. 28, n. 66.

9. Bain, *James Mill*, p. 368. Bruce Mazlish sees in Mill's position in the East India Company "no traumatic youthful agitation": "Work and career were relatively untroubled areas in John Stuart Mill's life" (*James and John Stuart Mill: Father and Son in the Nineteenth Century* [New York: Basic Books, 1975], pp. 198–99). Mazlish's reaction, which comes from a commentator aware of the subtleties of Oedipal conflict, suggests how successful Mill was in disguising his resentment. Henry Reeve, a contemporary observer, claimed that "Nothing could be more fortunate for a political philosopher than such an office" at the India House because it offered Mill the means of subsistence without "the wear and tear of professional life" ("*Autobiography*. By John Stuart Mill," *Edinburgh Review* 139 [1874]: 54).

10. Roebuck directly denied even this claim. He was particularly disappointed that Mill was writing for the *Monthly Repository* but did not have time to write for Roebuck's *Pamphlets for the People* (R. E. Leader, *Life and Letters of John Arthur Roebuck* [London: Edward Arnold, 1897], p. 75).

11. Bain, *John Stuart Mill*, p. 38.

12. A. W. Levi offered the first full reading of the crisis in these terms: "The 'Mental Crisis' of John Stuart Mill," *Psychoanalytic Review* 32 (1945): 86–101.

13. For the chronological difficulties in Mill's account, see Thomas, "John Stuart Mill and the Uses of Autobiography," p. 350; R. D. Cumming, "Mill's History of His Ideas," *Journal of the History of Ideas* 25 (1964): 235–56. See Loesberg, *Fictions*, chap. 3, for an account of the crisis in intellectual terms.

14. Bain, *John Stuart Mill*, p. 31n. Mill also received a special gratuity of £200 in March of 1827 as a distinction for his "zeal and assiduity" (William Foster, *The East India House: Its History and Associations* [London: John Lane and the Bodley Head, 1924], p. 199). See Martin Moir, "Introduction," 30: xiv.

15. Roebuck's description of his comments to Mill, in a letter to Henrietta Falconer, 17 September 1833, quoted by Sarah Wilks, "The Mill-Roebuck Quarrel," *Mill News Letter* 13, no. 2 (Summer, 1978): 10. The responses to Roebuck recorded in Mill's periodical writing in the 1830s are much more generous and approving; see especially "Notes on Newspapers" (1834), 6:191, 200.

16. Bain, *James Mill*, p. 207. As John Robson explains, it is "surprising that

[John Mill] did not become a lawyer" since others around him were following that path ("John Stuart Mill and Jeremy Bentham, with Some Observations on James Mill," *Essays in English Literature from the Renaissance to the Victorian Age,* ed. Millar MacLure and F. W. Watt [Toronto: University of Toronto Press, 1964], pp. 255–56). See William Thomas's essay on Mill (*The Philosophic Radicals: Nine Studies in Theory and Practice 1817–1841* [Oxford: Clarendon, 1979], chap. 4) for an excellent analysis of Mill's depression in relation to the disrepute into which the Philosophic Radicals had fallen in the late 1820s and 1830s; in this context, Mill's exclusion from an active political role would have seemed all the more inevitable and absolute. For a fine account of the context in which Mill was using the terms *slave* and *free,* see Catherine Gallagher, *The Industrial Reformation of English Fiction: Social Discourse and Narrative Form, 1832–1867* (Chicago: University of Chicago Press, 1985), part 1.

Most commentators treat the effect of Mill's crisis on his work, not his work as the cause of his crisis. In his introduction to the *Essays on England, Ireland and the Empire,* Joseph Hamburger states that Mill took up political journalism because he was barred from Parliament by his position in the India House and treats the effect of Mill's crisis on his political goals (6:xv–xxii). Similarly, an article in *Victorian Studies* convincingly examines the changes that the crisis made in Mill's thinking and their effect on his role as an India House official (Lynn Zastoupil, "J. S. Mill and India," 32 [1988]: 31–54). One exception is a note by J. Stanley Yake, who asserts that one of the causes of Mill's crisis was his realization that he could be only a "logical expounder" (12:113; "Mill's Mental Crisis Revisited," *Mill News Letter* 9, no. 1 [Fall 1973]: 6–7). Martin Moir notes that it is "perhaps unlikely that [Mill's] East India House experience played any direct part in this personal crisis," though he finds it "curiously appropriate" that the end of the period of crisis coincided with Mill's promotion to Assistant to the Examiner. In 1827–28, however, Mill was not "emerg[ing] from" the crisis (30:xvii), but suffering relapses into depression.

17. See Sharpless, *Literary Criticism of John Stuart Mill* (pp. 212–19) for an account of Mill's interest in literature as a repository of heroic lives to be imitated.

18. James Mill to Ricardo, 1817, qtd. in Thomas, *Philosophic Radicals,* p. 124; for Thomas on James Mill's *History,* see *Philosophic Radicals,* p. 117.

CHAPTER TWO: WIFE AND WORK

1. John Gross, *The Rise and Fall of the Man of Letters* (New York: Macmillan, 1969), pp. 23–37; T. W. Heyck, *The Transformation of Intellectual Life in Victorian England* (Chicago: Lyceum, 1982), chap. 2.

2. N. N. Feltes, *Modes of Production of Victorian Novels* (Chicago: University of Chicago Press, 1986), pp. 40–43.

3. Mill, *Essays on Some Unsettled Questions of Political Economy* (London: Parker,

1844). By contrast, a pamphlet he published in 1868, *England and Ireland*, identifies its author as "John Stuart Mill, M.P."

4. For a treatment of nineteenth-century attitudes toward the professions, see W. J. Reader, *Professional Men: The Rise of the Professional Classes in Nineteenth-Century England* (London: Weidenfeld and Nicolson, 1966). Reader notes that authors gained professional status in the census of 1861; clerks never did (p. 147). Trollope provides a telling perspective on Mill's career: in his *Autobiography*, he laments his exclusion from law and legislation—for such work, training is necessary—and he speaks of writing as "the only career in life within my reach. . . . Pens and paper I could command" (chap. 3).

5. Heyck, *Transformation*, chap. 8; for the various terms used to describe Mill, see Gross, *Rise and Fall*, p. 41; Collini, "Introduction," 21:viii.

6. See Maurice Cowling, *Mill and Liberalism* (Cambridge: Cambridge University Press, 1963), chaps. 1 and 6. Ben Knights, *The Idea of the Clerisy in the Nineteenth Century* (Cambridge: Cambridge University Press, 1978), chap. 5; Daniel Cottom, *Social Figures: George Eliot, Social History, and Literary Representation*, Theory and History of Literature, 44 (Minneapolis: University of Minnesota Press, 1987), chap. 1.

7. Harriet Grote, *The Personal Life of George Grote*, 2d ed. (London: John Murray, 1873), p. 49; Harriet Grote, *The Philosophical Radicals of 1832: Comprising the Life of Sir William Molesworth* (London: Savill and Edwards, 1866), p. 41.

8. For an extended treatment of the alignment of gender and vocation in the definition of the writer's work, see Mary Poovey, *Uneven Developments: The Ideological Work of Gender in Mid-Victorian England* (Chicago: University of Chicago Press, 1988), chap. 4.

9. Anne Mozley, *Bentley's Quarterly Review*, July 1859; qtd. in David Carroll, ed., *George Eliot: The Critical Heritage* (New York: Barnes and Noble, 1971), p. 90.

10. Harriet Martineau, *Autobiography* (1877; rpt. London: Virago, 1983), "My Only Political Plot," 2:258–64; for Martineau's ambitions as a writer, see *Autobiography* and Valerie Kossew Pichanick, *Harriet Martineau: The Woman and Her Work, 1802–76* (Ann Arbor: University of Michigan Press, 1980).

11. Jack Stillinger, "Who Wrote J. S. Mill's *Autobiography*?" *Victorian Studies* 27 (1983): 7–23.

12. Pichanick, *Harriet Martineau*, p. 38.

13. Bain, *John Stuart Mill*, pp. 93, 166.

14. Harriet Taylor, qtd. F. A. Hayek, *John Stuart Mill and Harriet Taylor: Their Correspondence and Subsequent Marriage* (Chicago: University of Chicago Press, 1951), pp. 99–100.

15. Carlyle, qtd. Hayek, p. 85; Grote, qtd. Hamburger, *Intellectuals in Politics*, p. 274.

16. James Mill to his son James Bentham Mill, qtd. Hayek, pp. 100–101. See also Loesberg, *Fictions*, pp. 58–60.

17. Francis E. Mineka, "The *Autobiography* and the Lady," *University of Toronto Quarterly* 32 (1963): 301–6.

18. Michael St. John Packe rightly defends James Mill against John Mill's accusations (*Life of John Stuart Mill*, pp. 24–26), though his advocacy of Harriet Taylor Mill as a wholly positive influence seems mistaken.

19. Alice Rossi, for instance, sees the Mills' marriage reflected in the ideal marriage envisioned in the *Subjection* ("Sentiment and Intellect: The Story of John Stuart Mill and Harriet Taylor Mill," in *Essays on Sex Equality* [Chicago: University of Chicago Press, 1970], p. 57). She offers a sympathetic account of Harriet Mill (pp. 19–45); the most evenhanded account is still Jack Stillinger's, "Introduction," *The Early Draft of John Stuart Mill's Autobiography* (Urbana: University of Illinois, 1961).

20. Herbert Spencer suggested the title *Supremacy of Women:* see his letter of 9 June 1869 in his unpublished correspondence with Mill, Special Collections, Northwestern University Library. In one of Harriet Taylor's more furious attacks on her future husband, she actually accused him of having become a Mrs. Grundy: his last letter to her had displayed the "puerility of thought & feeling of any utterly headless & heartless pattern of propriety old maid . . . good God" (qtd. Hayek, p. 153).

21. Avrom Fleishman, "Mill's *Autobiography:* Two Deities," in *Figures of Autobiography*, p. 149; James Olney, *Metaphors of the Self: The Meaning of Autobiography* (Princeton: Princeton University Press, 1972), p. 247; Loesberg, *Fictions*, chap. 3.

22. Bain, *John Stuart Mill*, p. 147.

23. Bain, *Autobiography*, pp. 209–10; R. H. Super, *Trollope at the Post Office* (Ann Arbor: University of Michigan Press, 1981), p. 59.

24. Bain, *John Stuart Mill*, p. 148.

25. For Mill's work at the India House, see: Martin Moir, "Introduction," 30:vii–liv; Eric Stokes, *The English Utilitarians and India* (Oxford: Clarendon, 1959), pp. 48–50; Abram L. Harris, "John Stuart Mill: Servant of the East India Company," *Canadian Journal of Economics and Political Science* 30 (1964): 185–202; Alan Ryan, "Utilitarianism and Bureaucracy," in G. Sutherland, ed., *Studies in the Growth of Nineteenth-Century Government* (London: Routledge and Kegan Paul, 1972), pp. 33–62; K. A. Ballhatchet, "The Home Government and Bentinck's Educational Policy," *Cambridge Historical Journal* 10 (1951): 224–29; Carl Dawson, "John Stuart Mill and the East India Company," *Shoin Literary Studies* 22 (1988): 1–12; Zastoupil, "J. S. Mill and India."

26. See Bain's account of James Mill's appointment (*James Mill*, pp. 167–85). William Thomas confirms Bain's view (*Philosophic Radicals*, p. 116).

27. For Grote's "astonishing" defense of Cleon, see Frank M. Turner, *The Greek Heritage in Victorian Britain* (New Haven: Yale University Press, 1981), p. 228; for analysis of both Mill's and Grote's use of Athens to reflect British political life, see Turner (p. 229) and Sparshott, "Introduction," 11:xxxiv.

Newman, qtd. in Ian Ker, *John Henry Newman: A Biography* (Oxford: Clarendon, 1988), p. 83.

28. Stefan Collini offers an excellent analysis of the "advantages" Mill found in his position as an "outsider" ("Introduction," 21:xii–xix). Bruce Kinzer finds "more self-deception than fine calculation or hypocrisy" in Mill's pose of disinterestedness during the 1865 election (28:xxi).

29. Carl Dawson, "John Stuart Mill and the East India Company," pp. 1–2.

30. Reader, *Professional Men* (p. 71) dates this development at 1860 or "thereabouts." Harold Perkin offers a persuasive treatment of this trend as the dominant development in the second half of the nineteenth century (*Origins of Modern English Society* [1969; London: Ark, 1986], chaps. 8 and 10).

31. In his illuminating introduction to Mill's *Writings on India,* Martin Moir makes a distinction between Mill's "official" pronouncements on behalf of the East India Company and his "personal views" (30:xl), and he turns to Mill's *Considerations on Representative Government* to demonstrate the congruity of those two standpoints (30:xlviii). Although Moir admits in a note that Mill "may also have been constrained by the circumstances of his own Company employment" in his views about India's future (30:xlv, n.95), Moir claims that Mill's defenses of the Company reveal him in "his character as a high-minded political thinker" (30:xliv). I would argue that the *Memorandum* and the five anonymous pamphlets that Mill wrote in 1858 are more "high-minded" than his theoretical statements because they are less influenced by the writer's disguised interest in the issues at hand.

32. "Parliamentary," *Judy* 1 (24 July 1867): 156; "No Thoroughfare," *Judy* 2 (25 March 1868): 275, 278–9; "Miss Mill Joins the Ladies," *Judy* 2 (25 November 1868): 46–7 [rpt. 29:vii].

CHAPTER THREE: ETHOLOGY AS POLITICS

1. Thomas Carlyle, *On Heroes, Hero Worship and the Heroic in History*, in *Works*, 5:154. Ben Knights points out that those who hoped to establish a clerisy attributed great power to the idea because that belief "implies the hegemony" of the clerisy, *The Idea of the Clerisy*, p. 151. Coleridge, *Collected Letters*, ed. Earl Leslie Griggs (Oxford: Oxford University Press, 1959), 4:585. For commentary, see Knights, p. 51.

2. For accounts of Mill's work on ethology, see L. S. Feuer, "John Stuart Mill as Sociologist: The Unwritten Ethology," in John M. Robson and Michael Laine, eds., *James and John Stuart Mill: Papers of the Centenary Conference* (Toronto: University of Toronto Press, 1976), pp. 86–110; John M. Robson, "Rational Animals and Others," in *James and John Stuart Mill: Papers*, pp. 143–60; David E. Leary, "The Fate and Influence of John Stuart Mill's Proposed Science of Ethology," *Journal of the History of Ideas* 43 (1982): 153–62. Feuer

credits Mill for "keeping his sociology free from ideology" (p. 110), a conclusion that Mill's commitment to the political implications of associationism calls into question. In "Mill's *Autobiography* as Political Theory," Eldon J. Eisenach treats that work as the fruition of Mill's desire to found a science of character because it is based on the inverse deductive method (*History of Political Thought* 8 [1987]: 111–29).

3. John M. Robson, *Improvement*, p. 7; Ann P. Robson, "Introduction," 22: xxxvi. Ann P. Robson's commentary on the influence of Bentham and James Mill on John Mill's early newspaper writing is excellent (22:xxxii–xli).

4. Bain noted tartly that botany, for Mill, was more sport than science (*John Stuart Mill*, p. 152).

5. Mill's relatively few essays in literary criticism reveal, for instance, a much wider range of reading in fiction than the letters give evidence of: one review of 1838, which treats the historical novel *Letters from Palmyra* by William Ware, cites and evaluates four novels by Brockden Brown and four others that John Neal published in the 1820s (1:434–35n).

6. For a discussion of Mill's position on this issue, see R. F. McRae, "Introduction," 7:xxix–xxxvi.

7. Bain, *Autobiography*, p. 164.

8. Martineau, *Autobiography*, 1:199–215. When George Jacob Holyoake tried to defend Mill's posthumous reputation against the charge that he had distributed birth-control literature in his youth, Holyoake could not bring himself to use those terms (*John Stuart Mill: As Some of the Working Classes Knew Him* [London: Trubner, 1873], pp. 16–20). See Francis E. Mineka, "John Stuart Mill and Neo-Malthusianism, 1873," *Mill News Letter* 8, no. 1 (Fall 1972): 3–10. Even in his own time, Mill's identity as a "walking book" untouched by sexual impulse was seen as a disqualification for his commentary on many subjects (Leslie Stephen, *The Life of Sir James Fitzjames Stephen* [London: Smith, Elder, 1895], pp. 316–17).

9. MacMinn, *Bibliography*, pp. 71–73.

10. James Mill, *The History of British India*, ed. William Thomas (1817; rpt. Chicago: University of Chicago Press, 1975), Preface, pp. 10, 13–14. J. H. Burns compares the sociology sketched in the *Logic* with James Mill's *History* ("The Light of Reason: Philosophical History in the Two Mills," in *James and John Stuart Mill*, pp. 3–20).

11. *Banter*, 2 December 1867, p. 164. Newman, *Apologia*, Note F., pp. 257–58. See Anschutz for an account of the way in which Mill practices "the necessary reticence of the politician" in his work on philosophy (p. 62).

12. Mill had copies of the correspondence with Comte (1841–43), his part of which he called "more a treatise than a letter," bound as a volume (Hayek, *John Stuart Mill and Harriet Taylor*, p. 114), and it provided many of the issues and conclusions that would appear later in *The Subjection of Women*. For a useful translation and account of this exchange, see Kenneth Thompson, *Auguste Comte: The Foundation of Sociology* (London: Thomas Nelson, 1976), pp. 189–

210. Robson (*Improvement,* p. 161) finds this failure admirable because Mill refused to "force organization on provisional materials"; that view is certainly just. Feuer attributes the failure to the "very comprehensiveness of Mill's inverse deductive method" ("John Stuart Mill as Sociologist," p. 89).

13. Bain, *On the Study of Character,* p. 13.

14. L. S. Hearnshaw explains that Mill's work on method in *A System of Logic* exhibits his "remarkable perspicacity," but that Bain played a more central role in the development of psychology as a science, although Mill's work on ethology "foreshadows the much later development of a psychology of personality." (*A Short History of British Psychology,* pp. 4–5).

CHAPTER FOUR: INFLUENCE AND AUTHORITY

1. Harriet Grote, *Personal Life of George Grote,* pp. 257, 275.

2. Frederick Denison Maurice, *Eustace Conway: or, The Brother and the Sister* (London: Bentley, 1834), 1:228. This point was, of course, the basis of Maurice's attacks on the Benthamites in both this novel and in his essay "Mr. James Mill," *Athenaeum* (1828), rpt. in *Sketches of Contemporary Authors* (1828; rpt. n.p.: Archon, 1970), p. 120.

3. Ryan, "Introduction," 9:x–xiv. Hamilton's editors state specifically that the lectures are, "with but slight alterations," the same as those that Hamilton gave in 1837–38 (Hamilton, *Lectures on Metaphysics and Logic,* H. L. Mansel and John Veitch, eds. [Edinburgh and London: Blackwood, 1859–60], 3:vii).

4. Mark Pattison, "J. S. Mill on Hamilton," *The Reader* 5 (20 May 1865): 562.

5. Bain, *John Stuart Mill,* p. 124. As John Robson puts it, Mill "was looking for a fight" ("Textual Introduction," 9:xcvi).

6. Robson, "Textual Introduction," 9:note, xcvi–xcvii. Robson's note on the organization of the *Examination* speaks frequently of a "leap" or "weak transition" between parts of Mill's argument.

7. Thomas Spencer Baynes, *An Essay on the New Analytic of Logical Forms* (Edinburgh: Sutherland and Knox, 1850, rpt. New York: Burt Franklin, 1971), p. 79.

8. Baynes, *Essay,* pp. vii, 28, 93–94. Pattison takes up these issues when he treats Hamilton as a mere imitator of Aristotle, and Mill as the innovator in the field ("J. S. Mill on Hamilton," p. 563).

9. Dianne F. Sadoff examines the relation between paternity and authority, *Monsters of Affection: Dickens, Eliot and Brontë on Fatherhood* (Baltimore: Johns Hopkins University Press, 1982). Edward W. Said discusses the relation between the writer's originality and authority in *Beginnings: Intention and Method* (New York: Basic Books, 1975), pp. 83–84.

10. In 1865 Mill told Grote that the *Autobiography* would be his "contribution" to his father's memory (16:1121). Contemporaries had questioned James Mill's originality and his influence; see Maurice, "Mr. James Mill," p. 122.

11. The idea that Bentham had gathered around him a group of "Bentham-ites" was, as William Thomas proves, "a product of later liberal myth-making" (*Philosophic Radicals,* p. 25). Both Thomas (pp. 97–98) and Hamburger (*Intellectuals in Politics,* pp. 11–15, 22–23) confirm John Mill's claims about his father's leadership.

12. James Mill, "Education," p. 100.

13. In describing his education to Thomas Carlyle, Mill repeated the claim he makes in the *Autobiography,* "I was not *crammed;* my own thinking faculties were called into strong though but partial play; & by their means I have been enabled to *remake* all my opinions" (12:128). A year later, however, he was more candid: "It was part of my former character, the character I am throwing off, that I seldom wished or ventured to *argue* with my *teachers:* . . . I was content to receive without giving" (12:183). For contemporary accounts that confirm the idea that cram was, indeed, the basis of Mill's education, see Stillinger, "Introduction," *Early Draft,* p. 16n.

14. Mill "was much too thoroughly versed in the doctrines he had been taught to throw them over; even had he wanted to, he had no other vocabulary in which to express himself" (William Thomas, *Mill* [Oxford: Oxford University Press, 1985], p. 36). Bain explains that when John Mill taught his siblings, "he took pains to explain their lessons, which their father never did" (*John Stuart Mill,* p. 28). See chapter 4 of John M. Robson's *The Improvement of Mankind* for a full account of the various influences on Mill.

15. James Mill, "Prisons and Prison Discipline," *Supplement to the Encyclopædia Britannica* (London: J. Innes, 1825), p. 4.

16. Mill, *Autobiography* (London: Longmans, Green, Reader, and Dyer, 1873), pp. 244–45.

17. Gertrude Himmelfarb uses this qualification as the basis of her contention that *On Liberty* is the work of the "other" John Stuart Mill (*On Liberty and Liberalism: The Case of John Stuart Mill* [New York: Knopf, 1974], p. 260), a contention that the rest of the argument in this chapter disputes.

18. For this commonplace of Mill criticism, see: Gertrude Himmelfarb, "Introduction," *On Liberty* (London: Penguin, 1985); Albert William Levi, "The Value of Freedom: Mill's Liberty (1859–1959)," and C. L. Ten, "Mill on Self-Regarding Actions," both reprinted in Spitz, ed., *On Liberty;* in particular, see pp. 198 and 243.

19. Michel Foucault, *Discipline and Punish: The Birth of the Prison,* trans. Alan Sheridan (New York: Random, 1979), pp. 195–228. See also Michael Ignatieff, *A Just Measure of Pain: The Penitentiary in the Industrial Revolution 1750–1850* (London: Penguin, 1978), pp. 109–13.

20. Jeremy Bentham, *Panopticon; or, The Inspection-House* (1791), in *The Works of Jeremy Bentham,* ed. John Bowring (Edinburgh: Tait, 1843), 4:66. Hereafter cited in the text by page number only.

21. John Robson assumes, as I do, that Mill's reference to having read

the "most important" of Bentham's works includes a reference to *Panopticon* (1:577–78).

22. Bentham, "Memoirs," in *Works,* 10:577. For a good account of James Mill's reluctance to see education in panoptical terms, see William Thomas, *Philosophic Radicals,* p. 143.

23. For a good account of the differences between Mill's and Bentham's concepts of liberty, see Douglas G. Long, *Bentham on Liberty: Jeremy Bentham's Idea of Liberty in Relation to His Utilitarianism* (Toronto: University of Toronto Press, 1977), pp. 115–18.

24. Bain, *The Senses and the Intellect* (London: Parker, 1855), preface, p. iv.

25. In a sense, *On Liberty* also looks to the past. What Mill seems to fear most is a resumption in the future of the legal sanctions against free expression that dogged so much of Bentham's career. Mill makes this point, albeit indirectly, by using examples of legal, not social, sanctions to point out the dangers of present tendencies.

26. For a full summary of contemporary responses to *On Liberty,* see J. C. Rees, *Mill and His Early Critics* (Leicester: Leicester University College, 1956), pp. 3–38. J. C. Rees also offers a good account of the reactions to Maurice Cowling's assertions about Mill's "moral totalitarianism" (*Mill and Liberalism,* p. xii): "The Reactions to Cowling on Mill," *Mill News Letter,* 1, no. 2 (Spring 1966): 2–11. More recent defenses can be found in C. L. Ten, *Mill on Liberty* (Oxford: Clarendon, 1980) and John Gray, *Mill on Liberty: A Defence* (London: Routledge and Kegan Paul, 1983).

27. *Eustace Conway,* 3:287. Coleridge, *The Friend,* ed. Barbara E. Rooke, *Collected Works* (Princeton: Princeton University Press, 1969), 1:185.

28. See also Hamburger ("Introduction," 6:xxxii–xxxiv) for an account of Mill's attempts to conceal the theoretical underpinnings of his ambitions for the Philosophic Radicals.

29. For commentary on this maneuver, see Maurice Cowling, "Mill and Liberalism," in J. B. Schneewind, ed., *Mill: A Collection of Critical Essays,* Modern Studies in Philosophy (Notre Dame: University of Notre Dame Press, 1969), p. 340.

30. *National Review* 8 (1859): 393–424; rpt. Spitz, ed., *On Liberty,* p. 123.

CHAPTER FIVE: SPECULAR REFLECTIONS

1. For Mill's piano playing, see F. A. Hayek, *John Stuart Mill and Harriet Taylor: Their Correspondence and Subsequent Marriage* (Chicago: University of Chicago Press, 1951), pp. 133, 183. The episode involving *Sartor Resartus* comes from Caroline Fox, *Memories of Old Friends,* ed. Horace N. Pym (London: Smith, Elder, 1882), p. 99. It should be compared to the more well-known incident involving Mill's reading of Shelley's "Ode to Liberty": "Nearly choking

with emotion, Mill said, 'It is almost too much for one'" (Lady Amberley's journal for 28 September 1870, *The Amberley Papers*, ed. Bertrand Russell and Patricia Russell [London: Hogarth, 1937], 2:375). For the documents relating Mill's break with his family, see Hayek, chap. 8. Documents from Hayek's volume are hereafter cited in the text.

2. For Mill's contentions with Spencer, see *Later Letters*, 15:846–47; 16:1089–91, 1110–11; *Logic*, 7:262–76. For Spencer's side of the debate, see "Mill *versus* Hamilton—The Test of Truth," *Fortnightly Review* 1 (1865): 531–50. For a fine analysis of the contradictions in Mill's ideal of the open mind, see Sparshott, "Introduction," 11:xliii, lxxiv–lxxv; for Mill's inability to learn from Darwin, see Ryan, "Introduction," 9:lxi.

3. Alan Ryan, *J. S. Mill* (London: Routledge and Kegan Paul, 1974), p. 233.

4. Auguste Comte, *Système de politique positive; Traité de sociologie, instituant la religion de l'humanité*, vol. 1 (Paris: Mathias, 1851), Dédicace, xviii. Hereafter cited in the text.

5. On the occasions when Harriet Mill responded with more generosity than her husband, Mill's acerbity was usually prompted by his sense that she had not been treated with the courtesy that she deserved (see, for instance, Mill's response to the "impudence" that Harriet Grote displayed in writing him a note [14:123,133] or Mill's failure to address his letter of condolence on the death of John Austin to his widow [Hayek, pp. 89–90]).

6. Mill told John Sterling that he thought that the essay on Coleridge should be written by "some one better versed in Coleridge" than himself, though he hoped that his own effort would not be "absurdly incomplete" (13:406). In fact, as Jonathan Arac pointed out to me, Mill emphasizes features in Coleridge that other commentators either puzzle over or ignore. See chapter 3, part 1 of Raymond Williams's *Culture and Society 1780–1950* (1958; New York: Harper and Row, 1966) for an account of what Mill recognized or failed to recognize in Coleridge. For an interpretation of "Coleridge" as a revelation of Mill's "ambiguous attitude to Coleridge's value and influence," see Christopher Turk, *Coleridge and Mill: A Study of Influence* (Aldershot: Avebury, 1988), chap. 10.

7. Oscar Wilde, "The Critic as Artist," *Intentions* (1891), rpt. in *The Artist as Critic: Critical Writings of Oscar Wilde*, ed. Richard Ellmann (New York: Random House, 1968), p. 365.

8. Georges Gusdorf, "Conditions and Limits of Autobiography," in Olney, ed., *Autobiography*, p. 32. George Eliot, *The Impressions of Theophrastus Such*, in *Works*, Illustrated Cabinet Edition (New York: Merrill and Baker, 1895–96), 8:3.

9. For this discussion of Coleridge, I am indebted to Sheila M. Kearns, "Autobiography Names Itself," *a\b: Auto/Biography Studies* 2 (1986–87): 6–13. Molly Rothenberg also offered some extremely helpful comments that clarified the issues raised by these quotations. For the relevant passages from Coleridge, see the *Logic*, ed. J. R. de J. Jackson, *Collected Works of Samuel Taylor*

Coleridge (Princeton: Princeton University Press, 1981), p. 84; *Biographia Literaria,* ed. James Engell and W. Jackson Bate, *Collected Works* (1983), 1:273.

10. Thomas De Quincey, *Confessions of an English Opium Eater* (1821), ed. Alethea Hayter (Harmondsworth: Penguin, 1971), p. 107. Subsequent references are to this edition. One of Mill's references to Piranesi (14:280) suggests that he was thinking of De Quincey's description of the artist's work, just as De Quincey was responding in this passage of his *Confessions* to Coleridge's description of Piranesi's *carceri.* Such complications, like those in the case of Mill and Comte, recall the dual definitions of assimilation as a process of registering influence or of recognizing similarities.

11. Philippe Lejeune has searched for a "textual sign" of autobiography, and although he has proceeded in his search no farther than the title page of the autobiographical work, finding in the author's signature the proof of the identity of narrator and subject ("The Autobiographical Pact," in *On Autobiography,* ed. Paul John Eakin, trans. Katherine Leary, Theory and History of Literature, 52 [Minneapolis: University of Minnesota Press, 1989], pp. 4, 20), such a sign depends too exclusively on the referentiality of autobiographical texts. An emphasis on the specular structure of such works would seem to be more productive. For a treatment of this issue, see my essay "The Mirror in *The Mill on the Floss:* Toward a Reading of Autobiography as Discourse," *Studies in the Literary Imagination* 23 (Fall 1990): 177–96. The primary post-structuralist statement of the specularity of autobiographical texts, indeed of all texts, is Paul de Man's "Autobiography as De-facement," *MLN* 94 (1979): 921: "The autobiographical moment happens as an alignment between the two subjects involved in the process of reading in which they determine each other by mutual reflexive substitution."

12. John Henry Newman, *Apologia pro Vita Sua,* ed. David J. DeLaura, Norton Critical Edition (New York: Norton, 1968), p. 96. Newman, *Autobiographical Writings,* ed. Henry Tristram (New York: Sheed and Ward, 1957), p. 26. John Ruskin, *Praeterita,* intro. Sir Kenneth Clark (London: Rupert Hart-Davis, 1949), p. 221. Charles Darwin, *Autobiography,* in Darwin and Huxley, *Autobiographies,* ed. Gavin de Beer (Oxford: Oxford University Press, 1974), p. 8.

13. John Sterling, *Arthur Coningsby* (London: Effingham Wilson, 1833), 1:62; 3:385. Charlotte Brontë, *Villette,* ed. Mark Lilly, intro. Tony Tanner (Harmondsworth: Penguin, 1979), p. 361.

14. For the association of autobiography and folklore, see Georges Gusdorf, "Conditions and Limits of Autobiography," pp. 32–33. Linda H. Peterson's *Victorian Autobiography: The Tradition of Self-Interpretation* (New Haven: Yale University Press, 1986) has codified the critical emphasis on British autobiography as a tradition of self-interpretation: she classifies conceptions of autobiography by their references to either mirrors or books, to either self-presentation or self-interpretation; according to this scheme, French autobiographies are explained by their association with mirrors; English, by their association with the bookish aims of self-interpretation (pp. 2–3). Analyses

of British autobiographies that take the mirror as their controlling metaphor for the genre typically treat twentieth-century works; see Shirley Neuman, "The Observer Observed: Distancing the Self in Autobiography," *Prose Studies* 4 (1981): 317–36. Neuman cites a passage from Wyndham Lewis's *Blasting and Bombardiering:* "My contacts with this contemporary [T. E. Hulme] is one of the best ways of reflecting myself. I am describing myself in describing him, just as in describing me he would be revealing his own peculiarities" (327). Such "reflections" are central even to the self-consciously self-interpretative autobiographies of Victorian writers. Linda H. Peterson herself offers proof of this point in her treatment of Margaret Oliphant's accounts of her contemporaries: "Audience and the Autobiographer's Art: An Approach to the *Autobiography* of Mrs. M. O. W. Oliphant," in *Approaches to Victorian Autobiography*, ed. George P. Landow (Athens: Ohio University Press, 1979), pp. 171–73.

15. Mark Spilka treats the relation between David and Uriah as a case of "projected feelings" in *Dickens and Kafka: A Mutual Interpretation* (Bloomington: Indiana University Press, 1963), p. 176, but he concludes that Uriah's "relation to David's inner life seems faint" (p. 194). For a discussion of Lucy Snowe's projections, see my "The Face in the Mirror: *Villette* and the Conventions of Autobiography," *ELH* 46 (1979), 262–89. Ruskin, *Praeterita*, p. 487. Newman, *Apologia*, p. 211. Paul de Man lists these "figures of Wordsworth's own poetic self" in "Autobiography as De-facement," p. 924.

16. Otto Rank, *The Double: A Psychoanalytic Study*, ed. and trans. Harry Tucker, Jr. (Chapel Hill: University of North Carolina Press, 1971). Jacques Lacan, "The Mirror Stage as Formative of the Function of the I," *Ecrits: A Selection*, trans. Alan Sheridan (New York: Norton, 1977), pp. 1–7. In "Psychoanalysis: The French Connection," Geoffrey Hartman asks, "Is there anything comparable to the mirror stage on the level of language?" (*Psychoanalysis and the Question of the Text* [Baltimore: Johns Hopkins University Press, 1978], p. 93). One answer would seem to be autobiographical narrative.

17. Thomas Carlyle, "Characteristics," in *Works* 28:20. Jonathan Loesberg offers perceptive commentary on this passage in *Fictions of Consciousness: Mill, Newman, and the Reading of Victorian Prose* (New Brunswick: Rutgers University Press, 1986), pp. 194–95.

18. See also Jerome Hamilton Buckley, *The Turning Key: Autobiography and the Subjective Impulse since 1800* (Cambridge: Harvard University Press, 1984), pp. 48–49. Buckley suggests that Mill's tears were less the result of relief at the idea of a dead father than of his "painful sense of difference" from the French youth who could love his siblings and his mother (p. 48). See also: James McDonnell, "'A Season of Awakening': An Analysis of Chapter Five of Mill's 'Autobiography,'" *Modern Language Review* 72 (1977): 780–81.

19. For Lacan, the mirror stage is fraught with risks, preparing as it does the basis of the alienation and rigid defenses of later experience, but this formulation does describe precisely the release that Mill experiences as he looks

into the mirror held up for him by Marmontel's *Memoirs*. As Lacan explains further, the mirror stage gives the infant not only a sense of integrity, but a sense of his relation to those around him ("The Mirror Stage," pp. 1–7).

20. Thomas Carlyle, *The Life of John Sterling, Works*, 11:268. Mill mentions both Julius Hare's "Memoir of John Sterling" (in Sterling's *Essays and Tales*, ed. Julius Charles Hare, 2 vols. [London: Parker, 1848] and Carlyle's *The Life of John Sterling* [London: Chapman and Hall, 1851] in his *Autobiography* [1:159]. Caroline Fox mentions in her *Memories of Old Friends* that Mill intended to write a biography of Sterling (p. 228). The accuracy of her accounts of the conversations of her contemporaries may be tested by comparing her notes on one of Carlyle's lectures on hero-worship with the printed text. Her account of Mill's explanation of his relation to Sterling, which uses the same words that Mill himself uses in his account of the friendship, is a case in point: "J. S. Mill says his acquaintance with Sterling began with a hard fight at the Debating Society . . . when he appeared as a Benthamite and Sterling as a Mystic; since then they have more and more approximated" (p. 78). Fox's *Memories* hereafter cited in the text.

21. Sterling to his son, qtd. in Anne Kimball Tuell, *John Sterling: A Representative Victorian* (New York: Macmillan, 1941), p. 69. For Bowring's comment on the "muddled" quality of Mill's thought, see Fox, *Memories*, p. 113; Bowring blames Wordsworth for this result. For information on Sterling's intellectual debts and realignments, see Tuell, pp. 198, 285, 299, 336. For Sterling on *The Election*, see Tuell, p. 39.

22. For Sterling's comments on Ireland, see the letter to Mill, 28 December 1843, qtd. Tuell, p. 128. For an account of Sterling's relations to General Torrijos, see Tuell, pp. 99–111; for Sterling's discouragement with public life, see Tuell, p. 116.

23. For the shift in Mill's dependency from his father to his wife, see chap. 2, note 21. Loesberg treats Mill's creation of Harriet Taylor in the *Autobiography* as an act of self-liberation (*Fictions of Consciousness*, p. 46).

24. See Fleishman, p. 152; Olney claims that Harriet Mill's highly emotional and intuitive nature transformed Mill from the machine that his father had created into a "man," pp. 247–53; cf. Loesberg's treatment of her intuitive qualities, pp. 47–48.

25. For Harriet Mill as John Mill's "ego ideal," see Fleishman, p. 152; Michael Palencia-Roth, "Mothers, Fathers and the Life of Reason: The Case of John Stuart Mill's *Autobiography*," *Comparative Civilizations Review* 4 (1980): 52.

26. Harold Laski quoting comments by Bain and Louis Blanc, qtd. Jack Stillinger, "Introduction," *Early Draft*, p. 24.

27. Francis Place, qtd. in Robson, *The Improvement of Mankind*, p. 62n. Compare Place's comment with James Mill's criticism that his son was like a "person who had not the organs of sense" (1:609).

CHAPTER SIX: REVISIONS IN THE LIFE
OF THOUGHT

1. If it was written in 1861 as an introduction to the brief section of the *Autobiography* that records Harriet Mill's death, the self-dismissive tone of this paragraph seems logical. Why it was not edited out of the text at a later stage of composition seems less clear. Many commentators have followed the lead of this paragraph in discounting the importance of this chapter. John M. Robson and Jack Stillinger rightly suggest that Mill's long account of his parliamentary career—to which he devoted more extensive comment than to his crisis—is "not easily justified on Mill's stated terms" and that "its main interest lies outside them" ("Introduction," 1:x). Cf. Kinzer, "Introduction," 28:xiv. One of the most acute commentators on both Mill's career and his written life, William Thomas, dismisses the section written in 1869 as "fragmentary and perfunctory" ("John Stuart Mill and the Uses of Autobiography," *History* 56 [1971]: 354).

2. For examination of this issue, see Paul John Eakin, *Fictions in Autobiography: Studies in the Art of Self-Invention* (Princeton: Princeton University Press, 1985), pp. 17–27; Gusdorf, "Conditions and Limits of Autobiography," in James Olney, ed., *Autobiography: Essays Theoretical and Critical* (Princeton: Princeton University Press, 1980), p. 38; and Louis A. Renza, "The Veto of the Imagination: A Theory of Autobiography," in Olney, ed., *Autobiography*, pp. 268–95.

3. During the election of 1865, however, when Mill was asked without warning to give a speech, his first of the campaign, he paid tribute to his father as one of the early liberals who had fought the good fight alone (28:15).

4. Matthew Arnold, *Culture and Anarchy: With Friendship's Garland and Some Literary Essays*, ed. R. H. Super, *Complete Prose Works* (Ann Arbor: University of Michigan Press, 1965), 5:133. "Who Are the Leaguers?" *Saturday Review*, 9 March 1868, p. 299. For Bradlaugh's recommendation of Drysdale's *Elements*, a work Mill refused to countenance, see Walter L. Arnstein, *The Bradlaugh Case: Atheism, Sex, and Politics among the Late Victorians* (1965; Columbia: University of Missouri Press, 1983), p. 343; David Tribe, *President Charles Bradlaugh, M.P.* (London: Elek, 1971), pp. 74–75. For John Bright's refusal to support Bradlaugh, see Hypatia Bradlaugh Bonner, *Charles Bradlaugh* (London: T. Fisher Unwin, 1902), 1:271; the *Times* praised Bright for his discretion in staying clear of Bradlaugh: Bright had demonstrated that he had "longer experience and in politics a sounder head" than Mill (16 October 1868, p. 6). Charles Bradlaugh, *The Autobiography of C. Bradlaugh: A Page in His Life*, new ed. (London: R. Forder, 1891), p. 28.

Bradlaugh's subsequent career justifies, at least from a conservative point of view, the fear he aroused in the 1860s. In the late 1870s he was tried with Annie Besant for publishing "obscene" birth-control material (see "A Dirty,

Filthy Book," ed. S. Chandrasekhar [Berkeley: University of California Press, 1981]). Finally elected to Parliament in 1880, he refused to take the oath of office; the stalemate that ensued lasted for five years. Bradlaugh's atheism was so celebrated that even after his death a spiritualist newspaper claimed that his ghost had returned to declare, "There is a God!" (David Berman, *A History of Atheism in England* [London: Croom Helm, 1988], p. 219).

5. For Helen Taylor's response to the letter in the *Daily News*, see Michael St. John Packe, *The Life of John Stuart Mill* (London: Secker and Warburg, 1954), p. 474. Packe justly notes that Helen Taylor sounds here remarkably like her mother. Establishing the authorship of the letter in which Mill dismisses the idea of an identification between himself and Bradlaugh does involve some problems. The letter is in Mill's hand (16:1522, n. 1), but the envelope is marked "reply by H.T." I presume that this instance, like others, of the "joint production" of a letter with Helen Taylor does, in fact, represent Mill's opinion.

6. For analysis, see Evelyn L. Pugh, "J. S. Mill's *Autobiography* and the Hyde Park Riots," *Research Studies* 50 (1982): 12–13.

7. W. F. Finlason, *The History of the Jamaica Case*, 2d ed. (London: Chapman and Hall, 1869), pp. 299, 306. Murchison, qtd. by Bernard Semmel, *Jamaican Blood and Victorian Conscience: The Governor Eyre Controversy* (Boston: Houghton Mifflin, 1963), p. 173.

8. Semmel, *Jamaican Blood and Victorian Conscience*, pp. 132–38.

9. George Jacob Holyoake, *Bygones Worth Remembering* (New York: E. P. Dutton, 1905), 2:265–66.

10. For contemporary accounts of the Hyde Park riots, see the *Times*, 26 July 1866, p. 12; Bonner, *Charles Bradlaugh*, 1:224–26; Sir Spencer Walpole, *The History of Twenty-Five Years* (London: Longmans, Green, 1904), 2:171–76; George Jacob Holyoake, *Sixty Years of an Agitator's Life* (London: T. Fisher Unwin, 1892), 2:186–90; R. H. Super's edition of *Culture and Anarchy* reprints Arnold's letters to his mother about the event, p. 385.

11. Pugh, 1–20. Despite the lack of any evidence to support Mill's claims, Pugh cannot bring herself to doubt his account because he was the "soul of integrity" (13). The silence of Mill's contemporaries on this point might reflect their respect or their embarrassment. Concerning a similar circumstance, Mill's distribution of birth-control literature in 1823, a friend who "was with him on the occasion" suggested that those who could correct or embellish the story should honor Mill's "possible wishes and feelings" by saying nothing (William Ellis to George J. Holyoake, 23 May 1874, qtd. by Francis E. Mineka, "John Stuart Mill and Neo-Malthusianism, 1873," *Mill News Letter* 8, no. 1 [Fall 1972], 8). The standard accounts of the Hyde Park riots simply accept Mill's version in the *Autobiography* (F. B. Smith, *The Making of the Second Reform Bill* [Cambridge: Cambridge University Press, 1966], p. 131; Maurice Cowling, *1867: Disraeli, Gladstone and Revolution* [Cambridge: Cambridge Uni-

versity Press, 1967], p. 262). Packe's *Life* follows the same pattern. Bruce L. Kinzer suggests that Mill "perhaps assigns too much weight to his intervention" (28:xxxiii).

No eyewitness to the events, as far as I can tell, supports Mill's account. To the contrary, the *Saturday Review* relates "President BEALES's boast that, had it not been for his magnanimity, London streets would have run with blood" ("The Reform League and Fenianism," 26 October 1867, p. 525). Sir Spencer Walpole, whose weakness at this crisis had been openly mocked, credits "the firm attitude of the Government" for the restoration of peace in London (*The History of Twenty-Five Years*, 2:176). Holyoake does credit Mill with protecting him during the subsequent meeting at the Agricultural Hall when Holyoake's colleagues were ready to demonstrate their anger at his supposed treason to their cause (*Sixty Years*, 2:189–90). An exhaustive contemporary history— William Nassau Molesworth's *The History of England from the Year 1830–1874*, new ed., 3 vols. (London: Chapman and Hall, 1874), 3:289,319—treats both the 1866 and 1867 attempts to meet in Hyde Park, but fails to mention Mill's involvment or even his service in the House of Commons.

12. *Hansard's Parliamentary Debates* (3d ser., 26 July 1866, col. 1541) and the *Times* (27 July 1866, p. 7) both record the laughter that followed Mill's announcement. As John M. Robson explains, one has to take the record of parliamentary speeches with a grain of salt (*What Did He Say? Editing Nineteenth-Century Speeches from Hansard and the Newspapers*, F. E. L. Priestley Lecture Series [Lethbridge: University of Lethbridge Press, 1988]). Yet, as Richard W. Davis has assured me, the addition of gratuitous sound effects was not part of the accepted mode of transcription. Pugh and Kinzer do not mention this humiliating fact in the accounts they offer of the episode.

13. For a similar conflation, see Mill's patently inaccurate claim that he thought of making his essay on liberty into a book as he climbed the steps of the Capitol (1:249). Gibbon and Mill become assimilated in this assertion.

14. Condorcet, *The Life of M. Turgot* (London: Printed for J. Johnson, 1787), p. 171. Subsequent references to this edition are in the text. Mill was called a "lost philosopher" in *Pall Mall Gazette*, 28 July 1866, p. 11. Roebuck's biography records the "general feeling" that Mill had failed to live up to the expectations aroused by his election to Parliament (Leader, *Life and Letters*, p. 307).

15. See also Robson and Robson, "Private and Public Goals," pp. 235–38; Hamburger, *Intellectuals in Politics*, pp. 98–99; Iris Wessel Mueller, *John Stuart Mill and French Thought* (Urbana: University of Illinois Press, 1956).

16. For treatment of such more conventional models in Victorian autobiography, see Linda H. Peterson, *Victorian Autobiography*.

17. The phrase is Michelet's; see Maurice Cranston, *Philosophers and Pamphleteers: Political Theorists of the Enlightenment* (Oxford: Oxford University Press, 1986), p. 156. Cranston points out the similarities in Turgot's and Condorcet's thought that would have prompted Condorcet to emphasize the ideals with which Mill could later identify. Condorcet was to Mill "the wisest and

noblest of men" (1:115) because they shared so many forward-looking ideas, including women's rights and the need for a "new aristocracy of the mind" within a democratic society (Cranston, pp. 151, 155). As a democrat, Condorcet also authorized Mill's admiration for Turgot, a monarchist.

18. "Mr. Mill as a Politician," *Saturday Review*, 11 August 1866, pp. 167–68. For Disraeli's response, see 28:xxxii.

19. For example, Paul Jay, *Being in the Text*, pp. 21–27. Such psychoanalytically inclined approaches are not always willing to grant that works of literature engage in regression; for a specific denial of this assertion, see Sadoff, *Monsters of Affection*, p. 2. This emphasis on regression explains why Lacan's conception of a mirror stage is so telling a commentary on the autobiographical act: the process of self-contemplation encourages the power of infantile desire to exert itself in the context of this literary version of the Imaginary.

20. Dickens, *David Copperfield*, ed. Trevor Blount (Harmondsworth: Penguin, 1966), p. 187. Herbert Spencer, *An Autobiography* (New York: D. Appleton, 1904), 2:291.

21. H. L. Mansel, in his defense of Hamilton, noted acutely that Mill had been "betrayed" by the "fatal charms of the goddess Necessity" (*The Philosophy of the Conditioned . . . on Sir William Hamilton's Philosophy and on Mr. J. S. Mill's Examination of that Philosophy* [London: Alexander Strahan, 1866], p. 183).

22. George Eliot, *Middlemarch*, ed. Bert Hornback, Norton Critical Edition (New York: Norton, 1977), pp. 17–18, 577. The fact that Will Ladislaw is "returned to Parliament by a constituency who paid his expenses" (p. 576) may reflect one of the more prominent facts about Mill's career.

AFTERWORD

1. Packe, *Life of John Stuart Mill*, p. 507.

2. Bentham, "Memoirs," in *Works*, 10:577; on James Mill's efforts to forward the scheme for Indian panopticons, see Stokes, *English Utilitarians and India*, p. 325 (n.I); on John Mill's limited opportunities, see Stokes, pp. 49–50, and Ballhatchet, "The Home Government," p. 228.

3. If India was for Britain, as Patrick Brantlinger has argued, a kind of "ideological safety valve," Mill's writing fulfilled a similar role for him (*The Rule of Darkness: British Literature and Imperialism, 1830–1914* [Ithaca: Cornell University Press, 1988], p. 35). Such a formulation would suggest, of course, that Mill's primary work was done for the East India Company. Writing was important only in that it allowed that work to go forward. Mill's compartmentalization of his career as a writer and of his work at the India House was admirably treated in two papers delivered at the 1988 MLA Convention, one by Sandhya Shetty and another by Carl Dawson (for the latter, see his "John Stuart Mill and the East India Company," p. 11). Martin Moir, however, claims

that Mill's writings on India were not "written in a special compartment of his mind closed off from his wider speculative thought" (30:xli).

4. The phrase is from John Morley's *Recollections* (New York: Macmillan, 1917), 1:55. For Mill's interest in the East India Company as "government of record," see Ryan, "Utilitarianism and Bureaucracy," pp. 38–42. For the emerging professional state, see Perkin, *Origins of Modern English Society*, chap. 10.

Index

Action, 68–69, 79, 88, 96, 283; man of action, 68, 78, 253, 276, 279, 281–82. *See also* Heroes; Theory
Adams, William Bridges, 5–7, 25, 230–31, 239
Amateurs, 81–83
Anonymity in publications, 25
"Armand Carrel," 281–83, 284–88
Arnold, Matthew, 267
Art: as practice, 219
Artist: definition, 219–20
Assimilation, 246, 254–55; definition, 224–26; Mill's early references to, 226; in letters, 230–31; in critical essays, 231–39; as specularity, 239–45. *See also Autobiography*: assimilation in
Associationism, 26, 133, 164, 229; Mill's training in, 17–19; conceptions of character, 19–24; reputation of, 21, 35, 36; introspection in, 21, 293; questioning of character, 21–25, 245; determinism of, 27–30, 35, 70–72, 165–66, 294; as basis of psychology, 138, 139; inadequacies of, 164–65; as panoptical psychological model, 204–5, 206–7
Atomism, 208–9
Auerbach, Nina, 304 (n. 4)

Auguste Comte and Positivism, 89–90, 223–25; as assimilative, 231–36
Augustine, Saint, 23, 32, 179
Austin, Charles, 59, 60, 62
Austin, John, 59, 60, 62; Mill studies law with, 56, 58, 66; as Mill's relative opposite, 238–39, 293
Authority, 169, 171, 178–79, 180, 207. *See also* Mill, John Stuart: character of, desire for influence and authority
Autobiography, 82, 183–84, 194, 237, 298–99; deceptive reticence of, ix, 48, 49, 49–63, 72, 83, 93, 94–96, 179, 197, 260–62, 272–73, 300; writing of, ix, 50, 64–65, 94–96; motivations for writing, x, 97, 179–80; on writing of *System of Logic,* 9–10, 186–87, 188–90; portrayal of James Mill, 14, 20, 97, 179–82, 191–92, 200; as associationist document, 18, 28, 29–30, 64, 255, 305–6 (n. 17); as account of life of theorist, 48; on Mill's vocation, 49–63; on employ at East India Company, 60–62, 100, 106; on crisis, 63–72, 95–96, 247–49; portrayal of Harriet Taylor Mill, 95–96, 192–95, 234–36, 254–57; account of *Examination,* 172; on

Autobiography, (continued)
  Comte, 188–89, 195; account of
  On Liberty, 195–96; assimilation
  in, 226–27, 247–58, 262, 266–
  67, 268, 278–89, 291–92, 293;
  account of parliamentary career,
  263–69, 272, 273, 290–91, 320
  (n. 1); account of Hyde Park crisis,
  274–76, 278–91 passim, 321–22
  (n. 11); referentiality of, 276–77,
  321–22 (n. 11)
Autobiography: referential nature of
  221, 262; specular nature of, 221,
  317 (n. 11), 317–18 (n. 14); specular structure of, 239–45, 259; difficulties of study of, 240, 244, 262;
  as objectification, 242–43; doubles
  in, 242–43; specular moments in,
  242–43; psychoanalytic theories
  of, 244–45, 289; Victorian, as
  self-interpretative, 244, 317–18
  (n. 14); as regressive, 289–91, 323
  (n. 19); as "self-life-writing," 303
  (n. 1). See also Assimilation

Bacon, Francis, 143–44
Baillie, Joanna: Constantine Paleologus, 54–56, 118, 286
Bain, Alexander, 15, 19–20, 21, 35,
  194, 214–15; on character, 4; as
  commentator on Mill's life, 63, 65,
  100, 101, 103, 303–4 (n. 3); on
  Harriet Taylor Mill, 93, 256; on
  ethology, 146, 163–64; on relative
  terms as doubles, 228–29
Ballot, 17, 212
Baynes, Thomas Spencer, 174–75,
  177–78
Bentham, Jeremy, xiii, 15, 30, 104,
  181, 230; Traité de législation, 32,
  34, 56–57, 189; as practical theorist, 47–48; as hero, 54; as reformer, 57–58; Rationale of Judicial

Evidence, 63, 65–66; shortcomings
  of, 129–30, 150, 166, 209, 245;
  character of, 164–65; portrayal
  in Autobiography, 180, 182, 197;
  influence on On Liberty, 196–97,
  203–8, 209, 212, 214; Panopticon,
  197–201, 204
Bentham, Samuel, 30, 200
"Bentham," 47–48, 229
Benthamites, 170, 180–82, 237
Birth control, 154–56, 268
Bouverie, E. P., 271
Bradlaugh, Charles, 266–69, 275,
  320–21 (n. 4)
Bright, John, 268
Brontë, Charlotte, 5, 87, 98; Villette,
  152, 243, 244, 251, 290
Buckle, Henry Thomas, 77
Byron, George Gordon, 68, 230, 249

Cairnes, John Elliott, 298
Cairns, John C., 280–81, 282
Carlyle, Thomas, 128, 219, 284, 299;
  on character, 6; on heroes, 6, 76,
  127; on Harriet Taylor Mill, 94;
  "Characteristics," 245; Life of John
  Sterling, 249, 250, 252, 253; Sartor
  Resartus, 256
Carrel, Armand, 230, 280–88; as
  ideal, 281–83; as Mill's relative
  opposite, 283–85, 287–88; assimilated with Turgot, 284–85; action
  in crisis, 286–87; contemporary
  reputation, 287–88
Cavaignac, Godefroy, 230, 287
Chadwick, Edwin, 270, 271
Chapman, John, 107
Character: Mill's preoccupation
  with, x–xi; in relation to circumstances, xi, 6, 19, 31, 35–36, 70–
  72, 117–18, 133, 144, 146–48,
  159, 165–66, 169, 220, 263, 292,
  294; Victorian conceptions of,

xiii, 3–6; Mill's definition of, 1–2; phrenology, 4; formation of, 6, 17–36, 140, 153, 164–65; in associationism, 19–24; continuity of, questioned by associationism, 21–25; self-determination of, 28, 71, 77–78, 165–66, 226, 255; national, 132, 137–38, 141, 145–46, 148–50, 152, 163; poet as type, 132–33; soldier as type, 132–34; difficulty of defining, 137–38; peasant as type, 150–51; of women, 159–60, 236; strength of, 206; art of, 219, 225–27, 294–95. *See also* Assimilation; Ethology; Women; Writing: identified with character

Christianity, 30, 212, 213

Class: bias of, 156–58

Classifications, 131–34, 197, 204–5, 229–30, 232, 237–38

Clergy, 90–91

Clerisy, 84, 100, 212; analogous to women, 89–90

Coleridge, Samuel Taylor, 84, 113, 212, 215, 250, 252; as man of letters, 9; as theorist, 47; magnum opus, 127; as relative opposite, 237–38; on self-consciousness, 240–41

"Coleridge," 229; as assimilation, 237–38

Collini, Stefan, 161

Comte, Auguste, 136, 162; on women and thinkers, 89–90; on working classes, 90; shortcomings of, 112, 129–30, 189, 195, 223–24, 231; influence on Mill, 188–89, 194; as Mill's relative opposite, 231–36; relation to Clotilde de Vaux, 233–36, 254–55

Condorcet, Marie Jean Antoine Nicolas Caritat, Marquis de, 278–80, 284–85, 286

Consciousness, 245; associationist conceptions of, 21–24. *See also* Self-consciousness

Considerations of Representative Government, 110–11, 112, 187

Cottier-tenancy, 148–49

Criticism: of writer's corpus, x; literary, definition of, xi, 219–20; as self-criticism, 225–26

Darwin, Charles, 233; *Autobiography*, 243, 290

Deduction, 141–42, 143, 176

Demosthenes, 55, 118

De Quincey, Thomas, 241–42, 244

Determinism, 27–31, 166, 212. *See also* Associationism, determinism of; Character, in relation to circumstances

"Diary" (1854), 7–8, 9, 10, 113

Dickens, Charles, 4–5, 13; *David Copperfield*, 243, 244, 245, 290

Diderot, Denis, 112

Disinterestedness, 105–6, 107–8, 110–11, 156–58, 239, 269

Dissertations and Discussions, 9, 46, 132, 285

Doubles, 228, 244–45, 246. *See also* Assimilation

Dumont, Pierre Etienne Louis, 91. *See also* Bentham, Jeremy, *Traité de législation*

Durham, Lord (John George Lambton), 31, 277

Early Draft: writing of, ix, 48, 64–65, 94–96; revisions of, 49, 85, 189, 251

East India Company, 103, 106–9, 300–301; India House routine, 101–2; as model of government, 110–11. *See also* Mill, James, employ at East India Company; Mill,

East India Company, *(continued)*
John Stuart, life of: employ at East
India Company
Economy (rhetoric), 162
Education, 114, 125, 135, 165; methods of, 14–16, 185; James Mill
on, 19; circumstances as, 146–
48; authority of teacher, 178–79;
Bentham's panoptical schemes for,
200–201, 204. *See also* Mill, James,
as teacher; Mill, John Stuart, life
of: education
Eliot, George, 87–88, 240; *Middlemarch,* 71, 239, 294–95
Empirical laws, 139–40, 141, 144
English: national character of, 132,
145–46, 208
*Essays on Some Unsettled Questions of
Political Economy,* 81–82, 187
Ethology, xiii, 191; in relation to reform, xi, 141–42, 144, 145, 146;
Mill's plans for, 65, 123–25, 144;
disappointment of Mill's plans
for, 124–25, 162–67; as heroic
endeavor, 127–28; applied to marginal groups, 128–29, 145, 158–
59; early essays in, 129, 130–34;
problems of data in, 133, 137–
38, 140–41, 160; treatment of, in
System of Logic, 134–44; "Political
Ethology," 138, 145; methodological problems of, 138–43;
as rhetorical tool, 145, 151–52,
167; Irish as subject of, 146–52;
working classes as subject of, 152–
59; women as subject of, 159–63;
Examination as example of, 168–
69; *On Liberty* as example, 214.
See also Character: in relation to
circumstances
Examination of Sir William Hamilton,
23, 223; as example of ethology,
168–69; motives for writing, 170–
72, 174–77; organization of, 173–

74; treatment of logic in, 174–76;
status of James Mill in, 182–83
Examiner, 11
Experientialism. *See* Associationism
Eyre, Gov. Edward, 270, 274

Faulkner, William, 10
Feltes, N. N., 81
Foucault, Michel, 197, 202, 203, 204
Fox, Caroline, 253, 258
Fox, William J., 93
French: national character of,
131, 132
French Revolution, 51–52, 286. *See
also* Girondins

Girondins, 52, 105, 281, 286
Gladstone, William Ewart, 116–17,
268, 274
Gosse, Edmund, 245
Grote, George, 19–20, 59, 60, 62,
230; *History of Greece,* 78, 101, 128,
166; on demagogues, 105; on *Examination,* 168; *Aristotle,* 297–98;
as Mill's relative opposite, 298
Grote, Harriet, 86, 94
"Grote's Aristotle," 297–98
Gusdorf, Georges, 240

Habits, 151, 208
Hamilton, Sir William, 168, 170–
78, 182–83, 263; on relativity of
knowledge, 228; as Mill's relative opposite, 292–93. *See also
Examination of Sir William Hamilton*
Hare, Julius, 249
Hartley, David, 18, 20, 204
Helvetius, Claude Adrien, 18, 204
Heroes: Carlyle on, 6, 76; James
Mill on, 76, 77; Macaulay on, 77–
78; writers as, 127–28. *See also*
Mill, John Stuart: character of,
admiration for heroes
Herschel, Sir John, 187, 189–90

House of Commons, 114. *See also*
Mill, John Stuart: life of: parlia-
mentary career
Humboldt, Wilhelm von, 83, 196
Hume, David, 21–22, 35
Hyde Park riots, 274–78

Ideas, 12, 20; primacy of, 169, 232.
See also Clerisy; Theory
Identity, xiii. *See also* Character
Improvement. *See* Reform
"Inaugural Address" (St. Andrews),
125
India House. *See* East India Com-
pany
Individuality, 2, 206
Influence, 169, 179–81, 184, 196;
Mill's, over others, 214–15, 275.
See also Authority; Originality
Intuitionism, 17, 18, 21, 240
Irish: as ethological subject, 146–52;
national character of, 148–49, 152

Jacotot, Joseph, 185
Jamaica Committee, 269, 270,
272, 273
James, William, 27, 35
Jobbery, 102–5
Journalists. *See* Writers
Judy, 114–17
Junius Redivivus, 5–7, 25, 230–
31, 239

Kearns, Sheila M., 240
Kingsley, Charles, 34–35
Kinzer, Bruce, 274
Knowledge: relativity of, 227–
29, 241

Lacan, Jacques, 244–45, 249
Lafayette, Marquis de, 54
Lake District, 32–34
Lewes, George Henry, 164
Liberals. *See* Mill, John Stuart, life

of: parliamentary career, relation
to Liberals
Liberty: as opposed to power, 97–
98; as authority, 196, 207
Locke, John, 18, 31
Loesberg, Jonathan, 23
Logic: reasoning in, 176; relative
opposites in, 228
London and Westminster Review, 80–81
London Debating Society, 59

Macaulay, Thomas Babington, 8,
59, 60, 150, 282; on heroes, 77–
78; as amateur, 83; on East India
Company, 106; on *On Liberty,* 211
Machines: human beings described
as, 2, 117–18, 201, 202, 300, 301
Mansel, Henry, 173
Marmontel, Jean François, 63, 247–
49
Marriage, 97–99, 115, 231
Martineau, Harriet, 88, 154
Matter, 25–27
Maurice, F. D., 250, 252; *Eustace
Conway,* 67, 170, 180
Men, 145–46, 160–62
Mill, George Grote, 91–93, 100–
101, 103
Mill, Harriet (née Burrow), 249,
257–58
Mill, Harriet Taylor, ix, 49, 70; as
determinant of Mill's career, 65,
86, 91, 93, 94, 98–99, 193, 254–
56; "joint productions," 91, 96,
156, 195–96, 236; as ideal, 96,
117–18, 234, 235–36, 255; criticisms of Mill, 99, 258–59, 310
(n. 20); death of, 123, 171, 256;
as original thinker, 192–94, 236;
compared to Clotilde de Vaux,
234–36; disapproval of Mill's associates, 235, 250; as Mill's double,
255, 256

205–8, 209; on authority, 170, 196, 207; apparent rejection of Utilitarianism, 202–3; as panoptical, 205–8, 209; rhetoric of, 211–13; motives for writing, 213–14; as example of ethological principles, 214

"On Genius," 187–88

"On the Definition of Political Economy," 134–35

Opposite, relative, 228

Opposition, 105–6, 109

Originality, 176–77, 187–88, 192, 206. *See also* Mill, John Stuart: character of, concern with originality

Otley, Jonathan, 33–34

Panopticon, 197–201, 202–4, 205–8, 213

Parker, John William, 81

Pattison, Mark, 171

Perception, 16, 239, 240–45, 258

Peterson, Linda H., 317–18 (n. 14)

Philosophes, 62

Philosophic Radicals, 62–63, 70, 93, 307 (n. 7), 308 (n. 16)

Phrenology, 4

Physiology, 163–64

Piranesi, Giambattista, 241–42

Plato, 165

Plutarch, 54

Poetry, 254; in relation to reform, 7, 68; in relation to character, 30, 31, 64

Poor Law, 151, 208, 210

Population control, 154–56, 268

Practice. *See* Theory

Principles of Political Economy, 102, 128, 187, 228–29; revisions of, 10, 153, 155, 157, 261; on theory, 46–47; on working classes, 152–59; reticence of, 154–55; on influence

and authority, 169; compared to *On Liberty*, 209–11

Professions, 80–83, 86, 107, 300–301, 309 (n. 4)

Property, 149–51, 152–53, 228

Psychology. *See* Associationism

Race, 43–44, 150

Rank, Otto, 244

Reading, 31–32, 33

Reform, 35–36, 49, 57–58, 66–67, 72–75, 112–15, 237. *See also* Ethology: in relation to reform; Mill, John Stuart: character of, attitude toward future

Reform Bill (1832), 72–75

Reform League, 275, 276, 277, 287

Robespierre, Maximilien François Marie Isidore de, 286

Revolution, 57–58, 73–74, 111–12, 115, 283. *See also* French Revolution; Girondins

Robson, John M., 33

Roebuck, John, 59, 60, 71, 95, 237; portrayal of, in *Early Draft*, 68–70; as man of action, 68, 78

Romilly, Samuel, 59, 62

Rousseau, Jean-Jacques, 53

Ruskin, John, 243, 244

Ryan, Alan, 23, 170, 171

Science: methods of, 135, 139–40, 141–44

Self-consciousness, 240–45, 247–48, 258, 259, 282. *See also* Assimilation

Semmel, Bernard, 272

Shelley, Percy Bysshe, 127, 230

Smiles, Samuel, 4

Sociology, 136, 138

Socrates, 80, 181–2

Southey, Robert, 87, 230

Spencer, Herbert, 21, 98, 215, 233, 290

Stephen, James Fitzjames, 77, 81

Stereotypes, Victorian, 43–44, 87–
89, 141, 189, 263–64. *See also*
Women: conventional attitudes
toward
Sterling, John, 73–75; *Arthur
Coningsby*, 67, 243; as Mill's relative
opposite, 230, 250–54; portrayal
in *Autobiography*, 249–54; man of
action, 253
Stewart, Dugald, 186
Strutt, Edward, 59, 60, 62
Stuart, Sir John, 50–51
Subject, xiii. *See also* Character: in
relation to circumstances
Subjection of Women, 194; on vocation, 86; on marriage, 97–99; as
ethological investigation, 159–63;
rhetorical tactics in, 161–62
System of Logic, 12, 22–23; writing of,
9–10, 16, 75, 85, 87, 102, 186–87;
stereotypes in, 43–44; on heroes,
77–78; revisions of, 77–78, 145;
on ethology, 123–24, 134–44;
theoretical goals of, 124, 128, 130;
on scientific methods, 139–40,
141–44; ignored by Baynes, 175;
cited in *Examination*, 175–76; as
work of originality, 188–91; compared to James Mill's *Analysis*, 191

Taylor, Helen, 193–94, 269, 298,
299, 321 (n. 5)
Taylor, John, 92, 257
Tennyson, Alfred, 290
Thackeray, William Makepeace,
80, 83
Theorist, 55; status of Victorian,
44–45, 46, 49, 306 (n. 2); identi-
fied with women, 115–16. *See also*
Mill, John Stuart: life of, career as
theorist; Writers
Theory, 44–49, 53, 56, 278. *See also*
Action

Thomas, William, 76
Tocqueville, Alexis Henri Charles
Maurice Clérel, Comte de, 211–13
Trollope, Anthony, 11, 82, 100
Turgot, Anne Robert Jacques, Baron
de l'Aulne, 278–81, 293; Morley
compares Mill to, 280; assimilated
with Carrel, 284–85

Utilitarianism, 48, 96, 213
Utilitarians, 170, 180–82, 237
Utilitarian Society, 59, 184

Vaux, Clotilde de, 233–36, 254–55
Vigny, Victor Alfred, Comte de,
131–34; as Mill's relative oppo-
site, 239
Villiers, Charles, 59, 60
Villiers, Thomas Hyde, 59, 60
Virtue, 165, 226

"Walking Tours," 16–17, 32–34
Walpole, Sir Spencer, 275, 276, 279
Whewell, William, 81, 187, 189
Wilde, Oscar, 238
Wisdom, popular, 141, 142–43,
163, 166
Women: conventional attitudes
toward, 44, 257, 263–64; marginality of, 86–90; passivity of,
87–89; fears about rights for,
90, 115, 162; desire for power in,
97–99; rights for, 114–17, 154,
161–62; character of, 159–60,
235–36, 304 (n. 4)
Wordsworth, William, 128, 150;
Prelude, ix, 244, 289; in relation
to Mill's crisis, 30, 64, 68, 70, 96,
249; Mill's imitations of, 32–33,
34, 298; Mill's visit to, 33, 34; "Intimations of Immortality," 68,
74, 298
Working classes, 90; freedom of,

29, 155–56; as ethological subject, 152–59; population control in, 154–56; character of, 156–57

Writers: reputation of, 7–8, 13; identified with women as marginal, 86–91; Victorian, 80–81, 83–84

Writing, 25, 181–82; identified with character, xi–xii, 2–3, 3–17, 24– 27, 34, 35, 36, 219–20, 221, 247, 297–99; as memorial to character, 8, 288, 291; as physical form, 8–9, 9–11, 13, 16–17, 24–27; as revision of character, 34, 227

"Writings of Alfred de Vigny," 131– 34